THE
COMPLETE
CAST-IRON
COOKBOOK

THE
COMPLETE
CAST-IRON
COOKBOOK

*More than 240 Delicious Recipes
for Your Cast-Iron Collection*

Dominique DeVito

CIDER MILL
PRESS

BOOK
PUBLISHERS
KENNEBUNKPORT, MAINE

13-Digit ISBN: 978-1604338225
10-Digit ISBN: 1604338229

This book may be ordered by mail from the publisher. Please include $5.99 for postage and handling.
Please support your local bookseller first!

Books published by Cider Mill Press Book Publishers are available at special discounts for bulk purchases in the United States by corporations, institutions, and other organizations. For more information, please contact the publisher.

Cider Mill Press Book Publishers
"Where good books are ready for press"
PO Box 454
12 Spring Street
Kennebunkport, Maine 04046

Visit us online!
www.cidermillpress.com

Typography: Avenir, Fairfield, Fenway Park, Gotham, Journal, Linotype Centennial, Minion, Neo Retro Draw, Neo Retro Fill, and Influence Medium

Image Credits: Page 229 (copyright) StockFood / Robbins, Heath; Page 331 (copyright) StockFood / Bill Milne Studio; Page 333 (copyright) StockFood / Leatart, Brian; Page 334 (copyright) StockFood / Short, Jonathan; Page 417 (copyright) StockFood / Norwood Browne, Angie; Page 418 (copyright) StockFood / Hwang, Kent; Page 433 (copyright) StockFood / Jackson, Richard; All other images used under official license from Shutterstock.com.

Printed in China

67890

CONTENTS

Equipment: 12" skillet or
7-quart Dutch oven

Different size skillets
or Dutch ovens may be
used but cooking times
will vary slightly

WHY CAST-IRON IS HERE TO STAY

There's nothing particularly attractive about a cast-iron skillet on the outside. It's all black, no shiny chrome, no flashy stainless steel, and it's heavy. And the handle gets hot. And if the pan hasn't been properly cared for, it can get rusty or look grungy, which is how many of them end up at flea markets, where the dust really shows because they're … black.

But boy oh boy is there something attractive about a cast-iron skillet that's in good shape and properly cared for. In sum, it is one of the best cooking tools you can have.

AND HERE'S WHY:

Cast-iron heats up, and distributes and holds heat, like no other pan, which gives you a greater range of temperatures to work with. For example, if you're sautéing onions in a stainless-steel skillet, it gets hot quickly, and it also loses its heat exponentially when the heat is lowered or the pan is removed from the heat. Sautéed onions are best when cooked slowly and evenly so they caramelize without burning. When your cast-iron skillet is good and hot, you can lower the heat and know that the temperature won't fall off so much that you have to keep playing with it as you continue to cook. And that's just one example.

Cast-iron skillets can go directly from the stove to the oven, and from the oven to the table, saving a lot of time at cleanup. Yes, the handles get hot, but they're an extension of the skillets themselves and so will never melt or fall off.

Another great thing about cast-iron is the material itself—iron. Women, especially, tend to be diagnosed with iron deficiencies. Beneficial iron leaches into foods cooked in a cast-iron skillet. It won't compensate for an iron deficiency, but it's helpful—and certainly better than the chemicals leaching from "nonstick" coatings, which have been shown to contribute to liver damage, developmental problems, cancer, and early menopause.

If you aren't sold yet, there's also the durability of cast-iron. These skillets are family heirlooms; they last as long as they're maintained properly. In fact, there's something wonderful about a cast-iron skillet that's been passed down from mother to daughter, father to son, grandparent to grandchild. There are stories in your family's cast-iron skillets, and there are stories you'll be telling about yours.

THE HISTORY OF CAST-IRON COOKWARE

Cast-iron is the product of pouring molten iron into a mold, letting it cool, and then refining it for its purpose (whether it be a pot, a bench, a piece of equipment, etc.). The Chinese were the first to develop foundries that could manage this practice, and it's estimated to date back to the 5th century BC. Here in the West, iron foundries are estimated to date back to the 11th century. Large cauldrons were some of the first cooking implements to come out of the foundries, and they were prized for being able to hold a lot, maintain temperatures, and sit solidly over a fire. Just as in ancient China, the process of making cast-iron pieces in the West involved pouring the hot metal into a mold made from sand and, when cast, removing the sand mold and grinding the piece to smooth its surfaces.

Fast-forward to our European ancestors in the mid-19th century, where cooking was done in hearths. The cookware was adapted so that pieces could be moved or repositioned more easily, and cast-iron cauldrons were built with longer handles and legs. Dutch ovens were forged to be placed directly on coals. As the oven itself evolved, the flat cast-iron skillet was created for use on an open "burner" or in the closed part of a cook stove.

AN AMERICAN REVOLUTION

Here in America, the first cast-iron foundry was established in 1619. Early settlers to the American colonies brought cookware with them, of course, and fashioned their hearths in the styles of what they were used to in their homelands. Cooking continued to be done in fireplaces or over open fires until modern plumbing made it possible to access water in the home. Cooks rejoiced, and running water became part of a true kitchen. Wood and coal fueled the fires that enabled cooking and heating until gas companies developed ways to produce ovens powered by gas in the 1900s. It didn't take too much longer for electric ovens to come onto the scene—in the 1930s—though they didn't become really popular until the price of electricity fell in the 1960s. Through all these developments, cast-iron remained the cookware of choice because it was still the most durable and practical.

It wasn't until after World War II that stainless steel and aluminum emerged as viable materials for pots and pans. The factories that had been making guns and tanks had a lot of it, and the fact that these metals were lighter than cast-iron and didn't rust made them attractive to homemakers. In quick succession all manner of pots and pans were formed with these metals, and a nonstick coating was developed to make their care even easier. Teflon® was approved by the U.S. Food and Drug Administration in 1960, and its popularity took off, pushing cast-iron to the back of the cabinet.

THE RESURGENCE OF ITS USE AND POPULARITY

It seems cooks started dragging cast-iron skillets out from the backs of their pantries in earnest by the late 2000s. The trend was confirmed when the *Los Angeles Times* published an article in November 2012 declaring, "Cast-iron enjoys a comeback among cooks." The author, Noelle Carter, attributed part of the resurgence to the fact that the company making the cookware—Lodge Manufacturing—had introduced pre-seasoned cast-iron. According to Lodge, this was an industry first that has now become an industry standard, as it eliminates having to continually season the cookware.

Personally I have skillets and Dutch ovens that I've inherited, and some that I've purchased. I've done my best to care for the cookware (as detailed in the next chapter), and have found that it always lives up to my expectations. My cast-iron cookware heats beautifully and without smoking, even without the addition of oil or fat; the things I cook in it don't stick to the surface; it's a joy to be able to start something on the stove and then finish it in the oven; and it seems to get better and better with use (which is not true of Teflon®-coated pans); and maybe best of all, my kids have

taken to using them and discovering their simplicity and practicality (though I have to remind them about not using soap to clean them).

With cast-iron cookware, you, too, will quickly learn that the variety of dishes you can prepare is only limited by your imagination!

WHICH PIECES FOR WHICH DISHES?

Now that cast-iron is popular again, you can find skillets and other pieces in a range of sizes. If you do an online search for cast-iron cookware, you'll find two names that come up a lot: Lodge and Williams-Sonoma. Lodge is a manufacturer, and you can buy pieces directly from them, or from retailers that sell their products. A manufacturer of enamel-coated cast-iron is the French company, Le Creuset. Williams-Sonoma sells it in many colors and sizes, and it's beautiful (if heavy). As with most things, you'll get what you pay for with your cast-iron, too. A simple skillet may look pricey compared to stainless steel or Teflon, but considering that you'll be using it almost daily for decades and it'll just keep getting better, it's a necessary investment. Lodge and Le Creuset are manufacturers you can completely trust.

Lodge makes skillets ranging from 3.5 inches in diameter up to 13.25 inches in diameter. They also make deep skillets, griddles (and covers), Dutch ovens, and specialized bakeware like cornstick pans and miniature cake pans.

You are welcome to experiment with any of the sizes, but for recipes in this book, I used a 12-inch skillet, or a 7-quart Dutch oven.

THE CARE & KEEPING OF YOUR CAST-IRON COOKWARE

You may already be familiar with a cast-iron skillet. It's the plain, black, one-piece pan that always seemed to be at the back of the cupboard. If you can remember where you saw that old pan, by all means, go get it. Acquiring a piece of cast-iron cookware from someone in your family is a way of keeping history alive. You'll be carrying on a tradition of cooking and serving foods that has lasted for generations. If, on the other hand, you're new to using cast-iron and you are the one to acquire it in your family, you can look forward to sharing its magic with your family and passing it on to your children or grandchildren.

Besides being an amazing piece of cookware, cast-iron does, indeed, last a lifetime (or more)— so long as it's properly cared for. It's simple enough to do, but it's important to do it properly, before and after every use. Here's how it is done.

SEASONING VERSUS PRE-SEASONED

The concept of seasoning a cast-iron skillet or other piece of cookware is to protect it from rusting and to aid in proper cooking. Part of the reason cast-iron fell out of favor with home cooks was that keeping the cookware properly seasoned was essential, and a chore. When Lodge introduced pre-seasoned cast-iron in the early 2000s, keeping the cookware seasoned became a whole lot easier. The cookware now has a nice sheen and a cooking surface that ensures great results right from the start. The seasoning process Lodge employs utilizes vegetable oil, just as cooks were instructed to do when seasoning their unseasoned cookware for the first time. And it doesn't hurt a pre-seasoned piece to get "re-seasoned" using the process outlined in the next section.

The important thing is the maintenance of the cookware. When it is washed (without soap), dried thoroughly (including the bottom, sides, and handles), and rubbed with enough vegetable oil to give it a smooth shine without appearing oily, then the cookware is ready for its next assignment.

SEASONING A NEW SKILLET

When I went shopping for a new cast-iron skillet, I came upon Lodge pans—a company that has been making cast-iron skillets since the late 1800s. They brand themselves as "America's Original Cookware." Since nothing stands completely still, they have recently developed a method to season their cookware so that it will last as it always has but with minimal (consistent) care. That's a good thing! What they do is coat the pan with vegetable oil and bake it in at very high heat, which is just what you need to do to an unseasoned pan. With a new Lodge seasoned piece, you can begin cooking with it almost immediately.

But let's start at the beginning, with an unseasoned skillet. Here's the procedure to bring it into use:

1. Wash with hot, soapy water.

2. Rinse and dry thoroughly.

3. If there's any rust on the pan, sand it lightly with fine-grained sandpaper. Apply Coca-Cola to the rust spots and leave on for 10 to 15 minutes. Wash again with soapy water, rinse, dry, and put the skillet on a burner over low heat to dry any excess moisture.

4. If there's no rust after drying the cookware all over, apply a light layer of cooking oil (vegetable oil, NOT olive oil, butter, or margarine!) all over the pan with a paper towel, rubbing even the handle. The pan should have a light sheen to it.

5. Place the skillet upside down on the middle rack of the oven and preheat the oven to 400° F (with the pan inside). Put a piece of foil or a baking dish on the lower rack to catch any dripping oil. Let the pan cook in the oven for about 2 hours.

6. Turn the oven off and let the pan cool (upside down) in the oven.

7. Take it out, wipe it down with a clean paper towel, and it's good to go.

8. If your pan has taken on a slightly brown color, you can repeat the process, which will further season the pan and darken its color, improving its appearance. This will also happen over time.

CARING FOR YOUR CAST-IRON

Rule #1: Never wash your seasoned pan with soapy water!

Rule #2: Never put a cast-iron pan in the dishwasher!

Why? Soap breaks down the protective seasoning, and you have to re-season the pan all over again. Leaving any kind of water on the pan will lead to rusting, which will demand re-seasoning from the beginning. It seems counterintuitive, especially when you're used to thinking "It's not clean unless it's been washed in (really) hot, soapy water," but it's actually a great thing about cast-iron.

After you've cooked in your skillet, clean it with hot water (no soap) and a plastic, rough-surfaced scrub brush. Dry the cookware completely after washing. Put a teaspoon of vegetable oil in the pan and, with a paper towel, rub it in all over the pan until it has a nice sheen.

Rule #3: Never use steel wool!

Cast-iron is a soft material compared to steel. Any particularly abrasive sponge on your cast-iron has the potential to scratch the surface enamel or strip your pan's seasoning.

If there's a mess that water and sponge cannot handle, you can create a scrubbing paste by adding coarse kosher salt to your hot water before using your scrub brush or sponge to loosen the food off. Stubborn residues may also be loosened from your cast-iron by soaking very briefly in water, but do not leave your pan submerged in water. You can also simmer the mess over medium-low heat to aid in loosening up more extreme grime.

Never clean your pan by burning it in a fire! The rapid heating of the metal can cause warps, cracks, red patchy scales, or brittleness that compromises the structure of your pan, and can sometimes make it unable to hold its protective seasoning.

Again, once scrubbed of leftovers, dry your cast-iron extremely well and rejuvenate the lovely sheen by rubbing in the vegetable oil, wiping the excess off with a clean paper towel.

Rule #4: Store your cast-iron in a dry place!

Good air circulation and a moisture-free environment will ensure your pan stays rust-free and clean until the next time you use it. If you need to stack it with other pans in your pantry or cupboard, put paper towels between the cookware to prevent scratches or other damage. Dutch ovens should be stored with their lids off, so that no moisture is trapped within.

Storing cast-iron within your oven is also a popular option, so that it is nearby and ready for use whenever you're cooking. Just be sure to remove any pans before pre-heating your oven (I couldn't tell you how many times I've discovered the pan I needed after the oven was warm)! Or you can leave it on your stovetop if you find you can't seem to cook a meal without it. An overhead rack is equally a good option, but if you have multiple cast-iron skillets, simply make sure that your cookware rack is well bolted to your ceiling and is prepared to handle the weight. Both of these options display your rustic, heirloom cookware proudly, and make a beautiful aesthetic statement for your kitchen.

GIVE IT A LOT OF LOVE

The best thing to do with your cast-iron skillet is USE IT! When you start using it for all the different things it can do (as evidenced by the diversity of recipes in this book), you'll probably find that the skillet lives on your stovetop, waiting for its next assignment. The more you use it, the better it gets. Nothing will stick to its surface. You can go from the frying pan to the fire, as it were, starting a dish on the stove and finishing it in the oven. You can cook your skillet over very high heat (or put it in the campfire), and it'll cook up the food you put in it beautifully (so long as you keep an eye on it).

In short, with regular use, the cast-iron skillet truly is a pan that will just keep cooking and cooking, getting better and better with age and use. Just like you and me!

The thing I've learned about cast-iron skillets is that, once you start using them regularly, they truly become your go-to cooking instruments. They're so versatile and so easy to use. They conduct heat beautifully, and the fact that they can go from stovetop to oven is a real bonus. Here's why: Flavor. And, yes, the overall look of the meal served in the cast-iron. There's something very elemental about it.

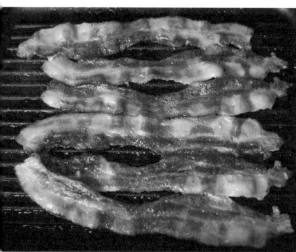

BREAKFAST TREATS & PASTRIES

There's something about the very word breakfast that makes your mouth water in anticipation. The association with fried eggs, sizzling bacon, crisp-edged potatoes, butter melting over hot pancakes—flavors and aromas that jump-start your day and make you feel like you can tackle anything. Another reason a real breakfast is so satisfying is because it's not every day that we're able to indulge. Who has the time during the week to make pancakes—or even eggs? I suspect very few of us, which is why breakfast is particularly delicious and delightful when it can happen in our homes. The recipes in this chapter are what a good breakfast is all about—hearty, filling, hot, salty, sweet—or all of these things! Using cast-iron cookware to cook breakfast also connects you to a tradition. You can imagine pioneers and homesteaders reaching for their skillets while wondering what was next as they headed West. You can imagine a farmer's wife cracking just-gathered eggs into a hot skillet in anticipation of her husband and children finishing the first round of milking and chores on the dairy farm. In our kitchens and lives, surrounded by the latest technology, there's nothing like breakfast prepared in a cast-iron pan. So get cooking!

EGGS IN A NEST

SERVES 2 ✦ ACTIVE TIME: 20 MINUTES ✦ START TO FINISH: 40 MINUTES

This is a dish that's as much about presentation as it is about taste, and both are fabulous. It's guaranteed to put a smile on your child's face in the morning.

4 pieces of sandwich bread

4 tablespoons butter

4 eggs

Salt and pepper to taste

1. Toast the bread on the light setting of the toaster, until it is just browned. Using a cookie cutter or the top of a small glass, perforate a hole in the center of each piece of toast.

2. Heat 2 tablespoons of the butter in the skillet over medium-high heat. Put two pieces of the toast with the holes in it in the pan. Cook for a couple of minutes on one side to get them golden, then flip them.

3. Crack the eggs into the holes. Lower the heat slightly, cover the pan, and cook until the egg is set, about 3 minutes. Serve the cooked pieces and repeat the cooking process with the other pieces of toast and eggs. Season with salt and pepper before serving.

Using cookie cutters of different shapes can be fun and festive, too.

CHEESY HASH BROWNS

SERVES 4 TO 6 ✦ ACTIVE TIME: 20 MINUTES ✦ START TO FINISH: 60 MINUTES

If you want gooey goodness without the fat from meat, this recipe is for you. Be careful not to overcook it or you'll go from gooey to chewy (which isn't bad, either).

4 tablespoons butter

4 large russet potatoes, shredded with a cheese grater and squeezed dry

1 teaspoon salt

½ teaspoon pepper, or to taste

6 eggs

½ cup milk

1 cup shredded cheese

1. Preheat the oven to 375° F.

2. Add the butter to the skillet and cook over medium-high heat. When the butter starts bubbling, add the potatoes and season with the salt and pepper. Press the potatoes into the bottom of the pan. Cook for about 5 minutes.

3. In a mixing bowl, whisk the eggs and milk together. Pour the eggs over the potatoes, shaking the pan to help them penetrate to the bottom. Sprinkle liberally with the cheese.

4. Transfer the skillet to the oven and cook until just set, about 10 minutes. Serve immediately.

The best cheeses to use in this recipe are those that melt well. This includes cheddar, Swiss, American, mozzarella, Monterey Jack, or Provolone. Use a blend of these cheeses if you want, so long as they are all shredded.

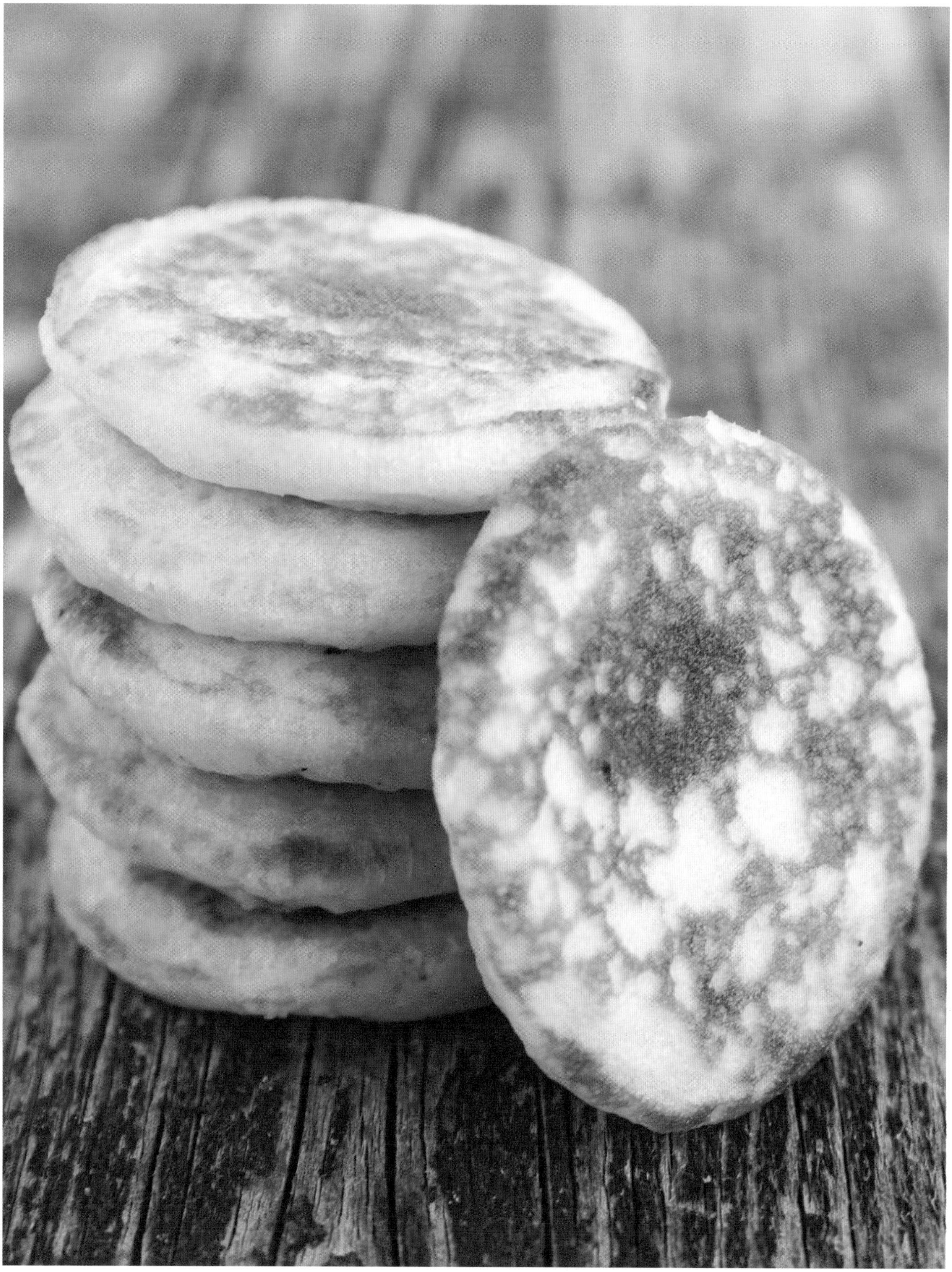

BLINIS

SERVES 6 TO 8 ✦ ACTIVE TIME: 60 MINUTES ✦ START TO FINISH: 60 MINUTES

These Russian pancakes are traditionally served with sour cream and caviar. They make great "fancy" breakfast pancakes that can be served with all sorts of different toppings (see sidebar).

½ cup whole wheat flour

1 tablespoon sugar

¼ teaspoon salt

½ teaspoon baking powder

2 eggs, beaten

2½ cups milk

2 tablespoons vegetable oil

1. In a large bowl, whisk together the flour, sugar, salt, and baking powder.

2. In a smaller bowl, combine the eggs and milk, stirring to combine. Add the liquid into the dry ingredients and stir to blend thoroughly.

3. Heat a skillet over medium-high heat and brush with some of the vegetable oil. Spoon just about a tablespoon of batter to form each blini. You should be able to fit about 4 at a time in the skillet. Cook for about 2 minutes a side (or less), flipping when the edges start to crisp. These cook up fast, so be careful not to overcook them.

4. Keep the blinis warm in the oven on very low heat until ready to serve.

If you like caviar of any kind, you have to try these with a dollop of sour cream or crème fraîche topped with caviar. Other great toppings include assorted jams; sour cream with a sprig of dill; scrambled eggs and hot sauce; scrambled eggs, bacon bits, and sour cream; honey–butter.

THE COMPLETE CAST-IRON COOKBOOK

MASHED POTATO BLINIS

SERVES 6 TO 12 (ABOUT 12 PANCAKES) ✦ ACTIVE TIME: 30 MINUTES ✦ START TO FINISH: 60 MINUTES

If it ever happens that you have leftover mashed potatoes (in our house it's rare, but can happen), then this is what you need to make with them. There's something otherworldly about these. The soft, buttery-chive mashed potato inside with a crispy crust outside explodes in your mouth.

2 cups mashed potatoes

3 oz. fresh chèvre (goat cheese)

2 tablespoons chives, finely chopped

2 eggs, beaten

2–3 tablespoons flour

Salt and freshly ground pepper to taste

3 tablespoons butter

1. Preheat the oven to 200° F.

2. In a large bowl, combine the mashed potatoes with the chèvre and chives. Add the eggs and stir. Add the flour 1 tablespoon at a time until the dough is the consistency of thick pancake batter. Season with salt and pepper.

3. Melt the butter in the skillet over medium-high heat. Make small pancakes with spoonfuls of batter, leaving room in between them. You should be able to fit 4 comfortably. Cook until browned on one side (about 2 minutes), flip and brown on the other side.

4. Place cooked pancakes on a plate, cover with foil, and put in the oven to keep warm until all are cooked and ready to serve.

Variations

You can serve these with so many toppings! Here are some favorites:

- Sour cream and caviar
- Sour cream and smoked salmon
- Smoked salmon and caviar
- Chunky applesauce
- Scrambled eggs with bacon pieces
- Fried eggs and salsa
- Sliced avocado and salsa
- Sliced avocado and smoked salmon

STICKY BUNS

SERVES 6 ✦ ACTIVE TIME: 90 MINUTES ✦ START TO FINISH: 2 HOURS

These take a bit of preparation time, but the result is sooo worth it! Your family or friends will wake up to the smell of these baking, and you'll soon have a kitchen full of people happily waiting for these to come out of the oven.

1 (26.4 oz.) package frozen biscuits

All-purpose flour for dusting

½ cup chopped pecans, toasted

1 teaspoon ground cinnamon

¼ teaspoon nutmeg

4 tablespoons butter, softened

¾ cup light brown sugar, firmly packed

1 cup confectioners' sugar

3 tablespoons half-and-half

½ teaspoon vanilla extract

1. Preheat the oven to 375° F.

2. Lightly dust a flat surface with flour. Spread the frozen biscuit dough out in rows of 4 biscuits each. Cover with a dish cloth and let sit for about 30 minutes until the dough is thawed but still cool.

3. While dough is thawing, toast the pecans. Spread the pieces on a cookie sheet and bake for about 5 minutes, stirring the pieces with a spatula about halfway through. Be sure not to overcook. Allow to cool. Put the pieces in a bowl and add the cinnamon and nutmeg, stirring to coat the nuts with the spices.

4. Sprinkle flour over the top of the biscuit dough, fold the dough in half, and then press it out to form a large rectangle (approximately 10 inches by 12 inches). Spread the softened butter over the dough.

5. Sprinkle the brown sugar over the butter, then the seasoned nuts. Roll the dough with the butter, sugar, and nuts in it, starting with a long side. Cut into 1-inch slices and place in a lightly greased skillet.

6. Place in the oven for about 30-35 minutes, until rolls in the center are cooked through. Remove from the oven and allow to cool.

7. Make the glaze by mixing the confectioners' sugar, half-and-half, and vanilla. Drizzle over the warm rolls and serve.

Variations

❀ Substitute toasted walnut or almond pieces instead of the pecans for a nuttier, earthier flavor.

❀ Substitute dark brown sugar instead of the light brown sugar if you want more of a molasses flavor.

❀ Save a few calories (not many!) by using low-fat milk instead of half-and-half, or skip the glaze entirely and either serve without it, or drizzle some maple syrup over the rolls.

CHEESY GRITS

SERVES 4 TO 6 ✦ ACTIVE TIME: 20 MINUTES ✦ START TO FINISH: 40 MINUTES

Done right, grits are a mouthful of special. No wonder they're a regular on the breakfast plates of Southerners.

2 cups whole milk

2 cups water

1 cup grits

1 teaspoon salt

1 teaspoon pepper

2 cups cheddar cheese, grated and packed

1. Preheat the broiler to high.

2. Bring the milk and water to a boil. Add the grits and cook, stirring constantly, until grits have thickened and are cooked through, about 15 minutes. Add the salt, pepper, and 1 cup of the cheese. Stir to combine.

3. Grease the skillet with some butter and add the grits. Sprinkle with the remaining cup of cheese. Put the skillet in the oven and allow the grits to toast under the broiler, about 2 minutes. Serve immediately.

If you want spicier grits, use 1 cup Pepper Jack cheese as half of the cheese you include. Or try other cheeses like Swiss, mozzarella, or fresh Parmesan.

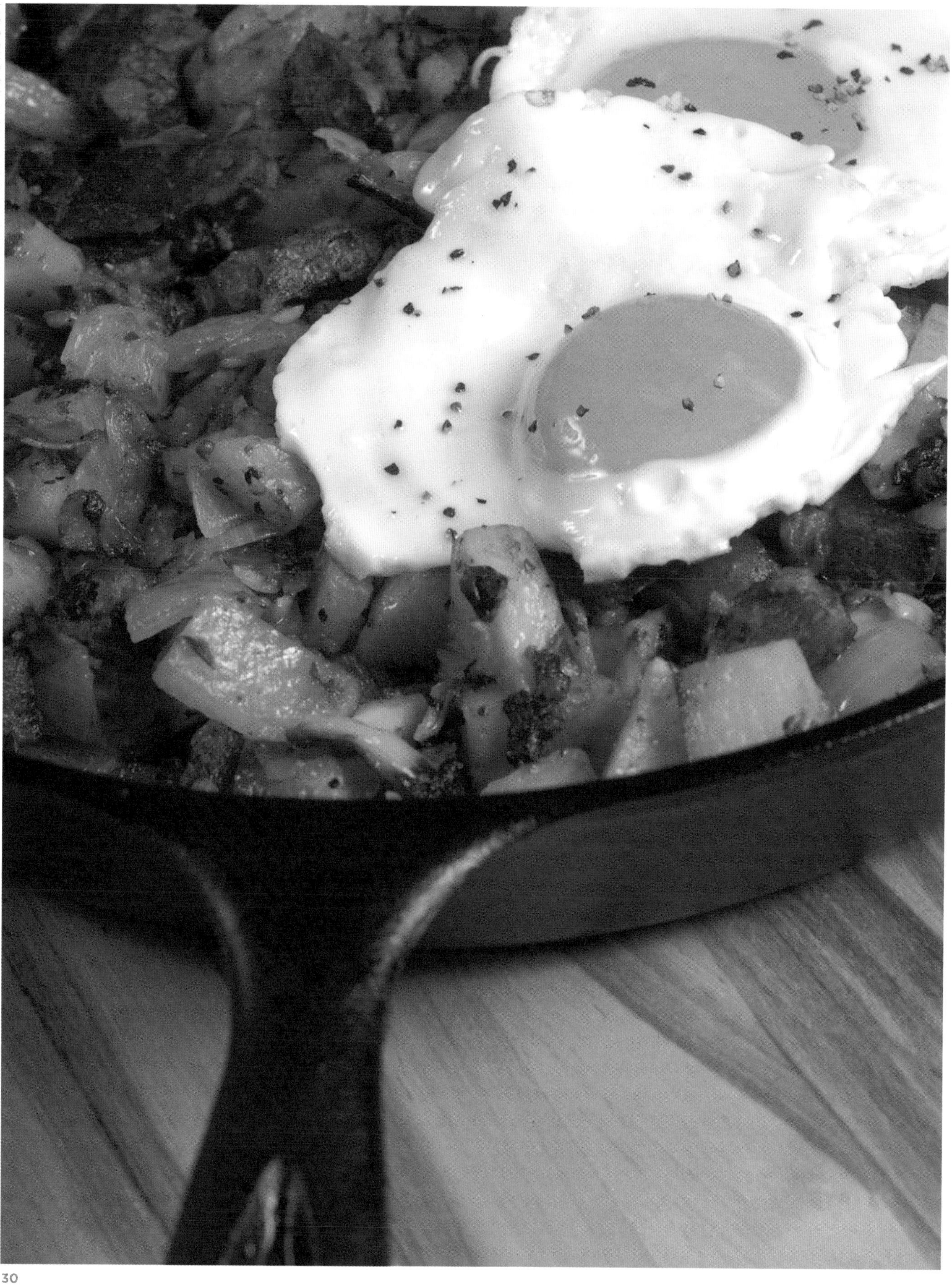

CORNED BEEF HASH

SERVES 4 TO 6 ✦ ACTIVE TIME: 40 MINUTES ✦ START TO FINISH: 90 MINUTES

If you like to eat this at a diner, wait until you make it yourself. It's so good!

2 large russet potatoes, peeled and cut into cubes

1 teaspoon salt, plus more for seasoning

3 tablespoons butter

½ Vidalia onion, diced

3 cloves garlic, minced

1 red bell pepper, cored and seeded, chopped fine

1 pound corned beef, cut into bite-sized pieces

½ teaspoon dried thyme

Freshly ground pepper to taste

1. Put the potatoes in a saucepan and cover with cold water. Add the 1 teaspoon of salt. Bring the water to a boil, then lower the heat and cook the potatoes about 10 minutes until partially cooked. (Cooking until soft will cause them to fall apart in the hash.) Drain them in a colander and rinse with cold water. Set aside.

2. Heat the butter in the skillet over medium-high heat. Add the onions, garlic, and pepper and cook, stirring, until the vegetables soften, about 3 minutes.

3. Add the potatoes and press them down into the skillet around the vegetables. Allow them to set and cook for about 5 minutes, then start turning sections over with a spatula while stirring in the corned beef. Sprinkle with the thyme, and season with salt and pepper. Continue to cook for about 5 minutes so that the potatoes are browned and the corned beef is warmed through. Season with additional salt and pepper if desired.

If you like eggs with your corned beef hash, once the potatoes are browned, make 4 to 6 indentations in the top of the hash and break the eggs into them. Lower the heat and cover the skillet. Continue cooking until the eggs are set, about 3 minutes.

BARBECUED CHICKEN HASH

SERVES 4 TO 6 ✦ ACTIVE TIME: 40 MINUTES ✦ START TO FINISH: 90 MINUTES

Got some leftover barbecued chicken? Serve up a Southern style breakfast with this flavorful hash.

2 large russet potatoes, peeled and cut into cubes

1 teaspoon salt, plus more for seasoning

3 tablespoons butter

1 Vidalia onion, diced

3 cloves garlic, minced

1 small jalapeño pepper, cored and seeded, sliced

1 pound cooked barbecued chicken, cut into bite-sized pieces

¼ cup barbecue sauce

Freshly ground pepper to taste

Salsa, sour cream, and sliced black olives to serve on the side

1. Put the potatoes in a saucepan and cover with cold water. Add the 1 teaspoon of salt. Bring the water to a boil, then lower the heat and cook the potatoes about 10 minutes until partially cooked. (Cooking until soft will cause them to fall apart in the hash.) Drain them in a colander and rinse with cold water. Set aside.

2. Heat the butter in the skillet over medium-high heat. Add the onion, garlic, and slices of jalapeño, and cook, stirring, until the vegetables soften, about 3 minutes.

3. Add the potatoes and press them down into the skillet around the vegetables. Allow them to set and cook for about 5 minutes, then start turning sections over with a spatula while stirring in the chicken and the barbecue sauce. Continue to cook for about 5 minutes so that the potatoes are browned and the meat is warmed through. Season with salt and pepper, and serve with sides of salsa, sour cream, and sliced black olives.

If you don't want to make this too hot, substitute a green bell pepper for the jalapeño pepper. People who want some spice can always add a favorite hot sauce to their serving.

HAM, HERB, AND TOMATO FRITTATA

SERVES 4 ✦ ACTIVE TIME: 20 MINUTES ✦ START TO FINISH: 40 MINUTES

Smoked ham provides an earthiness to this baked egg dish, which is also loaded with fresh herbs and tomatoes.

2 tablespoons butter

½ pound thick-sliced deli ham, cut into pieces

6 eggs

¼ cup milk or heavy cream

1 teaspoon salt

Freshly ground black pepper

6 cherry tomatoes, halved

½ cup fresh parsley, coarsely chopped

1 teaspoon fresh thyme, minced

1. Preheat the broiler to low.

2. Heat the skillet on medium-high heat. Melt the butter in the skillet, being careful not to let it burn. Add the ham to the pan and stir, cooking until just browned, about 3 minutes.

3. Whisk the eggs in a large bowl until combined. Add the milk or cream and stir. Add the salt and pepper.

4. Pour the egg mixture into the skillet. After a couple of minutes, as the eggs begin to set, add the cherry tomato halves and sprinkle the herbs over everything. Lower the heat to medium or low, cover, and cook until eggs are set, another 10 minutes. Place the skillet under the broiler for just a couple of minutes to "toast" the top.

5. Remove from the oven and allow to sit for a few minutes. Season with additional salt and pepper, if desired, and serve.

This is one of those frittatas into which you could add almost anything tasty in the fridge. Substitute cooked chicken pieces for the ham; sprinkle leftover sautéed greens over the eggs; add some chopped jalapeños for extra flavor and heat. Have fun experimenting.

HUEVOS RANCHEROS

SERVES 4 ✦ ACTIVE TIME: 25 MINUTES ✦ START TO FINISH: 40 MINUTES

Pretend you're in Mexico for the morning by serving this delicious—and filling—meal.

2 tablespoons
vegetable oil

4 (6-inch) corn tortillas

8 oz. refried beans

1 teaspoon butter

4 eggs

½ cup sharp cheddar
cheese, grated

½ cup Cotija or
grated Monterey
Jack cheese

½ cup fresh salsa

Jalapeño peppers, sliced
(optional)

Fresh cilantro
(optional)

1. Heat oil in a skillet over medium-high heat. Fry the tortillas, one at a time, until firm but not crisp. Transfer cooked tortillas to a plate lined with a paper towel, and separate with paper towels while cooking.

2. Put the refried beans and butter in a bowl and heat in the microwave for about 1 minute, stirring halfway through.

3. Fry the eggs in the skillet over easy and sprinkle with cheese when nearly cooked so that cheese melts.

4. Prepare the dish by placing a tortilla on a plate, topping with the beans, then the egg and cheese. Serve hot with salsa, jalapeños, and cilantro.

You can make this a one-dish meal. Cut the tortillas into ½-inch pieces and fry them, while stirring. When crisped, spoon the refried beans and butter over them, pressing them into the bottom of the skillet to brown. Break the eggs over the beans and cover so that the eggs start to set. Cook for about 2 minutes. Take off the lid and cover with cheese. Take the skillet off the heat, cover so that the cheese melts completely, and serve.

PECAN-CRUSTED MAPLE FRENCH TOAST

SERVES 4 ✦ ACTIVE TIME: 20 MINUTES ✦ START TO FINISH: 40 MINUTES

What better to do with leftover crusty bread than soak it in some fresh eggs and cream, sizzle it up in some butter, and encase it in pecans and maple syrup? Enjoy it with strong coffee and thick-sliced bacon, that's what!

4 eggs

½ cup heavy cream

¾ cup all-natural maple syrup

8 slices slightly stale, thick-cut bread

4 tablespoons butter

2 cups pecans, finely chopped

1 teaspoon cinnamon

1 teaspoon nutmeg

1. Preheat the oven to 200° F and place an oven-proof serving dish in it.

2. In a small bowl, combine the eggs, heavy cream, and ½ cup of the maple syrup. Whisk to thoroughly combine, or use an immersion blender.

3. Put pieces of bread in a 9x13-inch baking dish and cover with the egg mixture. Let the bread soak up the egg mixture for about 20 minutes, turning halfway so both sides can soak.

4. Combine chopped pecans, cinnamon, and nutmeg in a shallow dish and stir, before spreading out across dish. Dip each slice of soaked bread into the pecan-spice mixture, making sure every slice is covered on both sides.

5. Warm a skillet over medium heat. Add 2 tablespoons of the butter and as it melts, tilt the pan to coat it evenly. When the butter is heated but not browned, add 4 slices of the pecan-crusted bread. Allow to cook for about 4 minutes, then flip them. Drizzle the pieces with maple syrup while they're cooking on the other side, and after another 4 minutes or so, flip them again so the side with the maple syrup gets cooked for about a minute.

6. Transfer the cooked pieces to the serving dish in the oven. Repeat the cooking process for the remaining slices of bread.

7. Before serving, warm the remaining maple syrup (and some additional syrup) in a microwave-safe container for 30 seconds. Test the warmth. You don't want to over-warm it, just take the chill out. Serve the French toast with maple syrup.

The sugar in the maple syrup will also caramelize on the skillet, which is great as long as the heat is kept on medium, which won't burn the sugar but simply "toast" it.

BLUEBERRY SCONES

SERVES 4 TO 6 ✦ ACTIVE TIME: 30 MINUTES ✦ START TO FINISH: 50 MINUTES

These are delicious whenever you eat them, but they're especially good about 15 minutes after you take them out of the oven, slathered with butter!

3 cups flour

⅓ cup sugar

2½ teaspoons baking powder

½ teaspoon baking soda

1 teaspoon salt

¾ cup (1½ sticks) unsalted butter, chilled and cut into pieces

1 tablespoon orange zest

1 cup milk or half-and-half

1 cup fresh blueberries

1. Preheat the oven to 400° F. Position a rack in the middle of the oven.

2. In a large bowl, whisk together the flour, sugar, baking powder, baking soda, and salt. Add the butter pieces and mix with an electric mixer until just blended, or mix with a fork so that the dough is somewhat crumbly.

3. Stir in the orange zest and milk, and gently fold in the blueberries, being careful not to overmix.

4. With flour on your hands, transfer the dough to a lightly floured surface. Form the dough into a circle about ½-inch thick. With a long knife, cut the dough into 12 wedges.

5. Butter the skillet, and put the scone wedges in a circle in it, leaving some space between the pieces. Bake for 20 to 25 minutes, or until golden.

6. If desired, sprinkle with some additional sugar when just out of the oven.

Variations

✸ Substitute fresh cranberries for the blueberries, or use a blend of ½ cup blueberries and ½ cup cranberries.

✸ Substitute dried fruit for the blueberries: ½ cup dried cherries or dried sweetened cranberries.

Blueberries split when cooked and their juices can get a little messy. If you want a neater-looking scone, you can use dried blueberries. Reduce the amount used by about half, though, as their flavor is also more concentrated.

ROSEMARY BLACK PEPPER SCONES

SERVES 4 TO 6 ✦ ACTIVE TIME: 30 MINUTES ✦ START TO FINISH: 50 MINUTES

While these are a bit savory for an early breakfast, they are a hit for brunch, when they can very nicely complement a simple omelet and a Mimosa with fresh orange juice.

3 cups flour

2½ teaspoons baking powder

½ teaspoon baking soda

1 teaspoon salt

¾ cup (1½ sticks) unsalted butter, chilled and cut into pieces

1 tablespoon dried rosemary, crumbled

1 tablespoon freshly ground black pepper

1 cup milk or half-and-half

1. Preheat the oven to 400° F. Position a rack in the middle of the oven.

2. In a large bowl, whisk together the flour, baking powder, baking soda, and salt. Add the butter pieces and mix with an electric mixer until just blended, or mix with a fork so that the dough is somewhat crumbly.

3. Stir in the rosemary, black pepper, and milk, being careful not to overmix.

4. With flour on your hands, transfer the dough to a lightly floured surface. Form the dough into a circle about ½-inch thick. With a long knife, cut the dough into 12 wedges.

5. Butter the skillet, and put the scone wedges in a circle in it, leaving some space between the pieces. Bake for 20 to 25 minutes, or until golden.

CHEDDAR JALAPEÑO SCONES

SERVES 4 TO 6 ✦ ACTIVE TIME: 30 MINUTES ✦ START TO FINISH: 50 MINUTES

The spiciness of the jalapeño livens up any meal. I like to split the cooked scones in half and top with a spoonful of sour cream and some sliced avocado.

2 cups flour

1 teaspoon baking powder

½ teaspoon salt

1 teaspoon freshly ground black pepper

4 tablespoons butter, chilled, cut into pieces

¾ cup sharp cheddar cheese, grated

½ cup jalapeño peppers, sliced or chopped

½ cup milk

1 egg, beaten with a little milk

1. Preheat the oven to 400° F. Position a rack in the middle of the oven.

2. In a large bowl, whisk together the flour, baking powder, salt, and pepper. Add the butter pieces and mix with an electric mixer until just blended, or mix with a fork so that the dough is somewhat crumbly.

3. Stir in the cheese, peppers, and milk, being careful not to overmix.

4. With flour on your hands, transfer the dough to a lightly floured surface. Form the dough into a circle about ½-inch thick. With a long knife, cut the dough into 6 to 8 wedges.

5. Butter the skillet, and put the scone wedges in a circle in it, leaving some space between the pieces.

6. Brush with the beaten egg. Bake for 20 to 25 minutes, or until golden.

Variation

Ramp up the heat by substituting Pepper Jack cheese for the cheddar, or substitute a serrano pepper for the jalapeño. Wear gloves when working with hot peppers so you don't get the oils in your eyes or other thin-skinned areas, as they irritate and burn.

FRENCH TOAST

SERVES 3 TO 6 ✦ ACTIVE TIME: 20 MINUTES ✦ START TO FINISH: 40 MINUTES

French toast—a great way to use up bread that's on the verge of going stale—is so simple and so satisfying.

6 eggs

1 cup milk

½ teaspoon vanilla extract

Pinch of nutmeg (optional)

6 slices, thick-cut bread

4 to 6 tablespoons butter

1. In a mixing bowl, combine the eggs, milk, vanilla, and nutmeg (if desired).

2. Place the slices of bread in a baking dish. Pour the egg mixture over the bread, shaking the pan to distribute evenly. Flip the pieces of bread a couple of times to coat both sides with the mixture.

3. Heat 2 tablespoons butter in the skillet over medium-high heat. Add 2 slices of bread to the pan and cook until golden brown on each side, 2 to 3 minutes a side. Transfer the cooked pieces to a warm plate or keep warm in the oven while you cook the additional pieces.

4. Serve with maple syrup or jam.

Variation

If you want to make gluten-free French toast, just use gluten-free bread. It's as simple and delicious as that. You'll want one that's got some thickness to it and minimal crust.

The secret to great French toast is the choice of bread and the amount of egg mixture that saturates the bread. If you use a basic sandwich bread, you won't need as much egg mixture. If you use an egg-based bread like Challah, or a sourdough bread, you'll need more egg mixture as these kinds of bread are denser. They will also need to sit in the egg mixture longer. You'll need to adjust the recipe for the type of bread you're using, so be sure to have some extra eggs and milk on hand.

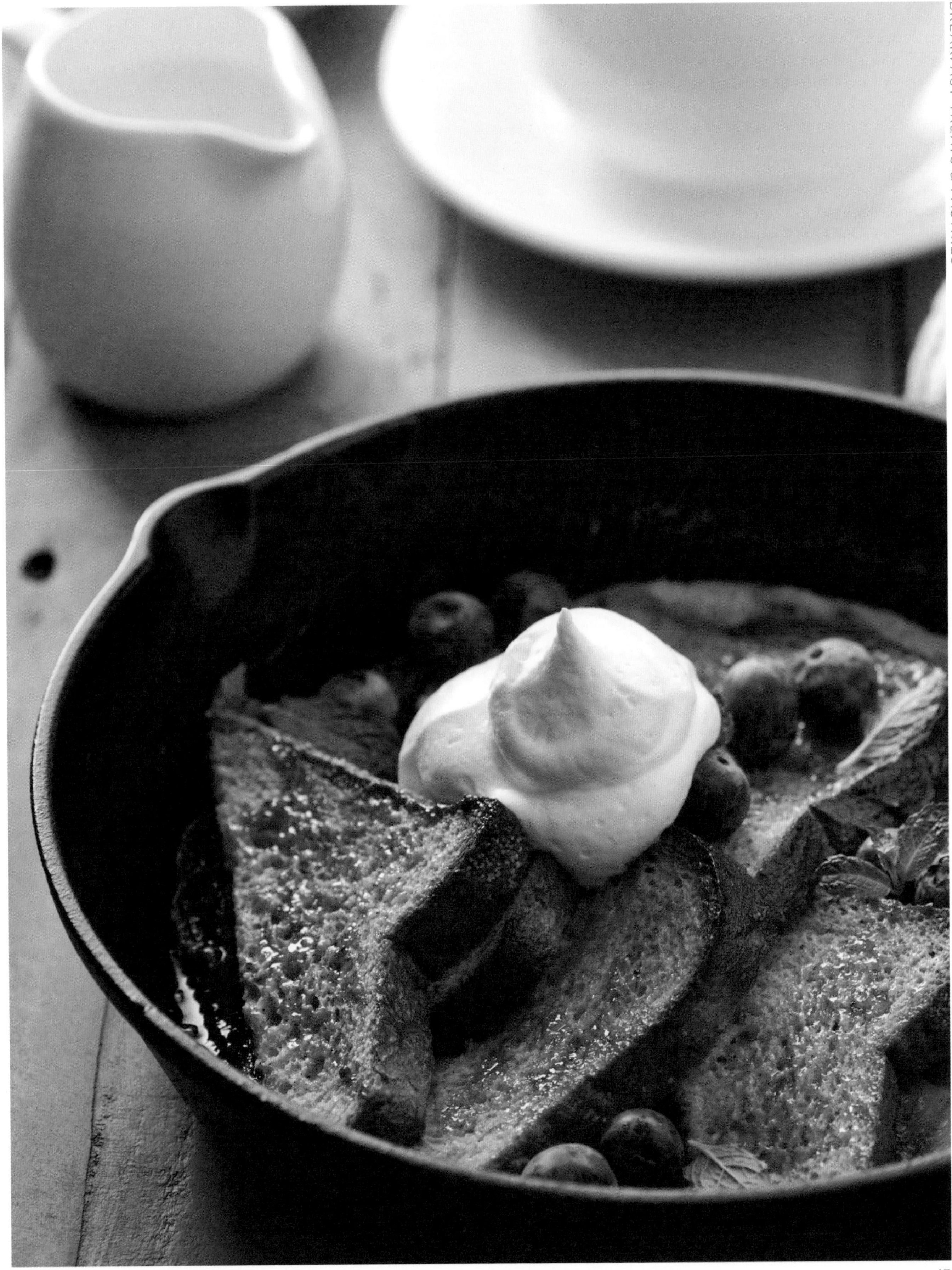

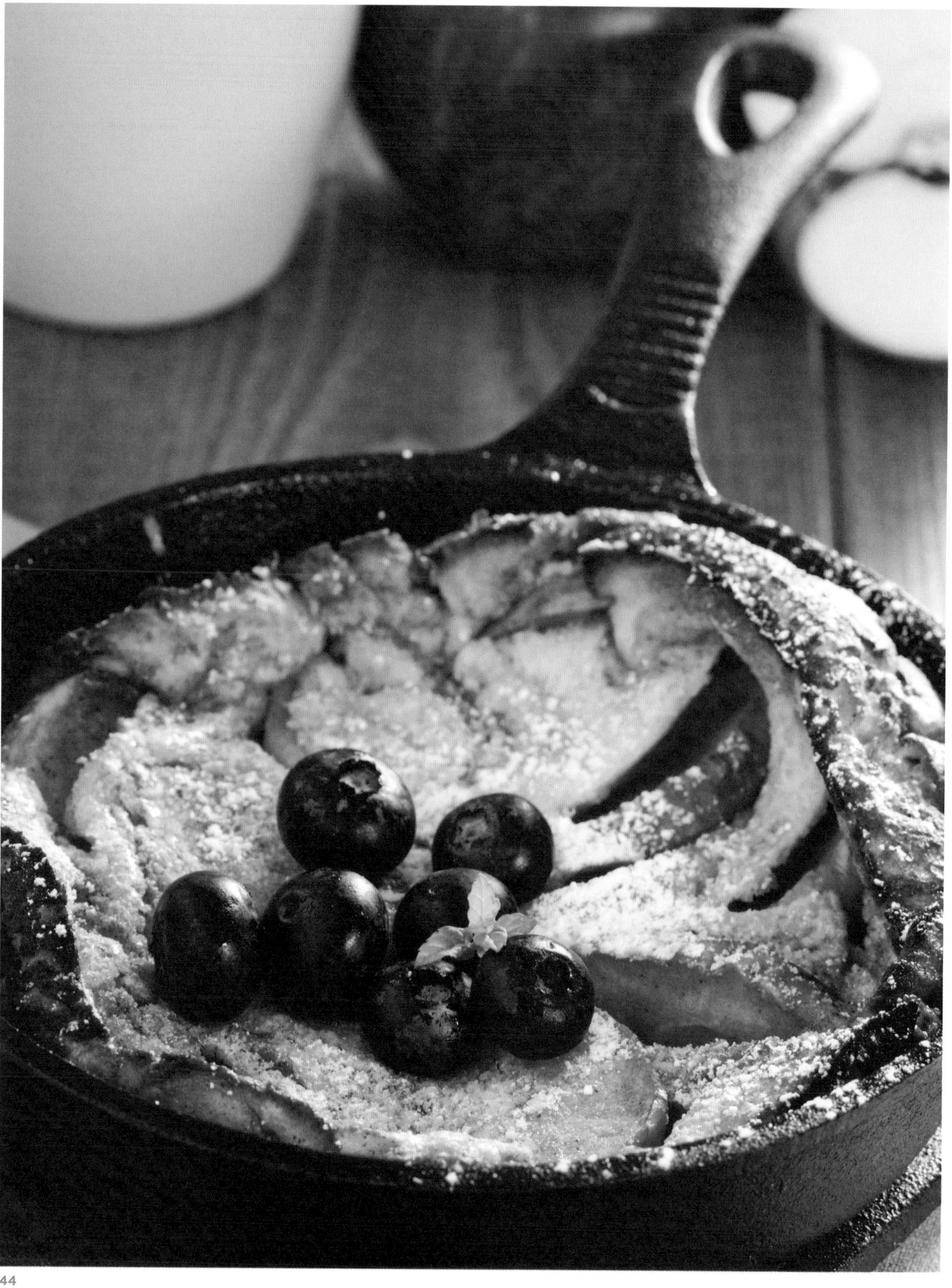

SKILLET APPLE PANCAKE

SERVES 4 TO 6   **ACTIVE TIME: 30 MINUTES**   **START TO FINISH: 60 MINUTES**

Make this the morning after you go apple picking. It's a great way to use up some of the apples and get your day off to a great start.

4 eggs

1 cup milk

3 tablespoons sugar

½ teaspoon vanilla extract

½ teaspoon salt

¾ cup flour

4 tablespoons butter

2 apples, peeled, cored, and thinly sliced

¼ teaspoon cinnamon

Dash of ground nutmeg

Dash of ground ginger

¼ cup light brown sugar

Confectioners' sugar for sprinkling (optional)

Preheat the oven to 425° F.

In a large bowl, whisk together the eggs, milk, sugar, vanilla, and salt. Add the flour and whisk to combine. Set the batter aside.

Heat the skillet over medium-high heat and add the butter, tilting the pan to thoroughly coat the bottom. Add the apple slices and top with the cinnamon, nutmeg, and ginger. Cook, while stirring, until apples begin to soften, about 5 minutes. Add the brown sugar and continue to stir while cooking for an additional few minutes until apples are very soft. Pat the cooked apples along the bottom of the skillet to distribute evenly.

Pour the batter over the apples, coating them evenly. Transfer the skillet to the oven and bake for about 20 minutes until the pancake is browned and puffy. Sprinkle with confectioners' sugar when fresh out of the oven if desired. Serve immediately.

Variation

To make a gluten-free version of this recipe, just substitute the ¾ cup of flour with ¾ cup Gluten Free All-Purpose Baking Flour from Bob's Red Mill and add 1 teaspoon of xanthan gum. Mix together before whisking into your wet ingredients.

You can vary the fruit-spice combo for this recipe in multiple ways. Consider making it with pears instead of apples, or using 1 of each. Add raisins to the apples or pears while cooking (about 1/2 cup), or try cranberries, blueberries, or dried cherries, along with toasted walnuts (about 1/2 cup).

SKILLET BERRY PANCAKE

SERVES 4 TO 6 ✦ ACTIVE TIME: 30 MINUTES ✦ START TO FINISH: 60 MINUTES

Just as making this with fresh apples is a way to celebrate after picking them, so is throwing together fresh summer berries to make this treat. (If they're not in season, you can use thawed frozen fruits and pretend it's summer.)

4 eggs

1 cup milk

3 tablespoons sugar

½ teaspoon vanilla extract

½ teaspoon salt

¾ cup flour

4 tablespoons butter

½ cup strawberries, sliced

½ cup blueberries

¼ cup honey

1. Preheat the oven to 425° F.

2. In a large bowl, whisk together the eggs, milk, sugar, vanilla, and salt. Add the flour and whisk to combine. Set the batter aside.

3. Heat the skillet over medium-high heat and add the butter, tilting the pan to thoroughly coat the bottom. Add the berries and honey. Cook, while stirring, until just softened and the honey coats the fruit, about 5 minutes. Shake the skillet gently to distribute the fruit evenly over the bottom.

4. Pour the batter into the skillet. Transfer the skillet to the oven and bake for about 20 minutes until the pancake is browned and puffy. Serve immediately.

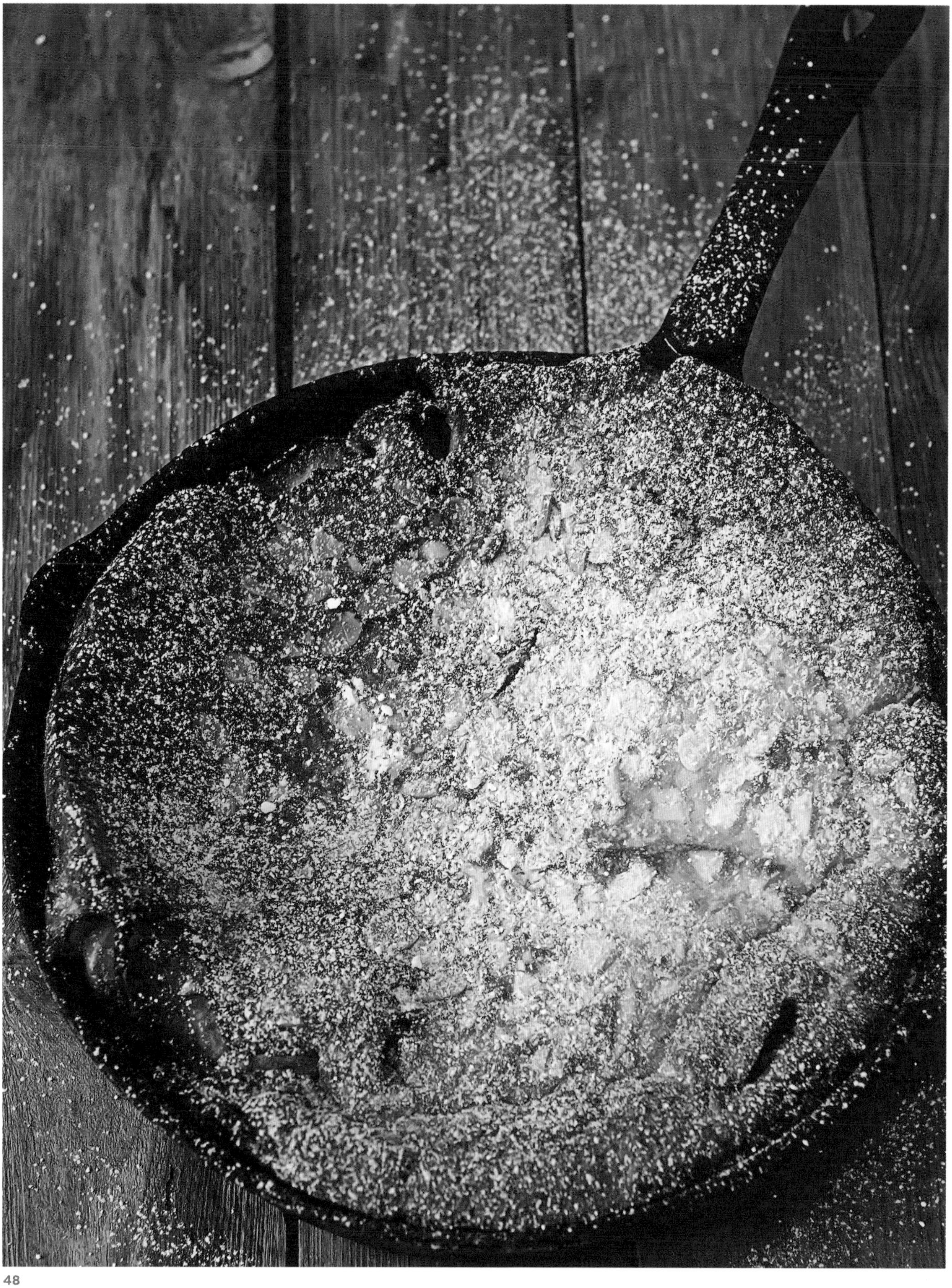

DAVID EYRE'S PANCAKE

SERVES 4 ✦ ACTIVE TIME: 30 MINUTES ✦ START TO FINISH: 30 MINUTES

A friend shared this recipe that she found in The New York Times *years ago. Turns out it has quite the following. It's more like a popover than a pancake, but it's really delicious. David Eyre was a writer/editor, so I'm happy to include this tribute to him and hopefully create a whole new following for it.*

½ cup flour

½ cup milk

2 eggs, lightly beaten

Pinch of nutmeg

4 tablespoons butter

2 tablespoons confectioners' sugar

Juice of ½ a lemon

1. Preheat the oven to 425° F.

2. In a bowl, combine the flour, milk, eggs, and nutmeg. Beat lightly; leave the batter a little lumpy.

3. Melt the butter in the skillet and, when very hot, pour in the batter.

4. Transfer the skillet to the oven and bake for 15 to 20 minutes, until golden brown.

5. Sprinkle with the sugar, return briefly to the oven, then remove. Sprinkle with lemon juice and serve.

This "pancake" is usually served with jam, which leads to all kinds of flavor options. Try anything from a sweet strawberry jam to a more pungent orange marmalade or fig spread. In the fall, an apple or pear butter would be perfect.

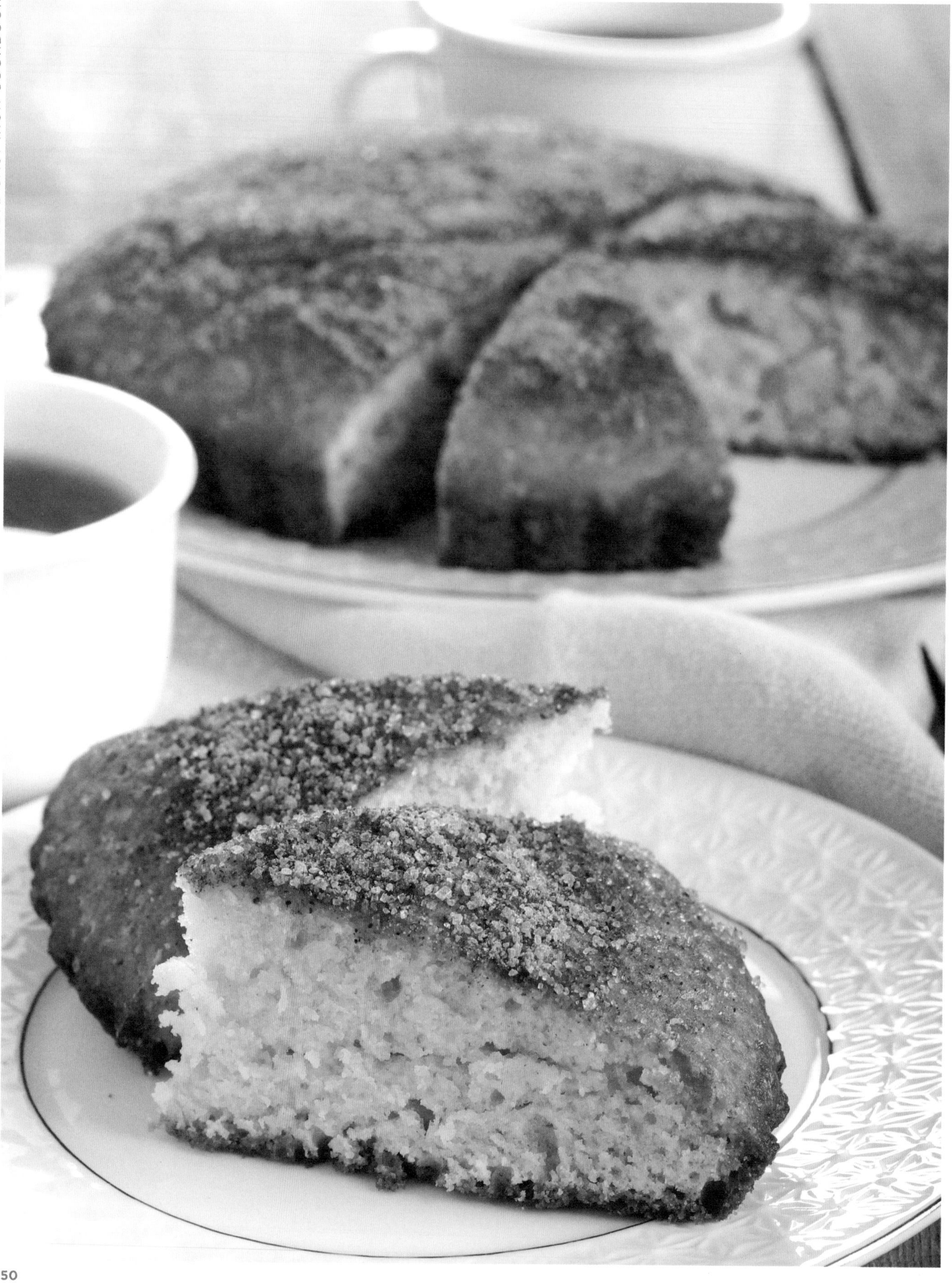

CINNAMON COFFEE CAKE

SERVES 6 TO 8 ✦ ACTIVE TIME: 90 MINUTES ✦ START TO FINISH: 2 HOURS

Some people sprinkle cinnamon over their coffee before brewing it. Cinnamon is not only wonderfully fragrant, but it is a natural antioxidant and anti-inflammatory and helps to fight infection.

For the Cake

1¾ cups flour

⅔ cup sugar

½ teaspoon baking soda

¼ teaspoon salt

¼ teaspoon ground cinnamon

8 tablespoons (1 stick) butter, softened

2 eggs

1 teaspoon vanilla extract

¾ cup buttermilk

For the Topping

1 cup flour

½ cup sugar

½ cup dark brown sugar

½ teaspoon cinnamon

¼ teaspoon salt

6 tablespoons unsalted butter, softened

1. Preheat the oven to 325˚ F.

2. To make the cake, whisk together the flour, sugar, baking soda, salt, and cinnamon in a large bowl. Add the butter and stir with an electric mixer until blended.

3. In a small bowl, whisk together the eggs, vanilla, and buttermilk. Pour into the flour mixture and blend on high speed until the batter is light and fluffy. Pour the batter into a greased skillet.

4. To make the topping, whisk together the flour, sugars, cinnamon, and salt in a bowl. Add the softened butter and combine to form a crumbly dough.

5. Dot the topping over the cake in the skillet. Put the skillet in the oven and bake for 45 minutes, until a knife inserted in the middle comes out clean. Allow to cool for about 10 minutes before serving.

BLUEBERRY COFFEE CAKE

SERVES 6 TO 8 ✦ ACTIVE TIME: 90 MINUTES ✦ START TO FINISH: 2 HOURS

One of the things I love about summer is how early it gets light in the morning. It's easy to get up at 5:30 or 6:00 a.m. when the sun is out, and that's the perfect time to make this coffee cake with summer-fresh, ripe blueberries. Of course, it's not so bad in the dead of winter, either, with blueberries you froze from the summertime. They don't even need to be thawed first.

For the Cake

1¾ cups flour

⅔ cup sugar

½ teaspoon baking soda

¼ teaspoon salt

8 tablespoons (1 stick) butter, softened

2 eggs

1 teaspoon vanilla extract

½ cup buttermilk

2 cups blueberries

For the Topping

1 cup flour

½ cup sugar

½ cup dark brown sugar

½ teaspoon ginger

¼ teaspoon salt

6 tablespoons unsalted butter, softened

½ cup crushed walnut pieces (optional)

1. Preheat the oven to 325° F.

2. To make the cake, whisk together the flour, sugar, baking soda, and salt in a large bowl. Add 6 tablespoons of butter and stir with an electric mixer until blended.

3. In a small bowl, whisk together the eggs, vanilla, and buttermilk. Pour into the flour mixture and blend on high speed until the batter is light and fluffy.

4. Over medium heat, melt the remaining 2 tablespoons butter in the skillet. Add the blueberries and shake to distribute evenly. Cook the blueberries in the butter for a couple of minutes, then pour the batter over them.

5. To make the topping, whisk together the flour, sugars, ginger, and salt in a bowl. Add the softened butter and combine to form a crumbly dough. Stir in the walnut pieces (if desired).

6. Dot the topping over the cake in the skillet. Put the skillet in the oven and bake for 45 minutes, until a knife inserted in the middle comes out clean. Allow to cool for about 10 minutes before serving.

APPLESAUCE OATMEAL BREAD

SERVES 6 TO 8 ◆ ACTIVE TIME: 30 MINUTES ◆ START TO FINISH: 90 MINUTES

This is an easy bread to make for a delicious after-school snack. It's practically cake, but with far less sugar. Adding flax seeds bumps up the nutritional goodness without compromising the flavor or texture of the bread.

¾ cup sugar

2 large eggs

½ cup vegetable oil

1 teaspoon vanilla extract

½ cup whole wheat flour

1 cup all-purpose flour

¼ teaspoon baking powder

½ teaspoon baking soda

1 teaspoon cinnamon

¼ teaspoon nutmeg

½ teaspoon salt

½ cup rolled oats

¾ cup chunky applesauce

¼ cup flax seeds (optional)

½ cup chopped walnuts or slivered almonds (optional)

1. Preheat the oven to 350° F. Put the skillet in the oven while it preheats.

2. In a large bowl, mix together the sugar, eggs, oil, and vanilla. In a separate bowl, combine the flours, baking powder, baking soda, cinnamon, nutmeg, and salt. Add the dry ingredients to the bowl of wet ingredients. Stir until thoroughly combined. Next, add the oats, applesauce, flax seeds (if desired), and nuts (if desired). Stir to combine.

3. Using pot holders or oven mitts, carefully remove the skillet from the oven. Pour the batter in and dust the top with additional oats and some brown sugar, if desired. Bake for 45 minutes until the bread sounds hollow when tapped on the top and a toothpick or knife inserted in the middle comes out clean.

4. Remove from the oven and let rest for about 5 to 10 minutes. Gently invert onto a plate. Allow to cool before cutting into wedges and serving.

PUMPKIN BANANA BREAD

MAKES 1 LOAF ✦ ACTIVE TIME: 30 MINUTES ✦ START TO FINISH: 2 HOURS

Whenever you can find something to add pumpkin to, go for it. Pumpkin is such a great source of Vitamin A, carotenoids, fiber, and more. It adds a ton of moisture to breads like this. The combination of pumpkin and banana is really yummy. If you like walnuts, be sure to add them, too. This is delicious as a bread to go with coffee, as a healthy breakfast on the go, or as a not-too-sweet dessert with a dollop of Greek yogurt on top of a slice.

8 tablespoons (1 stick) butter, softened

⅔ cup light brown sugar

2 tablespoons honey

2 large eggs

1 cup pumpkin purée (unsweetened)

1 cup very ripe bananas (about 2 or 3), mashed

2 tablespoons water

1 teaspoon vanilla extract

1½ cups flour (white or whole wheat)

¼ teaspoon baking powder

1 teaspoon baking soda

¾ teaspoon salt

½ teaspoon ground cinnamon

½ teaspoon ground nutmeg

½ cup walnuts, chopped (optional)

1. Preheat the oven to 350° F. Put the skillet in the oven while it preheats.

2. In a large bowl, beat together the butter, sugar, honey, eggs, pumpkin, bananas, water, and vanilla. In a separate bowl, whisk together the flour, baking powder, baking soda, salt, cinnamon, and nutmeg. Add the dry ingredients to the bowl of wet ingredients. Stir until thoroughly combined. Fold in the chopped walnuts, if desired.

3. Using pot holders or oven mitts, carefully remove the skillet from the oven. Pour in the batter and return the skillet to the oven. Bake for about 60 minutes, until the bread sounds hollow when tapped on the top and a toothpick or knife inserted in the middle comes out clean.

4. Remove from the oven and let rest for about 20 minutes. Gently invert onto a plate. Allow to cool before cutting into wedges and serving.

PALEO PUMPKIN BANANA BREAD

This is an easy recipe to convert to one that's Paleo, though we're leaving the skillet behind.

3 bananas, mashed

4 eggs

1 cup pumpkin purée (unsweetened)

¼ cup honey

⅓ cup coconut oil, melted

⅓ cup coconut flour

3 tablespoons arrowroot starch

1 teaspoon cinnamon

½ teaspoon baking soda

¼ teaspoon salt

1. Preheat the oven to 350° F.

2. Combine all the ingredients, stirring well. Grease a loaf pan with coconut oil before pouring the batter in.

3. Bake for about 50 minutes, until the bread sounds hollow when tapped on the top and a toothpick or knife inserted in the middle comes out clean.

4. Allow to cool before cutting into slices.

Variation

Increase the moisture and flavor of this bread by adding ½ cup flaked, unsweetened coconut.

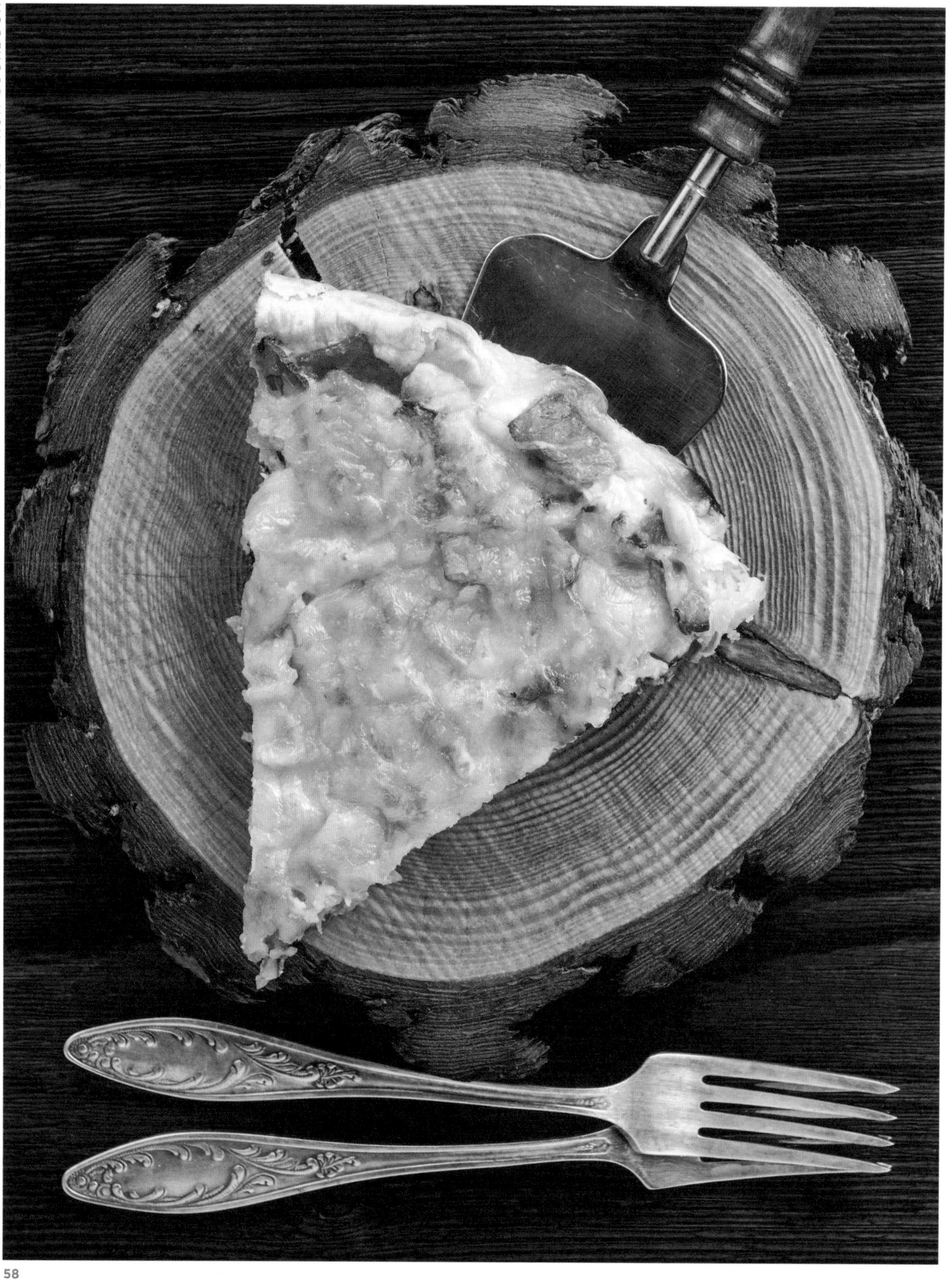

HAM AND CHEDDAR QUICHE

SERVES 6 TO 8 ✦ ACTIVE TIME: 40 MINUTES ✦ START TO FINISH: 90 MINUTES

What a combo! This quiche is rich with the salty goodness of fresh ham and the gooey deliciousness of cheddar cheese. The higher quality the ingredients you select are, the more flavorful it is, so don't skimp on this one.

1 baked crust
(see page 135)

2 tablespoons brown mustard

1 cup cooked ham, diced

1 cup sharp cheddar cheese, shredded

4 eggs

1½ cups whole milk or half-and-half

1 teaspoon salt

1 teaspoon ground pepper

Paprika (optional)

1. Preheat the oven to 350° F.

2. Working with the crust in the skillet, use a pastry brush or the back of a spoon to spread the mustard on the bottom and sides.

3. Sprinkle the ham pieces and shredded cheddar evenly over the bottom of the pie.

4. In a medium bowl, whisk the eggs until thoroughly combined. Add the milk, salt, and pepper and whisk to combine.

5. Pour the egg mixture over the meat and cheese, shaking the pan gently to distribute evenly and settle the liquid. If desired, sprinkle the top with paprika.

6. Put the skillet in the oven and bake for 35 to 40 minutes or until the quiche is puffy and golden brown, and the eggs are set.

7. Allow to sit for 10 minutes before slicing and serving.

BACON AND ZUCCHINI QUICHE

SERVES 6 TO 8 ✦ ACTIVE TIME: 45 MINUTES ✦ START TO FINISH: 90 MINUTES

Crisp, salty bacon is the perfect complement to zucchini in this late-summer quiche. I like to add a garlic-herb chèvre to further highlight these ingredients.

1 baked crust
(see page 135)

½-¾ pound thick-cut
bacon, cut into pieces

1 small zucchini,
cut into thin rounds

1 clove garlic, minced

4 eggs

1½ cups half-and-half

½ teaspoon salt

½ teaspoon freshly
ground pepper

3-5 oz. garlic-herb
chèvre

1. Preheat the oven to 350° F.

2. In a skillet, sauté the bacon pieces until just crispy, about 10 minutes. Use a slotted spoon to gather the pieces and put them on a plate lined with a paper towel to drain.

3. Add the zucchini pieces and garlic to the bacon fat, reduce the heat, and stir. Cook until zucchini is just soft, about 10 minutes.

4. Sprinkle the bacon pieces on the bottom of the crust, and use a slotted spoon to put the zucchini over it. Dot the mixture with the garlic-herb chèvre.

5. In a medium bowl, whisk the eggs until thoroughly combined. Add the half-and-half, salt, and pepper, and whisk to combine.

6. Pour the egg mixture over the other ingredients, shaking the pan gently to distribute evenly.

7. Put the skillet in the oven and bake for 35 to 40 minutes or until the quiche is puffy and golden brown and the eggs are set. Use pot holders or oven mitts to take the skillet out of the oven.

8. Allow to sit for 10 minutes before slicing and serving.

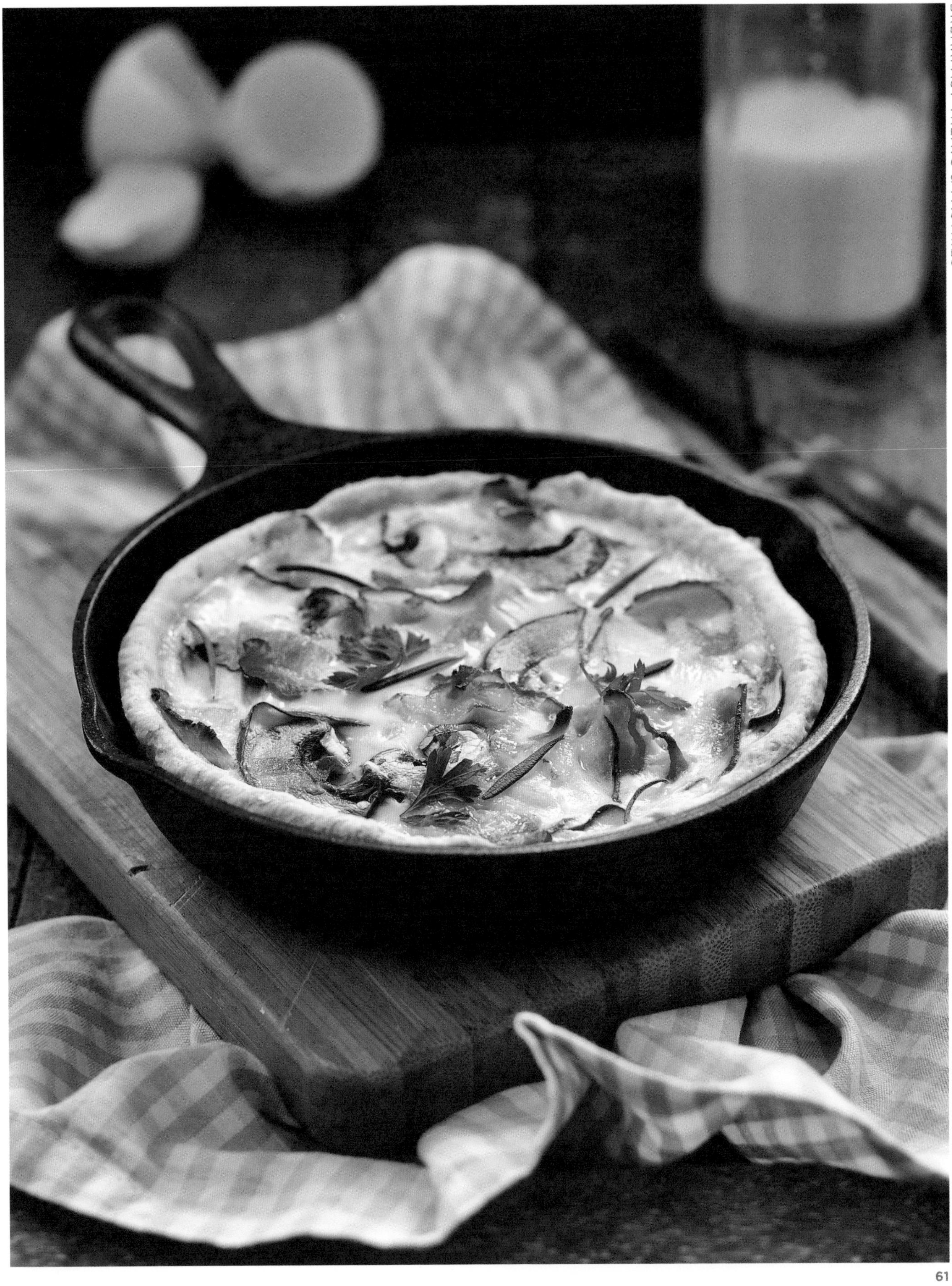

BEET AND CHÈVRE QUICHE

SERVES 6 TO 8 ✦ ACTIVE TIME: 45 MINUTES ✦ START TO FINISH: 2 HOURS

I love beets. They're beautiful and they're good for you. And they taste great. All good reasons to cook them up and put them in a quiche, where their color, texture, and flavor all work beautifully. Add fresh goat cheese (chèvre) and a hint of thyme, and you have an elegant, easy, and fabulous meal.

1 flaky pastry crust recipe for a single crust (see page 136)

4 or 5 red or golden beets (or a combination), peeled and sliced thin

2 tablespoons yellow onions, minced

1 teaspoon olive oil

6 eggs

1½ cups whole milk

2 teaspoons dried thyme

2 cloves garlic, pressed

4 oz. fresh goat cheese (chèvre)

1. Preheat the oven to 400° F.

2. Put the beet slices and minced onions in a pouch of heavy duty aluminum foil. Drizzle with olive oil and close up securely. Put the pouch in the oven and roast the beets and onions for about 20 minutes until soft, checking after 10 to 15 minutes. Remove pouch from oven and let sit while you prep the other ingredients.

3. In a large bowl, whisk the eggs until thoroughly combined. Add the milk, thyme, and garlic, and whisk to combine.

4. Carefully open the pouch of beets and onions and distribute over the pie crust. Pour the egg mixture over this, and dot with pieces of the goat cheese.

5. Cover the skillet with foil and bake for 40 minutes. Remove foil from skillet and continue to bake another 10 to 15 minutes or until the quiche is golden brown and the eggs are set. A knife inserted in the center should come out clean.

6. Allow to sit for about 30 minutes before slicing and serving.

CRAB QUICHE

SERVES 6 TO 8 ✦ ACTIVE TIME: 40 MINUTES ✦ START TO FINISH: 90 MINUTES

This recipe harkens back to the cuisine of my parents—decadent ingredients in cream and vermouth. It's easy to see why it was so popular once you taste this. It's a great Sunday brunch recipe to serve along with a big green salad and a bottle of French rosé!

1 flaky pastry crust recipe for a single crust (see page 136)

3 tablespoons unsalted butter

2 tablespoons scallions, tender parts only, thinly sliced

4 eggs

2 cups half-and-half

2 tablespoons dry vermouth

½ teaspoon salt

¼ teaspoon cayenne pepper

1 pound lump crab meat, thawed and drained if frozen

1. Preheat the oven to 350° F.

2. In a skillet over medium heat, melt butter and add scallions. Cook for about 5 minutes until scallions are tender.

3. In a large bowl, whisk eggs until thoroughly combined. Add the half-and-half, vermouth, salt, and cayenne pepper, and whisk to combine. Stir the cooked scallion mixture and the crab meat into the egg mix, and pour everything into the pie crust, shaking the pan gently to distribute evenly.

4. Put the skillet in the oven and bake for about 40 minutes or until the quiche is golden brown and the eggs are set. A knife inserted in the center should come out clean.

5. Allow to sit for about 20 minutes before slicing and serving.

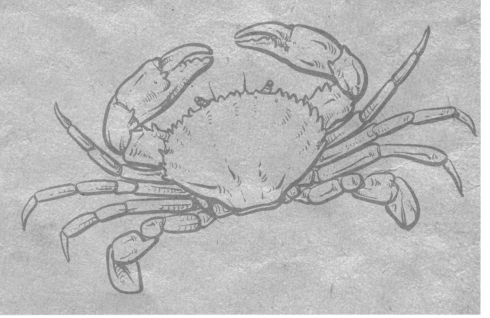

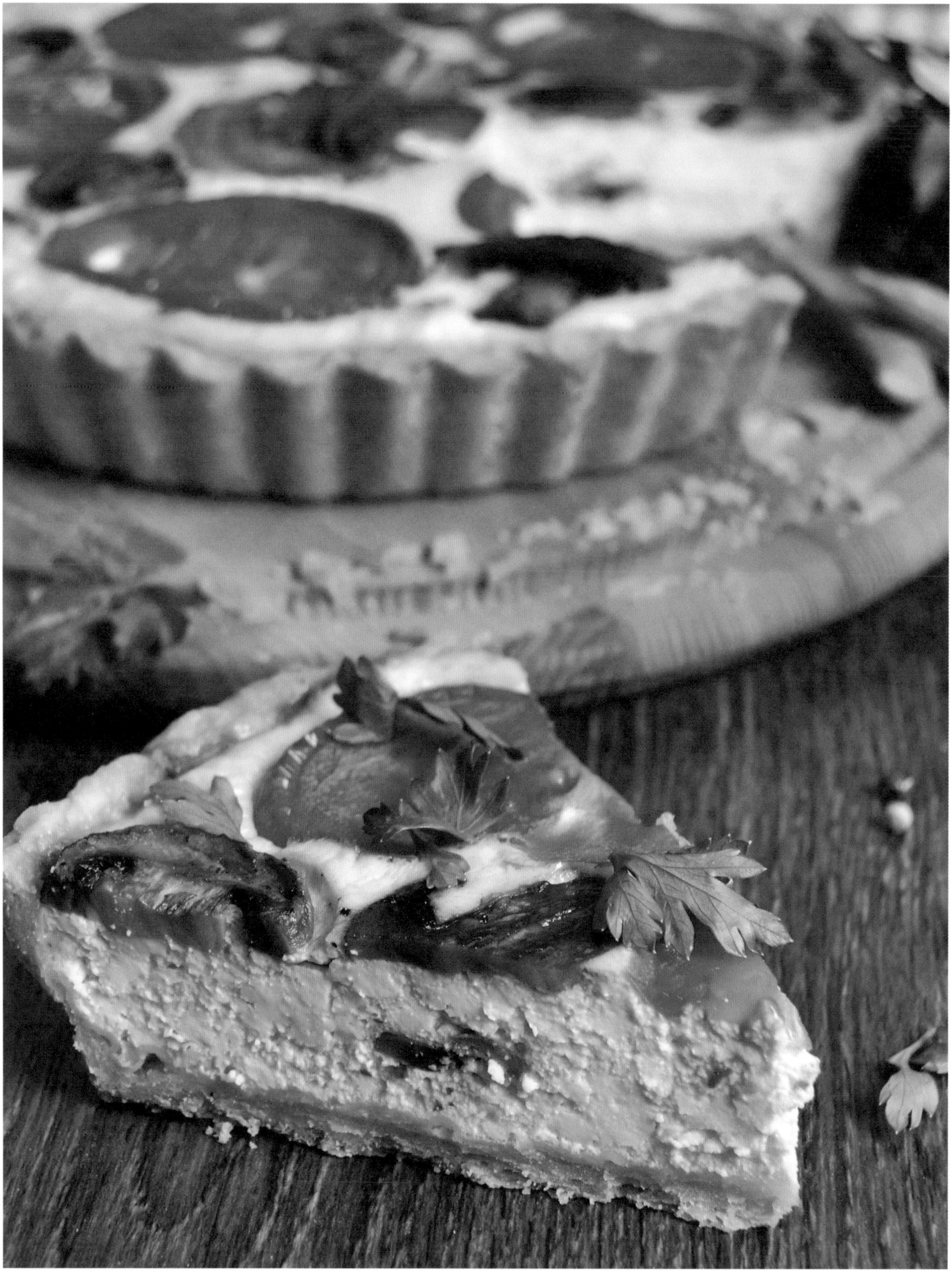

SAUSAGE AND FETA QUICHE

SERVES 6 TO 8 ✦ ACTIVE TIME: 45 MINUTES ✦ START TO FINISH: 90 MINUTES

This is a really yummy combination, made all the better by adding some Kalamata olives. If you can't get to Greece, make this quiche and find a sunny spot. You'll be transported.

1 baked crust
(see page 135)

2 tablespoons olive oil

½ pound Italian sausage

¼ cup red onion, diced

1 small tomato, seeds removed, diced

¼ cup Kalamata olives, halved

½ cup feta cheese, crumbled

4 eggs

2 cups whole milk

1 teaspoon salt

1 teaspoon fresh ground pepper

1. Preheat the oven to 350˚ F.

2. In a skillet, heat the olive oil over medium heat and add the sausage meat. Cook, while stirring, to break up the meat into crumbles. When it is no longer pink throughout, use a slotted spoon to transfer the meat onto a plate lined with a paper towel to drain.

3. Add the onion to the skillet and stir, cooking for about 3 minutes. Add the sausage back to the pan, and add the tomato and olives. Stir to combine and remove from the heat. Allow to cool slightly.

4. In a large bowl, whisk the eggs until thoroughly combined. Add the milk, salt, and pepper, and whisk to combine. Fill the crust with the meat and vegetables. Sprinkle the crumbled feta evenly over the mixture. Pour the egg mixture over the other ingredients, shaking the pan gently to distribute evenly.

5. Put the skillet in the oven and bake for 30 to 40 minutes or until the quiche is puffy and golden brown, and the eggs are set. A knife inserted in the center should come out clean.

6. Allow to sit for about 20 minutes before slicing and serving.

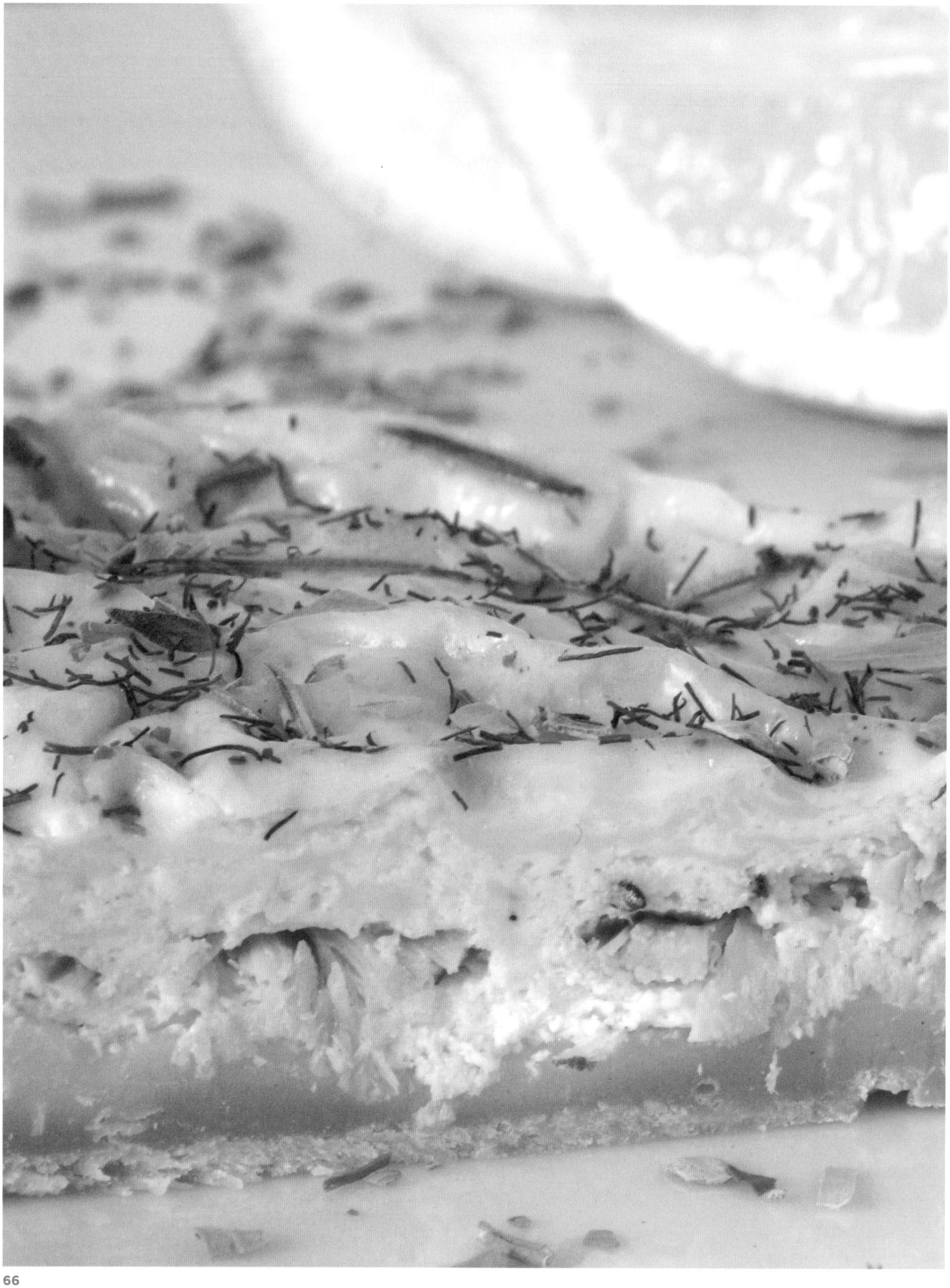

SMOKED SALMON AND DILL QUICHE

SERVES 6 TO 8 ✦ ACTIVE TIME: 30 MINUTES ✦ START TO FINISH: 90 MINUTES

Any good deli in New York City will serve smoked salmon for breakfast—typically on a bagel with a schmear of cream cheese, a few capers, and a sprig of dill. What a treat! Putting smoked salmon and dill in a quiche makes for a breakfast dish that is still fantastic for fans of the fish, but is mellower and therefore more palatable for those who might not be.

1 flaky pastry crust recipe for a single crust (see page 136)

1 teaspoon Dijon mustard

1 pound smoked salmon, cut or torn into nickel-sized pieces

4 eggs

1 cup half-and-half

1 teaspoon salt

½ teaspoon ground black pepper

1 tablespoon dill, finely minced

1 (3 oz.) package cream cheese, cut into small cubes

1. Preheat the oven to 350° F.

2. Working with the crust in the skillet, brush the mustard over the bottom of the dough. Place the salmon pieces in the pie.

3. In a large bowl, whisk the eggs until thoroughly combined. Add the half-and-half, salt, and pepper, and whisk to combine. Add the dill and mix well.

4. Pour the egg mixture over the salmon pieces, shaking the pan gently to distribute evenly. Sprinkle the cubes of cream cheese evenly on top.

5. Put the skillet in the oven and bake for 35 to 40 minutes or until the quiche is puffy and golden brown, and the eggs are set.

6. Allow to sit for 10 minutes before slicing and serving.

BROCCOLI-CHEDDAR QUICHE

SERVES 6 TO 8 ✦ ACTIVE TIME: 45 MINUTES ✦ START TO FINISH: 90 MINUTES

This is a recipe that features broccoli paired with cheddar. It's delicious heated or at room temperature, and, served with a salad, makes a great meal.

1 flaky pastry crust recipe for a single crust (see page 136)

1 teaspoon Dijon mustard

1¼ cups cheddar cheese, grated/shredded

3 cups broccoli florets and stems

6 eggs

1 cup half-and-half

1 teaspoon salt

½ teaspoon ground black pepper

½ cup Parmesan cheese, grated

1. Preheat the oven to 350˚ F.

2. In a saucepan, steam the broccoli pieces until cooked but still crisp, about 15 minutes. Drain, and rinse with cold water, and set aside to dry.

3. Working with the crust in the skillet, brush the mustard over the bottom of the dough. Next, use about ¼ cup of the cheddar cheese and sprinkle it over the dough. Place the broccoli pieces in the pie.

4. In a large bowl, whisk the eggs until thoroughly combined. Add the half-and-half, salt, and pepper, and whisk to combine. Add the remaining cheddar cheese and mix well.

5. Pour the egg mixture over the broccoli pieces, shaking the pan gently to distribute evenly. Sprinkle the Parmesan over everything.

6. Put the skillet in the oven and bake for 35 to 40 minutes or until the quiche is puffy and golden brown, and the eggs are set.

7. Allow to sit for 10 minutes before slicing and serving.

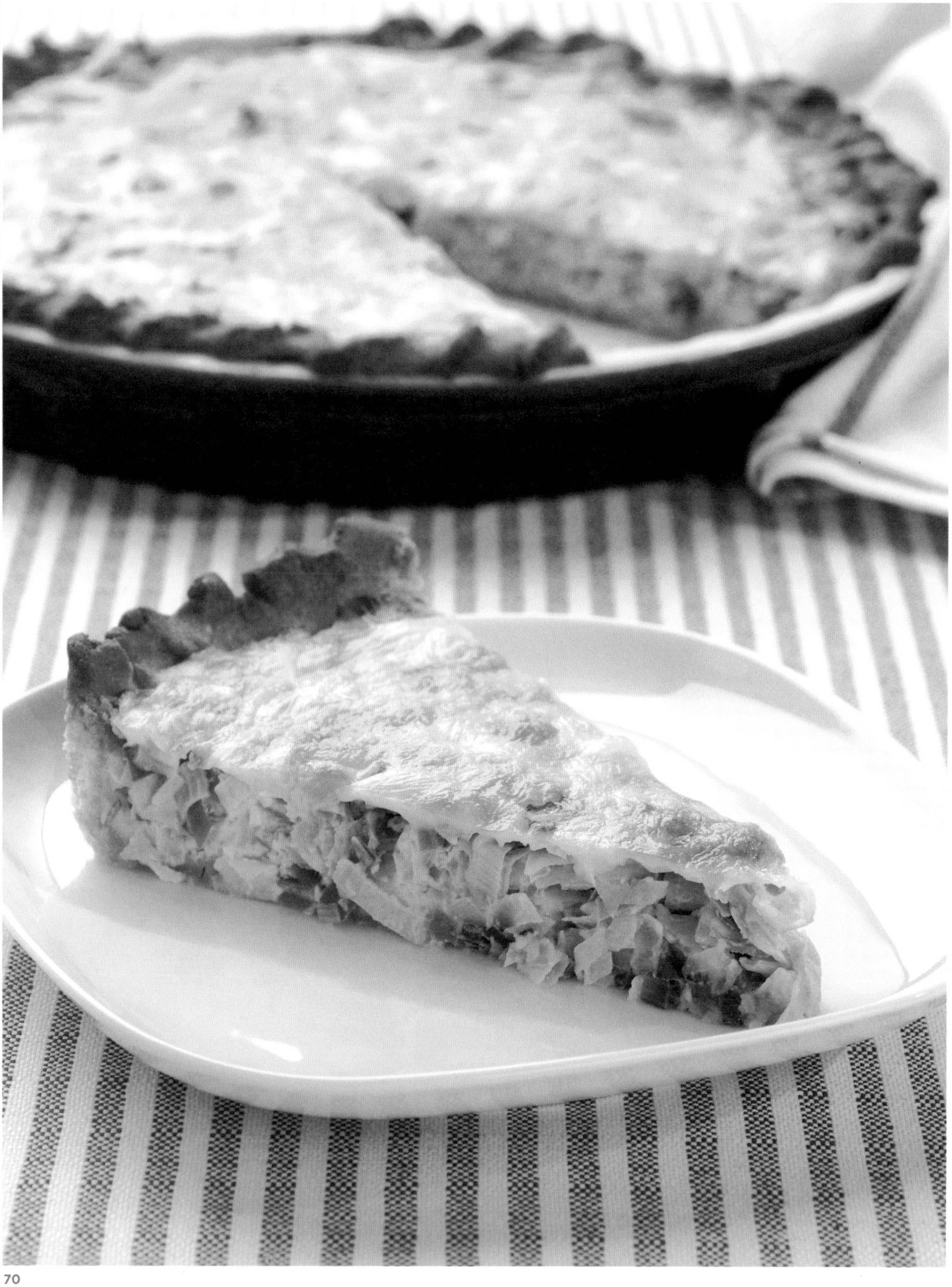

QUICHE WITH SAUTÉED LEEKS

SERVES 6 TO 8 ✦ ACTIVE TIME: 30 MINUTES ✦ START TO FINISH: 90 MINUTES

The leeks in this recipe are sautéed until soft and golden, which brings out their delectable mild onion flavor. Swiss or Gruyere cheese is the perfect complement. This is an easy-to-make quiche that is nonetheless quite elegant. It goes great with a green salad.

1 flaky pastry crust recipe for a single crust (see page 136)

3 large leeks, white and light green parts only

2 tablespoons olive oil

4 eggs

1 cup whole milk or half-and-half

½ to ¾ cup Swiss or Gruyere cheese, shredded

Salt and pepper to taste

1. Preheat the oven to 400° F.

2. Prepare the leeks by cutting the white and light green parts only into thin slices. Separate the rings in a colander, and rinse thoroughly to remove any sand or grit. Pat dry.

3. In a skillet, heat the olive oil over medium-high heat. Add the leeks and cook, stirring, for 1 minute to 2 minutes. Lower the heat and continue to cook so that the leeks become tender and golden, not overly browned, about 10 to 15 minutes. Stir frequently.

4. In a large bowl, whisk the eggs until thoroughly combined. Add the half-and-half, and whisk to combine. Add the shredded cheese and mix well. Season with salt and pepper.

5. Spread the sautéed leeks over the crust in the cast-iron skillet. Pour the egg mixture over the leeks, shaking the pan gently to distribute evenly.

6. Put the skillet in the oven and bake for about 40 minutes or until the quiche is puffy and golden brown, and the eggs are set.

7. Allow to sit for 10 minutes before slicing and serving.

MUSHROOM AND SWISS CHEESE QUICHE

SERVES 6 TO 8 ✦ ACTIVE TIME: 30 MINUTES ✦ START TO FINISH: 90 MINUTES

If you want a delicious, earthy quiche that will hit the spot on a cool autumn day, then this is it. Swiss cheese is the perfect partner for mushrooms, and the cornmeal crust is a great choice for this, as it adds some texture. You can use a flaky pastry crust, too.

1 cornmeal crust
(see page 141)

4 tablespoons butter

½ pound mushrooms,
sliced thin (a mixture
of portobello, shiitake,
and white mushrooms
is ideal)

1 small leek, white part
only, sliced thin

4 eggs

2 cups whole milk

1 teaspoon salt

½ teaspoon pepper

⅛ teaspoon nutmeg

1 cup Swiss cheese,
shredded

1. Preheat the oven to 350° F.

2. In a skillet over medium heat, melt the butter and add the mushrooms and leek. Cook, while stirring, until vegetables are soft, about 5 minutes.

3. In a large bowl, whisk eggs until thoroughly combined. Add milk, salt, pepper, and nutmeg, and whisk to combine.

4. Sprinkle half of the Swiss cheese on the crust. Distribute the mushroom/leek mixture over the cheese. Pour the egg mixture over everything and shake the skillet gently to evenly distribute the liquid. Sprinkle the remaining Swiss cheese on top.

5. Put the skillet in the oven and bake for 30 to 40 minutes or until the quiche is puffy and golden brown, and the eggs are set.

6. Allow to sit for about 20 minutes before slicing and serving.

CRUSTS & BREADS

Wait until you taste the mouthwatering breads and delectable pies that will be coming out of your oven when you start baking with the cast-iron skillet! You'll find that things are cooked more evenly, yielding the best-tasting breads, pies, and more. This chapter includes some basic breads and useful crusts for recipes that are sure to become family favorites—as well as gluten-free options!

BISCUITS

SERVES 4 TO 6 ✦ ACTIVE TIME: 20 MINUTES ✦ START TO FINISH: 40 MINUTES

For fluffy buttermilk biscuits, you need to work with a very hot skillet. The golden brown crust on the bottom is as much of a delight as the airy, warm dough.

2 cups flour

1 teaspoon sugar

1 teaspoon salt

1 tablespoon baking powder

8 tablespoons butter, cut into pieces

½ cup buttermilk, plus 2 tablespoons

1. Preheat oven to 450° F.

2. In a large bowl, combine the flour, sugar, salt, and baking powder.

3. Using a fork or pastry knife, blend in 6 tablespoons of the butter to form a crumbly dough. Form a well in the middle and add ½ cup of the buttermilk. Stir to combine and form a stiff dough. Using your fingers works best! If it seems too dry, add 1 tablespoon more of the buttermilk, going to 2 tablespoons if necessary.

4. Put 2 tablespoons butter in the skillet and put the skillet in the oven.

5. Put the dough on a lightly floured surface and press out to a thickness of about 1 inch. Cut out biscuits using an inverted water glass. Place the biscuits in the skillet and bake for about 10 minutes, until golden on the bottom.

Biscuits can be served with savory or sweet additions. You can make mini ham sandwiches by splitting the biscuits, putting some mayonnaise and grainy mustard on them, and putting in a slice of fresh-baked ham. You can fill them with scrambled eggs and bacon bits. Or you can slather them with butter and your favorite jam or honey. Or just eat them as is.

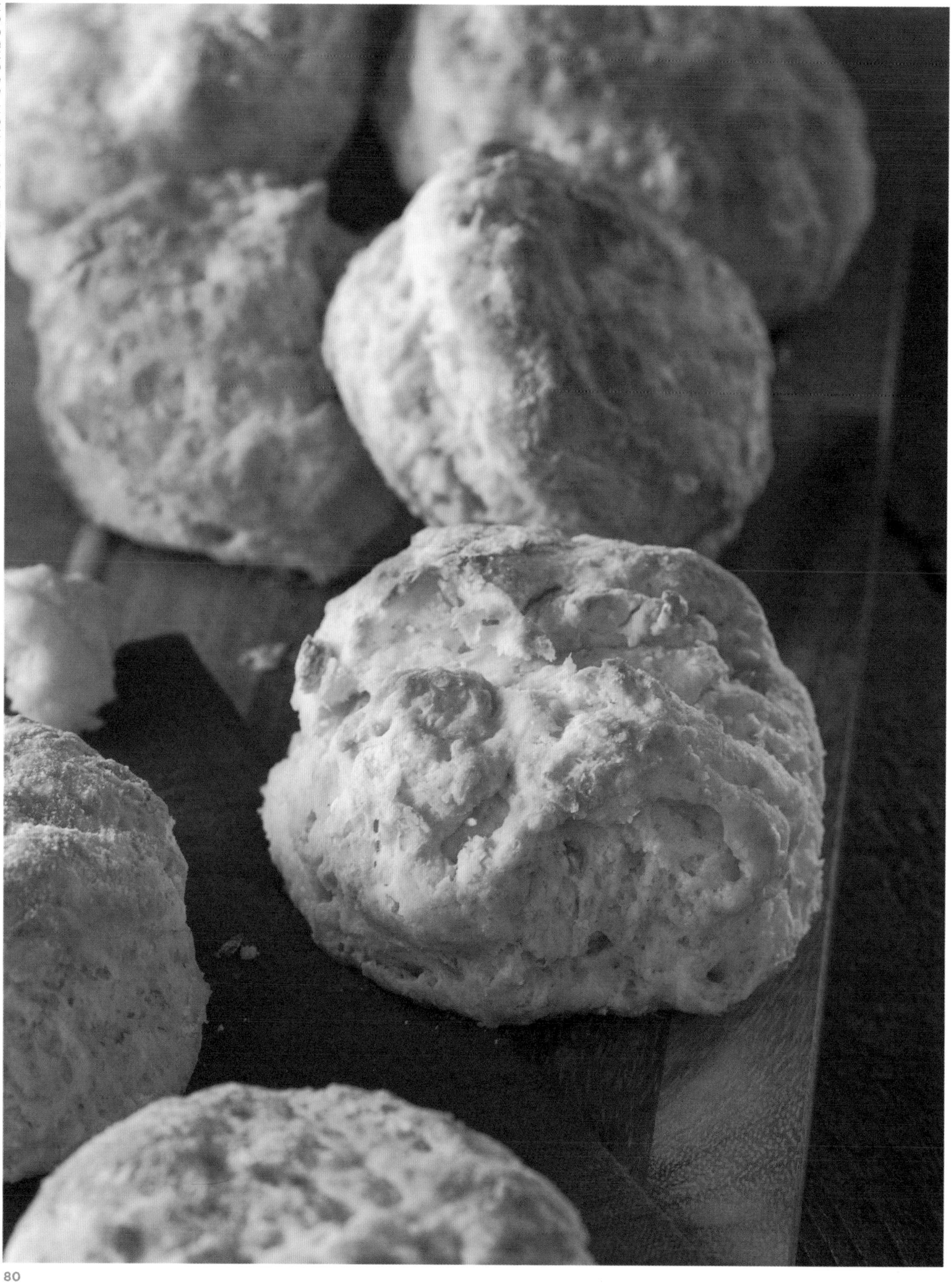

GLUTEN-FREE BISCUITS

SERVES 4 TO 6   ACTIVE TIME: 20 MINUTES   START TO FINISH: 40 MINUTES

It is possible to make delicious gluten-free biscuits, though they'll be a bit more crumbly than those made with regular flour.

1½ cups rice flour

⅓ cup potato starch

3 tablespoons tapioca flour

1 tablespoon baking powder

3 teaspoons maple sugar, or 1 tablespoon maple syrup

2 teaspoons cream of tartar

¼ teaspoon salt

1 teaspoon xanthan gum

7 tablespoons butter

½ cup buttermilk, plus 2 tablespoons

Preheat oven to 450° F.

In a large bowl, combine the flours, potato starch, baking powder, sugar, cream of tartar, salt, and xanthan gum. Using a fork or pastry knife, blend in 5 tablespoons of the butter to form a crumbly dough.

Form a well in the middle and add ½ cup buttermilk. Stir to combine and form a stiff dough. Using your fingers works best! If it seems too dry, add 1 tablespoon more of the buttermilk, going to 2 tablespoons if necessary.

Put 2 tablespoons butter in the skillet and put the skillet in the oven.

Put the dough on a lightly floured surface and press out to a thickness of about 1 inch. Cut out biscuits using an inverted water glass. Place the biscuits in the skillet and bake for about 10 minutes, until golden on the bottom.

DINNER ROLLS

MAKES ABOUT A DOZEN ROLLS ✦ ACTIVE TIME: 1 HOUR ✦ START TO FINISH: 3 HOURS

These classic dinner rolls are light, flaky, and buttery perfection.

1¼ cups whole milk, heated to 110° F

3 tablespoons sugar

1 tablespoon active dry yeast

8 tablespoons (1 stick) unsalted butter

¾ teaspoon salt

2 eggs at room temperature, lightly beaten

3½ cups cake or bread flour (not all-purpose flour)

1. In a small bowl, combine ½ cup warm milk and the sugar. Sprinkle the yeast over it, stir, and set aside so the yeast can proof (about 10 minutes).

2. While the yeast is proofing, melt the butter in the skillet over low to medium heat, and remove from heat when melted.

3. When the yeast mix is frothy, stir in 3 tablespoons of the melted butter, the remaining milk, the salt, and the eggs. Then stir in the flour, mixing until all ingredients are incorporated. Transfer to a lightly floured surface and knead the dough for 5 to 10 minutes until it is soft, springy, and elastic.

4. Coat the bottom and sides of a large mixing bowl (ceramic is best) with butter. Place the ball of dough in the bowl, cover loosely with plastic wrap, put it in a naturally warm, draft-free location, and let it rise until doubled in size, about 45 minutes to 1 hour.

5. Prepare a lightly floured surface to work on. Punch down the dough in the bowl and transfer it to the floured surface. Warm the skillet containing the butter so that it is melted again.

6. Break off pieces of the dough and shape them into 2-inch balls with your hands. Roll the balls in the butter in the skillet, and leave them in the skillet.

7. Cover the skillet loosely with a clean dish towel, put it in the warm, draft-free spot, and let the rolls rise until doubled in size, about 30 minutes. While they're rising, preheat the oven to 350° F.

8. When the rolls have risen and the oven is ready, cover the skillet with aluminum foil and bake in the oven for 20 minutes. Remove the foil and finish cooking, another 15 minutes or so, until the rolls are golden on top and light and springy. Serve warm.

It's important to proof the yeast before adding it to your recipe to ensure that it is fresh and active. If it is, it reacts with the sugar and liquid and creates tiny bubbles. It also releases a smell that is described (appropriately enough) as "yeasty"—the smell you get from fresh-baked bread. Yeast reacts with sugar to release carbon dioxide and, eventually, alcohol. This is the basis of making beer and wine, too. But with baking, the fermentation process stops when the live cells are cooked in the oven.

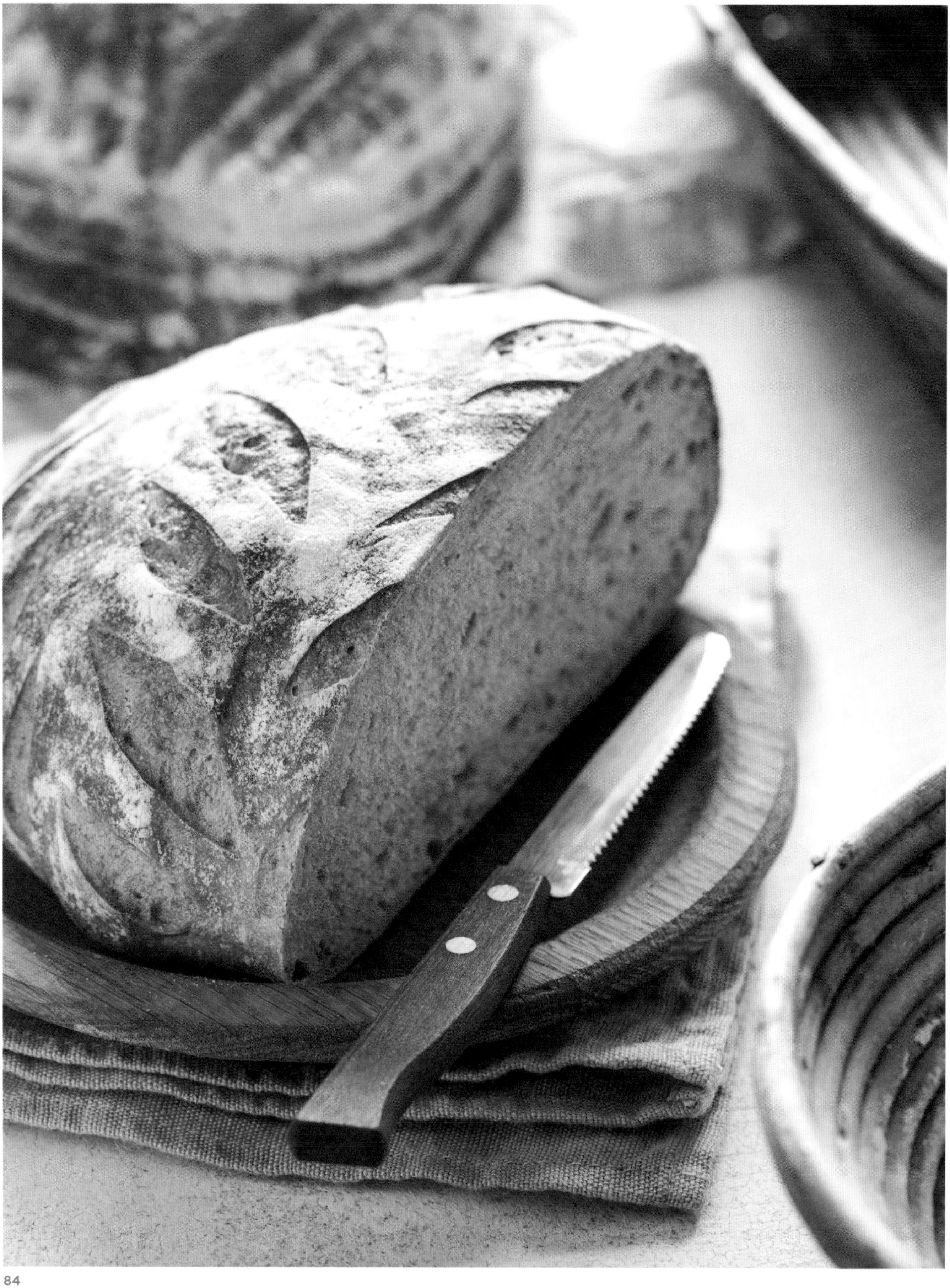

NO-KNEAD BREAD

I recommend using a 7-quart cast-iron Dutch oven for this recipe. This delicious bread is a great way to upgrade a pimento cheese sandwich—there is really nothing easier. Just remember that you need to give it up to two days, so plan ahead!

½ tablespoon active dry yeast

¼ teaspoon sugar

1½ cups water (110 to 115° F)

1½ teaspoons kosher salt

3 cups all-purpose flour, plus more for kneading and dusting

1. In a large bowl, add the yeast and sugar and top with the warm water. Stir to dissolve the yeast. Cover the bowl with plastic wrap and allow to proof for about 15 minutes. Add the salt and flour. Stir until just blended with the yeast, sugar, and water. The dough will be sticky.

2. Cover the bowl with plastic wrap and set aside for at least 15 hours and up to 18 hours, preferably in a place that's 65 to 70° F.

3. The dough will be bubbled when you go to work with it. Lightly dust a work surface with flour and scoop the dough out onto it. Dust your fingers with flour so they don't stick to the dough. Fold it gently once or twice.

4. Transfer the dough to a clean bowl that is room temperature and cover with a dish towel. Let rise another 1 to 2 hours until doubled in size.

5. While the dough is on its final rise, preheat the oven to 450° F, placing the Dutch oven inside with the lid on so it gets hot. When the oven is ready and dough has risen, carefully remove the lid and gently scoop the dough from the bowl into the Dutch oven. Cover and bake for 20 minutes. Remove the lid and continue to bake for another 25 minutes until the top is golden and it sounds hollow when tapped.

6. Remove Dutch oven from oven and use tea towels to carefully transfer bread to a rack or cutting board. Allow to cool at least 20 minutes before serving.

BASIC WHITE BREAD

MAKES 1 SMALL ROUND ✦ ACTIVE TIME: 25 MINUTES ✦ START TO FINISH: 3 HOURS

I was skeptical of the recipes I found for baking bread in a cast-iron Dutch oven. They called for heating the cookware in the oven while the oven preheated (to a very high 450° F) and leaving the lid on for part of the baking time. But the photos looked good, so I dove in. This was the first recipe I made, and it was a great success. I'm definitely a convert. Hope you will be, too.

¼ teaspoon active dry yeast

¼ teaspoon sugar

1½ cups water (110 to 115° F)

1 teaspoon kosher salt

3 cups all-purpose flour, plus more for kneading and dusting

1. Put the yeast and sugar in a measuring cup and add about ½ cup warm water in a drizzle. Hot water will kill the yeast, so it's important that the water be warm without being hot. Cover the measuring cup with plastic wrap and set it aside for about 15 minutes. If the yeast doesn't foam, it is not alive and you'll need to start over.

2. When the yeast is proofed, pour it into a large bowl and add the additional cup of warm water. Stir gently to combine. Add the salt to the flour, and add the flour to the yeast mixture. Stir with a wooden spoon until combined. The dough will be wet and sticky.

3. Put a dusting of flour on a flat surface and lift out the dough. With flour on your hands and more at the ready, begin kneading the dough so that it loses its stickiness. Don't overdo it, and don't use too much flour; just enough that it becomes more cohesive.

4. Place the dough in a large bowl, cover the bowl with plastic wrap, and allow to rise untouched for at least 1 hour, and up to several hours. Gently punch it down, re-cover with the plastic, and allow to rise again for another 30 minutes or so.

5. While the dough is on its final rise, preheat the oven to 450° F. Put a piece of parchment paper on the bottom of the Dutch oven and put it in with the lid on so it gets hot. When the oven is ready and dough has risen, carefully remove the lid and gently scoop the dough from the bowl into the pot. Cover and bake for 15 minutes. Remove the lid and continue to bake for another 15 to 20 minutes until the top is golden and it sounds hollow when tapped.

6. Remove the pot from the oven and use tea towels to carefully remove the bread. Allow to cool before slicing.

WHEAT BREAD

SERVES 4 TO 6 ✦ **ACTIVE TIME: 20 MINUTES** ✦ **START TO FINISH: 60 MINUTES**

When you discover how easy it is to make such a tasty loaf of bread with all-purpose flour, you'll want to start experimenting with other flavors and textures that can be found in flours, nuts, and so on. Here's a wheat bread recipe that uses enough all-purpose flour to ensure adequate rising and fluffiness upon baking.

¼ teaspoon instant yeast

¼ teaspoon sugar

1½ cups water (110 to 115° F)

1 teaspoon kosher salt

2 cups whole wheat flour

1 cup all-purpose flour, plus more for kneading and dusting

1. Put the yeast and sugar in a measuring cup and add about ½ cup warm water in a drizzle. Hot water will kill the yeast, so it's important that the water be warm without being hot. Cover the measuring cup with plastic wrap and set it aside for about 15 minutes. If the yeast doesn't foam, it is not alive and you'll need to start over.

2. When the yeast is proofed, pour it into a large bowl and add the additional cup of warm water. Stir gently to combine. Add the salt to the flours, and add the flours to the yeast mixture. Stir with a wooden spoon until combined. The dough will be wet and sticky.

3. Put a dusting of flour on a flat surface and lift out the dough. With flour on your hands and more at the ready, begin kneading the dough so that it loses its stickiness. Don't overdo it, and don't use too much flour; just enough that it becomes more cohesive.

4. Place the dough in a large bowl, cover the bowl with plastic wrap, and allow to rise untouched for at least 1 hour, and up to several hours. Gently punch it down, re-cover with the plastic, and allow to rise again for another 30 minutes or so.

5. While the dough is on its final rise, preheat the oven to 450° F. Put a piece of parchment paper on the bottom of the Dutch oven and put it in with the lid on so it gets hot. When the oven is ready and dough has risen, carefully remove the lid and gently scoop the dough from the bowl into the pot. Cover and bake for 15 minutes. Remove the lid and continue to bake for another 15 to 20 minutes until the top is golden and it sounds hollow when tapped.

6. Remove the pot from the oven and use tea towels to carefully remove the bread. Allow to cool before slicing.

Variations

❀ Making this with a seeded crust really boosts the flavor and adds texture, too. A nice combination is toasted sesame seeds and poppy seeds. When the dough is in the Dutch oven and ready to be baked, sprinkle generously with the seeds, pressing lightly to help the seeds adhere.

❀ Gluten-Free Variation: Make a gluten-free whole grain loaf by mixing one 20 oz. bag of Bob's Red Mill Hearty Whole Grain Bread mix with 1¾ cups water, 2 eggs, ¼ cup vegetable oil, and 2 teaspoons cider vinegar. There's an envelope of yeast in the package. Allow it to proof in the water, mix in the other ingredients, knead, and allow to rise about 45 minutes before baking in the Dutch oven as you would for the Wheat Bread recipe.

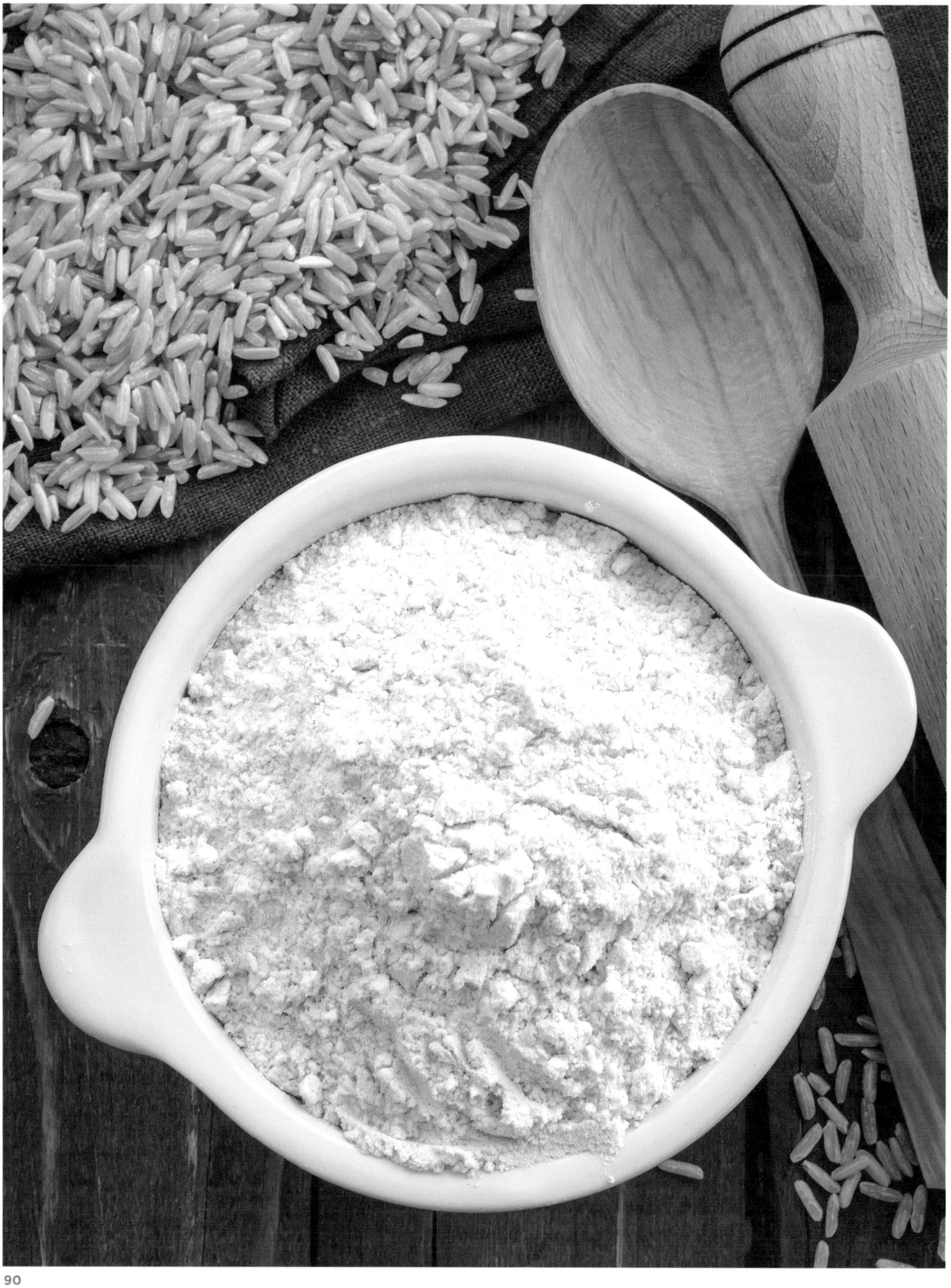

GLUTEN-FREE BREAD

MAKES 1 SMALL ROUND ✦ ACTIVE TIME: 25 MINUTES ✦ START TO FINISH: 3 HOURS

We are fortunate to live in a time when gluten-free options are numerous. If you love bread and can't or don't want to eat gluten, make this recipe and dig in! You'll be amazed at the result—an equally crusty yet fluffy loaf that tastes great!

½ teaspoon instant yeast

¼ teaspoon sugar

1½ to 2½ cups water (110 to 115˚ F)

1 teaspoon kosher salt

1½ teaspoons xanthan gum

3 cups Bob's Red Mill Gluten-Free Flour, plus more for kneading and dusting

⅓ cup Bob's Red Mill Sweet White Rice Flour

1. Put the yeast and sugar in a measuring cup and add about ½ cup warm water in a drizzle. Hot water will kill the yeast, so it's important that the water be warm without being hot. Cover the measuring cup with plastic wrap and set it aside for about 15 minutes. If the yeast doesn't foam, it is not alive and you'll need to start over.

2. When the yeast is proofed, pour it into a large bowl and add an additional cup of warm water. Stir gently to combine. Add the salt and xanthan gum to the flours, and add the flours to the yeast mixture. Stir with a wooden spoon until combined. Add up to an additional cup of warm water to accommodate the rice flour, which is tackier than regular flour. The dough should be wet and sticky.

3. Put a dusting of flour on a flat surface and lift out the dough. With flour on your hands and more at the ready, begin kneading the dough so that it loses its stickiness. Don't overdo it, and don't use too much flour; just enough that it becomes more cohesive.

4. Place the dough in a large bowl, cover the bowl with plastic wrap, and allow to rise untouched for at least 1 hour, and up to several hours. Gently punch it down, re-cover with the plastic, and allow to rise again for another 30 minutes or so.

5. While the dough is on its final rise, preheat the oven to 450˚ F. Put a piece of parchment paper on the bottom of the Dutch oven and put it in with the lid on so it gets hot. When the oven is ready and dough has risen, carefully remove the lid and gently scoop the dough from the bowl into the pot. Cover and bake for 15 minutes. Remove the lid and continue to bake for another 15 to 20 minutes until the top is golden and it sounds hollow when tapped.

6. Remove the pot from the oven and use tea towels to carefully remove the bread. Allow to cool before slicing.

SEEDED BREAD

MAKES 1 SMALL ROUND ✦ ACTIVE TIME: 25 MINUTES ✦ START TO FINISH: 3 HOURS

As you master breadmaking in the cast-iron Dutch oven, you can experiment in all kinds of ways. If you like toasted sesame seeds, this is a real treat.

¼ teaspoon instant yeast

¼ teaspoon sugar

1½ cups water (110 to 115° F)

1 teaspoon kosher salt

3 cups all-purpose flour, plus more for kneading and dusting

1 egg yolk, beaten with 1 tablespoon water

½ cup sesame seeds

1. Put the yeast and sugar in a measuring cup and add about ½ cup warm water in a drizzle. Hot water will kill the yeast, so it's important that the water be warm without being hot. Cover the measuring cup with plastic wrap and set it aside for about 15 minutes. If the yeast doesn't foam, it is not alive and you'll need to start over.

2. When the yeast is proofed, pour it into a large bowl and add the additional cup of warm water. Stir gently to combine. Add the salt to the flour, and add the flour to the yeast mixture. Stir with a wooden spoon until combined. The dough will be wet and sticky.

3. Put a dusting of flour on a flat surface and lift out the dough. With flour on your hands and more at the ready, begin kneading the dough so that it loses its stickiness. Don't overdo it, and don't use too much flour; just enough that it becomes more cohesive.

4. Place the dough in a large bowl, cover the bowl with plastic wrap, and allow to rise untouched for at least 1 hour, and up to several hours. On a gently floured surface, turn out the dough and gently punch it down. Put a large piece of parchment paper in the bowl in which the bread was rising before. Return the dough to the bowl on the parchment paper, cover with plastic wrap, and allow to rise again for another 30 minutes or so.

5. While the dough is on its final rise, preheat the oven to 450° F. Put a piece of parchment paper on the bottom of the Dutch oven and put it in with the lid on so it gets hot. When the oven is ready and dough has risen, carefully remove the lid and gently scoop the dough from the bowl into the pot, brush with the egg wash, and sprinkle generously with the sesame seeds. Cover and bake for 15 minutes. Remove the lid and continue to bake for another 15 to 20 minutes until the top is golden and it sounds hollow when tapped.

6. Remove the pot from the oven and use tea towels to carefully remove the bread. Allow to cool before slicing.

Variation

Substitute unsalted sunflower seeds or pepitas (pumpkin seeds) for the sesame seeds.

GARLIC ROSEMARY ROLLS

**SERVES 6 TO 8 (ABOUT 8 ROLLS) ✦ ACTIVE TIME: 90 MINUTES ✦
START TO FINISH: 3 HOURS**

If you're a fan of garlic as my family is, you will swoon at the scent these rolls give off as they're baking. Better yet is the taste. Mangia!

1 packet active dry yeast (2¼ teaspoons)

1 cup water (110 to 115° F)

1 tablespoon sugar

2 tablespoons butter, melted

1 teaspoon salt

2 cloves garlic, minced

4 cups flour

1 teaspoon fresh rosemary leaves, chopped, or 2 teaspoons dried, crushed rosemary

1 egg, lightly beaten

Sea salt to taste

1. In a large bowl, mix the yeast, warm water, and sugar and let the yeast proof for about 10 minutes, until foamy.

2. Next add the 1 tablespoon of butter, salt, garlic, and half the flour. Mix until a sticky dough forms. Continue to add flour, mixing to form a soft dough. Add the rosemary with the last addition of flour.

3. Coat the bottom and sides of a large mixing bowl (ceramic is best) with butter. Place the ball of dough in the bowl, cover loosely with plastic wrap, put it in a naturally warm, draft-free location, and let it rise until doubled in size, about 45 minutes to 1 hour.

4. Put the skillet in the oven and preheat the oven to 400° F.

5. Transfer the dough to a lightly floured surface. Divide into 8 pieces and form into balls.

6. Remove the skillet from the oven and melt the remaining tablespoon of butter in it. Place the rolls in the skillet, turning to cover them with butter. Wash the rolls with the beaten egg and sprinkle with sea salt.

7. Bake in the oven until golden and set, about 40 minutes.

Make cheesy garlic-rosemary rolls by sprinkling Parmesan or Pecorino Romano cheese on the tops after washing with the beaten egg. Skip the sea salt.

ROASTED GARLIC BREAD

MAKES 1 SMALL ROUND ✦ ACTIVE TIME: 25 MINUTES ✦ START TO FINISH: 3 HOURS

Be forewarned: If you love garlic (as I suspect you do if you want to make this recipe), the smell of this bread baking will make you drool. Once you can slice into it, eat it as-is, toast it, top with a thin smear of pesto, or serve it as a wonderful substitute for traditional garlic bread.

1 head garlic

¼ cup olive oil

¼ teaspoon instant yeast

¼ teaspoon sugar

1½ cups water (110 to 115° F)

1 teaspoon kosher salt

3 cups all-purpose flour, plus more for kneading and dusting

1. Preheat the oven to 375° F.

2. Take as much of the paper skin off the head of garlic as possible without separating the cloves. With a sharp knife, cut off only as much of the top of the head as necessary to expose the cloves in their sleeves. Put the garlic cut side up on a piece of heavy duty aluminum foil or in a garlic roaster. Pour the olive oil over the top of the head of garlic. Fold the aluminum foil up and over the garlic to cover it, crimping any edges together, or put the lid on the garlic roaster. Roast in the oven for 50 to 60 minutes.

3. Open the foil or roaster and allow the garlic to cool slightly. Extract the roasted cloves from their sleeves by squeezing the bottom so the cloves pop out. Put them on a plate or in a shallow bowl. Reserve the cooking oil.

4. Put the yeast and sugar in a measuring cup and add about ½ cup warm water in a drizzle. Hot water will kill the yeast, so it's important that the water be warm without being hot. Cover the measuring cup with plastic wrap and set it aside for about 15 minutes. If the yeast doesn't foam, it is not alive and you'll need to start over.

5. When the yeast is proofed, pour it into a large bowl and add the additional cup of warm water. Stir gently to combine. Add the salt to the flour, and add the flour to the yeast mixture. Stir with a wooden spoon until combined. The dough will be wet and sticky.

6. Put a dusting of flour on a flat surface and lift out the dough. With flour on your hands and more at the ready, begin kneading the dough so that it loses its stickiness. Don't overdo it, and don't use too much flour; just enough that it becomes more cohesive. Add the roasted garlic cloves while you're kneading the dough.

7. Lightly grease a large bowl with some of the garlic-infused olive oil and place the dough in it. Cover the bowl with plastic wrap, and allow to rise untouched for at least 1 hour, and up to several hours. Gently punch it down, re-cover with the plastic, and allow to rise again for another 30 minutes or so. Brush the surface with the remaining garlic-infused oil.

8. While the dough is on its final rise, preheat the oven to 450° F. Put a piece of parchment paper on the bottom of the Dutch oven and put it in with the lid on so it gets hot. When the oven is ready and dough has risen, carefully remove the lid and gently scoop the dough from the bowl into the pot. Cover and bake for 15 minutes. Remove the lid and continue to bake for another 15 to 20 minutes until the top is golden and it sounds hollow when tapped.

9. Remove the pot from the oven and use tea towels to carefully remove the bread. Allow to cool before slicing.

Variation

Add ¼ cup fresh rosemary during the kneading process to complement the garlic and add another layer of flavor.

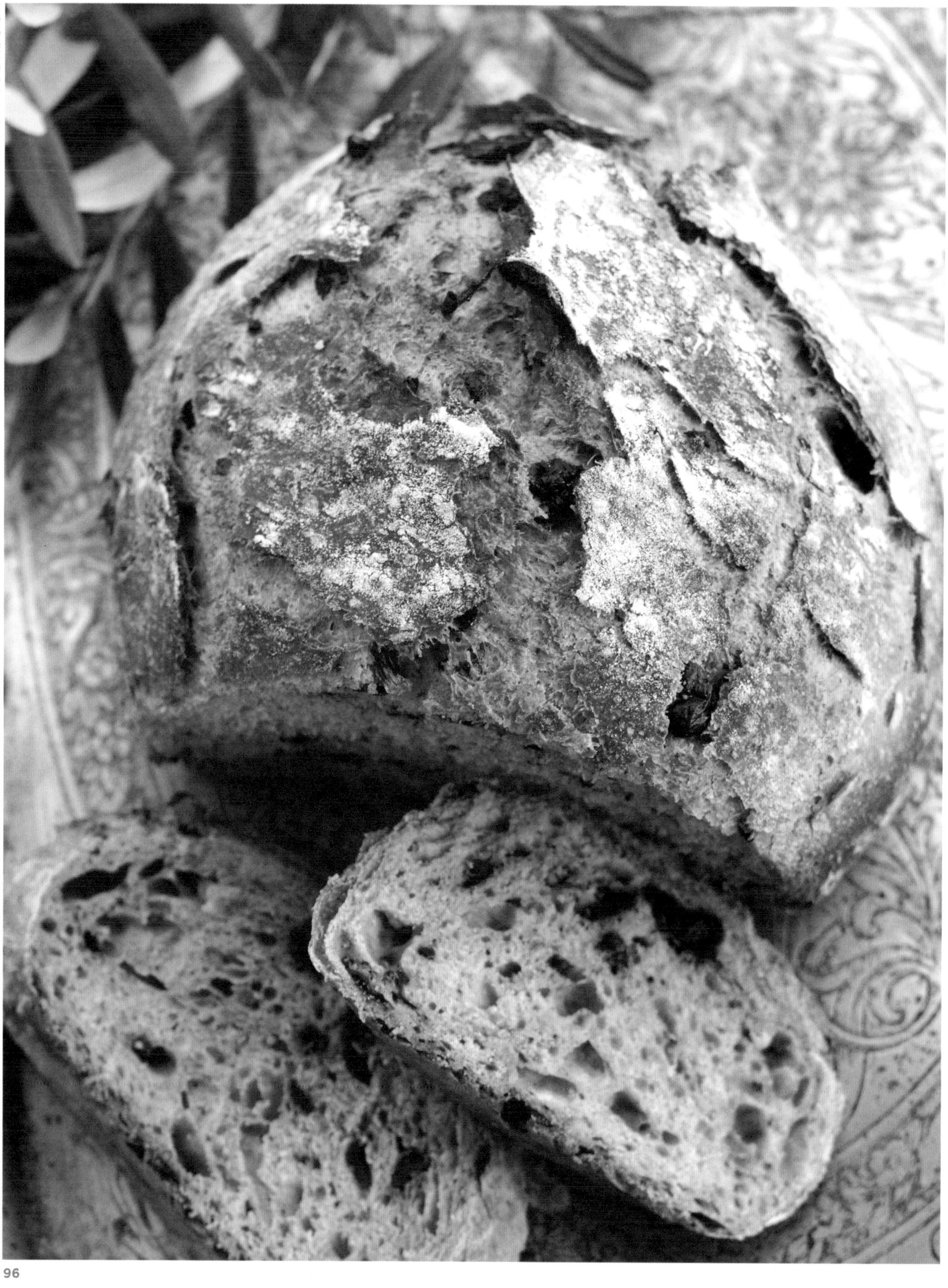

OLIVE LOAF

MAKES 1 SMALL ROUND   **ACTIVE TIME: 25 MINUTES**   **START TO FINISH: 3 HOURS**

I love the earthy-salty flavor of dark olives like Kalamatas. They are delicious in bread, too. Rather than taking the time to slice a lot of Kalamata olives, I like to use a top-shelf tapenade (olive) spread, which is easy to spread and distribute in the dough.

¼ teaspoon instant
yeast

¼ teaspoon sugar

1½ cups water
(110 to 115° F)

1 teaspoon kosher salt

3 cups all-purpose
flour, plus more for
kneading and dusting

½ cup tapenade
(olive spread) or
½ cup Kalamata olives

1 tablespoon olive oil

1. Put the yeast and sugar in a measuring cup and add about ½ cup warm water in a drizzle. Hot water will kill the yeast, so it's important that the water be warm without being hot. Cover the measuring cup with plastic wrap and set it aside for about 15 minutes. If the yeast doesn't foam, it is not alive and you'll need to start over.

2. When the yeast is proofed, pour it into a large bowl and add the additional cup of warm water. Stir gently to combine. Add the salt to the flour, and add the flour to the yeast mixture. Stir with a wooden spoon until combined. The dough will be wet and sticky.

3. Put a dusting of flour on a flat surface and lift out the dough. With flour on your hands and more at the ready, begin kneading the dough so that it loses its stickiness. Don't overdo it, and don't use too much flour; just enough that it becomes more cohesive. Incorporate the tapenade or olive pieces while you're kneading.

4. Place the dough in a large bowl, cover the bowl with plastic wrap, and allow to rise untouched for at least 1 hour, and up to several hours. Gently punch it down, re-cover with the plastic, and allow to rise again for another 30 minutes or so. Brush with the olive oil.

5. While the dough is on its final rise, preheat the oven to 450° F. Put a piece of parchment paper on the bottom of the Dutch oven and put it in with the lid on so it gets hot. When the oven is ready and dough has risen, carefully remove the lid and gently scoop the dough from the bowl into the pot. Cover and bake for 15 minutes. Remove the lid and continue to bake for another 15 to 20 minutes until the top is golden and it sounds hollow when tapped.

6. Remove the pot from the oven and use tea towels to carefully remove the bread. Allow to cool before slicing.

CHOCOLATE-CINNAMON BREAD

**MAKES 1 SMALL ROUND ✦ DUTCH OVEN: 4.5 QUART ✦
ACTIVE TIME: 25 MINUTES ✦ START TO FINISH: 3 HOURS**

This is like an exotic pain au chocolat—*crunchy and crispy on the outside, fluffy yet chocolaty and spicy on the inside. Be patient when it comes out of the oven and allow the bread to cool for 15 to 20 minutes so that it slices easily and cleanly.*

¼ teaspoon active dry yeast

¼ teaspoon sugar

1½ cups lukewarm water (90 to 100° F)

2 tablespoons unsalted butter

1 cup semi-sweet chocolate morsels

1 teaspoon ground cinnamon

3 cups all-purpose flour, plus more for kneading and dusting

1 teaspoon salt

1. Put the yeast and sugar in a measuring cup and add about ½ cup lukewarm water in a drizzle. Hot water will kill the yeast, so it's important that the water be warm without being hot. Cover the measuring cup with plastic wrap and set it aside for about 15 minutes. If the yeast doesn't foam, it is not alive and you'll need to start over.

2. Cut the butter into thin slices and put it with the chocolate morsels in a medium-sized, microwave-safe bowl. Melt the chocolate and butter in the microwave, working in 20-second increments. After each 20 seconds, stir the butter and chocolate. Microwave just until melted, about 40 to 60 seconds. Stir in the cinnamon and set aside to cool. It must be cool when added to the dough.

3. When the yeast is proofed, pour it into a large bowl and add the additional cup of lukewarm water. Stir gently to combine. Add the salt to the flour, and add the flour to the yeast mixture. Stir with a wooden spoon until combined. The dough will be wet and sticky.

4. Put a dusting of flour on a flat surface and lift out the dough. With flour on your hands and more at the ready, begin kneading the dough so that it loses its stickiness. Don't overdo it, and don't use too much flour—just enough that it becomes more cohesive. While kneading, add the chocolate mixture in increments, using as much as you want. You may choose not to use it all. Work it into the dough gently.

5. Place the dough in a large bowl, cover the bowl with plastic wrap, and allow to rise untouched for at least 1 hour, and up to several hours. Gently punch it down, re-cover with the plastic, and allow to rise again for another 30 minutes or so.

6. While the dough is on its final rise, preheat the oven to 450° F. Put a piece of parchment paper on the bottom of the Dutch oven and put it in with the lid on while the oven reaches 450° F. When the oven is ready, use pot holders to remove the lid of the Dutch oven, scoop the dough from the bowl to the pot, put the lid back on, and close the oven door.

7. Bake with the lid on for 15 minutes, then remove the lid. Allow to bake for another 15 to 20 minutes until the top is golden and the bread sounds hollow when tapped.

8. Remove the pot from the oven and use tea towels to carefully remove the bread. Allow to cool before slicing.

Variation

Add a subtle yet delightful heat to the bread by adding 1 teaspoon cayenne pepper along with the cinnamon.

WHOLE WHEAT CRANBERRY-PECAN BREAD

MAKES 1 SMALL ROUND ✦ ACTIVE TIME: 25 MINUTES ✦ START TO FINISH: 3 HOURS

This is a delicious and dense bread that is especially good toasted and served with fresh butter or cream cheese. It also makes a great complement to soft cheeses when cut into small pieces and served instead of crackers.

¼ teaspoon instant yeast

¼ teaspoon sugar

1½ cups water (110 to 115° F)

1 teaspoon kosher salt

2 cups whole wheat flour

1 cup all-purpose flour, plus more for kneading and dusting

1 cup dried cranberries

1 cup pecans, chopped

1. Put the yeast and sugar in a measuring cup and add about ½ cup warm water in a drizzle. Hot water will kill the yeast, so it's important that the water be warm without being hot. Cover the measuring cup with plastic wrap and set it aside for about 15 minutes. If the yeast doesn't foam, it is not alive and you'll need to start over.

2. When the yeast is proofed, pour it into a large bowl and add the additional cup of warm water. Stir gently to combine. Combine the whole wheat flour and the all-purpose flour in a bowl. Add the salt to the flours, and add the flours to the yeast mixture. Stir with a wooden spoon until combined. The dough will be wet and sticky.

3. Put a dusting of all-purpose flour on a flat surface and lift out the dough. With flour on your hands and more at the ready, begin kneading the dough so that it loses its stickiness. As you're kneading, add in the cranberries and pecans so that they're distributed evenly in the dough. Don't overdo it, and don't use too much flour; just enough that it becomes more cohesive.

4. Place the dough in a large bowl, cover the bowl with plastic wrap, and allow to rise untouched for at least 1 hour, and up to several hours. Gently punch it down, re-cover with the plastic, and allow to rise again for another 30 minutes or so.

5. While the dough is on its final rise, preheat the oven to 450° F. Put a piece of parchment paper on the bottom of the Dutch oven and put it in with the lid on so it gets hot. When the oven is ready and the dough has risen, carefully remove the lid and gently scoop the dough from the bowl into the pot. Cover and bake for 15 minutes. Remove the lid and continue to bake for another 15 to 20 minutes until the top is golden and it sounds hollow when tapped.

6. Remove the pot from the oven and use tea towels to carefully remove the bread. Allow to cool before slicing.

SIMPLY SENSATIONAL IRISH SODA BREAD

MAKES 1 LOAF ✦ ACTIVE TIME: 30 MINUTES ✦ START TO FINISH: 90 MINUTES

Make this on a weekend morning when you have some extra time, then have slices of it later in the day with a cup of coffee or tea.

4 cups flour

½ cup sugar

⅛ teaspoon salt

3¼ teaspoons baking powder

½ teaspoon baking soda

2 tablespoons caraway seeds

2 large eggs, lightly beaten

1½ cups buttermilk

8 oz. golden raisins

1. Preheat the oven to 450° F.

2. Combine the flour, sugar, salt, baking powder, baking soda, and caraway seeds. Add the beaten eggs and stir to combine. Gradually add the buttermilk until the dough is sticky and messy. Stir in the raisins.

3. Generously butter the skillet. Scoop and spread the dough in it.

4. Bake for about 1 hour, until the top is crusty and brown and the bread sounds hollow when tapped. Insert a toothpick in the center, too, to be sure the dough is cooked through. The toothpick should come out clean.

5. Serve with fresh butter and orange marmalade.

It wouldn't be St. Patrick's Day without Irish soda bread. According to the Culinary Institute of America, "With a history spanning more than two centuries, soda bread is a traditional Irish specialty. The first loaf, consisting of little more than flour, baking soda, salt, and sour milk, made its debut in the mid-1800s when baking soda found its way into Irish kitchens." They don't mention the raisins or caraway seeds, but I consider these essential!

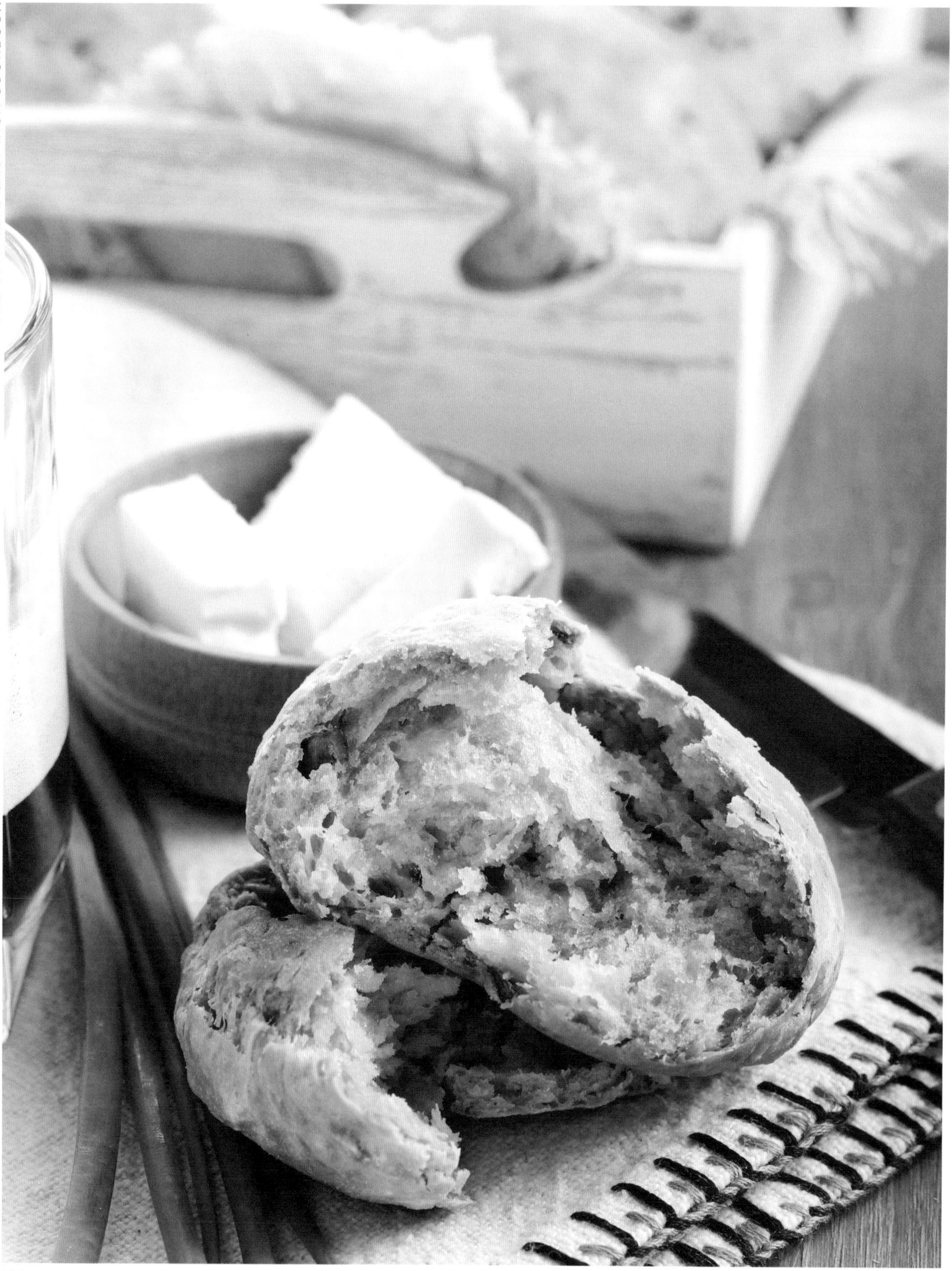

CHEESY CHIVE SODA BREAD

MAKES 1 LOAF ✦ ACTIVE TIME: 40 MINUTES ✦ START TO FINISH: 90 MINUTES

If you're looking for a savory version of a simple soda bread to serve with soup or stew, this is a great recipe.

3 cups white flour

2 cups spelt flour

¾ cup rolled oats (not instant)

2 tablespoons sugar

1 tablespoon baking powder

1 teaspoon salt

1 teaspoon baking soda

8 tablespoons (1 stick) butter, melted and cooled

2½ cups buttermilk

1 large egg, lightly beaten

¼ cup chives, chopped

1¼ cups sharp white cheddar cheese, grated

Freshly ground black pepper to taste

1. Preheat the oven to 350° F.

2. In a large bowl, combine the flours, oats, sugar, baking powder, salt, and baking soda. Whisk to combine thoroughly. In another bowl, combine the butter, buttermilk, and egg.

3. Add the buttermilk mixture to the flour mixture and stir vigorously to blend. The dough will be sticky. Stir in the chives and 1 cup of the grated cheese.

4. Liberally grease the skillet with butter. Scoop and spread the dough into the skillet. Sprinkle the black pepper pepper over the top, then sprinkle the remaining cheese over it. Using a sharp knife, make an "x" in the center of the dough, about ½-inch deep, to settle the cheese further into the dough as it cooks.

5. Bake in the oven for about 1 hour and 15 minutes until golden on top and a toothpick inserted in the center comes out clean. Allow to sit in the skillet for a few minutes before serving.

Soda bread doesn't keep so well, so if you happen to have any left over, be sure to wrap it tightly in plastic wrap. Store it in the refrigerator. It will last for about 3 days this way. The bread makes great toast!

FOCACCIA

SERVES 4 TO 6 ✦ ACTIVE TIME: 90 MINUTES ✦ START TO FINISH: 3 HOURS

This is essentially a raised flatbread—like a crustier pizza—to which all kinds of yummy things can be added. It's become synonymous with Italian cuisine, and it's certainly popular in Italy, but it's also made throughout the Mediterranean region. You can find it in grocery stores, but there's nothing like a fresh piece right out of the skillet, still warm, with the exact toppings you want. This one is a simple salt/Parmesan focaccia.

1 packet active dry yeast (2¼ teaspoons)

2 teaspoons salt

2 cups water (110 to 115° F)

4 to 4½ cups flour, plus more for dusting and kneading

3 tablespoons olive oil, plus more for drizzling over bread before baking

Sea salt (coarse grained) and freshly ground black pepper to taste

Parmesan cheese, grated, for topping

1. Proof the yeast by mixing it with the warm water. Let sit for 10 minutes until foamy.

2. In a bowl, combine the flour, salt, and yeast mix. Stir to combine. Transfer to a lightly floured surface and knead the dough until it loses its stickiness, adding more flour as needed, about 10 minutes.

3. Coat the bottom and sides of a large mixing bowl (ceramic is best) with olive oil. Place the ball of dough in the bowl, cover loosely with plastic wrap, put it in a naturally warm, draft-free location, and let it rise until doubled in size, about 45 minutes to 1 hour.

4. Preheat the oven to 450° F.

5. When risen, turn the dough out onto a lightly floured surface and divide it in half. Put a tablespoon of olive oil in the skillet, and press one of the pieces of dough into it. Drizzle some olive oil over it and sprinkle with salt and pepper, then with Parmesan cheese. Cover loosely with plastic wrap and let rise for about 20 minutes. With the other piece, press it out onto a piece of parchment paper, follow the same procedure to top it, and let it rise.

6. Put the skillet on the middle rack of the oven and bake for 25 to 30 minutes until golden and hot. Remove from oven and let rest for 5 minutes before removing from skillet to cool further. Wipe any crumbs off the skillet, coat with more olive oil, and transfer the other round to the skillet. Bake for about 25 minutes, remove from skillet, and let cool.

7. If desired, you can put the extra dough in a plastic bag and store it in the refrigerator for up to 3 days to use later.

ITALIAN HERB FOCACCIA

SERVES 4 TO 6 ◆ **ACTIVE TIME: 90 MINUTES** ◆ **START TO FINISH: 3 HOURS**

Infused with oregano, thyme, and basil—and garlic, too—this herbed focaccia is sensational dipped into olive oil infused with red peppers, or topped with an olive tapenade.

1 teaspoon active dry yeast

1 cup water (110 to 115° F)

2 to 2½ cups flour, plus more for dusting and kneading

1 teaspoon salt

½ teaspoon dried oregano

½ teaspoon dried thyme

¼ teaspoon dried basil

1 clove garlic, minced

3 tablespoons olive oil, plus more for drizzling over bread before baking

Sea salt (coarse grained) and freshly ground black pepper to taste

Parmesan cheese, grated, for topping

1. Proof the yeast by mixing it with the warm water. Let sit for 10 minutes until foamy.

2. In a bowl, combine the flour, salt, oregano, thyme, and basil, and stir into yeast mix. Stir to combine. Stir in the garlic. Transfer to a lightly floured surface and knead the dough until it loses its stickiness, adding more flour as needed, about 10 minutes.

3. Coat the bottom and sides of a large mixing bowl (ceramic is best) with olive oil. Place the ball of dough in the bowl, cover loosely with plastic wrap, put it in a naturally warm, draft-free location, and let it rise until doubled in size, about 45 minutes to 1 hour.

4. Preheat the oven to 450° F.

5. Put a tablespoon of olive oil in the skillet, and press the dough into it. Drizzle some olive oil over it and sprinkle with salt and pepper, then with Parmesan cheese. Cover loosely with plastic wrap and let rise for about 20 minutes.

6. Put on the middle rack of the oven of the oven and bake for 25 to 30 minutes until golden and hot. Remove from oven and let rest for 5 minutes before removing from skillet to cool further.

CARAMELIZED ONION AND LEEK FOCACCIA

SERVES 4 TO 6 ✦ ACTIVE TIME: 2 HOURS ✦ START TO FINISH: 3 HOURS

I'm a sucker for caramelized onions, which are onions that have been sautéed in butter and oil until soft and browned. They lose their bite, and are transformed into something almost sweet. The addition of leeks makes for a more subtle and slightly sweeter topping.

8 tablespoons (1 stick) butter

3 tablespoons olive oil

1 medium yellow onion, peeled and sliced thin

1 large leek, white and light green part only, sliced thin and rinsed of any grit

1 teaspoon active dry yeast

1 cup water (110 to 115° F)

2 to 2½ cups flour, plus more for dusting and kneading

1 teaspoon salt

1 teaspoon freshly ground black pepper, plus more for topping

Sea salt (coarse grained), for topping

Parmesan cheese, grated, for topping

1. In a skillet (cast-iron or otherwise), melt butter and 2 tablespoons of oil over medium-low heat. When melted, add the onion and leek slices. Increase the heat to medium-high and cook, stirring, until onions and leeks start to soften, about 5 minutes. Reduce heat to low and allow to cook, stirring occasionally, until cooked down and browned, about 10 to 15 minutes. Set aside.

2. Proof the yeast by mixing it with the warm water. Let sit for 10 minutes until foamy.

3. Combine the flour, salt, and pepper, and stir into yeast mix. Stir to combine well. Dough will be sticky. Transfer to a floured surface and knead the dough until it loses its stickiness, adding more flour as needed, about 10 minutes.

4. Coat the bottom and sides of a large mixing bowl (ceramic is best) with olive oil. Place the ball of dough in the bowl, cover loosely with plastic wrap, put it in a naturally warm, draft-free location, and let it rise until doubled in size, about 45 minutes to 1 hour.

5. Preheat the oven to 450° F.

6. Put a tablespoon of olive oil in the skillet, and press the dough into it. Top with the caramelized onion/leek mix. Season generously with sea salt and pepper, then with Parmesan cheese. Cover loosely with plastic wrap and let rise for about 20 minutes.

7. Put the skillet on the middle rack of the oven and bake for 25 to 30 minutes until golden and hot. Remove from oven and let rest for 5 minutes before removing from skillet to cool further.

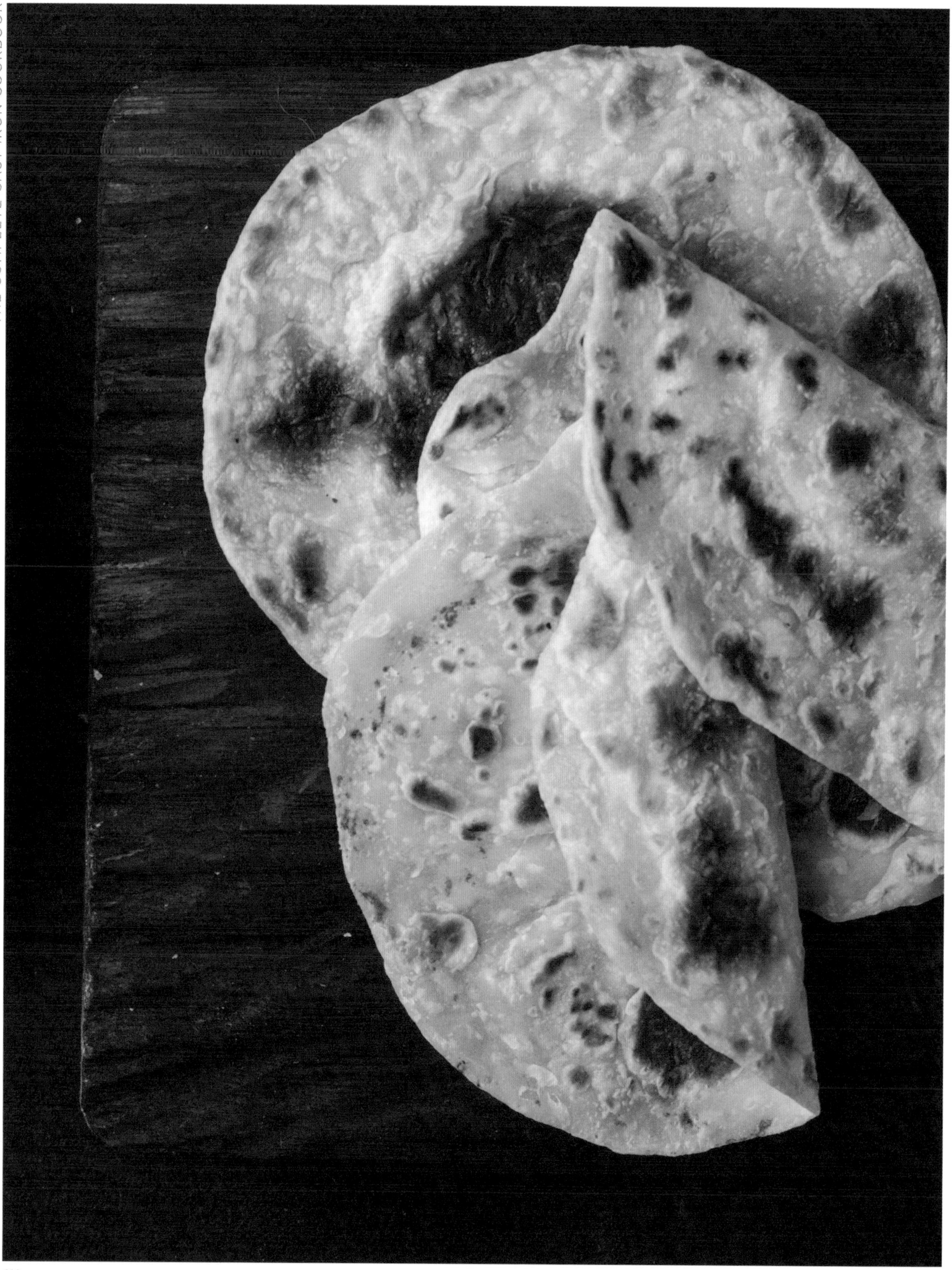

TORTILLAS

We are covering flatbreads from around the world, so now, on to Mexico! These are even simpler to make than the ones that involved yeast. There's no need to let the dough rise for tortillas—simply mix, knead, and shape—all with your hands, which is really fun. Then cook. Oh, and eat!

3 cups flour, plus more for dusting

1 teaspoon salt

2 teaspoons baking powder

3 tablespoons Crisco shortening or 4 tablespoons butter, chilled

1½ cups water at room temperature

1. Put the flour in a large bowl. Mix in the salt and baking powder.

2. Add the shortening (or butter), and, using your fingers, blend it into the flour mix until you have a crumbly dough. Add 1 cup of the water and work it in, then gradually add the remaining ½ cup, working it in with your hands, so that you create a dough that's not too sticky.

3. Lightly flour a work surface and turn out the dough. Knead it for about 10 minutes until it's soft and elastic. Divide it into 12 equal pieces.

4. Using a lightly floured rolling pin, roll each piece out to almost the size of the bottom of the skillet.

5. Heat the skillet over high heat. Add a tortilla. Cook for just 15 seconds a side. Keep the cooked tortillas warm by putting them on a plate covered with a damp tea towel. Serve warm.

A homemade tortilla begs for a filling of sliced, grilled meat with shredded cheese, chopped tomatoes, chopped red onions, chopped lettuce, and sliced jalapeños.

PITA BREAD

MAKES 16 PITAS ✦ ACTIVE TIME: 60 MINUTES ✦ START TO FINISH: 2 HOURS

Here's an easy recipe for another flatbread that originated in the Mediterranean region, purportedly ancient Greece, as the word pita itself is Greek. It is popular around the world, but especially in Middle Eastern countries.

1 packet active dry yeast (2¼ teaspoons)

2½ cups water (110 to 115° F)

3 cups flour, plus more for dusting

1 tablespoon olive oil

1 tablespoon salt

3 cups whole wheat flour

1. Proof the yeast by mixing with the warm water. Let sit for about 10 minutes until foamy.

2. In a large bowl, add the yeast mix into the regular flour and stir until it forms a stiff dough. Cover and let the dough rise for about 1 hour.

3. Add the oil and salt to the dough and stir in the whole wheat flour in ½-cup increments. When finished, the dough should be soft. Turn onto a lightly floured surface and knead it until it is smooth and elastic, about 10 minutes.

4. Coat the bottom and sides of a large mixing bowl (ceramic is best) with butter. Place the ball of dough in the bowl, cover loosely with plastic wrap, put it in a naturally warm, draft-free location, and let it rise until doubled in size, about 45 minutes to 1 hour.

5. On a lightly floured surface, punch down the dough and cut into 16 pieces. Put the pieces on a baking sheet and cover with a dish towel while working with individual pieces.

6. Roll out the pieces with a rolling pin until they are approximately 7 inches across. Stack them between sheets of plastic wrap.

7. Heat the skillet over high heat and lightly oil the bottom. Cook the individual pitas about 20 seconds on one side, then flip and cook for about a minute on the other side, until bubbles form. Turn again and continue to cook until the pita puffs up, another minute or so. Keep the skillet lightly oiled while processing, and store the pitas on a plate under a clean dish towel until ready to serve.

Pitas are delicious, somewhat chewy bread pockets that can be filled with just about anything. In summer, I like to smear the inside with fresh hummus, and top with chopped carrots, lettuce, tomatoes, and hot sauce. Make a grilled cheese sandwich by putting some butter, slices of Swiss cheese, slices of American cheese, and slices of tomatoes inside, wrapping the sandwich in foil, heating it inside the foil on the skillet or on a grill for about 5 minutes a side, then unwrapping it and lightly toasting it directly on the hot pan.

NAAN

MAKES 4 TO 8 SERVINGS (8 PIECES) ✦ ACTIVE TIME: 60 MINUTES ✦
START TO FINISH: 3 TO 4 HOURS

This is the bread that is traditionally served with Indian cuisine, from spicy to saucy. It's cooked in a tandoor (clay oven) in India, but the cast-iron skillet turns out a very good replication!

1½ teaspoons active dry yeast

½ tablespoon sugar

1 cup water (110 to 115° F)

3 cups all-purpose flour or 1½ cups all-purpose and 1½ cups whole wheat pastry flour, plus more for dusting

¼ teaspoon salt

1 teaspoon baking powder

½ cup plain yogurt

4 tablespoons unsalted butter, melted

¼ cup olive oil

1. Proof the yeast by mixing it with the sugar and ½ cup of the warm water. Let sit for 10 minutes until foamy.

2. In a bowl, combine the remaining water, flour, salt, baking powder, and yeast mix. Stir to combine. Add the yogurt and 2 tablespoons of the butter and stir to form a soft dough.

3. Transfer to a lightly floured surface and knead the dough until it is springy and elastic, about 10 minutes.

4. Coat the bottom and sides of a large mixing bowl (ceramic is best) with butter. Place the ball of dough in the bowl, cover loosely with plastic wrap, put it in a naturally warm, draft-free location, and let it rise until doubled in size, about 1 to 2 hours.

5. Punch down the dough. Lightly flour a work surface again, take out the dough and, using a rolling pin, make a circle of it and cut it into 8 slices (like a pie).

6. Heat the skillet over high heat until it is very hot (about 5 minutes). Working with individual pieces of dough, roll them out to soften the sharp edges and make the pieces look more like teardrops. Brush both sides with olive oil and, working one at a time, place the pieces in the skillet.

7. Cook for 1 minute, turn the dough with tongs, cover the skillet, and cook the other side for about a minute (no longer). Transfer cooked naan to a plate and cover with foil to keep warm while making the additional pieces. Serve warm.

Variations

❋ You can add herbs or spices to the dough or the pan to make naan with different flavors.

❋ Add ¼ cup chopped fresh parsley to the dough.

❋ Sprinkle the skillet lightly with cumin, coriander, or turmeric (or a combination) before cooking the pieces of naan.

❋ Use a seasoned olive oil to brush the pieces before cooking—one with hot pepper flakes or roasted garlic.

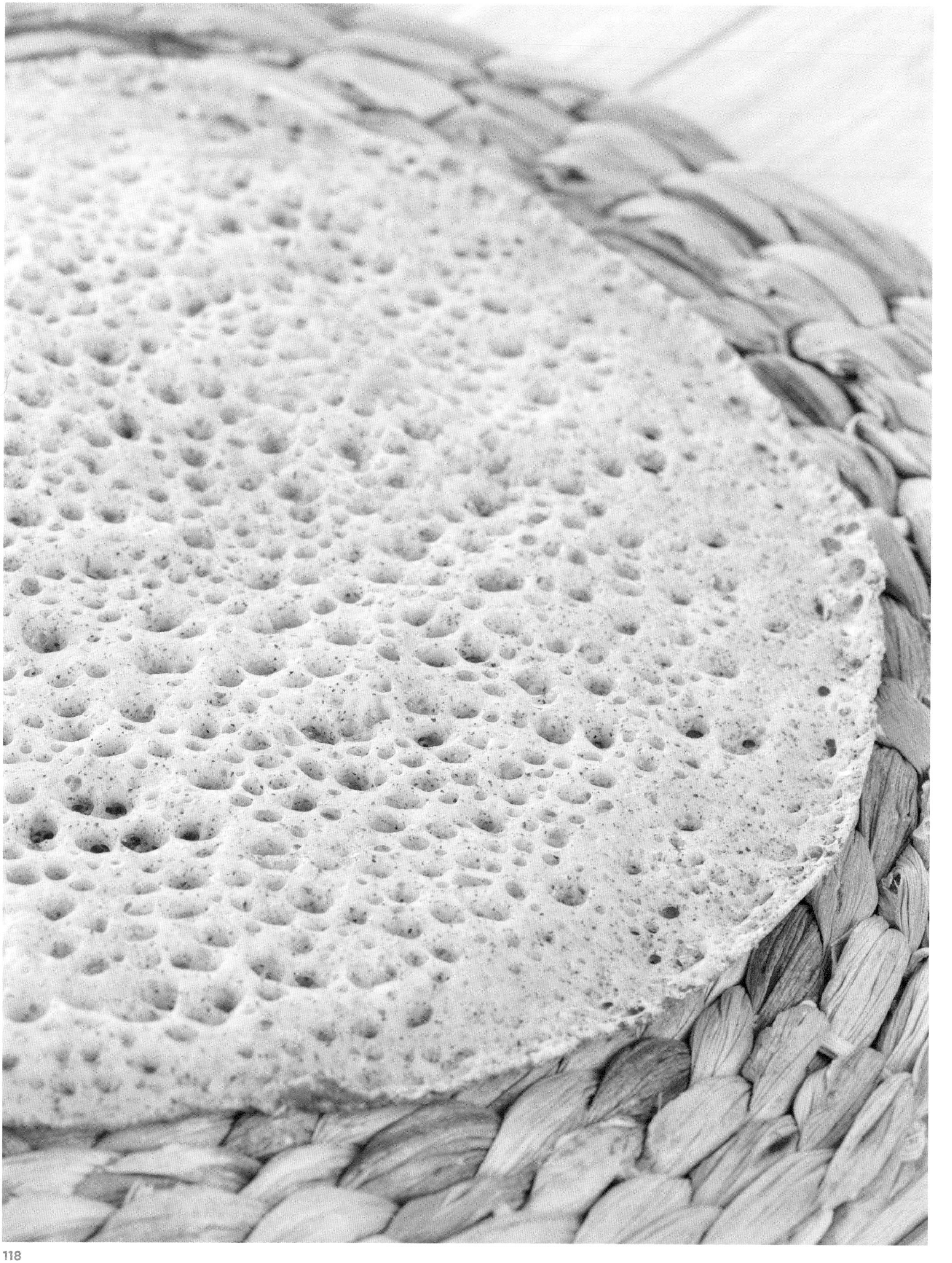

ETHIOPIAN INJERA

MAKES 1 INJERA ✦ ACTIVE TIME: 60 MINUTES ✦ START TO FINISH: 3 DAYS

If you've ever eaten at an Ethiopian restaurant, you'll remember that the centerpiece of the meal is a thick, spongy bread that's placed in the middle of the table. The dishes go around it, and you eat by ripping apart the bread and scooping up the other foods. I like to use it as almost a polenta or spongy pizza crust, topping with whatever leftovers I can reasonably pile on. While the ingredients are minimal, you have to plan ahead for the day you want to serve the injera, as the "flour" needs to sit for several days to break down the grain.

½ teaspoon active
dry yeast

2 cups water
(110 to 115° F)

1½ cups ground teff
(put the seeds in a food
processor or blender
to reduce to "flour")

Salt

Vegetable oil

1. Proof the yeast by mixing with the warm water. Let sit for about 10 minutes until foamy.

2. Put the ground teff in a bowl and add the yeast mixture. Mix thoroughly until a stiff dough forms. Put a dish towel over the bowl and stick it in a draft-free, fairly warm place in your kitchen. Let it sit for 2 to 3 days. It will bubble and turn brown and smell sour.

3. When ready to make the injera, add salt to the mix until some of the sour "bite" has dissipated. The mix at this time should resemble pancake batter.

4. Heat the skillet over medium heat and brush with vegetable oil. Pour enough batter on the pan to coat the bottom. You want it to be thinner than a pancake but thicker than a crepe. Tilt to spread the batter over the bottom of the skillet. Cook until holes form in the bread and the edges crisp up and lift away from the pan. The bread should not be flipped so be sure to let it cook thoroughly.

5. When cooked, lift it out with a spatula and put it on a plate or platter to cool. Place plastic wrap between injeras if you cook a batch of them. Serve warm with bowls of things like sautéed vegetables, grilled pieces of meats, creamed spinach, sautéed mushrooms, authentic Ethiopian dishes you can make— or the Indian dishes you can find in grocery stores.

Thank goodness for Bob's Red Mill. They are bringing exotic grains from around the world to grocery stores here in the United States. One of those grains is teff, a wheat-like grain that's cultivated almost exclusively in Ethiopia. Teff is the smallest grain in the world, and it looks almost like poppy seeds (100 teff grains equal the size of a kernel of wheat!). It's full of iron, and it's gluten free. Bob's Red Mill website has recipes for teff, so you won't have to use the bag just to make injera—unless you want to.

PIZZA DOUGH

**SERVES 2 (ABOUT 4 LARGE SLICES) ✦ ACTIVE TIME: 30 MINUTES ✦
START TO FINISH: UP TO 3 DAYS**

This is breadmaking at its simplest: flour, water, salt, and yeast. There's actually a cookbook with that title! With this super-easy recipe, you can create amazing pizzas that can be completely individualized with almost anything you have in the fridge or pantry, from traditional cheese to "gourmet." And while the flavor will become more complex and the crust crispier if you allow the dough to rise for a couple of hours (or up to 3 days in the refrigerator), you can also roll it out and bake it within 15 minutes of making it.

¾ cup water
(110 to 115° F)

1 teaspoon active
dry yeast

2 cups all-purpose
flour, plus more for
dusting

1½ teaspoons salt

1 tablespoon olive oil

Toppings

Traditional pizza
toppings include
the base of marinara
topped with mozzarella
cheese, as well as
ricotta cheese, Italian
seasonings, garlic,
fresh tomatoes,
pepperoni, sausage,
meatballs, spinach,
olives, mushrooms,
peppers, onions—
almost anything!

1. If you'll be making pizza within the hour, preheat the oven to 450° F.

2. In a large bowl, add the warm water and yeast, stirring to dissolve the yeast. Stir in the flour and salt and mix until the dough is just combined. It will be sticky.

3. Turn out on a floured surface and start kneading until the flour is incorporated, adding more if necessary to make the dough malleable and smooth, but not overdone.

4. If cooking immediately, allow the dough to rest for 15 minutes. While it's doing so, put the skillet in the oven. Prepare the toppings for the pizza. If preparing ahead of time, place dough in the refrigerator for up to 3 days.

5. After 15 minutes or when ready, put a piece of parchment paper under the dough. Start rolling and pushing it out to form a 9-inch disk that will fit in the skillet. If it bounces back, let it rest before pushing or rolling it out again.

6. When the disk is formed, use pot holders or oven mitts to remove the skillet from the oven. Add the olive oil and brush to distribute over the bottom. Transfer the dough to the skillet and add the toppings.

7. Bake for 12 to 15 minutes until the crust starts to brown and the toppings are hot and bubbling. Use caution taking the hot skillet from the oven. Allow to cool for 5 minutes before lifting or sliding the pizza out and serving.

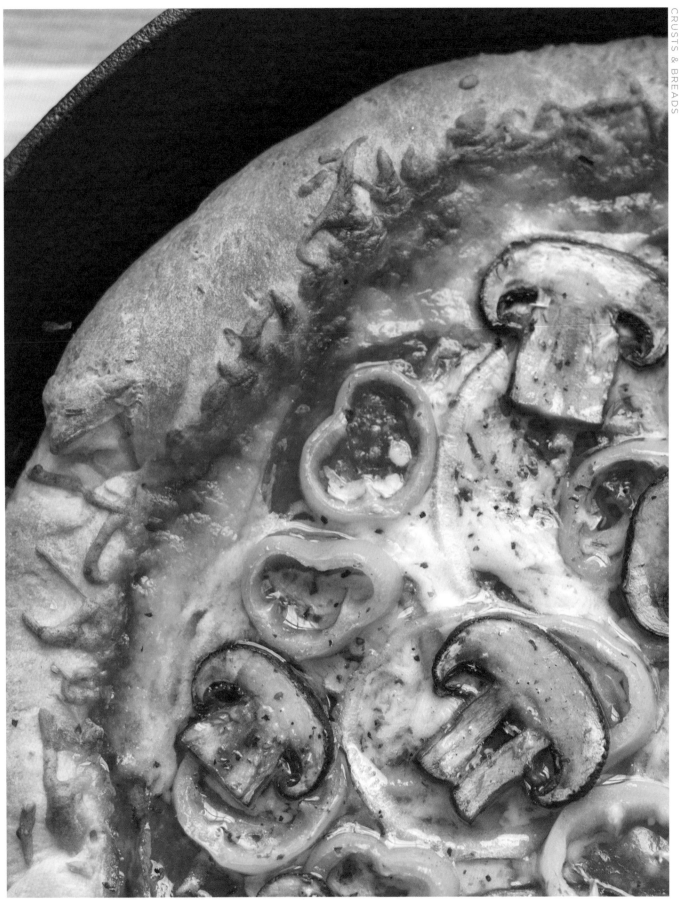

PALEO PIZZA DOUGH

**SERVES 2 (ABOUT 4 LARGE SLICES) ✦ ACTIVE TIME: 30 MINUTES ✦
START TO FINISH: 30 MINUTES TO 3 DAYS**

Paleo Bonus: You can make a great paleo-friendly pizza crust with that most wonderful of vegetables, cauliflower! Here's how:

1 head cauliflower

**2 eggs, lightly beaten
(or use just whites
if you prefer)**

**1 tablespoon Italian
seasoning**

**Salt and pepper
to taste**

1. Preheat the oven to 450° F.

2. Use a food processor to render the cauliflower florets into a rice-like consistency.

3. Fill a large pot about ⅓ full of water, bring to a boil, and cook the cauliflower in it until soft, about 5 minutes. Allow to drain thoroughly, then transfer cooked cauliflower to a clean dish towel and squeeze out as much water as possible. Put the cooked, dried cauliflower in a bowl.

4. Add the eggs, Italian seasoning, salt, and pepper and mix thoroughly. If preparing ahead of time, place dough in the refrigerator for up to 3 days.

5. Take enough of the "dough" and, on a piece of parchment paper, shape it into a circle that will fit in the skillet. Lightly grease the skillet with coconut oil. Use a spatula to carefully transfer the crust to the skillet. Bake for about 10 minutes, until golden. Remove from the oven, allow to cool slightly, add toppings, and bake again for 10 to 12 minutes.

WHOLE WHEAT PIZZA DOUGH

If you like an earthier-tasting crust with the added health benefits of whole wheat, this is another easy recipe to follow. Because pizza dough needs to be elastic, it's best to keep some of the regular flour in the blend. The honey helps activate the yeast, and mellows the whole wheat flavor just a bit.

¾ cup water
(110 to 115° F)

½ teaspoon honey

1 teaspoon active
dry yeast

1½ cups wheat flour

½ cup all-purpose
flour, plus more for
dusting

1½ teaspoons salt

1 tablespoon olive oil

1. If you'll be making pizza within the hour, preheat the oven to 450° F.

2. In a large bowl, add the warm water, honey, and yeast, stirring to dissolve the yeast. Stir in the flours and salt and mix until the dough is just combined. It will be sticky.

3. Turn out on a floured surface and start kneading until the flour is incorporated, adding more if necessary to make the dough malleable and smooth, but not overdone.

4. If cooking immediately, allow the dough to rest for 15 minutes. While it's doing so, put the skillet in the oven. Prepare the toppings for the pizza. If preparing ahead of time, place dough in the refrigerator for up to 3 days.

5. After 15 minutes or when ready, put a piece of parchment paper under the dough. Start rolling and pushing it out to form a 9-inch disk that will fit in the skillet. If it bounces back, let it rest before pushing or rolling it out again.

6. When the disk is formed, use pot holders or oven mitts to remove the skillet from the oven. Add the olive oil and brush to distribute over the bottom. Transfer the dough to the skillet and add the toppings.

7. Bake for 12 to 15 minutes until the crust starts to brown and the toppings are hot and bubbling. Use caution taking the hot skillet from the oven. Allow to cool for 5 minutes before lifting or sliding the pizza out and serving.

GARLIC KNOTS

MAKES ABOUT 3 DOZEN ✦ ACTIVE TIME: 45 MINUTES ✦ START TO FINISH: 90 MINUTES

Use the pizza dough recipe to make the knots themselves. They'll get that great cast-iron crust when they bake, then they can be bathed with garlic-parsley butter and put on a plate. Don't expect them to hang around for long, which is why this is a double batch of dough.

For the Knots

1½ cups water
(110 to 115° F)

2 teaspoons active
dry yeast

4 cups all-purpose
flour, plus more for
dusting

2 teaspoons salt

1 tablespoon olive oil

For the Garlic-Parsley Sauce

8 tablespoons (1 stick)
unsalted butter

8 cloves garlic, minced

⅓ cup parsley leaves,
finely chopped

2 teaspoons salt

Parmesan cheese, grated
(optional)

1. In a large bowl, add the warm water and yeast, stirring to dissolve the yeast. Stir in the flour and salt and mix until the dough is just combined. It will be sticky.

2. Turn out on a floured surface and start kneading until the flour is incorporated, adding more if necessary to make the dough malleable and smooth, but not overdone.

3. Lightly grease a bowl and put the dough in it. Allow to rise for about an hour. Preheat the oven to 450° F.

4. Transfer to a lightly floured surface and push and stretch the dough into a large rectangle. If it resists, let it rest before stretching it further. Cut the rectangle into strips, and tie the strips into knots. Spread the tablespoon of olive oil over the bottom of the skillet. Tuck the knots into the skillet so they are slightly separated. Bake for about 15 minutes until golden brown.

5. While the knots are baking, prepare the garlic-parsley sauce. In a saucepan on medium heat, melt the butter. Add the garlic and reduce the heat to medium-low. Allow to cook, stirring occasionally, for about 3 minutes. This takes some of the pungency out of the garlic and also infuses the butter with the flavor. Stir in the chopped parsley and salt.

6. When the garlic knots come out of the oven, place a tea towel over your hand to pull them off the skillet and put them in a large mixing bowl. Scoop a large spoonful of the garlic-parsley sauce over the knots and toss to coat, adding a bit more if necessary. Use another spoon to transfer the coated knots to a plate. Sprinkle with Parmesan if desired and serve.

7. Continue to work in batches in the skillet until the dough is used up, or save some of the dough in the refrigerator for up to 3 days. The sauce can also be refrigerated for several days and reheated.

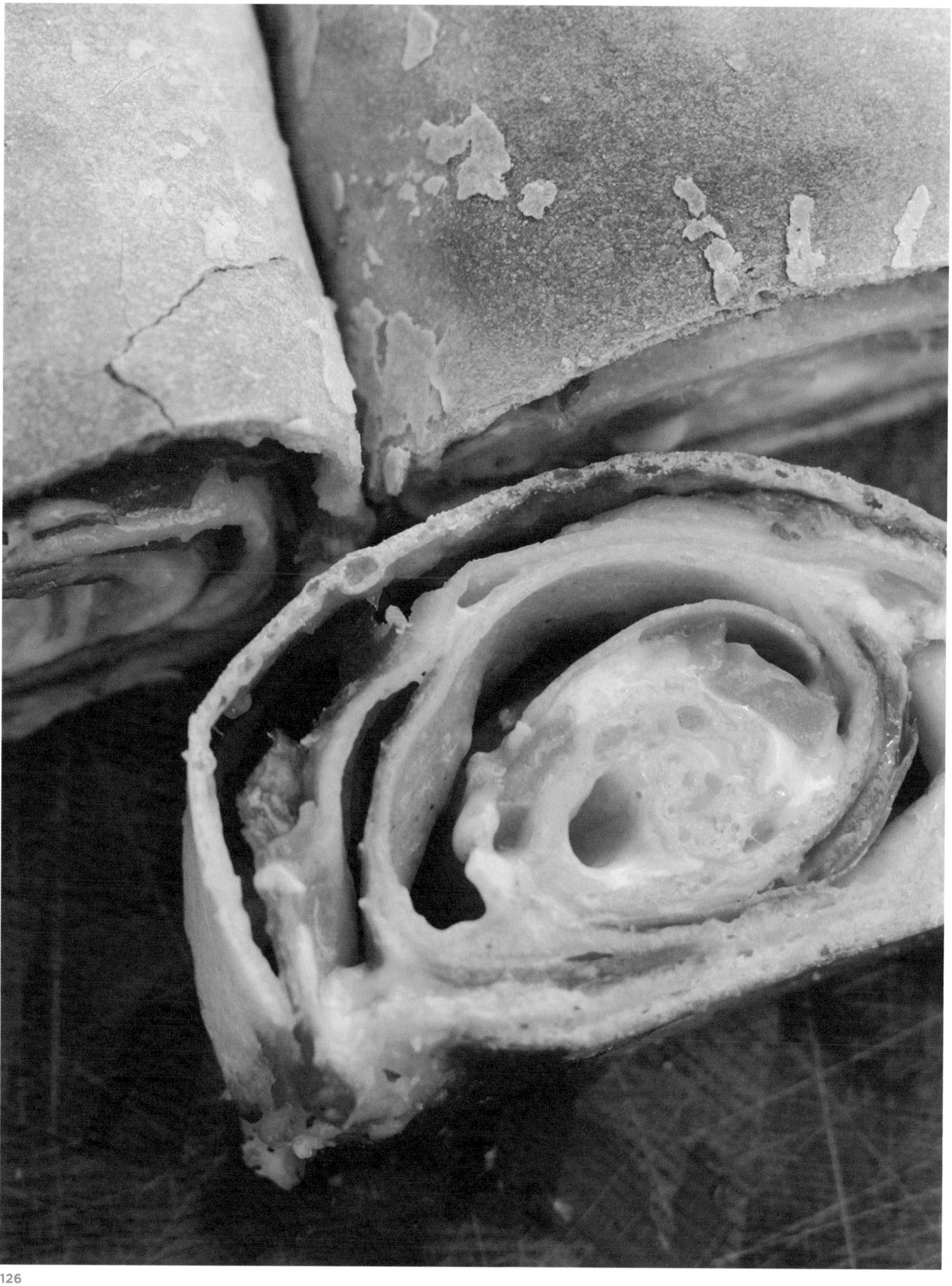

PEPPERONI BREAD

SERVES 6 TO 8 ✦ ACTIVE TIME: 60 MINUTES ✦ START TO FINISH: 3 HOURS

This is a favorite during football season, when the game hasn't actually started until this makes an appearance in front of the TV. Start in the morning for an afternoon game, as the dough needs to rise several times. But it's so delicious!

1¼ cups water
(110 to 115° F)

1 tablespoon sugar

1 oz. active dry yeast

1 tablespoon butter, melted

1½ teaspoons salt

3½ cups flour, plus more for dusting

Salt and pepper to taste

½ pound pepperoni, slivered

2 cups mozzarella cheese, grated

1 teaspoon hot pepper flakes

1 teaspoon dried oregano

1 teaspoon garlic powder

1. Proof the yeast by mixing it with the water and sugar in a large bowl and then stirring. Let sit until foamy, about 10 minutes. Add the salt and about half the flour to form a sticky dough. Cover the bowl with plastic wrap or a clean dish towel and let rise in a warm, draft-free place until it is double in size, about 1 hour.

2. Punch down the dough and add more flour to make it less sticky. Transfer to a floured surface and work the dough until it's smooth and elastic. Transfer to a lightly greased bowl and let sit for about 15 minutes.

3. On the floured surface, roll the dough out into a rectangle about 14x16 inches. Sprinkle with salt and pepper, spread the pieces of pepperoni around the dough, then cheese, and top with a sprinkling of hot pepper flakes, oregano, and garlic powder. Roll up, pinching the ends to secure filling.

4. Grease the skillet with the butter and lay the roll in it in a coil, working from the edges toward the center. Cover with a clean dish towel and let it rise again for about 1 hour. Preheat the oven to 375° F.

5. Bake the pepperoni bread for about 30 minutes, until golden on top and bubbling in the center. Serve immediately.

Variation

It's easy to make this into a full-blown Meat Lover's Bread. In addition to the pepperoni, add about ¼ to ½ cup of any or each of diced pancetta, diced smoked ham, crumbled cooked bacon, sautéed sausage, or diced cooked meatballs.

SAUSAGE, PEPPER, AND ONION CALZONE

SERVES 4 TO 6 ✦ ACTIVE TIME: 1 HOUR ✦ START TO FINISH: 2 HOURS

Eating one of these is like being at an Italian street fair. Load it up so that the ingredients and juices overflow when you eat it. Fabuloso!

For the Dough

1½ cups water
(110 to 115° F)

2 teaspoons active
dry yeast

4 cups all-purpose
flour, plus more for
dusting

2 teaspoons salt

For the Filling

3 tablespoons olive oil

3 cloves garlic, minced

1 medium onion, sliced

1 teaspoon red pepper
flakes (optional)

1 green pepper, seeds
removed, sliced into
strips

1 red pepper, seeds
removed, sliced into
strips

1 pound hot Italian
sausage, sliced into
thin rounds

½ teaspoon oregano

Salt and pepper to taste

2 cups mozzarella
cheese, shredded

1. Make the dough by combining the warm water and yeast in a large bowl, stirring to dissolve the yeast. Stir in the flour and salt and mix until the dough is just combined. It will be sticky.

2. Turn out on a floured surface and start kneading until the flour is incorporated, adding more if necessary to make the dough malleable and smooth, but not overdone.

3. Lightly grease a bowl and put the dough in it. Allow to rise while you prepare the filling and preheat the oven, about 30 minutes.

4. Preheat the oven to 400° F.

5. Make the filling. In a large skillet over medium-high heat, cook the onions and garlic in the oil for about 2 minutes. Add the sausage slices and continue cooking until browned, another 5 minutes. Reduce the heat to medium, add the pepper slices, and stir to combine. Reduce the heat to low and continue cooking, stirring occasionally, until the pepper slices have softened and caramelized slightly in the oil, 10 to 15 minutes. Season with oregano, red pepper flakes, if using, salt, and pepper. Set aside but do not refrigerate.

6. On a lightly floured surface, turn out the dough and separate it into two equal pieces. Roll each piece into a 12-inch circle.

7. Place one circle in the skillet. The dough should extend about halfway up the side. Spread the sausage and peppers over it, then top with the mozzarella cheese. Place the other dough circle over the filling and crimp to seal the edges together with your fingers. Cut 4 slits in the top.

8. Bake for 25 minutes until the crust is a lovely golden brown. Use pot holders or oven mitts to remove the skillet. Allow to cool for about 10 minutes before slicing and serving. Serve with additional marinara sauce if desired.

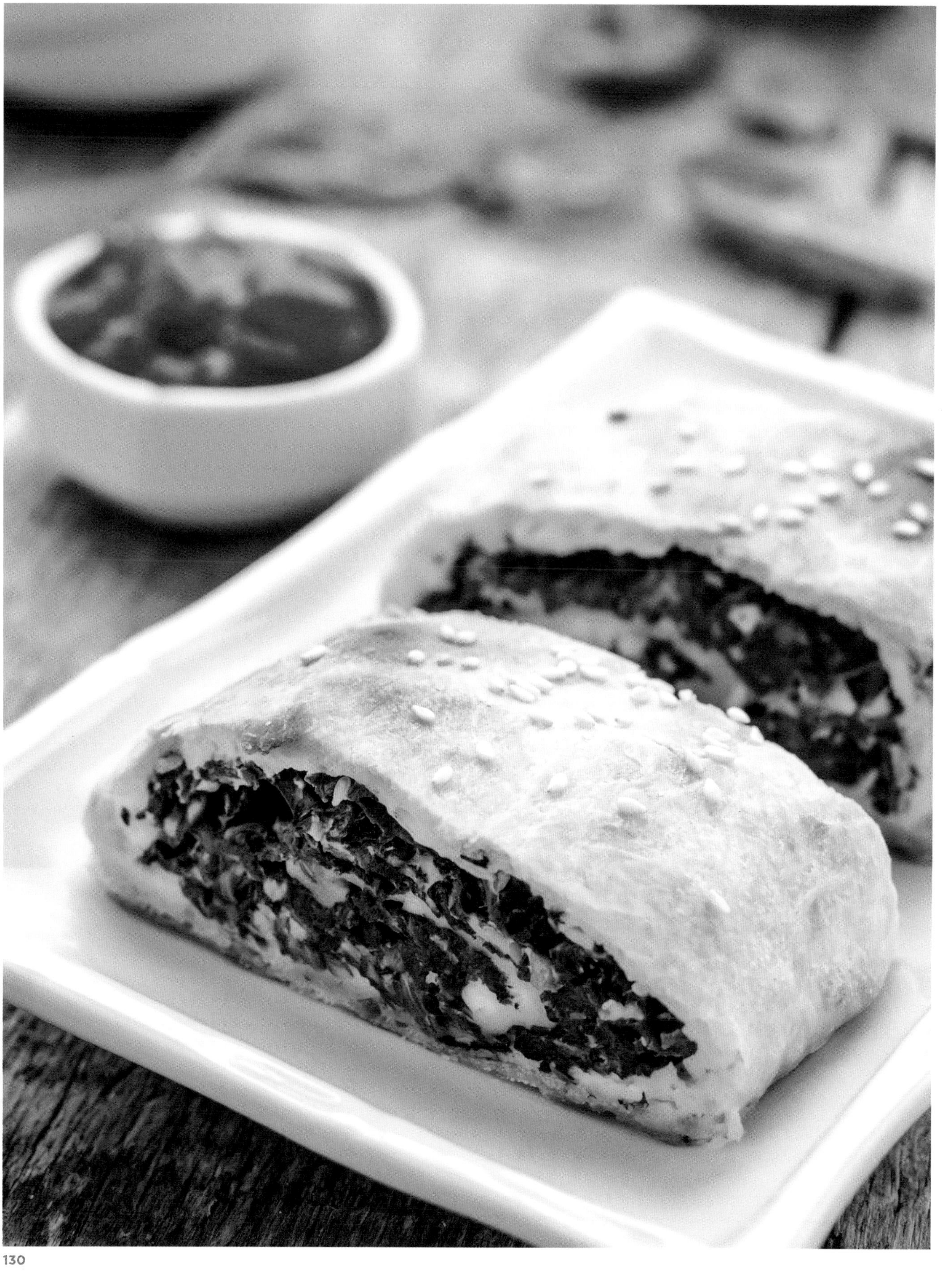

SPINACH AND RICOTTA CALZONE

SERVES 4 TO 6 ✦ ACTIVE TIME: 1 HOUR ✦ START TO FINISH: 2 HOURS

Such a great combination! The resulting pizza "pie" is gooey with cheese and plenty of lovely green spinach. I like to spice this up with hot pepper flakes, but you can serve them on the side if you prefer.

For the Dough

1½ cups water
(110 to 115° F)

2 teaspoons active
dry yeast

4 cups all-purpose
flour, plus more for
dusting

2 teaspoons salt

For the Filling

2 tablespoons olive oil

3 cloves garlic, minced

1 teaspoon red pepper
flakes (optional)

1 (16 oz.) package frozen
chopped spinach leaves

Salt and pepper
to taste

2 cups fresh ricotta
cheese

1 egg, lightly beaten

½ cup Parmesan cheese,
grated

1. Make the dough by combining the warm water and yeast in a large bowl, stirring to dissolve the yeast. Stir in the flour and salt and mix until the dough is just combined. It will be sticky.

2. Turn out on a floured surface and start kneading until the flour is incorporated, adding more if necessary to make the dough malleable and smooth, but not overdone.

3. Lightly grease a bowl and put the dough in it. Allow to rise while you prepare the filling and preheat the oven, about 30 minutes.

4. Preheat the oven to 400° F.

5. Make the filling. Put the olive oil, garlic, and red pepper flakes, if using, in a large skillet over medium-high heat. Add the frozen spinach. Stir while cooking as the spinach thaws, coating the leaves with the oil and garlic, about 5 minutes. Reduce the heat to medium-low and cover, stirring occasionally, until the spinach is cooked through, another 15 minutes. Season with salt and pepper. Set aside but do not refrigerate. In a bowl, mix together the ricotta, egg, and Parmesan cheese.

6. On a lightly floured surface, turn out the dough and separate it into two equal pieces. Roll each piece into a 12-inch circle.

7. Place one circle in the skillet. The dough should extend about halfway up the side. Spread the cooked spinach evenly over the dough, then dollop with the ricotta cheese mix. Use a spatula or the back of a large spoon to distribute the ricotta. Place the other dough circle over the filling and crimp to seal the edges together with your fingers. Cut 4 slits in the top.

8. Bake for 25 minutes until the crust is a lovely golden brown. Use pot holders or oven mitts to remove the skillet. Allow to cool for about 10 minutes before slicing and serving.

EGGPLANT, OLIVES, ONIONS, AND ANCHOVIES CALZONE

SERVES 4 TO 6 ✦ ACTIVE TIME: 1 HOUR ✦ START TO FINISH: 2 HOURS

Here's a calzone inspired by the flavors of Greece. For a clean, just-right taste, use anchovies marinated in oil, not anchovy paste, which is too salty and can be somewhat bitter.

For the Dough

1½ cups water
(110 to 115° F)

2 teaspoons active
dry yeast

4 cups all-purpose
flour, plus more for
dusting

2 teaspoons salt

For the Filling

3 tablespoons olive oil

1 small eggplant, cubed

3 cloves garlic, minced

½ teaspoon red
pepper flakes

4 to 6 anchovy fillets
in oil (not anchovy
paste)

½ cup black olives,
pitted and halved

2 cups mozzarella
cheese, shredded

Parmesan cheese, grated

1. Make the dough by combining the warm water and yeast in a large bowl, stirring to dissolve the yeast. Stir in the flour and salt and mix until the dough is just combined. It will be sticky.

2. Turn out on a floured surface and start kneading until the flour is incorporated, adding more if necessary to make the dough malleable and smooth, but not overdone.

3. Lightly grease a bowl and put the dough in it. Allow to rise while you prepare the filling and preheat the oven, about 30 minutes.

4. Preheat the oven to 400° F.

5. Make the filling. In a large skillet, heat 1 tablespoon of oil over medium-high heat. Add the eggplant cubes and cook, stirring, until softened and browned, about 6 to 8 minutes. Use a slotted spoon and transfer the pieces to a plate covered with a paper towel to absorb extra oil. Add 2 tablespoons of oil to the hot pan and add the garlic and red pepper flakes. Cook until the garlic bits dance in the oil, about 2 minutes. Add the anchovy fillets and the olives and stir to combine, cooking for an additional minute or 2. Add the eggplant pieces and stir to combine.

6. On a lightly floured surface, turn out the dough and separate it into two equal pieces. Roll each piece into a 12-inch circle.

7. Place one circle in the skillet. The dough should extend about halfway up the side. Spread the eggplant/olive mixture evenly over the dough, then sprinkle the mozzarella over everything. Place the other dough circle over the filling and crimp to seal the edges together with your fingers. Cut 4 slits in the top.

8. Bake for 20 to 25 minutes until the crust is a lovely golden brown. Use pot holders or oven mitts to remove the skillet. Allow to cool for about 10 minutes before slicing and serving with grated Parmesan cheese.

PALEO PIE CRUST

You can make any pie a "Paleo pie" with a few key ingredient swaps, starting with the perfect Paleo crust! This recipe makes a delicious Paleo-friendly pie crust (single crust).

½ cup each rice, tapioca, and potato starch flours

2 teaspoons xanthan gum

½ teaspoon salt

Dash of sugar

4 tablespoons lard, ghee, or coconut oil

4 or 5 tablespoons very cold water

1. Combine the flours, xanthan gum, salt, and sugar. Work the fat into the flour.

2. When a crumbly dough forms, add the water 2 tablespoons at a time, working it with your fingers until it holds together.

3. Transfer to a lightly floured surface and form a patty. Wrap in plastic and refrigerate about 1 hour before rolling.

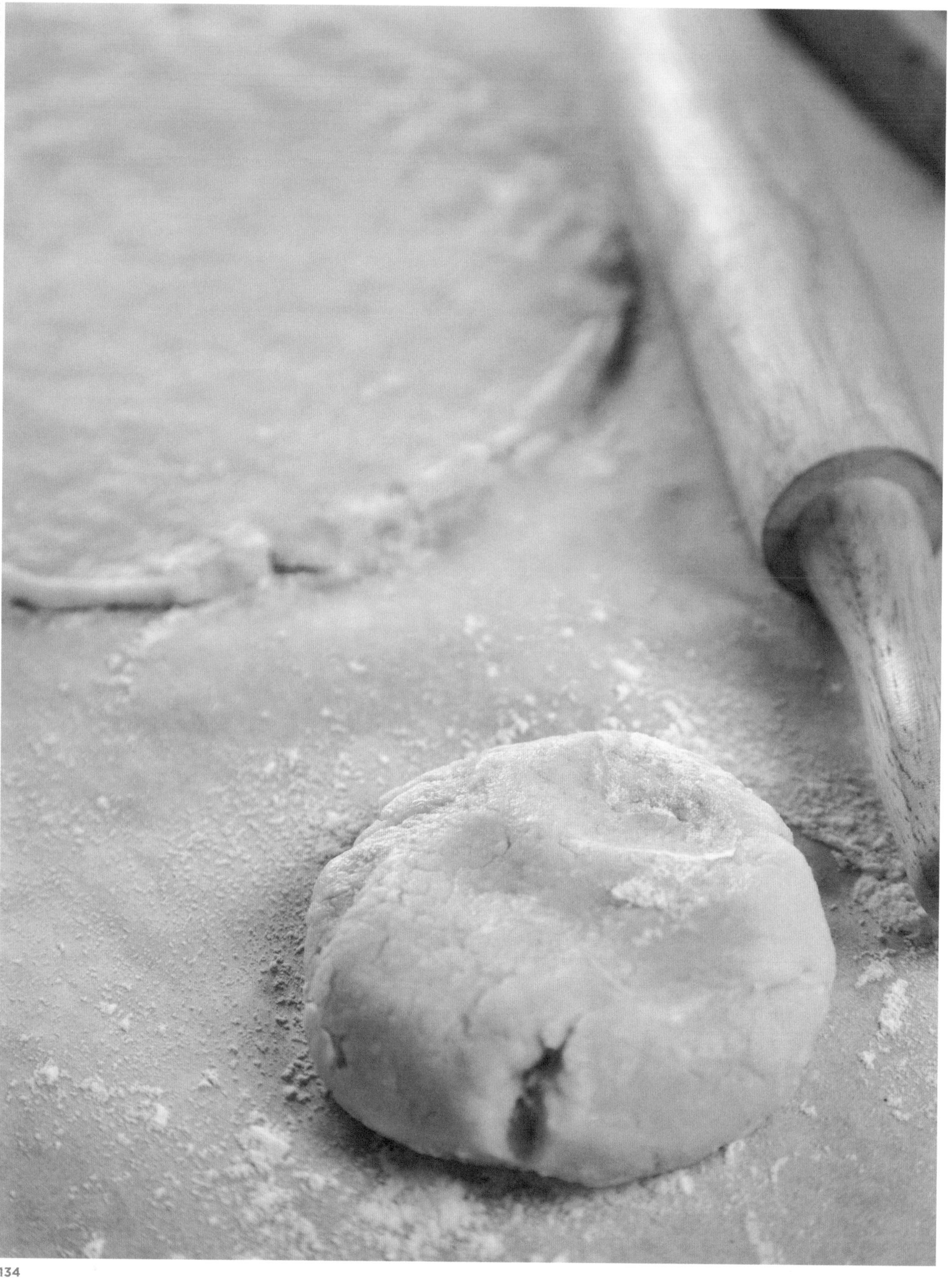

BAKED CRUST

MAKES 1 12-INCH CRUST ✦ ACTIVE TIME: 20 MINUTES ✦ START TO FINISH: 2 HOURS

Many of the pies in this cookbook call for a simple, single baked crust. It's fast and easy to put together and the result is delicious.

1¼ cups flour, plus more for dusting

¼ teaspoon salt

½ cup (1 stick) unsalted butter, chilled and cut into small pieces, plus 1 tablespoon butter for greasing the skillet

4 to 6 tablespoons cold water

1. In a large bowl, combine the flour and salt. Add the butter and work it into the flour mixture with a pastry blender or 2 knives until the dough resembles coarse meal. Add 3 tablespoons cold water to start, and using your hands or a fork, work the dough, adding additional tablespoons of water until the dough just holds together when you gather it in your hands.

2. Working on a lightly floured surface, gather the dough and form it into a solid ball or disk. Wrap tightly in plastic wrap and refrigerate for about an hour. The dough can be refrigerated for a couple of days or frozen for a couple of months.

3. Preheat the oven to 450° F. Take the dough out of the refrigerator to allow it to warm up a bit but work with it cold. Put the refrigerated dough on a lightly floured surface, and with a lightly dusted rolling pin, flatten the dough into a circle, working both sides to extend it to a 10- to 12-inch round.

4. Grease the cast-iron skillet with 1 tablespoon of butter.

5. Carefully position the crust in the skillet so it is evenly distributed, pressing it in lightly. Crimp the edges. Use a fork to prick the crust on the bottom and sides. Line with foil or parchment paper, and fill with uncooked rice as a weight.

6. Bake for 10 to 12 minutes until lightly browned. Transfer to a wire rack to cool before filling.

FLAKY PASTRY CRUST

MAKES 2 9- TO 12-INCH CRUSTS ✦ ACTIVE TIME: 30 MINUTES
START TO FINISH: 2–3 HOURS

This is the traditional pie crust recipe, and while it's tempting to take a shortcut and use a piecrust mix or even a pre-made crust, there truly is nothing as delicious as a crust made from scratch. Once you get the hang of it, too, you'll find making the crust as enjoyable and therapeutic as indulging in the pie.

2½ cups flour, plus more for dusting

1 teaspoon salt

¼ cup vegetable shortening

½ cup (1 stick) butter, chilled and cut into small pieces (if using unsalted butter, increase salt to 1¼ teaspoons), plus 1 tablespoon butter for greasing the skillet

6 to 8 tablespoons cold water

1. In a large bowl, combine the flour and salt. Add the shortening, and using a fork, work it in until the mixture forms a very coarse meal. Add the butter and work into the dough with a pastry blender or your fingers until the dough is just holding together. Don't overwork the dough; there can be chunks of butter in it. Add 4 tablespoons cold water to start, and using your hands or a fork, work the dough, adding additional tablespoons of water until the dough just holds together when you gather it in your hands.

2. Working on a lightly floured surface, gather the dough and form it into a solid ball. Separate into equal parts and form into disks. Wrap each tightly in plastic wrap and refrigerate for 30 to 60 minutes. Dough can be refrigerated for a couple of days or frozen for a couple of months.

3. Take the dough out of the refrigerator to allow it to warm up a bit but work with it cold. Put the refrigerated dough on a lightly floured surface, and with a lightly dusted rolling pin, flatten the dough into 2 circles, working both sides to extend each to a 9- to 12-inch round.

4. Grease the cast-iron skillet with 1 tablespoon of butter.

5. Carefully position the crust in the skillet so it is evenly distributed, pressing it in lightly and allowing the dough to extend over the side.

6. If making a single-crust pie, crimp the edges as desired. If filling and adding a top crust, leave the extra dough so it can be crimped with the top crust. Fill the pie as directed, and then roll out the top crust so it is just bigger than the diameter of the top of the skillet. For an extra flaky pastry crust, refrigerate the assembled pie for about 30 minutes before baking.

7. When ready to bake, cut a slit or hole in the middle of the top crust for heat to escape. Brush the crust with milk, which will turn it a nice brown color. Bake as directed.

GLUTEN-FREE CRUST

MAKES 1 10-INCH CRUST ✦ ACTIVE TIME: 20 MINUTES ✦ START TO FINISH: 90 MINUTES

Achieving something somewhat flaky is the trick with a gluten-free crust. This comes very close, and it's delicious, too. Double the recipe for a two-crust pie.

1¼ cups gluten-free multi-purpose flour blend

1 tablespoon sugar

½ teaspoon xanthan gum

½ teaspoon salt

6 tablespoons unsalted butter, chilled and cut into small pieces, plus 1 tablespoon butter for greasing the skillet

1 large egg

2 teaspoons fresh squeezed lemon juice

1 to 2 tablespoons cold water

1. In a large bowl, combine the flour blend, sugar, xanthan gum, and salt. Add the butter and work it into the flour mixture with a pastry blender or your fingers to form a coarse meal that includes whole bits of butter.

2. In a small bowl, whisk the egg and lemon juice together briskly until very foamy. Add to the dry ingredients and stir until the dough holds together. If dough isn't quite holding, add 1 tablespoon of cold water at a time until it does. Shape into a disk, wrap tightly in plastic wrap, and refrigerate for 30 to 60 minutes or overnight.

3. When ready to make the pie, take dough out of the refrigerator and allow to rest at room temperature for about 10 minutes before rolling. Working on a flat surface dusted with gluten-free flour, roll the dough into a 10-inch disk.

4. Grease the cast-iron skillet with 1 tablespoon of butter.

5. Carefully position the crust in the skillet so it is evenly distributed, pressing it in lightly. Crimp the edges. Fill and bake as directed.

SWEET & SAVORY CORNMEAL CRUST

MAKES 1 10-INCH CRUST ✦ ACTIVE TIME: 20 MINUTES ✦ START TO FINISH: 90 MINUTES

A crust that includes cornmeal will have more texture and flavor than a crust made from simple all-purpose flour. This distinctive texture and flavor is a perfect complement to savory fillings when prepared without sugar, and makes a great base for sweet pies as well. It's easy to make, too!

¾ cup all-purpose flour, plus more for dusting

¾ cup yellow cornmeal

3 tablespoons sugar if making a sweet crust

½ teaspoon salt

½ cup (1 stick) unsalted butter, chilled and cut into small pieces, plus 1 tablespoon butter for greasing the skillet

1 egg, slightly beaten

1. In a large bowl, thoroughly combine the flour, cornmeal, sugar if making a sweet crust, and salt. Add the butter and work it into the flour mixture with a pastry blender or your fingers to form coarse meal. Add the egg and continue to blend until the dough comes together.

2. Shape into a disk, cover tightly with plastic wrap, and refrigerate for 30 minutes.

3. Preheat the oven to 375° F. Take the dough out of the refrigerator to allow it to warm up a bit but work with it cold. Put the refrigerated dough on a lightly floured surface, and with a lightly dusted rolling pin, flatten the dough into a circle, working both sides to extend it to a 10-inch round.

4. Grease the cast iron skillet with 1 tablespoon of butter.

5. Carefully position the crust in the skillet so it is evenly distributed, pressing it in lightly. Crimp the edges. Use a fork to prick the crust on the bottom and sides. Line with foil or parchment paper, and fill with uncooked rice as a weight.

6. Bake for 10 to 12 minutes until lightly browned. Transfer to a wire rack to cool before filling.

GRAHAM CRACKER CRUST

MAKES 1 10-INCH CRUST ✦ ACTIVE TIME: 20 MINUTES ✦ START TO FINISH: 45 MINUTES

I'm a fan of crushing graham crackers to make this crust, but you can also purchase graham cracker crumbs in the baked goods aisle of your grocery store. Either works, as the cracker is held together with butter and sugar. There are so many fillings that complement the flavor and texture of a graham cracker crust. Experiment and enjoy.

1½ cups graham cracker crumbs

2 tablespoons sugar

1 tablespoon maple syrup

5 tablespoons unsalted butter, melted, plus 1 tablespoon butter for greasing the skillet

1. Preheat the oven to 375° F.

2. In a large bowl, combine graham cracker crumbs and sugar. Stir to combine. Add maple syrup and melted butter and stir to thoroughly combine.

3. Liberally grease the skillet with the butter. Pour the dough into the skillet and lightly press into shape. Line with tin foil and fill with uncooked rice. Bake for 10 to 12 minutes until golden.

4. Allow to cool on a wire rack before filling.

Variations

✸ Chocolate Graham Cracker Crust—Use chocolate graham crackers instead of plain.

✸ Cinnamon Graham Cracker Crust—Use cinnamon graham crackers instead of plain or add ½ teaspoon ground cinnamon and ¼ teaspoon ground ginger to the basic graham cracker crust mix.

✸ Hint of Heat Graham Cracker Crust—Add ¼ to ½ teaspoon cayenne pepper to the graham crackers before adding sugar, syrup, and butter.

PECAN NUT CRUST

So simple and elegant and delicious, nut crusts are a great gluten-free alternative to traditional crusts. They're a great base for everything from creamy, earthy fillings like pumpkin to decadent chocolate cream and even frozen yogurt with fruit.

1½ cups raw pecans

1½ tablespoons honey

2 tablespoons unsalted butter, chilled and cut into small pieces, plus 1 tablespoon butter for greasing the skillet

1. Preheat the oven to 400° F.

2. Put the pecan pieces in a food processor and pulse until you have a coarse, crumbly meal. Alternately, you can put the pieces in a large, thick plastic bag and mash them with a rolling pin or meat tenderizer.

3. Transfer the crushed nuts to a bowl and add the honey and butter, mixing with a pastry blender, fork, or your fingers until a coarse meal is formed. There can be chunks of butter.

4. Liberally grease the skillet with the butter. Transfer the nut mixture to the skillet and gently press it into the pan to form a crust.

5. Put the skillet on top of a cookie sheet to catch any oil that may drip from the nuts. Bake for 10 to 12 minutes, until browned and toasty. Remove from the oven and allow to cool completely on a wire rack.

Variations

✹ Almond Crust—Substitute 1½ cups raw almonds for pecans.

✹ Walnut Crust—Substitute 1½ cups raw walnut pieces for pecans

✹ Hazelnut Crust—Use ¾ cup raw hazelnuts with ¾ cup almonds or pecans.

✹ Mixed Nut—Use a blend of all these nuts.

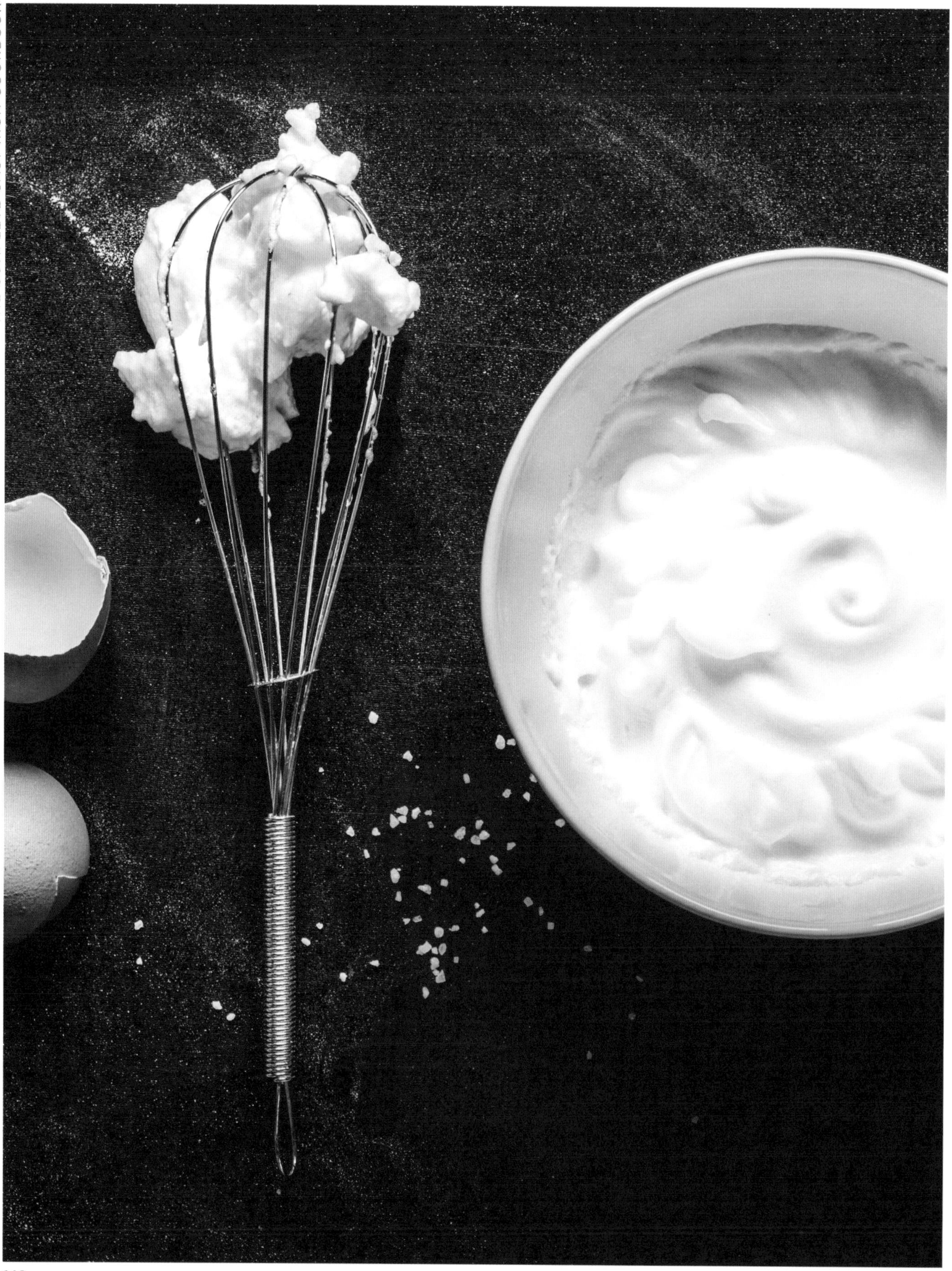

MERINGUE PIE SHELL

MAKES 1 12-INCH CRUST ✦ ACTIVE TIME: 30 MINUTES ✦ START TO FINISH: 90 MINUTES

Making this crust is a great way to use up egg whites left over from another recipe, or just because! The baking time is long and slow, but the result is a light, delicious, gluten-free shell that's perfect for creamy or fruit fillings.

3 egg whites at room temperature

¼ teaspoon cream of tartar

¾ cup sugar

½ teaspoon vanilla extract

1 tablespoon butter for greasing the skillet

1. Preheat the oven to 225° F.

2. In a large bowl, beat egg whites and cream of tartar on high speed until foamy. Beating constantly, add sugar 2 tablespoons at a time, beating after each addition until sugar is thoroughly dissolved. Beat until whites are glossy and stand in stiff peaks. Add and beat in vanilla.

3. Grease the skillet with the butter and spread the meringue over it, working it up the sides to form a rim.

4. Bake for 60 to 90 minutes until meringue is firm and a toothpick inserted in center comes out clean. Turn off the oven and allow to dry and crisp in the cooling oven for at least 1 hour. Remove from oven, cool completely on a wire rack, and fill as desired.

ENTREES

When you're looking for something that's loaded with flavor to be the centerpiece of your meal, flip through this chapter. The cast-iron skillet's versatility and practicality shine through when used to cook meats, fish, and casseroles. You'll find everything here from amazing crab cakes to simple meat-and-veggie-stuffed pot pies and satisfyingly juicy meats. The cast-iron skillet does an amazing job of browning on the outside while retaining moisture on the inside. It can go from stove to oven and handle the heat from both, which means there are fewer pans and dishes to fuss with when you're preparing a main course. And so, without further ado, here are some recipes to whet your appetite and excite your senses.

BEST. BURGERS. EVER.

MAKES 3 TO 4 BURGERS ✦ ACTIVE TIME: 30 MINUTES ✦ START TO FINISH: 30 MINUTES

I won't argue that a burger hot off the grill isn't a delicious thing. It's a staple of American dining. But if you want the Best. Burger. Ever., you won't produce it on the grill. You'll make it in a cast-iron skillet. Period. Why? Because the fat in the meat creates its own sauce, helping to brown and flavor the meat as it cooks. All of this drips off the grill. The cast-iron holds the heat steady and hot, too, turning the surface of the burger the perfect, crispy dark brown from side to side. If your mouth is watering now, wait until you make these at home.

1 pound ground beef

Salt and pepper to taste

Hamburger buns (not too bready)

Slices of cheese (optional)

Lettuce, tomato, onion (optional)

Ketchup, mustard, pickles, mayonnaise (optional)

1. Refrigerate the hamburger meat until ready to use.

2. When it's time to make the burgers, first brush your skillet with a thin sheen of oil, and heat it over medium-high heat. Take the meat out of the fridge and form the patties. Don't overhandle the meat, simply take a handful of it (about 3 oz.), and gently form into a patty. Make 3 or 4, depending on how many will fit in the skillet.

3. Put the patties in the skillet and don't touch them. Let them start to cook on the medium-high heat. They'll spatter and sizzle. That's fine. Sprinkle some salt on them, and grind some pepper over them (but not too much). Let them cook on one side for about 3 minutes.

4. When you flip the burgers, if you want cheese on one or all of them, put it on now. The cheese should blanket the meat, not be an afterthought.

5. Leave the burgers to cook on this side just as you did the other side. The skillet takes care of even distribution of the heat. Wait 3 or 4 minutes. Scoop the burger off the skillet with the spatula, slide it onto a bun, top with whatever you like, and dig in. Best. Burgers. Ever.

The kind of meat you use matters. The meat-to-fat ratio should be about 80-20. Most ground beef found in the grocery store is 85-15 or 90-10. If you have to go with one of these, choose the fattier proportion. The best thing to do, though, is ask the meat department to grind the meat for you. You want a chuck cut with a good amount of fat in it. The fat should show up as almost chunky in the meat, not pulverized to look like pale red mush. Trust me on this one.

JUICY TURKEY BURGERS

SERVES 4 TO 6 ✦ ACTIVE TIME: 20 MINUTES ✦ START TO FINISH: 60 MINUTES

I love the idea of using ground turkey to reduce the fat in recipes where I'd normally use ground beef. Unfortunately, the taste is never the same, and it's for that very reason: less fat! It turns out that shredded zucchini can moisten—and flavor—ground turkey, making for a very satisfying (and low-fat) experience.

Olive oil

½ cup onion, finely diced

2 cloves garlic, pressed

¾ cup plain bread crumbs

1 teaspoon tamari (or soy sauce)

½ teaspoon fresh ground pepper

1 teaspoon salt

¼ teaspoon dried sage

1 tablespoon fresh parsley, finely chopped

½ cup zucchini, grated or shredded in a food processor

¼ cup mozzarella cheese, grated

1 pound ground turkey

1. Heat the skillet over medium-high heat and coat with about a teaspoon of olive oil. Add the onion and garlic and cook, stirring, until the onion is translucent, about 3 minutes. Remove from heat and transfer the onion mix to a large bowl.

2. Add the bread crumbs, tamari, pepper, salt, sage, parsley, zucchini, and mozzarella. Combine well. Add the turkey and stir to mix the ingredients together.

3. Form the meat into patties, wrap in plastic, and refrigerate for 30 minutes.

4. Heat the skillet over medium-high heat and add about a teaspoon of olive oil. Place the patties in the skillet and cook for about 4 minutes per side. Do not overflip or flatten the patties while cooking.

5. Because you want the turkey cooked through the center, reduce the heat to medium and cover the skillet. Continue to cook for another 3 to 4 minutes. Press down gently on one of the patties to see if the juice is running clear. If it's still pink, continue to cook another minute or so.

6. Season with additional salt and pepper, and serve on hamburger buns with toppings of your choice.

COUNTRY FRIED STEAKS AND GRAVY

SERVES 2 ✦ ACTIVE TIME: 40 MINUTES ✦ START TO FINISH: 2 HOURS

Try your hand at one of the most iconic Southern inventions—the Country Fried Steak! You'll get the best results if you use the best ingredients: farm-fresh for the meat and cream, if at all possible. Enjoy!

For the Steak

2 ¼-pound round steaks or cube steaks

Kosher salt

1 cup flour

½ teaspoon freshly ground black pepper

1 cup peanut, vegetable, or canola oil

2 tablespoons unsalted butter, cut into pieces

For the Gravy

2 tablespoons pan drippings

2 tablespoons flour

¾ cup milk

Kosher salt

Freshly ground black pepper

1. Preheat oven to 200° F.

2. Prep steaks by patting dry, then seasoning both sides with kosher salt.

3. Add flour and pepper to a shallow dish or bowl before dredging the steaks in it. Make sure they are evenly coated.

4. Heat the skillet over medium-high heat until hot. Add the oil and the butter, coating the bottom of the pan. Put the steaks on the pan and sear on both sides, cooking for about 5 minutes a side.

5. Transfer steaks to a platter in the oven and keep warm as you make the gravy.

6. Turn the heat down and pour out all but 2 tablespoons of the leftover pan drippings. Mix in about 2 tablespoons of flour, creating a roux. Continue to stir while turning the heat back up to medium.

7. Once the roux is smooth, slowly add the milk, stirring constantly until incorporated. If the gravy is too thick, add more milk. If too thin, continue to cook it until it reduces. Season with a sprinkle of salt and plenty of black pepper.

8. Put the steaks on a plate and pour the gravy over them.

GAME DAY CHILI

SERVES 4 TO 6 ✦ ACTIVE TIME: 20 MINUTES ✦ START TO FINISH: 40 MINUTES

This hearty dish's roots may be Southwestern, but it is welcome at tailgates across the entire nation.

Vegetable oil

½ onion, diced

1 pound ground beef

1 (15.5 oz.) can kidney beans, drained and rinsed

1 (15.5 oz.) can diced tomatoes, with juice

3 oz. (½ can) tomato paste

⅓ cup chili powder

1 tablespoon garlic powder

1 teaspoon cumin

½ teaspoon oregano

1 teaspoon cayenne pepper

Salt and pepper to taste

1. Heat the skillet over medium-high heat. Add a scant teaspoon of vegetable oil to just coat the pan, and add the onion, stirring to cook, until translucent, about 2 minutes. Add the ground beef, stirring to break it up as you cook it. Brown the meat so that it's cooked through, about 10 minutes.

2. Drain the meat over a colander in the sink. Put the meat back in the skillet.

3. Over medium heat, stir in the beans, tomatoes, tomato paste, chili powder, garlic powder, cumin, oregano, and cayenne. Combine thoroughly and bring the mix to a gentle boil. Season with salt and pepper. Continue to cook on low for 10 to 15 minutes. Serve hot in bowls.

Corn chips are one of my guilty pleasures, so I always take the opportunity to garnish my chili with crumbled corn chips (or I use them as scoops for the chili). At our table, we also put out bowls of shredded cheddar cheese, sour cream, jalapeño slices, and thinly sliced scallions. Some like to serve chili with rice, which is good, too.

CAROLINA CRAB CAKES WITH REMOULADE SAUCE

MAKES 6 CAKES ✦ ACTIVE TIME: 60 MINUTES ✦ START TO FINISH: 90 MINUTES

With these cakes, if you want great flavor, you have to go for top-quality crab meat. This is the kind that's in the refrigerated section of your store's fish department. Don't buy crab meat that's canned like tuna. It has neither the flavor nor the consistency needed for these cakes.

For the Crab Cakes

1 pound lump crab meat (preferably blue crab)

¼ cup onion, minced

½ cup bread crumbs

1 teaspoon Worcestershire sauce

1 teaspoon Old Bay seasoning

2 tablespoons hot sauce

1 teaspoon dried parsley flakes

1 tablespoon mayonnaise

1 tablespoon milk

1 large egg, lightly beaten

Salt and freshly ground pepper to taste

¼ cup oil (preferably peanut, but olive is fine)

Lemon wedges

For the Remoulade Sauce

1 cup mayonnaise

2 tablespoons mustard (preferably Creole, otherwise whole grain or Dijon will do)

1 teaspoon Cajun seasoning

1 tablespoon sweet paprika

1 tablespoon pickle juice or fresh lemon juice (your preference)

1 tablespoon Louisiana-style hot sauce, plus more to taste

1½ teaspoons garlic, minced

2 tablespoons fresh parsley, finely chopped (optional)

Salt and freshly ground black pepper to taste

1. In a medium bowl, combine the ingredients for the remoulade sauce and mix well. Cover and chill in the refrigerator.

2. In a large bowl combine crab meat, onion, bread crumbs, Worcestershire sauce, Old Bay seasoning, hot sauce, parsley flakes, and mayonnaise. Mix the milk into the egg and add to the crab mix, blending gently but thoroughly. Season with salt and pepper. If mix seems dry, add some more mayonnaise.

3. Heat the skillet over medium-high heat. Add the oil. It should be about ¼-inch deep. When oil is hot, add 3 or 4 individual heaping spoonfuls of crab mix to the skillet, pressing down on the tops of each to form a patty (cake). Brown the cakes on each side for about 3 minutes. Try to turn the cakes over just once. If you're worried about them not getting cooked through, put a lid on the skillet for a minute or so after they've browned on each side.

4. Transfer the cakes to a plate and cover with foil to keep them warm while you cook the next batch.

5. Serve on a platter with lemon wedges and remoulade sauce on the side.

SALMON CAKES

MAKES 6 TO 8 CAKES ✦ ACTIVE TIME: 60 MINUTES ✦ START TO FINISH: 90 MINUTES

I use canned salmon for this recipe. The quality isn't as high as using fresh salmon, but it's quite good. With the healthy add-ins, and the fact that the end product is a cake that will be topped with a dressing like tartar or cocktail sauce, the canned salmon is great for ease of use and taste.

2 (14.75 oz.) cans of salmon (preferably Red Salmon over Pink Salmon)

2 large eggs, lightly beaten

4 tablespoons bread crumbs

¼ cup onion, minced

1 teaspoon Frank's Red Hot sauce

1 teaspoon dried parsley flakes

Salt and freshly ground pepper to taste

2 tablespoons oil (preferably peanut, but olive is fine)

Lemon wedges

1. Drain the liquid from the cans of salmon, and empty the fish into a bowl, flaking it apart with a fork. Add the eggs, bread crumbs, minced onion, hot sauce, and parsley flakes and stir, combining well. Season with salt and pepper.

2. Heat the skillet over medium-high heat. Add 1 tablespoon of the oil. Add 3 or 4 individual heaping spoonfuls of fish mix to the skillet, pressing down on the tops of each to form a patty (cake). Brown the cakes on each side for about 5 minutes. Try to turn the cakes over just once. If you're worried about them not getting cooked through, put a lid on the skillet for a minute or so after they've browned on each side.

3. Transfer the cakes to a plate and cover with foil to keep them warm while you cook the next batch. Serve on a platter with lemon wedges.

Variations

Salmon cakes can be served many ways:

● Eat them as you would hamburgers, on a bun with lettuce, tomato, red onion, and, instead of ketchup or mustard, tartar or cocktail sauce.

● Serve a cake on top of a green salad with a lemon-dill dressing on the side.

● Make mini cakes and serve as finger foods with toothpicks and dipping sauces.

PORK CHOPS WITH CIDER AND APPLES

SERVES 4 ✦ ACTIVE TIME: 3 HOURS ✦ START TO FINISH: 4 HOURS

Apples are the perfect accompaniment to pork, and the lovely glaze created in the skillet adds another element of deliciousness. I prefer chops with the bones in, but boneless chops are fine, too.

4 pork chops, about ½-inch thick, bone-in or boneless

Salt and pepper to taste

2 tablespoons olive oil

2 shallots, thinly sliced

3 cloves garlic, minced

3 tablespoons flour

1½ cups apple cider

2 tablespoons fresh parsley, chopped

1 teaspoon dried sage

1 teaspoon fresh thyme

2 tablespoons butter

3 large apples, cored, peeled and sliced

1 tablespoon sugar

½ teaspoon cinnamon (if desired)

1. Preheat the oven to 350° F.

2. Season the chops with salt and pepper. Heat the skillet over medium-high heat. Add the olive oil and coat the bottom. Add the chops and sear on both sides, about 3 minutes a side. Transfer to a plate.

3. Add the shallots and garlic to the skillet and stir, cooking, until onion is translucent, about 3 minutes.

4. Reduce the heat to low and stir in the flour, cooking for about a minute. Slowly add the cider, using a whisk to combine it with the flour and onions. Whisk constantly as you slowly add and incorporate the cider. When it is all mixed, increase the heat to medium, stir occasionally, and bring to a boil. Keep at a boil for a few minutes.

5. Stir in the parsley, sage, and thyme, then add the chops. When the sauce returns to a boil, remove the skillet from the burner, cover it, and put the skillet in the oven. Bake for 1½ hours until the chops are very tender.

6. When the chops have about 20 minutes of cooking time left, prepare the apples.

7. Heat another skillet over medium-high heat and add the butter. When it is melted, add the apple slices. Reduce the heat to low and cook, stirring occasionally, until they start to soften. Sprinkle them with the sugar and cinnamon (if desired), and continue to cook until soft.

8. Serve the chops with the apples, drizzling some of the sauce from the skillet over both.

If you make this after apple picking, like we do, pick up some cider donuts for dessert.

FRIED CHICKEN

SERVES 4 ✦ ACTIVE TIME: 60 MINUTES ✦ START TO FINISH: 90 MINUTES

If you want the texture and flavor of deep-fried chicken without the mess, try this recipe. The cornflakes are essential!

3 chicken legs (drumsticks and thighs together, cut to make 3 drumsticks and 3 thighs)

¼ cup flour

Salt and pepper to taste

1 cup milk

1 tablespoon white vinegar

2 eggs, lightly beaten

1½ cups cornflakes, finely crushed

½ cup plain bread crumbs

1 teaspoon paprika

1 cup vegetable oil

1. Preheat the oven to 400° F. Place the skillet in the oven to get it hot.

2. Rinse and dry the chicken pieces.

3. In a shallow bowl or cake pan, whisk together the flour with some salt and pepper. Combine the milk and the vinegar and let the combination sit for 10 minutes (to create buttermilk). When ready, mix the milk in a bowl with the beaten eggs. In another large bowl, combine the cornflakes, bread crumbs, paprika, and 2 tablespoons of the vegetable oil.

4. Coat the chicken pieces one at a time by dipping each in the flour, then the milk mixture, then the crumb mixture, being sure to coat all sides. When coated, put the pieces on a plate, cover with plastic wrap, and refrigerate for about 15 minutes.

5. Remembering how hot it's going to be (wear oven mitts!), take the skillet out of the oven and put the remaining oil in it. Heat it on low until hot. Add the cold chicken pieces and turn in the hot oil until both sides are coated.

6. Put the skillet back in the oven and bake for about 30 minutes, turning the pieces after 15 minutes. The chicken is done when the juices run clear when pierced with a knife. Serve immediately.

LIVER AND ONIONS

SERVES 4 TO 6 ✦ ACTIVE TIME: 40 MINUTES ✦ START TO FINISH: 7 HOURS

My family thinks I'm crazy because I get very excited when I see a beautiful piece of calf's liver. I can smell and practically taste its pungent, buttery goodness, slathered with sautéed onions. My mother used to make it for my family as a treat, and it was delicious every time. Serve this with homemade mashed potatoes, which are the perfect food to soak up the oil and butter from the liver and onions. And if you want to be completely decadent, serve creamed spinach, too.

1 pound calf's liver (not beef liver, which is not as tender)

1½ cups milk

5 tablespoons butter

2 onions, thinly sliced

½ cup flour

Salt and freshly ground pepper to taste

Chopped fresh parsley for garnish

Fresh parsley, chopped, for garnish

1. To prep the liver, put it in a glass bowl and cover with the milk. Cover the bowl with plastic wrap and refrigerate the meat for 5 to 6 hours.

2. Heat skillet over medium heat. Add the 3 tablespoons of butter. When butter is melted, add onion slices. Stir to separate and coat with the butter. Cook over medium heat just until onions begin to soften, about 6 minutes. Reduce the heat to low and cook, stirring occasionally for 30 to 40 minutes.

3. While the onions are cooking, remove the liver from the milk. Cut into 2 pieces and pat dry with paper towels. Put the flour on a plate and season with salt and pepper. Gently press the liver pieces into the flour to coat them. Shake off excess.

4. Heat another cast-iron skillet over medium heat. Add the remaining butter. When hot but not browned, add the liver pieces. Sauté the pieces for about 2 to 3 minutes a side so that they are browned on the outside but slightly pink inside. Be careful not to overcook them.

5. When done, transfer the liver to a plate and pile on the sautéed onions. Sprinkle the chopped fresh parsley over the plate and serve.

Calf liver is milder than beef liver. Even so, soaking liver in milk is a way to remove any bitterness.

SIMPLE SKILLET SALMON

SERVES 4 TO 6 ✦ ACTIVE TIME: 20 MINUTES ✦ START TO FINISH: 30 MINUTES

Start with super-fresh fish, and keep it simple—butter, lemon, salt, and pepper—and you can create a succulent dish that is ready in no time.

3 to 4 pounds of salmon fillets

2 tablespoons unsalted butter, cut in pieces, softened

1 lemon

Salt and pepper to taste

1 tablespoon olive oil

1. Rinse the fillets with cold water to ensure that any scales or bones are removed. Dry them on paper towels. Rub the butter on both sides of the fillets, squeeze lemon over them, and season with salt and pepper.

2. Heat the skillet over medium-high heat and add the tablespoon of olive oil. Add the fillets, flesh side down. Cook on one side for about 3 minutes, then flip them and cook for 2 minutes on the other side. Remove the pan from the heat and let the fish rest in it for a minute before serving. The skin should peel right off.

There are different cuts of salmon: steaks and fillets. The steaks are cut from the meat around the backbone, and they contain that bone in the middle. Fillets are cut from the flesh that extends from the head to the tail of the fish. For this recipe, use fillets.

SMOKY MOUNTAIN ROASTED TROUT

with Fennel and Vidalia Onion

SERVES 2 ✦ ACTIVE TIME: 60 MINUTES ✦ START TO FINISH: 2 HOURS

Roasting the whole trout on a bed of onions and fennel creates a sweetness of flavor and crispness of skin that make for a flavorful and satisfying—and very nutritious—meal.

2 tablespoons olive oil

1 Vidalia onion, sliced thin

2 heads of fennel, fronds removed, sliced thin

2 brown or brook trout, about 1 pound total, cleaned

Salt and pepper to taste

Lemon slices

1. Preheat the oven to 450° F.

2. Heat the skillet over medium-high heat. In a bowl, combine the olive oil, onion, and fennel. Add the vegetables to the skillet and cook, stirring, until they soften and start to brown, about 20 minutes. Flatten and spread the vegetables in the skillet. Lightly oil the fish on both sides, season with salt and pepper, and place the fish on the bed of vegetables.

3. Put the skillet in the oven and bake for 25 minutes.

4. To serve, remove the fish from the skillet and fillet them by making an incision from head to tail, holding the head firmly, and lifting gently to pull the skeleton away from the bottom of the fish. Once boned, put the fillets on a plate and serve with the vegetables on the side. Garnish with lemon slices.

SIMPLY SENSATIONAL CHILI CON CARNE

SERVES 4 TO 6 ✦ ACTIVE TIME: 20 MINUTES ✦ START TO FINISH: 40 MINUTES

Chili is another dish that has as many variations as people who like to cook and eat it. This one is basic and elemental so that, if you want, you can embellish it with spicier or more exotic seasonings, different cuts of meat, and so on.

Vegetable oil

½ onion, diced

1 pound of steak tips

1 (15.5 oz.) can kidney beans, drained and rinsed

1 (15.5 oz.) can diced tomatoes, with juice

3 oz. (½ can) tomato paste

⅓ cup chili powder

1 tablespoon garlic powder

1 teaspoon cumin

½ teaspoon oregano

1 teaspoon cayenne pepper

Salt and pepper to taste

1. Heat the skillet over medium-high heat. Add about a teaspoon of vegetable oil to just coat the pan, and add the onion, stirring to cook, until translucent, about 2 minutes. Add the steak tips and stir occasionally as you cook them. Brown the meat so that it's cooked through, about 10 minutes.

2. Over medium heat, stir in the beans, tomatoes, tomato paste, chili powder, garlic powder, cumin, oregano, and cayenne. Combine thoroughly and bring the mix to a slow boil. Season with salt and pepper. Continue to cook on low for 10 to 15 minutes. Serve hot in bowls.

CAJUN BLACKENED TILAPIA

SERVES 4 ✦ ACTIVE TIME: 40 MINUTES ✦ START TO FINISH: 90 MINUTES

The cast-iron skillet is perfect for blackening fish, as it requires high heat and quick cooking. Although the result is delicious, the blackening process creates a lot of smoke, so be sure to turn the oven fan on or open the windows before you start cooking.

For the Tilapia

1 stick butter, melted

4 boneless tilapia fillets, about 4 oz. each

1 lemon, cut into 4 wedges

For the Blackened Seasoning

2 tablespoons paprika

1 tablespoon onion powder

3 tablespoons garlic powder

2 tablespoons cayenne pepper

1½ teaspoons celery salt

1½ tablespoons finely ground black pepper

1 tablespoon dried thyme

1 tablespoon dried oregano

1 tablespoon ground chipotle

1. In a bowl, combine all the spices for your blackened seasoning and set aside.

2. Heat the skillet over high heat for about 10 minutes until very hot. While the skillet heats up, rinse the fillets and then pat dry with paper towels. Dip the fish fillets in the melted butter, covering both sides, and then press the blackened seasoning generously into both sides.

3. Put the fish in the skillet and cook for about 3 minutes a side, placing a bit of butter on top while the other side is cooking. Serve with lemon wedges.

Tilapia is a wonderful fish for blackening, as it is a firm-fleshed fish that is fairly bland and thus benefits from seasoning. You can blacken any kind of fish, though. Others that taste great prepared this way are catfish, tuna, grouper, halibut, and trout.

CHICKEN FAJITAS

SERVES 6 TO 8 ✦ ACTIVE TIME: 30 MINUTES ✦ START TO FINISH: 5 HOURS

The trick is to bring this dish to the table while the meat and veggies are still sizzling. You'll want to be sure you have all the sides prepped ahead of time so you can go straight from stove to table with this. You'll want tortillas, guacamole, salsa, sliced jalapeños, sliced black olives, and sour cream.

For the Chicken

½ cup orange juice

1 lime, squeezed (about 3 tablespoons juice)

4 cloves garlic, minced

1 jalapeño pepper, ribs and seeds removed, diced

2 tablespoons fresh cilantro, chopped

1 teaspoon cumin

1 teaspoon dried oregano

Salt and pepper to taste

3 tablespoons olive oil

3 to 4 boneless, skinless chicken breasts, cut into strips

For the Vegetables

2 tablespoons olive oil

1 red onion, thinly sliced

1 red bell pepper, ribs and seeds removed, thinly sliced

1 green bell pepper, ribs and seeds removed, thinly sliced

1 yellow bell pepper, ribs and seeds removed, thinly sliced

2 jalapeño peppers or serrano chiles, ribs and seeds removed, sliced thin

3 cloves garlic, minced

¼ cup fresh-squeezed lime juice

½ cup fresh cilantro, chopped

Salt and pepper to taste

1. Prepare the chicken. In a bowl, combine orange juice, lime juice, garlic, jalapeño, cilantro, cumin, oregano, salt, and pepper. When thoroughly combined, add the olive oil. Put the chicken pieces in the mix, stir, cover with plastic wrap, and refrigerate for about 4 hours.

2. About an hour before you want to eat, get the sides prepared so you'll have them on hand when the dish is sizzling.

3. Heat the skillet over medium-high heat. Remove the chicken from the marinade with a slotted spoon and put it in the skillet, stirring and turning the pieces so they brown on all sides. Cook thoroughly, about 8 to 10 minutes. Transfer the cooked chicken to a platter and cover loosely with foil to keep warm.

4. Prepare the vegetables. Reduce the heat to medium, add the oil, and then add the onion, peppers, jalapeño, and garlic. Cook, while stirring, for 3 to 5 minutes until vegetables soften. Add the lime juice and cilantro and cook for a few minutes more. Season with salt and pepper.

5. While vegetables are still sizzling, push them to one side of the pan and put the chicken on the other side. Serve immediately.

You can use the same ingredients to make steak fajitas, but substitute 1 pound of flank steak for the chicken, and marinate it overnight. Don't slice the steak until it has been cooked.

SAUSAGE AND PEPPERS

SERVES 4 TO 6 ✦ ACTIVE TIME: 40 MINUTES ✦ START TO FINISH: 60 MINUTES

This combination is so delicious. It includes onions, as well. Sauté everything until it is crispy and caramelized, and serve in large sandwich rolls.

4 tablespoons olive oil

1 pound sweet Italian sausages

4 cloves garlic, thinly sliced

3 bell peppers, your choice of color, thinly sliced

2 hot peppers like Italian, poblano, or Hungarian Hot Wax (or 1 jalapeño), ribs and seeds removed, thinly sliced

1 large onion, thinly sliced

Salt and pepper to taste

1. Preheat oven to 350° F.

2. Heat the skillet over medium-high heat. Add 1 tablespoon of olive oil. Sauté the sausages in the oil until golden brown on all sides—about 3 minutes a side. Transfer the sausages to a plate.

3. Add the remaining oil, and add the garlic, peppers, and onion. Cook, stirring, while the vegetables soften, about 5 to 6 minutes. Return the sausages to the skillet.

4. Put the skillet in the oven and bake for about 15 minutes, until sausages are cooked through and the vegetables are tender and slightly crunchy on the outside. Season with salt and pepper. Serve in long sandwich buns, and hot pepper flakes if desired.

STEAK FRITES

SERVES 2 ✦ ACTIVE TIME: 30 MINUTES ✦ START TO FINISH: 2 HOURS

A hot, juicy steak… yummy. A mound of hot, crispy French fries… fabulous! Now combine them, and you'll understand why this dish is on the menu at nearly every bistro in France. And you can create them both in your skillet.

For the Fries

1 pound Yukon Gold potatoes, peeled, washed, and cut into thin strips

3 cups peanut oil (Although increasingly difficult to find, peanut is the best oil to fry in. If you can't find it, vegetable oil is a suitable substitute.)

Salt and pepper to taste

For the Steak

2 small steaks (sirloin, rib eye, or shell are the best choices), about 1 inch thick

3 tablespoons unsalted butter

Salt and pepper to taste

Fresh parsley for garnish

1. Preheat the oven to 200° F.

2. Prepare everything ahead of time so you can cook the steaks immediately after the fries. If you wait too long, the fries will get soft. Line a baking sheet with paper towels (for the fries when they're cooked). Put the steaks on a plate in the refrigerator (keep them cold until ready for to go in the pan). Make sure your potato strips are clean and dry.

3. Put the oil in the skillet and add the potatoes. Bring the oil to a boil over medium-high heat (careful of splattering). As the oil gets hotter, the potatoes will get limp and just start to brown (about 15 minutes). At this point, start turning them with tongs to get all of the sides crispy and browned. Cook another 5 minutes or so.

4. Transfer the fries to the baking sheet and sprinkle with salt. Put in the oven to keep warm, covering with additional paper towels so they stay crisp.

5. Drain the fat from the skillet into a heat-proof glass container (like a measuring cup). Put the skillet back on the burner and add the butter. Take the steaks out of the fridge. When the butter is hot but not smoking, put the steaks in the skillet. Sear them over the high heat for a minute per side, then reduce the heat to medium. Sprinkle with salt and pepper and turn them every few minutes. They're cooked in about 8 minutes (so that they're somewhat rare and juicy inside).

6. Transfer the steaks to plates, and pile the French fries next to them. Garnish with parsley. *Voila!*

STEAK AU POIVRE

SERVES 2 · ACTIVE TIME: 40 MINUTES · START TO FINISH: 2 HOURS

After making the Steak Frites (page 179), the natural progression was to experiment and create the other classic French bistro fare, Steak Au Poivre (with pepper). You'll get the best results if you use the best ingredients: farm-fresh for the meat, shallots, chives, and cream, if at all possible. Bon appetit!

2 boneless strip steaks (about 8 oz. each)

Kosher salt

1 tablespoon whole black peppercorns

1 teaspoon vegetable oil

2 small shallots, minced

2 tablespoons unsalted butter, cut into pieces

⅓ cup cognac or other brandy

½ cup heavy cream

Rosemary sprigs for garnish (optional)

1. Preheat oven to 200° F.

2. Prep steaks by patting them dry, then seasoning both sides with kosher salt.

3. Put the peppercorns in a sealed plastic bag and working on a hard, flat surface, pound them with a meat tenderizer or mallet to crush them. Pour them onto a plate and press both sides of both steaks into them, distributing peppercorns evenly over the meat.

4. Heat the skillet over medium-high heat until hot. Add the oil, coating the bottom of the pan. Put the steaks in the pan and sear on both sides, cooking for about 3 minutes a side for medium-rare.

5. Transfer steaks to a platter in the oven and keep warm as you make the sauce.

6. With the skillet on medium heat, add a tablespoon of the butter, let it melt, and add the shallots. As they sauté, stir up the bits stuck to the bottom of the pan. Cook until shallots are browned, about 3 minutes. Pour the cognac in the pan, swirl it around, and using a long-handled lighter, ignite it. The flame will subside in a minute or so. Continue to cook sauce until it is nearly boiling, while stirring constantly.

7. Add the cream and any juices from the platter the steaks are on. Reduce the heat and cook the sauce until somewhat reduced, about 5 minutes. Stir in the last tablespoon of butter.

8. Put the steaks on a plate and pour the sauce over them. Garnish with rosemary, if desired.

SEAFOOD PAELLA

SERVES 4 TO 6 ◆ ACTIVE TIME: 90 MINUTES ◆ START TO FINISH: 2 HOURS

Paella is a rice dish that hails from Valencia in Spain. Its yellow hue comes from saffron threads, and it is chock-full of everything good: rice, meat, fish, and vegetables. This recipe is made with more seafood than meat, and it's for a smaller serving size than a platter that would normally feed a party.

4 cups chicken broth

2 tablespoons olive oil, as needed

1 onion, diced

4 cloves garlic, minced

1 teaspoon smoked paprika

½ teaspoon saffron threads, crushed

2½ cups short-grain rice

2 ripe tomatoes, seeded and chopped

1 cup dry white wine

1 teaspoon salt

Freshly ground black pepper

1 cup frozen peas

½ pound calamari, cut into 1-inch pieces

8 oz. Spanish chorizo, cut into ¼-inch rounds

½ pound small shrimp, peeled and deveined

16 mussels, scrubbed and debearded

1. Preheat the oven to 425° F.

2. In a saucepan, bring the chicken broth to a simmer over medium heat.

3. Heat the skillet over medium-high heat. Add the olive oil, onion, and garlic, and cook, stirring occasionally, until the onion is translucent, about 3 minutes. Add the paprika and saffron, and cook, while stirring, for another minute.

4. Add the rice, stirring to coat, then stir in the tomatoes and wine. Bring to a boil and cook until the liquid is reduced by half, about 2 minutes. Add the hot chicken broth and peas, stir, then bring to a boil and cook for 5 minutes. Season with salt and pepper.

5. Add the peas, calamari, and chorizo and stir to combine. Put the skillet in the oven and bake for about 30 minutes, until the calamari are soft. Scatter the shrimp and mussels over the top of the paella and return to the oven. Cook until the shrimp are opaque and the mussels have opened, 5 to 10 minutes.

6. Keep an eye on the dish so the seafood on top doesn't overcook.

7. Remove from the oven, discard any mussels that didn't open, let rest for about 5 minutes, and serve.

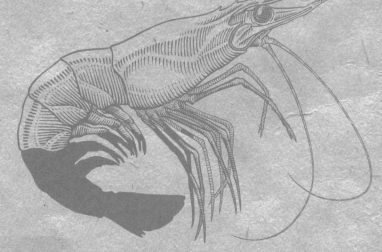

CHICKEN-QUINOA CASSEROLE

SERVES 4 TO 6 ✦ ACTIVE TIME: 45 MINUTES ✦ START TO FINISH: 90 MINUTES

Using frozen vegetables in this recipe is a real time-saver. The turmeric adds a delicate spiciness, too.

1 tablespoon olive oil

½ onion, diced

2 cloves garlic, minced

1 pound boneless, skinless chicken breast, cut into 1-inch pieces

½ cup frozen vegetables (peas, beans, carrots, corn)

1 teaspoon turmeric

½ teaspoon salt

½ teaspoon black pepper

12 oz. crushed tomatoes or chopped tomatoes in puree

1 cup water

1 cup quinoa

¼ cup parsley, chopped

½ cup feta cheese, crumbled

1. Heat the skillet over medium-high heat. Add the olive oil, onion, and garlic and cook for 2 minutes or until translucent.

2. Add the chicken pieces and frozen vegetables and continue to cook, stirring, until chicken pieces are browned, about 8 minutes. Stir in the turmeric and season with salt and pepper.

3. Add the tomatoes and water, and bring to a boil. Stir in the quinoa, reduce the heat to medium, and cook for 15 to 20 minutes until quinoa is cooked and most of the liquid has evaporated. Stir in the parsley and sprinkle with feta cheese. Serve.

Quinoa is a "super food" that has been a part of the human diet for several thousand years, since the Incas deemed it fit for human consumption. It is a seed that is prepared like a grain. It contains all nine amino acids and is rich in lysine, iron, magnesium, and riboflavin. Quinoa also has more fiber than grains. On its own, its flavor is somewhat nuttier than brown rice and its texture is grainier. It is a great base for vegetables and grilled meat or fish.

LAMB CHOPS WITH ROSEMARY AND LEMON

SERVES 4 ✦ ACTIVE TIME: 15 MINUTES ✦ START TO FINISH: 30 MINUTES

Lamb chops are an indulgence, for sure, so if you're going to splurge, be sure to follow this recipe when preparing them. The rosemary, garlic, and lemon seasoning brings out the earthy goodness of the chops.

4 tablespoons fresh-squeezed lemon juice

2 tablespoons fresh rosemary leaves, chopped

2 cloves garlic, pressed

Salt and pepper to taste

8 lamb chops

1. Preheat the broiler on high. Position a rack to be about 5 to 7 inches away from the heat. Put the skillet in the oven so it gets hot.

2. In a bowl, combine the lemon juice and rosemary. Press the garlic into the mix and season with salt and pepper. Using your hands, rub the chops in the mix, being sure to coat both sides and distribute evenly. Put the chops on a platter.

3. When the skillet is hot, take it out and position the chops in it so they fit. Return skillet to the rack under the broiler and cook for about 5 minutes. Since the skillet is already hot, the lamb is cooking on both sides at once.

4. Remove from the oven, let rest for a minute, and serve.

MOUSSAKA

SERVES 4 TO 6 ✦ ACTIVE TIME: 90 MINUTES ✦ START TO FINISH: 2 HOURS

This Greek dish is an incredible blend of lamb, eggplant, and spices. Topped with a cheesy crust, this is a great alternative to shepherd's pie.

For the Filling

1 large eggplant, ends trimmed and cut into cubes

¼ cup salt

4 cups cold water

⅓ cup olive oil

1 pound ground lamb

1 onion, diced

3 cloves garlic, minced

½ cup dry red wine

8 oz. can tomato sauce

2 tablespoons fresh parsley, chopped

1 teaspoon dried oregano

½ teaspoon cinnamon

Salt and pepper to taste

For the Crust

5 eggs

6 tablespoons butter

⅓ cup flour

2½ cups milk

⅔ cup Parmesan cheese, grated

⅓ cup fresh dill, chopped (or substitute parsley)

1. Preheat the oven to 350° F.

2. Prep the eggplant by putting the cold water in a bowl and adding the salt. When dissolved, add the eggplant cubes and stir. Cover the bowl with plastic wrap and let the cubes soak for about 20 minutes. After soaking, drain in a colander and rinse the eggplant with cold water. Squeeze the cubes to wring out the water, place them on a pile of paper towels, and blot them as dry as possible. Set aside.

3. While the eggplant is soaking, heat the skillet over medium-high heat. Add a tablespoon of oil to coat the bottom. Brown the ground lamb in the skillet until cooked, about 4 minutes. Use a slotted spoon to transfer the cooked meat to a bowl. Set aside.

4. Cook the prepared eggplant. Heat the skillet over medium-high heat again. Add ¼ cup of olive oil and add the cubes, stirring frequently, until they start to soften, about 5 minutes. Use the slotted spoon to add the cooked eggplant to the bowl with the lamb in it.

5. Put the skillet back on the heat and add the rest of the oil. Cook the onion and garlic together, while stirring constantly, until the onion is translucent, about 3 minutes. Add the lamb and eggplant and stir to combine. Add the wine, tomato sauce, parsley, oregano, and cinnamon. Stir to combine, lower the heat to low, and simmer for about 15 minutes, stirring occasionally. Season with salt and pepper.

6. Next, make the crust. In a large bowl, beat the eggs lightly. Heat another skillet or saucepan over medium heat, melt the butter, lower the heat slightly, and add the flour, stirring to combine and form a paste. Slowly add the milk, while stirring with a whisk. Bring to a boil over low heat while whisking constantly. When the mixture reaches a boil, remove from the heat. Add about half the hot mix into the eggs and stir briskly, then pour the tempered eggs into the skillet or saucepan and mix into the rest of the hot flour/milk mix. Add the cheese and dill (or parsley) and stir.

7. Even out the top of the lamb-and-eggplant mixture, then top with the flour-egg-and-cheese mixture. Put the skillet in the oven. Bake for 35 to 45 minutes until the crust is set and golden brown.

8. Allow to rest for about 5 minutes before serving.

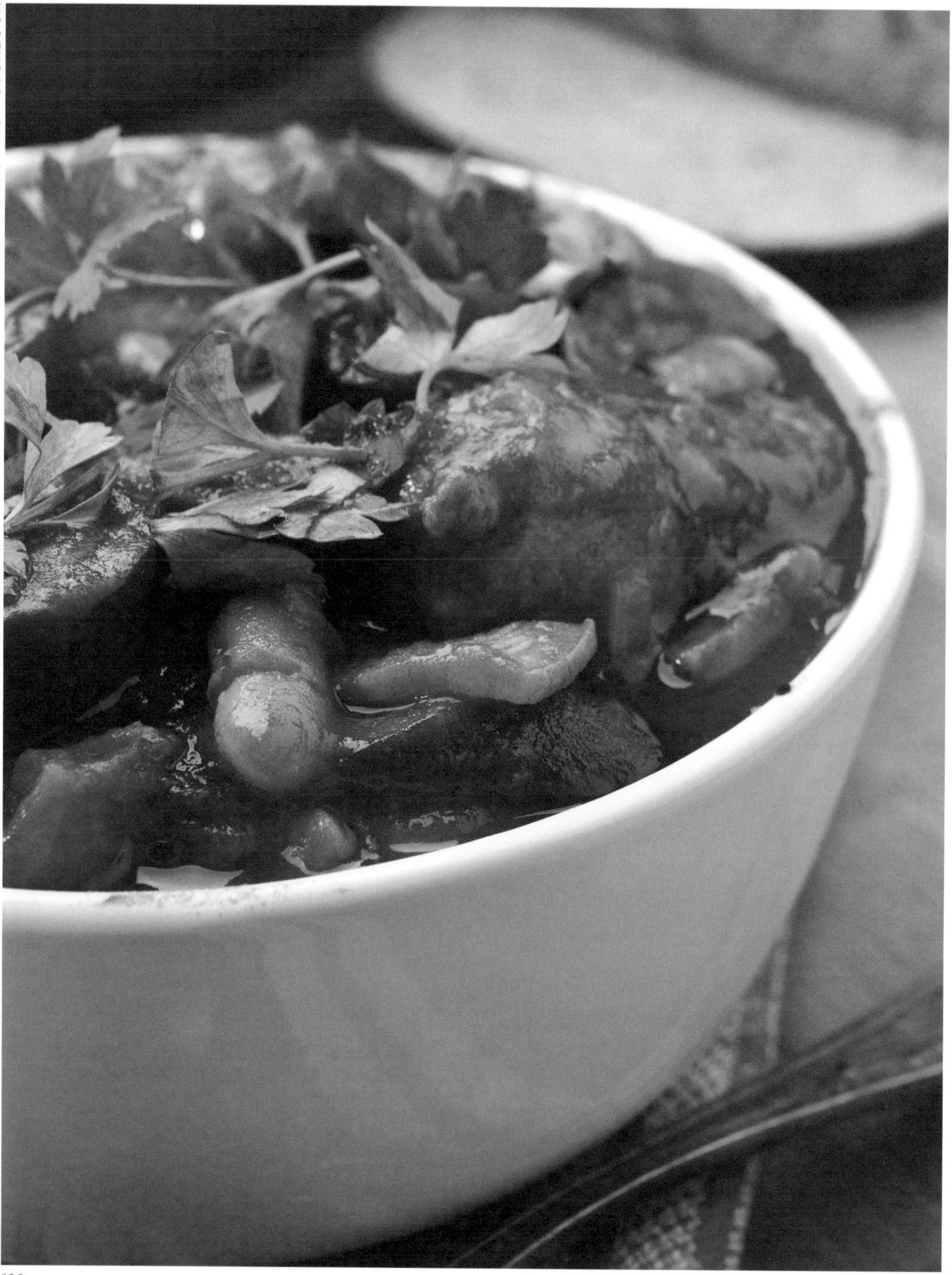

SPICY SAUSAGE STEW WITH SUMMER VEGETABLES

SERVES 4 TO 6 ✦ ACTIVE TIME: 35 MINUTES ✦ START TO FINISH: 60 MINUTES

When everything looks so good at the farmer's markets in the late summer, it's easy to end up with a lot of vegetables and few ideas of how to combine them. This dish showcases the flavors of peppers, corn, and tomatoes, with just the right amount of spice.

2 tablespoons butter

1 onion, diced

2 cloves garlic, minced

1 pound Italian sausage, cut into slices

2 teaspoons chili powder

½ teaspoon cayenne pepper

2 red peppers, diced

3 ears of corn, shucked and cleaned, kernels removed

1 small zucchini, cut into half-moons about ¼ inch thick

4 tomatoes, seeds removed, cut into chunks

Salt and pepper to taste

Parsley for garnish (optional)

1. Heat the skillet over medium-high heat. Add the butter. When it is melted, add the onion and garlic and cook, while stirring, until translucent and slightly browned, about 5 minutes.

2. Add the meat and stir, browning on all sides, about 3 minutes. Stir in the spices. Top with the peppers, corn, zucchini, and tomato pieces. Stir and season with salt and pepper.

3. Cover the skillet, reduce the heat to medium, and cook, covered, for about 20 minutes, checking it occasionally to make sure there is enough liquid and that it's at a gentle simmer, not a rolling boil. Garnish with parsley if desired. Serve immediately.

BEEF STROGANOFF

SERVES 4 TO 6 ✦ ACTIVE TIME: 40 MINUTES ✦ START TO FINISH: 90 MINUTES

This was a favorite of my family's when I was growing up, so I made it for mine as they were growing up. I'm happy to say that they've liked mine as much as I liked my mother's. The dish itself is Russian (Stroganov), made with pieces of beef served in a rich sauce that includes sour cream (Smetana). It reportedly became popular in the mid-1800s.

1 tablespoon olive oil

1 pound stew beef, cut into strips

1 small onion, minced

2 cloves garlic, pressed

½ cup mushroom caps, sliced

1½ cups beef broth

¼ cup dry sherry

1 tablespoon Worcestershire sauce

¼ cup flour

½ cup sour cream

Salt and pepper to taste

1. Heat olive oil in the skillet over medium-high heat. Add the beef strips so they fit in the skillet (or work in batches). Fry them in the skillet, while turning so that all sides get browned, about 3 minutes. Transfer the beef pieces to a plate and cover with foil to keep warm.

2. Add a bit more oil if necessary, and sauté the onion, garlic, and mushrooms until soft, about 5 minutes. In the skillet, add the beef broth, sherry, and Worcestershire sauce. Bring to a boil, scraping the browned bits of meat and vegetables off the bottom of the pan. Put the flour in a bowl and add some of the heated sauce, using a whisk to form a paste. Add a bit more sauce to the bowl, and when the sauce is incorporated with the flour, transfer all of it into the skillet and stir until incorporated. Continue to cook until the sauce thickens.

3. Reduce the heat and add the sour cream. Add the beef back to the skillet. When everything is hot, season with salt and pepper, and serve.

This dish must be served over egg noodles. Nothing else will do. Chop some fresh parsley to use as a garnish if desired, and have some bread available to lap up the extra sauce.

SKILLET WINGS

MAKES 3 TO 6 SERVINGS ✦ ACTIVE TIME: 30 MINUTES ✦ START TO FINISH: 60 MINUTES

These are a double whammy of sauteed goodness baked to perfection in a very hot oven. Invite over your wing-loving friends and see if they don't agree that these are the best ever.

6 whole chicken wings

1 tablespoon butter

1 tablespoon vegetable oil

Salt and pepper for seasoning

⅛ teaspoon cayenne pepper

7 oz. Frank's Red Hot sauce

1. Preheat the oven to 500° F.

2. With a sharp knife, cut the wings at the joint so that you have three sections: the single-boned section, the double-boned section, and the tip. Discard the tips.

3. When the oven is almost to 500° F, put the skillet over medium-high heat and add the butter and oil. When this gets hot, add the wing sections and stir. Season with salt and pepper, sprinkle with cayenne, stir again, then coat the wings with a portion of the hot sauce (use just enough to coat the wings).

4. Put the skillet in the oven. Cook the wings for a couple of minutes, remove the skillet (wear oven mitts!), flip over each wing section, and coat with additional hot sauce. Put the skillet back in the oven and cook for another 2 minutes. Repeat this procedure for about 20 minutes, basting with the hot sauce in the skillet, until the wings are fully cooked and crispy all over.

5. Serve with the traditional blue cheese dip and a side of celery and carrot sticks.

If you like fiery wings, you'll want to up the heat in this recipe. Instead of Frank's Red Hot sauce and a hint of cayenne pepper, look for the kicked-up styles of Frank's, including a hot wing sauce and an extra-hot sauce. If you have a favorite hot sauce besides Frank's, give it a try. The secret to these great wings is the sautéing then baking.

BEEF BRISKET

SERVES 6 TO 8 ✦ ACTIVE TIME: 30 MINUTES ✦ START TO FINISH: 9 HOURS

Brisket is the cut of meat that's taken from the cow's breast. It is a tough piece of meat that needs a long, slow cooking time—but it's worth it, because the slow cooking tenderizes the meat and brings out the flavor. A little prep time, and the meat can cook in the skillet in the oven for a solid 8 hours, leaving you free to do other things.

8-pound brisket, with a layer of fat on it or with marbling of fat

1 teaspoon vegetable oil

Salt and pepper

1. Preheat the oven to 250° F.

2. Heat a large cast-iron skillet over medium-high heat. When it's hot, add the vegetable oil, and then put the brisket in fat side down so it starts to cook. Sear the meat on both sides, about 3 minutes a side, and season with salt and pepper.

3. Put the skillet in the oven with the brisket facing fat side up. Cook for 8 hours, checking on it every few hours to be sure it isn't drying out (this is unlikely).

4. Cook until the meat is very tender, falling apart at the touch of a fork.

Some serious BBQ competitions feature brisket, and different chefs have different "secret ingredients" to transform this cut. Some use barbecue rubs with everything from cayenne to cumin to special peppers. Some start with the heat high and then lower it. If you want a flavored brisket, explore putting a rub together. You'll need to add it as you would the salt and pepper in this recipe. But I prefer to serve the basic brisket with different barbecue sauces on the side.

BLACK BEAN BURGERS

SERVES 4 TO 6 ✦ ACTIVE TIME: 90 MINUTES ✦ START TO FINISH: 2 HOURS

For those times when you want a break from meat but want the great taste and texture of a juicy hamburger, try making these black bean burgers. Be sure you have ripe tomatoes and avocadoes to put on them when serving.

1 (15 oz.) can black beans, drained and rinsed

⅓ cup scallions

¼ cup roasted red peppers, chopped

¼ cup cooked corn

¼ cup plain bread crumbs

1 egg, lightly beaten

2 tablespoons cilantro, chopped

½ teaspoon cumin

½ teaspoon cayenne pepper

½ teaspoon freshly ground black pepper

1 teaspoon fresh-squeezed lime juice

1 tablespoon olive oil

Hamburger buns

Tomato slices

Avocado slices

Red onion, thinly sliced

1. In a food processor or blender, combine half the beans with the scallions and roasted red peppers. Pulse until you have a thick paste. Transfer to a large bowl.

2. Add the corn, bread crumbs, egg, cilantro, cumin, cayenne, pepper, and lime juice. Stir to blend. Add the remaining beans and stir vigorously to get all ingredients to stick together. Cover bowl with plastic wrap and let sit at room temperature for about 30 minutes.

3. Heat skillet over medium-high heat. Form mixture into 4 to 6 patties. Add oil to skillet and, when hot, add the patties. Cook, covered, about 5 minutes per side.

4. Serve immediately on hamburger buns with slices of tomato, avocado, and red onion.

VEAL PARMIGIANA

What I like about using veal cutlets for this dish is that they are thinner than chicken cutlets, with a bigger flavor, too. Use fresh mozzarella and shred it yourself; it tastes much better. And of course, don't forget hot pepper flakes on the side!

½ cup flour

Salt and pepper to taste

½ cup bread crumbs (Italian seasoned)

¼ cup Parmesan cheese, grated, plus more for sauce

1 egg

½ cup milk

4 veal cutlets

3 tablespoons olive oil

2 cloves garlic, peeled and halved

4 oz. mozzarella cheese, shredded

1 (24 oz.) jar marinara sauce (or 3 cups home-made)

1. Preheat the oven to 450˚ F.

2. In a shallow bowl, season the flour with salt and pepper.

3. In another shallow bowl, mix the bread crumbs and Parmesan cheese.

4. In a third shallow bowl, whisk the egg with the milk until combined.

5. Line a plate with wax paper. Dip the cutlets in flour, then in the egg-and-milk mixture, then the bread crumb mix, coating both sides. Place the breaded cutlets on the wax paper until ready to cook.

6. Heat the skillet over medium-high heat and add the olive oil. When it's hot, add the cutlets and the garlic pieces. Brown the cutlets in the oil, cooking for 2 to 3 minutes per side. Remove the wax paper, and put the cutlets on the plate.

7. Lower the heat to medium and add the marinara sauce, stirring until sauce bubbles. Reduce heat to low and simmer for about 10 minutes.

8. Put the cutlets in the skillet and sprinkle with additional Parmesan. Divide the shredded mozzarella between the cutlets, put it on top of each, and put the skillet in the oven. Cook until cheese melts and begins to brown, about 5 minutes. Serve immediately.

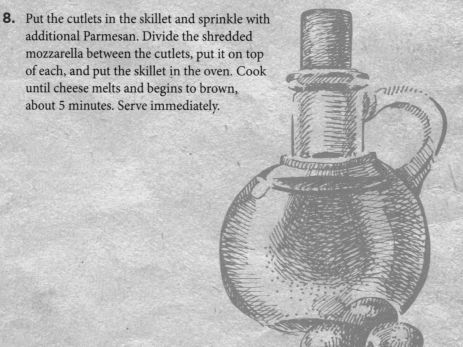

VEAL FRANCESE

MAKES 4 CUTLETS ◆ ACTIVE TIME: 30 MINUTES ◆ START TO FINISH: 45 MINUTES

If Veal Parmigiana is a down-to-earth comfort food, rich with tomatoes and cheese, then Veal Francese is the elegant uptowner, with a nuanced sauce of butter, lemon, and wine. If given a choice, I'd take both.

4 veal cutlets

Salt and pepper to taste

¼ cup flour

1 egg

1 lemon, halved, seeds removed

2 tablespoons butter

1 tablespoon vegetable oil

2 cloves garlic, peeled and halved

⅓ cup dry white wine

1. In a shallow bowl, season the flour with salt and pepper. Put the egg in a separate shallow bowl and beat in 1 tablespoon of fresh-squeezed lemon juice.

2. Heat the skillet over medium-high heat. Add the butter and oil together. When the butter is melted, add the garlic and stir. Dip a cutlet in the egg blend, then in the flour, coating lightly on both sides. Put the cutlet in the skillet. Do the same with the remaining cutlets. Sauté for just a couple of minutes on each side, until lightly browned, and transfer the cutlets to a plate.

3. With the heat lowered to medium, squeeze the juice from half the lemon into the skillet, then add the wine. Increase the heat and bring the liquid to a rolling boil, scraping the browned bits up from the bottom. Cook the sauce so that it reduces and lightens as it boils, about 5 minutes.

4. To serve, dip the cutlets in the sauce, put on a plate, and serve with the remaining sauce at the table.

GENERAL TSO CHICKEN

SERVES 4 • **ACTIVE TIME: 1½ HOURS** • **START TO FINISH: 2 HOURS**

When our family goes for Chinese food, someone always orders this dish. I got curious about how it could be made at home, since it seems a natural for the cast-iron skillet. This recipe works—and it includes one of our favorite sauces, Sriracha!

1 large egg

1½ teaspoons toasted sesame oil

¼ cup low-sodium soy sauce, plus 1 tablespoon

¼ cup cornstarch, plus 1 tablespoon

1 pound skinless, boneless chicken thighs, cut into bite-sized pieces

1 tablespoon vegetable oil, plus more for frying

2 tablespoons fresh ginger, finely chopped

3 cloves garlic, minced

1 cup chicken broth

2 teaspoons Sriracha

3 tablespoons sugar

3 scallions, thinly sliced

1. Carefully crack the egg over a medium-sized bowl, separating the white and yolk so the white goes into the bowl. Put the yolk in a cup and refrigerate for another use. Add the sesame oil, 1 tablespoon of soy sauce, and ¼ cup cornstarch. Whisk to combine. Add the chicken pieces and marinate at room temperature for about 30 minutes.

2. In a small saucepan, heat the tablespoon of oil over medium-high heat. Add the ginger and garlic and stir for about a minute. Add in the broth, Sriracha, sugar, remaining soy sauce, and tablespoon of cornstarch, and whisk to combine the ingredients. Continue to whisk until the sauce gets thick and glossy. Reduce the heat to low and cover to keep it warm.

3. Heat the cast-iron skillet over medium-high heat and add about ½ inch of oil. When hot, add the chicken one piece at a time so it doesn't splatter too much. Turn the pieces with a slotted spoon so that they brown on all sides. Cook until crispy, about 5 minutes. As the pieces are cooked, transfer them to a plate lined with paper towels to drain.

4. When all the pieces are cooked, stir them into the sauce with the scallions. Serve hot.

This dish is usually served with a bowl of white rice and a side of steamed broccoli. We prefer brown rice, but we do think steamed broccoli makes the meal. To coordinate the three parts, make the rice ahead of time and reheat on the stove over a low flame. The broccoli can be partially steamed ahead of time and then finished with additional steaming of about 10 minutes.

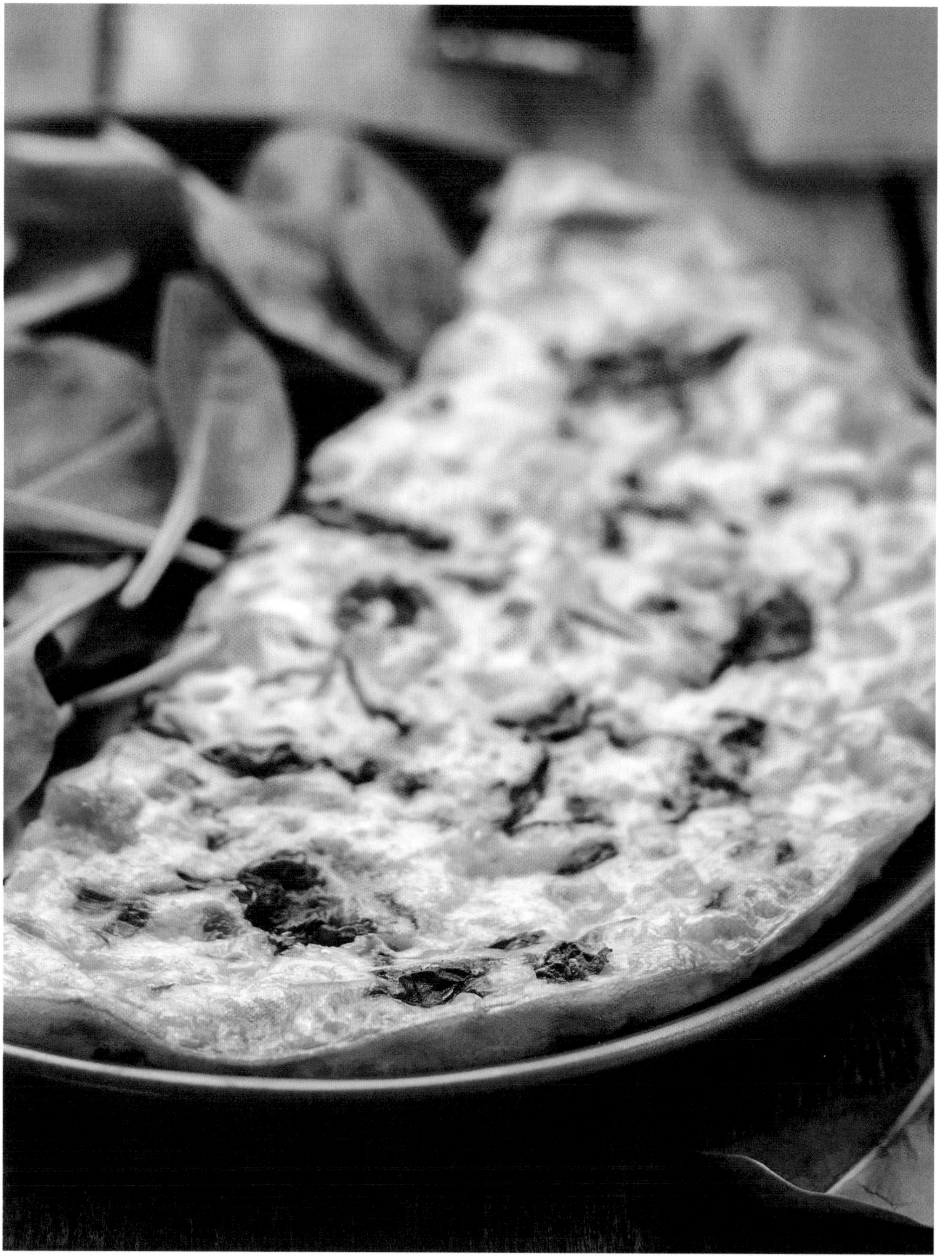

SPINACH FRITTATA

SERVES 4 ✦ ACTIVE TIME: 20 MINUTES ✦ START TO FINISH: 30 MINUTES

This delicious combination gives a nod to Greek cuisine with the addition of feta cheese. Serve this for brunch with other classic Greek foods, like olives, pita wedges, and tzatziki sauce (see recipe below).

6 eggs

2 tablespoons butter

¼ cup red onion, chopped

1 clove garlic, minced

2 cups fresh spinach leaves, coarse stems removed, roughly chopped

½ cup feta cheese

Salt and pepper to taste

1. Preheat the broiler to low.

2. In a small bowl, beat the eggs with a whisk until combined.

3. Heat skillet over medium-high heat. Melt the butter in the skillet and add the onion and garlic, stirring to cook until onion is translucent, about 3 minutes.

4. Add the spinach and stir so the leaves wilt. Sprinkle the feta over the mixture.

5. Pour the eggs over everything and shake the pan to evenly distribute them. Sprinkle with salt and pepper. Cover the skillet and let cook until set, about 10 minutes. Place the skillet in the oven under the broiler to "toast" the top, about 2 minutes.

6. Allow to stand for a couple of minutes and serve. Season with additional salt and pepper.

Tzatziki Sauce is a simple blend of cucumbers, yogurt, garlic, and lemon juice, and it's a refreshing accompaniment to egg and meat dishes. To make it, peel, remove the seeds from, and finely chop half of a cucumber. Wrap it in a cheesecloth or paper towel and squeeze it to get the liquid out. Put the pieces in a bowl. Add 2 cups plain Greek yogurt, 2 tablespoons fresh-squeezed lemon juice, 4 cloves of garlic (pressed), and salt and pepper to taste. Refrigerate for at least 1 hour before serving, longer if possible. If desired, you can add fresh dill.

MAINLY MUSHROOM FRITTATA

SERVES 4 ◆ ACTIVE TIME: 20 MINUTES ◆ START TO FINISH: 40 MINUTES

If you love mushrooms (and I sure do!), you'll love this frittata. The mushrooms are moist and earthy, the perfect base for Swiss cheese and eggs.

3 tablespoons butter

½ onion, diced

1 pound mushrooms, picked over and sliced or chopped

1 teaspoon salt

½ teaspoon pepper

1 tablespoon dry vermouth (optional)

8 eggs

½ cup milk or half-and-half

1 cup Swiss cheese, shredded

⅓ cup fresh parsley, chopped

1. Melt the butter in the skillet over medium-high heat. Add the onion and cook, stirring, until translucent, about 3 minutes. Add the mushrooms, lower the heat slightly, and cook, while stirring occasionally, until soft, 5 to 10 minutes. Drain the liquid from the pan. Season the mushrooms with the salt and pepper, and add the vermouth if desired.

2. Preheat the broiler to low. In a bowl, whisk the eggs and the milk until combined. Pour the egg mixture over the mushrooms and onion. Sprinkle the cheese all around the top, and then sprinkle the parsley over everything. Cover the skillet and let cook until set, about 10 minutes. Place the skillet in the oven under the broiler and "toast" the top, about 2 minutes. Remove from the oven and let sit for a few minutes before serving.

The selection of mushrooms in grocery stores is getting bigger and bigger. You can use one kind of mushroom for this dish, or you can use several kinds together. For example, you could use sliced white mushrooms, and you won't need to do much prep work. Or you could choose portobellos, which have a meatier texture and flavor. There are also shiitake or cremini mushrooms. If you mix the mushrooms, just be sure to cut them into similarly sized pieces so they cook evenly.

209

VEGETABLE FRITTATA

SERVES 4 ✦ ACTIVE TIME: 20 MINUTES ✦ START TO FINISH: 40 MINUTES

Make this veggie-loaded egg dish as a hearty breakfast or a light dinner. It's a perfect thing to cook up with fresh ingredients bought at the local farmer's market.

6 eggs

3 tablespoons butter

½ onion, minced

2 cloves garlic, minced

2 carrots, sliced thin

½ small zucchini, sliced thin

½ red pepper, seeded and sliced thin

⅓ cup parsley, chopped fine

Salt and pepper to taste

1 teaspoon red pepper flakes, if desired

1. Preheat the broiler to low.

2. In a bowl, whisk the eggs until combined.

3. Heat the skillet over medium-high heat. Melt the butter in the skillet. Add the onion and garlic and cook, stirring, until the onion is translucent, about 3 minutes.

4. Add the carrots and zucchini slices, lower the heat to medium, and cook, stirring occasionally, until softened, about 5 minutes. Add the red pepper and continue to cook, about 5 minutes. Add the parsley.

5. Pour the eggs over the vegetables. Shake the skillet to distribute evenly. Season with salt and pepper, and sprinkle with red pepper flakes if desired. Cover and cook until eggs are set, about 10 minutes.

6. Put the skillet in the oven and cook for a few minutes to "toast" the top. Remove from the oven and let sit for a few minutes before serving.

There are so many delicious ingredients in this frittata that it's practically a one-pan meal. Make it even heartier by adding sweet potatoes. Wash a large sweet potato and pierce it all over with a fork. Put it on a paper towel in the microwave and cook for 3 minutes. Using a dish towel because it will be hot, turn the potato over and cook another 2 or 3 minutes. Allow to cool for a minute or so, and cut the potato into bite-sized pieces. Add it to the frittata after the red peppers. Arugula, spinach, and tomatoes are also nice additions.

SMOKED SALMON FRITTATA

SERVES 4 ✦ ACTIVE TIME: 20 MINUTES ✦ START TO FINISH: 30 MINUTES

Salmon is a high-protein, low-fat food that adds lots of texture and—best of all—taste! Combined with the sweetness of leeks, this recipe is one you'll want to reserve for a special brunch.

2 leeks, white part only

2 tablespoons olive oil

1 tablespoon butter

8 eggs

½ cup cream or half-and-half

1 teaspoon salt

Freshly ground black pepper to taste

4 oz. smoked salmon, chopped

3 oz. package cream cheese, softened and cut into bits

1. Preheat the broiler to low.

2. Slice the white part of the leeks into thin slices. Put them in a colander, separating the circles. Rinse thoroughly to be sure there is no fine dirt or sand. Dry the leeks on paper towels.

3. Heat the oil and the butter in a skillet over medium-high heat. Add the leeks and cook, stirring until translucent and tender, 3 to 5 minutes. Reduce the heat to low.

4. In a bowl, whisk the eggs until well blended, and add the cream, salt, and pepper. Pour the eggs over the leeks in the skillet and increase heat to medium. Place pieces of salmon and cream cheese on top of the eggs. Cover the skillet and let cook until set, about 10 minutes. Place the skillet in the oven under the broiler to "toast" the top, about 2 minutes. Remove from the oven and let sit for a few minutes before serving.

If you like dill, it makes an excellent garnish for this very tasty frittata. Finely chop some sprigs and sprinkle them over the dish when it is cool. Another tasty addition is pieces of steamed asparagus, which can be sprinkled throughout at the same time as the salmon and cream cheese.

STUFFED PORK CHOPS

SERVES 4 ✦ ACTIVE TIME: 60 MINUTES ✦ START TO FINISH: 90 MINUTES

When cool temperatures have you thinking about ways to roast meats with dried fruits and nuts, this recipe will appeal to everything you're craving.

4 boneless pork chops

Salt and pepper to taste

2 tablespoons olive oil

½ onion, minced

1 cup bread pieces from a thick, crusty bread like a baguette or sourdough loaf

½ cup dates, pitted and chopped

¼ cup walnuts, coarsely chopped

2 tablespoons port wine

2 tablespoons fresh sage, chopped

2 cups chicken broth

½ cup dry white wine

1. Preheat the oven to 400° F.

2. Rinse and pat dry the pork chops. Using a long, sharp knife, cut an incision into the meat to form a pocket. Season the chops with salt and pepper all over.

3. Heat the skillet over medium-high heat. Add the olive oil and onion and cook, stirring, until onion is soft, about 3 minutes. Reduce the heat to medium and add the bread cubes, dates, walnuts, port wine, and sage, stirring gently to combine. Cook for a couple of minutes until well blended. Remove pan from the heat.

4. Fill the chops with the stuffing. Brush the skillet with oil, put it over medium-high heat, and add the chops, searing on both sides for about 3 minutes. Add the chicken broth and wine. Put the skillet in the oven and roast for about 20 minutes or until pork is cooked through. Baste with the pan juices after about 10 minutes. Let the chops rest for about 5 minutes before serving.

SUPER-EASY SPARERIBS

SERVES 2 TO 4 ✦ ACTIVE TIME: 2 HOURS ✦ START TO FINISH: 2 HOURS

Oven roasting in a skillet renders tender ribs with no hassle. Make these on a cold winter night, and you can pretend you're at a summertime picnic.

2 pounds pork spareribs

Salt and pepper for seasoning

Juice from ½ lemon

1 to 2 cups barbecue sauce (optional)

1. Preheat the oven to 350° F.

2. Wash and dry the ribs, cutting into sections that will fit in the skillet. Season both sides with salt and pepper.

3. Put the ribs in the skillet, sprinkle with fresh-squeezed lemon juice, and put the skillet in the oven. Bake for about 90 minutes, turning halfway through cooking time.

4. For the second half of the cooking time, brush with barbecue sauce, if desired, and turn again for the last 15 minutes, putting barbecue sauce on the other side of the ribs. Serve immediately.

CREPES

SERVES 8 TO 10 (ABOUT 16 CREPES) ✦ ACTIVE TIME: 60 MINUTES ✦
START TO FINISH: 6 HOURS

These are very thin pancakes that can be filled with any number of things. The batter can be made with or without sugar, depending on whether you want to fill them with savory or sweet ingredients. Making them for the first time is intimidating, as it involves getting the right amount of batter on a skillet that's heated to the right temperature, but once you get the hang of it, it's a very satisfying experience that yields great results!

4 tablespoons butter

3 eggs

⅛ teaspoon salt

1 cup whole milk (possibly more)

1 cup flour (minus 2 tablespoons)

1. Heat the skillet over low heat and melt 2 tablespoons of the butter very slowly.

2. In a large mixing bowl, whisk the eggs until smooth. Add the salt and milk and whisk together until well blended. Whisk in the flour and, while whisking, add the melted butter. Keep whisking until the batter is smooth and there are no lumps. Cover the bowl with plastic wrap or a clean dish towel, put in a cool, dark place, and let rest for 3 or 4 hours before making the crepes.

3. You'll need a spatula that won't scratch the surface of the skillet. Have that and a ladle for scooping out the batter ready by the stove.

4. Heat the skillet over medium-high heat and melt a slice of the remaining 2 tablespoons of butter in it. Stir the crepe batter to blend again. When the skillet is hot but not smoking (the butter should not brown), use the ladle to scoop about ¼ cup of batter into the skillet. When the batter hits the pan, tilt it gently to spread the batter evenly over the bottom. When the bottom is covered, cook for just over 1 minute and then flip the crepe over and cook the other side for about half the time. Tilt the skillet over a plate to slide the crepe out.

5. You should be able to make several crepes per slice of butter, but gauge how dry the pan is, and if you think it needs butter, add some. If the pan gets too hot and the butter browns, wipe it out with a paper towel and start over.

6. Continue making the crepes until all the batter is used up. As they cool on the plate, put pieces of waxed paper between them to keep them from sticking together. If you're not going to use them right away, wrap the stack in aluminum foil and keep them in the refrigerator or freeze them.

Variations

- To make dessert crepes, add 3 tablespoons of sugar when you add the flour, and 2 tablespoons Cognac (or 1 tablespoon vanilla) once the batter is mixed.

- For dessert crepes, smother a warm crepe with chocolate-hazelnut spread sprinkled with crushed, roasted, and salted peanuts or cashews. You can also spread a cooled dessert crepe with cream cheese and your favorite jam. Or spread a dessert crepe with a thin layer of peanut butter and top with thinly sliced bananas.

- Fill savory crepes with a variety of cooked meats, poultry, or fish, in a sauce. For example, you can use pieces of leftover chicken in a cream sauce with peas and mushrooms. Roll a generous spoonful up in the crepe, tuck it into a baking dish (with others), sprinkle with shredded cheese, and bake in the oven at 350° F for about 10 minutes.

- Cook some spicy Italian sausage, spread some ricotta on the crepe, add the sausage, season with salt and pepper, roll up and put in a baking dish, cover with marinara and shredded mozzarella, and bake at 350° F for about 15 minutes.

CHICKEN AND MUSHROOM CREPES

SERVES 8 TO 10 (ABOUT 16 CREPES) ✦ ACTIVE TIME: 60 MINUTES ✦ START TO FINISH: 6 HOURS

Make this filling with leftover chicken and transform what might be a boring dinner into an elegant dining experience.

For the Crepes

4 tablespoons butter

3 eggs

⅛ teaspoon salt

1 cup whole milk (possibly more)

1 cup flour (minus 2 tablespoons)

For the Filling

4 tablespoons butter

1 pound mushrooms, stems removed and cut into pieces

1 to 2 cups cooked chicken, cut into small pieces

1 can cream of mushroom soup

2 tablespoons Madeira or vermouth

⅓ cup milk

2 tablespoons parsley, chopped

Salt and pepper to taste

1. Heat the skillet over low heat and melt 2 tablespoons of the butter very slowly.

2. In a large mixing bowl, whisk the eggs until smooth. Add the salt and milk and whisk together until well blended. Whisk in the flour and, while whisking, add the melted butter. Keep whisking until the batter is smooth and there are no lumps. Cover the bowl with plastic wrap or a clean dish towel, put in a cool, dark place, and let rest for 3 or 4 hours before making the crepes.

3. While the crepe batter is settling, prepare the filling. Wipe down your skillet and melt the butter over medium heat. Add the mushroom pieces and cook, stirring frequently, until softened and lightly browned, about 5 to 8 minutes. Add the chicken pieces, mushroom soup, Madeira or vermouth, and milk. Stir to combine and continue to cook until well blended, about 3 minutes. Stir in the chopped parsley. Add salt and pepper to taste. Put the mixture into a bowl, cover, and refrigerate until the crepes are cooked and ready to be filled.

4. When the crepe batter is ready, you'll need a spatula that won't scratch the surface of the skillet. Have that and a ladle for scooping out the batter ready by the stove.

5. Heat the skillet over medium-high heat and melt a slice of the remaining 2 tablespoons of butter in it. Stir the crepe batter to blend again. When the skillet is hot but not smoking (the butter should not brown), use the ladle to scoop about ¼ cup of batter into the skillet. When the batter hits the pan, tilt it gently to spread the batter evenly over the bottom. When the bottom is covered, cook for just over 1 minute and then flip the crepe over and cook the other side for about half the time. Tilt the skillet over a plate to slide the crepe out.

6. You should be able to make several crepes per slice of butter, but gauge how dry the pan is, and if you think it needs butter, add some. If the pan gets too hot and the butter browns, wipe it out with a paper towel and start over.

7. Continue making the crepes until all the batter is used up. As they cool on the plate, put pieces of waxed paper between them to keep them from sticking together.

8. Preheat the oven to 350° F. Take the chicken-and-mushroom mixture out of the refrigerator and bring to room temperature.

9. Lightly grease a 9 x 13 inch baking dish. Working with one crepe at a time, put a generous scoop of the filling in the middle and fold the crepe up around the filling. Place the crepe in the baking dish so that the folded part faces down. When the baking dish is filled with stuffed crepes, cover the dish with foil and bake for about 30 minutes until the filling is bubbling and hot.

10. Remove the foil and let cool for a few minutes before serving.

ITALIAN CREPES

SERVES 8 TO 10 (ABOUT 16 CREPES) ✦ **ACTIVE TIME: 60 MINUTES** ✦
START TO FINISH: 6 HOURS

I'm not sure that the French would think this is a good idea, but as far as flavor combinations go, it works. Using crepes instead of pizza dough essentially produces a less bready calzone. Mangia!

For the Crepes

4 tablespoons butter

3 eggs

⅛ teaspoon salt

1 cup whole milk (possibly more)

1 cup flour (minus 2 tablespoons)

For the Filling

1 pound Italian sausage, sweet, hot, or a combination

4 cloves garlic, minced

1 package frozen spinach, thawed and squeezed dry

1 (15.5 oz.) can diced tomatoes, drained

Salt and pepper to taste

8 oz. ricotta cheese

2 cups mozzarella cheese, shredded

1. Heat the skillet over low heat and melt 2 tablespoons of the butter very slowly.

2. In a large mixing bowl, whisk the eggs until smooth. Add the salt and milk and whisk together until well blended. Whisk in the flour and, while whisking, add the melted butter. Keep whisking until the batter is smooth and there are no lumps. Cover the bowl with plastic wrap or a clean dish towel, put in a cool, dark place, and let rest for 3 or 4 hours before making the crepes.

3. While the crepe batter is settling, prepare the filling. Wipe down your skillet, warm over medium-high heat, and cook the sausage until it's only slightly pink inside. Drain the residual fat and add the garlic. Lower the heat to medium and cook until the sausage is cooked through, while stirring frequently, about 5 minutes. Add the spinach and tomatoes and stir to combine. Season with salt and pepper. Transfer to a bowl, cover, and refrigerate until ready to make the crepes.

4. When the crepe batter is ready, you'll need a spatula that won't scratch the surface of the skillet. Have that and a ladle for scooping out the batter ready by the stove.

5. Heat the skillet over medium-high heat and melt a slice of the remaining 2 tablespoons of butter. Stir the crepe batter to blend again. When the skillet is hot but not smoking (the butter should not brown), use the ladle to scoop about ¼ cup of batter into the skillet. When the batter hits the pan, tilt it gently to spread the batter evenly over the bottom. When the bottom is covered, cook for just over 1 minute and then flip the crepe over and cook the other side for about half the time. Tilt the skillet over a plate to slide the crepe out.

6. You should be able to make several crepes per slice of butter, but gauge how dry the pan is, and if you think it needs butter, add some. If the pan gets too hot and the butter browns, wipe it with a paper towel and start over.

7. Continue making the crepes until all the batter is used up. As they cool on the plate, put pieces of waxed paper between them to keep them from sticking together.

8. Preheat the oven to 350° F. Take the sausage-and-spinach mixture out of the refrigerator and stir in the ricotta cheese. Season with additional salt and pepper if desired.

9. Lightly grease a 9 x 13 inch baking dish. Working with one crepe at a time, put a generous scoop of the filling in the middle and fold the crepe up around the filling. Place the crepe in the baking dish so that the folded part faces down. When the baking dish is filled with the stuffed crepes, sprinkle them with the mozzarella. Cover the dish with foil and bake for about 20 minutes. Remove the foil and cook for another 5 to 10 minutes until the cheese is bubbly and just browned. Serve immediately.

SHEPHERD'S PIE

SERVES 4 TO 6 ✦ ACTIVE TIME: 45 MINUTES ✦ START TO FINISH: 90 MINUTES

I'm not sure how this recipe came to be called a "pie" since it doesn't really have a crust. Instead, it has a top layer of mashed potatoes, which blankets the beef mixture and helps keep it juicy. In that sense, it works like a pie. Semantics aside, it's one of the best comfort foods you can make.

6 russet potatoes, peeled and cubed

½ teaspoon salt

½ cup (8 tablespoons) butter, cut into individual tablespoons

½ to ¾ cup milk, or ½ cup milk and ¼ cup plain yogurt

Salt and pepper to taste

1 tablespoon olive oil

½ yellow onion, finely chopped

1 pound ground beef

1 (15 oz.) can of petit pois (peas), drained, or 2 cups high-quality frozen peas

½ of a 15 oz. can of corn, drained (optional)

1. Preheat the oven to 350° F.

2. After peeling and cubing the potatoes, give them a final rinse to get all the dirt off. Put the potato pieces in a large saucepan or pot and cover with cold water. Add the salt. Bring the water to a boil, reduce to a simmer, and cook the potatoes until soft, about 20 minutes. When they can be easily pierced with a sharp knife, they're cooked.

3. Drain the potato pieces and put them in a large bowl. Add 6 tablespoons of the butter and ½ cup of the milk and use a potato masher to make the mashed potatoes. Add additional milk or yogurt to get a creamy but not soupy consistency. Season with salt and pepper and set aside.

4. Warm the cast-iron skillet over medium heat, add the tablespoon of olive oil, and cook the onion, stirring to just soften, about 2 minutes. Add the ground beef and stir to break apart while it browns. When there is just a little pinkness left in the meat, drain the fat from the skillet. Stir in the peas and, if desired, the corn kernels. Season with salt and pepper.

5. Spread the mashed potatoes over the meat and vegetables, distributing the potatoes evenly and smoothing the top. Cut the remaining 2 tablespoons of butter into slivers and dot the potatoes with them.

6. Cover with foil and bake for 30 minutes. Remove the foil and cook another 10 minutes until the potatoes are just browned.

7. Allow to cool for 5 minutes before serving.

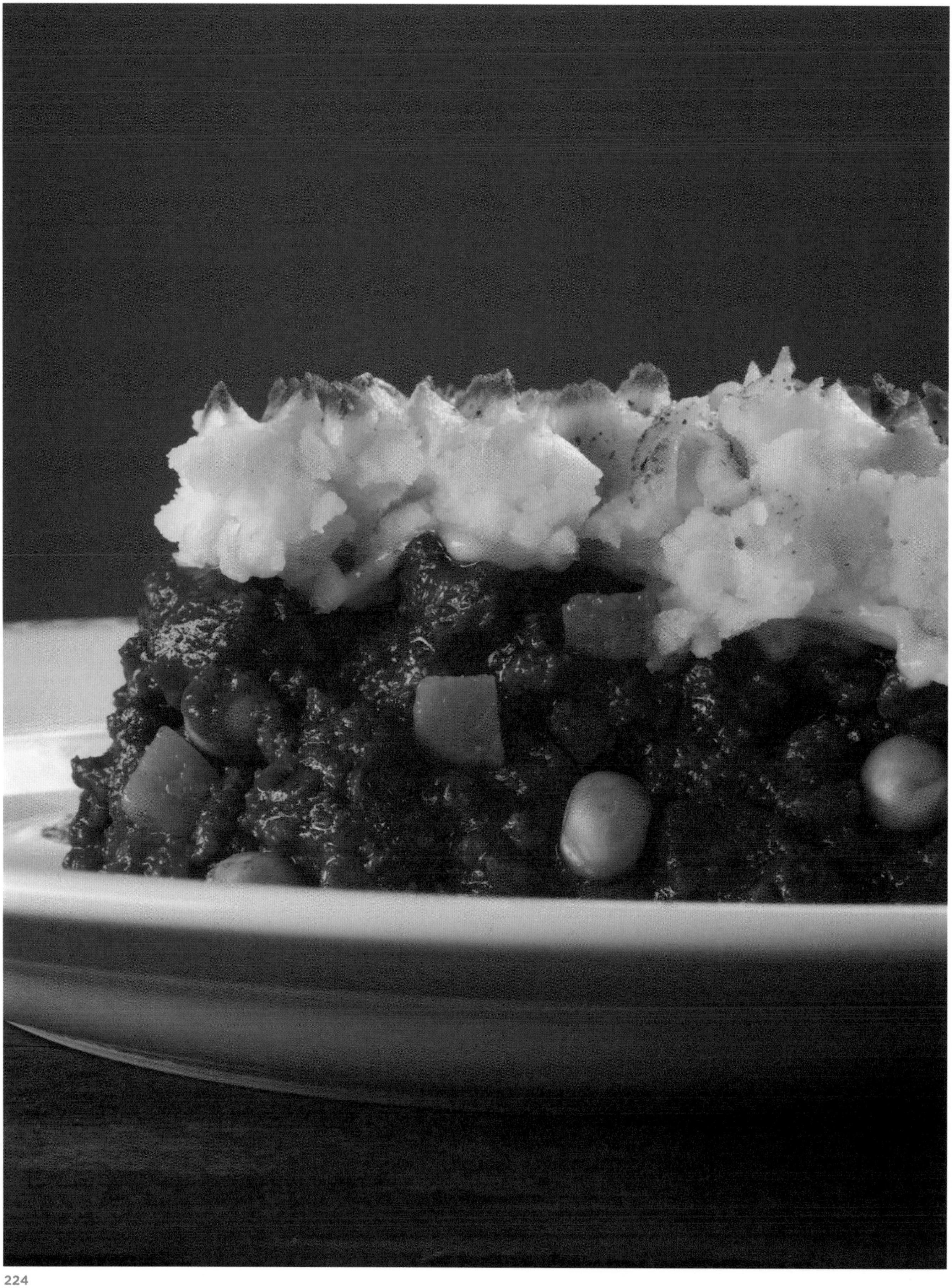

BEEF BOURGUIGNON SHEPHERD'S PIE

SERVES 4 TO 6 ✦ ACTIVE TIME: 60 MINUTES ✦ START TO FINISH: 90 MINUTES

This is a decadent shepherd's pie, with loads of butter and cream. Celebrate its richness and don't skimp when purchasing the ingredients.

6 russet potatoes, peeled and cubed

½ teaspoon salt

½ cup (8 tablespoons) butter

¾ cup half-and-half

½ cup white cheddar cheese, shredded

Salt and pepper to taste

3 slices bacon, cut into ½-inch pieces

2 tablespoons olive oil

1½ pounds stew beef, cut into chunks

1 carrot, peeled, washed, and sliced

½ yellow onion, diced

½ cup white mushrooms, sliced

1 tablespoon flour

1½ cups dry red wine

1 cup beef broth

1 tablespoon tomato paste

1 clove garlic, smashed

¼ teaspoon dried thyme

1 bay leaf

1. Preheat the oven to 325° F.

2. After peeling and cubing the potatoes, give them a final rinse to get all the dirt off. Put the potato pieces in a large saucepan or pot and cover with cold water. Add the salt. Bring the water to a boil, reduce to a simmer, and cook the potatoes until soft, about 20 minutes.

3. Drain the potato pieces and put them in a large bowl. Add 6 tablespoons of the butter and the half-and-half, and use a potato masher to make the mashed potatoes. Stir in the shredded cheese. Add additional half-and-half to get a creamy but not soupy consistency. Season with salt and pepper and set aside.

4. In the cast-iron skillet, sauté the bacon in 1 tablespoon of oil for about 3 minutes, until it starts to lightly brown. Remove with a slotted spoon and place a plate lined with a paper towel.

5. Next, cook the beef pieces in the oil and bacon fat, turning to brown on all sides. Use the slotted spoon to put the beef with the bacon. Put the carrot, onion, and mushrooms in the skillet and cook, while stirring, until just softened, about 3 minutes. Put the beef and bacon into the skillet with the vegetables. Add the flour and continue to cook and stir for another 5 minutes.

6. Stir in the wine and the broth, then the tomato paste, garlic, thyme, and bay leaf. The liquid should barely cover the meat and vegetables. Bring to a low boil over medium heat. Season with salt and pepper, cover tightly with foil, and place in the oven for 3 hours, until the meat is tender.

7. Return the skillet to the stove, remove the foil, and simmer over low heat for 5 to 10 minutes to reduce the sauce. Skim off any fat and remove the bay leaf. Increase the oven temperature to 350° F.

8. Spread the mashed potatoes over the beef and vegetables, distributing the potatoes evenly and smoothing the top. Cut the remaining 2 tablespoons of butter into slivers and dot the potatoes with them.

9. Cover with foil and bake for 20 minutes. Remove the foil and cook another 10 minutes until the potatoes are just browned.

INSIDE-OUT NACHO SHEPHERD'S PIE

SERVES 4 TO 6 ✦ ACTIVE TIME: 45 MINUTES ✦ START TO FINISH: 90 MINUTES

Talk about a winning one-dish meal for the family! This pot pie tastes like the best loaded nachos you've ever had, already mixed up, hot, and gooey. Try it, you'll love it!

1 cornmeal crust (see page 141)

1 pound ground beef

½ yellow onion, chopped fine

2 cloves garlic, crushed

½ cup black olives, sliced

¼ to ½ cup jalapeño peppers, sliced (depending on how hot you like it)

½ cup corn kernels (no sugar added)

1 (15 oz.) can diced tomatoes

1½ cups sharp cheddar cheese, shredded

1 cup sour cream

Salt and pepper to taste

1 egg

1 tablespoon water

1. Preheat the oven to 350° F.

2. In the cast-iron skillet, add the ground beef and the onion, sautéing until the meat is just browned and the onion is softened. Drain the fat from the meat.

3. Return the skillet to the heat and add the garlic, olives, jalapeño peppers, corn kernels, and diced tomatoes. Stir well to combine. Reduce heat to low.

4. In a bowl, stir together the cheddar cheese and the sour cream. Gently stir this into the ground beef mixture. Season with additional salt and pepper if desired. Remove from heat.

5. Top the meat mixture with the cornmeal crust. Garnish with some jalapeño slices, if desired. Beat egg with the tablespoon of water and brush the egg wash over the crust.

6. Put the skillet in the oven and bake for 25 to 30 minutes until the crust is golden and the filling is bubbly.

MUSHROOM AND CHARD SHEPHERD'S PIE

SERVES 4 TO 6 ✦ ACTIVE TIME: 45 MINUTES ✦ START TO FINISH: 90 MINUTES

Here's a great recipe for a pot pie that's filling and earthy but has no meat in it. It's topped with mashed potatoes, which makes it more of a meal. Serve with a big green salad for a special brunch or a light dinner.

6 russet potatoes, peeled and cubed

½ teaspoon salt

½ cup (8 tablespoons) butter, cut into individual tablespoons

½ to ¾ cup milk, or ½ cup milk and ¼ cup plain yogurt

Salt and pepper to taste

3 tablespoons butter

1 small onion, finely chopped

1 pound assorted mushrooms, rinsed and chopped, to yield approximately 3 cups

1 bunch Swiss chard, washed and chopped (or substitute 4 cups fresh spinach leaves, stems removed)

1 tablespoon Worcestershire sauce

1. Preheat the oven to 350° F.

2. After peeling and cubing the potatoes, give them a final rinse to get all the dirt off. Put the potato pieces in a large saucepan or pot and cover with cold water. Add the salt. Bring the water to a boil, reduce to a simmer, and cook the potatoes until soft, about 20 minutes. When they can be easily pierced with a sharp knife, they're cooked.

3. Drain the potato pieces and put them in a large bowl. Add 6 tablespoons of the butter and ½ cup of the milk and use a potato masher to make the mashed potatoes. Add additional milk or yogurt to get a creamy but not soupy consistency. Season with salt and pepper and set aside.

4. In the cast-iron skillet, melt the butter over medium heat. Add the onion and cook, until just softened, about 3 minutes. Add the mushrooms, the chopped stems of the chard (not the leaves), and the Worcestershire sauce. Cook for about 3 minutes, while stirring frequently, then reduce the heat to low and continue to cook for another 5 minutes or so, until the mushrooms and chard stems are soft. If the mixture seems dry, add a tablespoon of olive oil.

5. Increase the heat to medium and add the chard leaves. Cook, while stirring constantly, until the leaves wilt, about 3 minutes. Remove the skillet from heat and season with salt and pepper.

6. Spread the mashed potatoes over the mixture, distributing the potatoes evenly and smoothing the top. Cut the remaining 2 tablespoons of butter into slivers and dot the potatoes with them.

7. Cover with foil and bake for 25 minutes. Remove the foil and cook another 10 minutes until the topping is just browned and the filling is bubbly.

LOBSTER SHEPHERD'S PIE

SERVES 4 TO 6 ✦ ACTIVE TIME: 45 MINUTES ✦ START TO FINISH: 90 MINUTES

I love this recipe because it takes "fancy" food—lobster—and makes it into something down-to-earth yet elegant. It makes a wonderful dinner for a date night, and it also shines at a Sunday brunch with family and friends.

6 russet potatoes, peeled and cubed

½ teaspoon salt

10 tablespoons butter, cut into individual tablespoons

½ to ¾ cup milk, or ½ cup milk and ¼ cup plain yogurt

Salt and pepper to taste

6 large leeks, white and light green parts only, halved lengthwise, cut into ½-inch pieces, and rinsed well

2 tablespoons flour

1 cup chicken or vegetable broth

3 cups cooked lobster meat

¾ cup canned peas, drained

½ cup canned corn, drained

1 tablespoon dry sherry

1. Preheat the oven to 350° F.

2. After peeling and cubing the potatoes, give them a final rinse to get all the dirt off. Put the potato pieces in a large saucepan or pot and cover with cold water. Add the salt. Bring the water to a boil, reduce to a simmer, and cook the potatoes until soft, about 20 minutes. When they can be easily pierced with a sharp knife, they're cooked.

3. Drain the potato pieces and put them in a large bowl. Add 6 tablespoons of the butter and ½ cup of the milk and use a potato masher to make the mashed potatoes. Add additional milk or yogurt to get a creamy but not soupy consistency. Season with salt and pepper and set aside.

4. In the cast-iron skillet, melt 2 tablespoons of butter and cook the leeks over medium heat, stirring to just soften, about 2 minutes. Reduce the heat to low and cover. Cook an additional 5 to 8 minutes, stirring occasionally, until tender.

5. Stir in the flour, and cook for 1 minute. Add the broth, raise the heat to medium-high, and bring to a boil. Reduce heat to low, and let simmer, uncovered, for 2 minutes.

6. Stir in lobster, peas, corn, and sherry and remove the skillet from heat.

7. Spread the mashed potatoes over the mixture, distributing the potatoes evenly and smoothing the top. Cut the remaining 2 tablespoons of butter into slivers and dot the potatoes with them.

8. Cover with foil and bake for 30 minutes. Remove the foil and cook another 10 minutes until the potatoes are just browned.

9. Allow to cool slightly before serving.

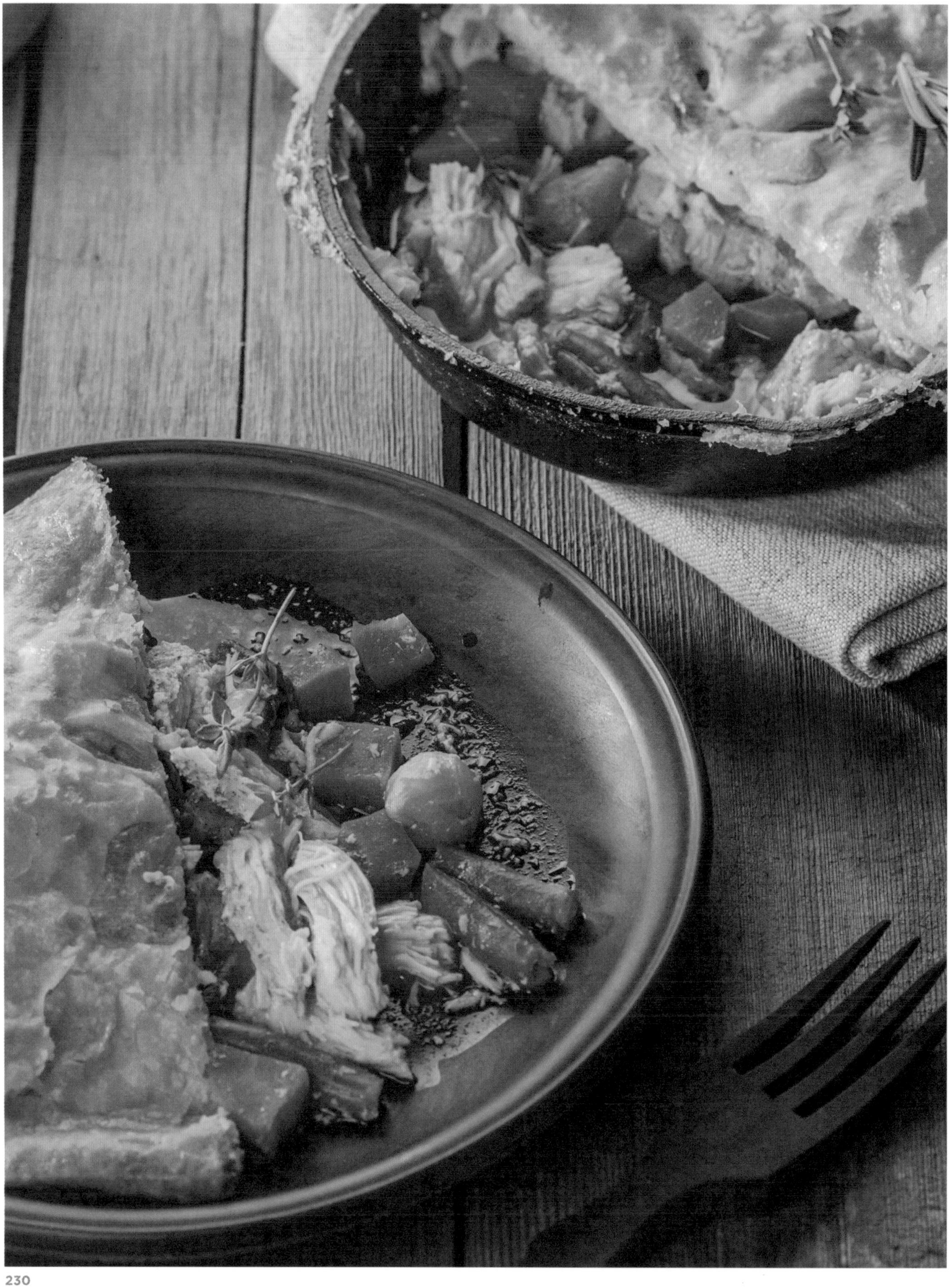

CHICKEN POT PIE

SERVES 4 TO 6 ✦ ACTIVE TIME: 60 MINUTES ✦ START TO FINISH: 2 HOURS

When you have leftover chicken, reach for this recipe. Simply prepare the chicken mixture in the skillet, top with a crust, bake, and you have a delicious and satisfying meal.

1 flaky pastry crust recipe for a single crust (see page 136)

2 tablespoons olive oil

½ yellow onion, diced

1 clove garlic, chopped

1 carrot, peeled and chopped

2 tablespoons butter, cut into smaller slices

2 tablespoons flour

1¼ cups milk at room temperature

1½ cups cooked chicken, cut into bite-sized pieces

¾ cup frozen green bean pieces

Salt and pepper to taste

½ teaspoon cayenne (optional)

1 tablespoon half-and-half

1. Preheat the oven to 350° F.

2. In a small skillet (not the cast-iron skillet), heat the olive oil. Add the onion and garlic and stir, while cooking, for about 2 minutes. Add the carrot slices. Reduce the heat to low, cover, and cook, while stirring occasionally, until the carrots start to soften and the onion caramelizes, about 5 minutes. Set aside.

3. Before starting to make the white sauce, be sure the milk is at room temperature. If it's not, microwave it so that it's just warm, about 15 to 20 seconds. Have the milk ready.

4. In the cast-iron skillet melt the butter over medium heat. Sprinkle the flour over it and stir quickly yet gently to blend. Reduce the heat slightly so the butter doesn't burn. Stir until the butter and flour form a soft paste.

5. Add just a little of the warm milk and stir constantly to blend it in. Add more milk in small increments, working after each addition to stir it into the flour-and-butter mixture smoothly. Work this way until all the milk has been incorporated. Continue to stir the sauce, while cooking over low heat, until it thickens, about 5 minutes.

6. Add the chicken pieces, green beans, and vegetable mixture from the other skillet. Season with salt and pepper. If you want a hint of heat, add the cayenne pepper.

7. On a lightly floured surface, roll out the crust so it will fit over the filling. Lay it gently on top, push down slightly to secure, and cut 3 or 4 slits in the middle. Brush the crust with the half-and-half.

8. Put the skillet in the oven and bake for 30 to 40 minutes, until the crust is browned and the filling is bubbly.

9. Allow to cool slightly before serving.

TURKEY AND SWEET POTATO POT PIE

SERVES 4 TO 6 ✦ **ACTIVE TIME: 45 MINUTES** ✦ **START TO FINISH: 90 MINUTES**

This is a fun pot pie to make after Thanksgiving, when there tends to be leftover turkey and sweet potatoes. Feel free to add any other vegetable leftovers to the filling, such as green beans, creamed onions, or peas. If you're inspired, add the cumin. It adds an exotic flavor and gives the filling a nice, deep yellow color.

1 flaky pastry crust recipe for a single crust (see page 136)

2 tablespoons olive oil

½ yellow onion, diced

1 clove garlic, chopped

1 small sweet potato, peeled and cut into small cubes

½ teaspoon thyme

2 tablespoons butter, cut into smaller slices

2 tablespoons flour

1¼ cup milk at room temperature

1½ cups cooked turkey, cut into bite-sized pieces

1 cup frozen peas

Salt and pepper to taste

½ teaspoon cumin (optional)

1 tablespoon half-and-half

1. Preheat the oven to 350° F.

2. In a small skillet (not the cast-iron skillet), heat the olive oil. Add the onion and garlic and stir, while cooking, for about 2 minutes. Add the sweet potato pieces and the thyme. Reduce the heat to low, cover, and cook, while stirring occasionally, until the sweet potatoes soften and the onion caramelizes, about 5 minutes. Set aside.

3. Before starting to make the white sauce, be sure the milk is at room temperature. If it's not, microwave it so that it's just warm, about 15 to 20 seconds.

4. In the cast-iron skillet, melt the butter over medium heat. Sprinkle the flour over it and stir quickly yet gently to blend. Reduce the heat slightly so the butter doesn't burn. Stir until the butter and flour form a soft paste.

5. Add just a little of the warm milk and stir constantly to blend it in. Add more milk in small increments, working after each addition to stir it into the flour-and-butter mixture smoothly. Work this way until all the milk has been incorporated. Continue to stir the sauce, while cooking over low heat, until it thickens, about 5 minutes.

6. Add the turkey pieces, peas, and vegetable mixture from the other skillet, along with any other leftovers you think would taste good. If needed, add some additional milk so the filling isn't too thick. Season with salt, pepper, and, if desired, cumin.

7. On a lightly floured surface, roll out the crust so it will fit over the filling. Lay it gently on top, push down slightly to secure, and cut 3 or 4 slits in the middle. Brush the crust with the half-and-half.

8. Put the skillet in the oven and bake for 30 to 40 minutes, until the crust is browned and the filling is bubbly.

9. Allow to cool slightly before serving.

BEEF AND MUSHROOM POT PIE

SERVES 4 TO 6 ✦ ACTIVE TIME: 45 MINUTES ✦ START TO FINISH: 90 MINUTES

When you're looking for something to pair with a big, dry red wine and it's a chilly fall day, remember this dish. Prepare it early in the day, bake about an hour before you're ready for dinner, and this pot pie will be the perfect companion to that special bottle.

1 flaky pastry crust recipe for a single crust (see page 136)

3 tablespoons flour

1 teaspoon salt, plus more for seasoning

1 teaspoon pepper, plus more for seasoning

1 teaspoon paprika

½ cup stew beef, cut into chunks

2 tablespoons olive oil

½ yellow onion, diced

2 carrots, peeled and sliced

1 celery stalk, leaves removed, diced

1 cup mushrooms, sliced

½ cup beef broth

¾ cup stout beer

2 cloves garlic, crushed

½ teaspoon thyme

½ teaspoon rosemary

1 bay leaf

1 egg

1 tablespoon water

1. Preheat the oven to 400° F.

2. In a large bowl, whisk together the flour, salt, pepper, and paprika. Add the beef pieces and toss to coat well. Set aside.

3. In the cast-iron skillet, heat the oil over medium-high heat. Add the floured meat pieces and stir, while cooking, until just browned on the outside. Add the garlic and stir. Add the onion, carrots, celery, and mushrooms, and stir while cooking for about 2 minutes. After a minute, add the broth, beer, garlic, thyme, rosemary, and bay leaf. Stir and bring to a boil, then reduce the heat to low and simmer for 10 to 12 minutes, while stirring occasionally, until meat and vegetables are tender. Remove from heat and allow to cool, about 30 to 40 minutes. Remove the bay leaf. Season with additional salt and pepper, if desired.

4. On a lightly floured surface, roll out the crust so that it will just cover the meat mixture. Lay it gently on top, push down slightly to secure, and cut 4 or 5 slits in the middle. Beat egg with 1 tablespoon of water and brush the egg wash on the crust.

5. Bake for about 30 to 40 minutes or until crust is browned and filling is bubbly.

6. Allow to cool slightly before serving.

LAMB POT PIE

SERVES 4 TO 6 ✦ **ACTIVE TIME: 45 MINUTES** ✦ **START TO FINISH: 90 MINUTES**

An earthy, vegetable-rich lamb stew topped with a flaky, buttery crust. A great dish to end a long, cold day.

1 flaky pastry crust recipe for a single crust (see page 136)

3 tablespoons flour

1 teaspoon salt, plus more for seasoning

1 teaspoon pepper, plus more for seasoning

2 pounds boneless lamb meat from leg or shoulder, cut into ½-inch cubes

2 tablespoons olive oil

2 cups fat-free chicken broth

1 large potato, peeled, washed, and cut into bite-sized pieces

1½ cups frozen broccoli florets

1 cup frozen peas and carrots

3 cloves garlic, finely chopped

¾ teaspoon paprika

¼ cup parsley, chopped

1 egg

1 tablespoon water

1. Preheat the oven to 400° F.

2. In a large bowl, whisk together the flour, salt, and pepper. Add the lamb pieces and toss to coat well. Set aside.

3. In the cast-iron skillet, heat the oil over medium-high heat. Add the floured meat pieces and cook, while stirring, until just browned on the outside. Add the garlic and cook for a minute or 2. Add the broth, potato, broccoli, and peas and carrots. Bring to a boil, then reduce the heat to low and simmer for 10 minutes, while stirring occasionally. Stir in the paprika and parsley, and season with additional salt and pepper.

4. On a lightly floured surface, roll out the crust so that it will just cover the meat mixture. Lay it gently on top, push down slightly to secure, and cut 4 or 5 slits in the middle. Beat egg with 1 tablespoon of water and brush the egg wash on the crust.

5. Put the skillet in the oven and bake for 30 minutes, until the crust is browned and the filling is bubbly.

6. Allow to cool slightly before serving.

CHICKEN AND ARTICHOKE HEART POT PIE

SERVES 4 TO 6 ✦ ACTIVE TIME: 45 MINUTES ✦ START TO FINISH: 90 MINUTES

You could call this a pot pie Italiano, as the marinade for the artichoke hearts adds to the flavor of the dish.

1 flaky pastry crust recipe for a single crust (see page 136)

2 tablespoons olive oil from the jar of artichoke hearts

½ yellow onion, diced

1 clove garlic, chopped

1 (6 oz.) jar quartered, marinated artichoke hearts, drained and chopped

½ teaspoon oregano

½ teaspoon dried red pepper flakes (optional)

2 tablespoons butter, cut into smaller slices

2 tablespoons flour

1¼ cup milk at room temperature

1½ cups cooked chicken, cut into bite-sized pieces

1 cup frozen peas

Salt and pepper to taste

1 tablespoon half-and-half

1. Preheat the oven to 350˚ F.

2. In a small skillet (not the cast-iron skillet), heat the oil from the artichoke hearts. Add the onion and garlic and stir, while cooking, for about 2 minutes. Add the artichoke hearts, oregano, and, if desired, hot pepper flakes. Reduce the heat to low, cover, and cook, while stirring occasionally, until the vegetables soften and caramelize, about 5 minutes. Set aside.

3. Before starting to make the white sauce, be sure the milk is at room temperature. If it's not, microwave it so that it's just warm, about 15 to 20 seconds. Have the milk ready.

4. In the cast-iron skillet, melt the butter over medium heat. Sprinkle the flour over it and stir quickly yet gently to blend. Reduce the heat slightly so the butter doesn't burn. Stir until the butter and flour form a soft paste.

5. Add just a little of the warm milk and stir constantly to blend it in. Add more milk in small increments, working after each addition to stir it into the flour-and-butter mixture smoothly. Work this way until all the milk has been incorporated. Continue to stir the sauce, while cooking over low heat, until it thickens, about 5 minutes.

6. Add the chicken pieces, peas, and vegetable mixture from the other skillet. Season with salt and pepper.

7. On a lightly floured surface, roll out the crust so it will fit over the filling. Lay it gently on top, push down slightly to secure, and cut 3 or 4 slits in the middle. Brush the crust with the half-and-half.

8. Put the skillet in the oven and bake for 30 to 40 minutes, until the crust is browned and the filling is bubbly.

9. Allow to cool slightly before serving.

MUSHROOM, SPINACH, AND LEEK GALETTE

SERVES 4 TO 6 ✦ ACTIVE TIME: 30 MINUTES ✦ START TO FINISH: 90 MINUTES

Caramelized leeks are even sweeter than onions, and are a great complement to the earthy mushrooms and bright spinach that top this galette.

1 flaky pastry crust recipe for a single crust (see page 136)

4 tablespoons butter

2 leeks, white and light green parts only, washed and thinly sliced

1½ cups mushrooms (all white mushrooms or a combination of types), sliced

4 cups baby spinach leaves

½ cup Parmesan cheese, grated

1 tablespoon half-and-half

1. Preheat the oven to 375° F.

2. In the cast-iron skillet, melt 2 tablespoons of the butter over medium heat and add the leeks. Cook, while stirring, until the leeks soften, about 2 minutes. Add the remaining 2 tablespoons of butter and the mushrooms, and stir to combine. Allow to cook over low heat, stirring occasionally, until the mushrooms are soft and the leeks are caramelized, about 10 minutes.

3. Raise the heat to medium and add the baby spinach, stirring as the leaves wilt. When wilted, remove the skillet from heat. Transfer the vegetables to a bowl but leave the melted butter in the skillet.

4. On a lightly floured surface, roll out the crust so that it is about 1 inch larger than the bottom of the pan and lay the pastry crust in the pan.

5. Place the vegetable mixture in the center. Fold the extra crust over the filling. Sprinkle with Parmesan cheese and brush the crust with the half-and-half.

6. Put the skillet in the oven and bake for 20 to 30 minutes until the crust is golden and puffy.

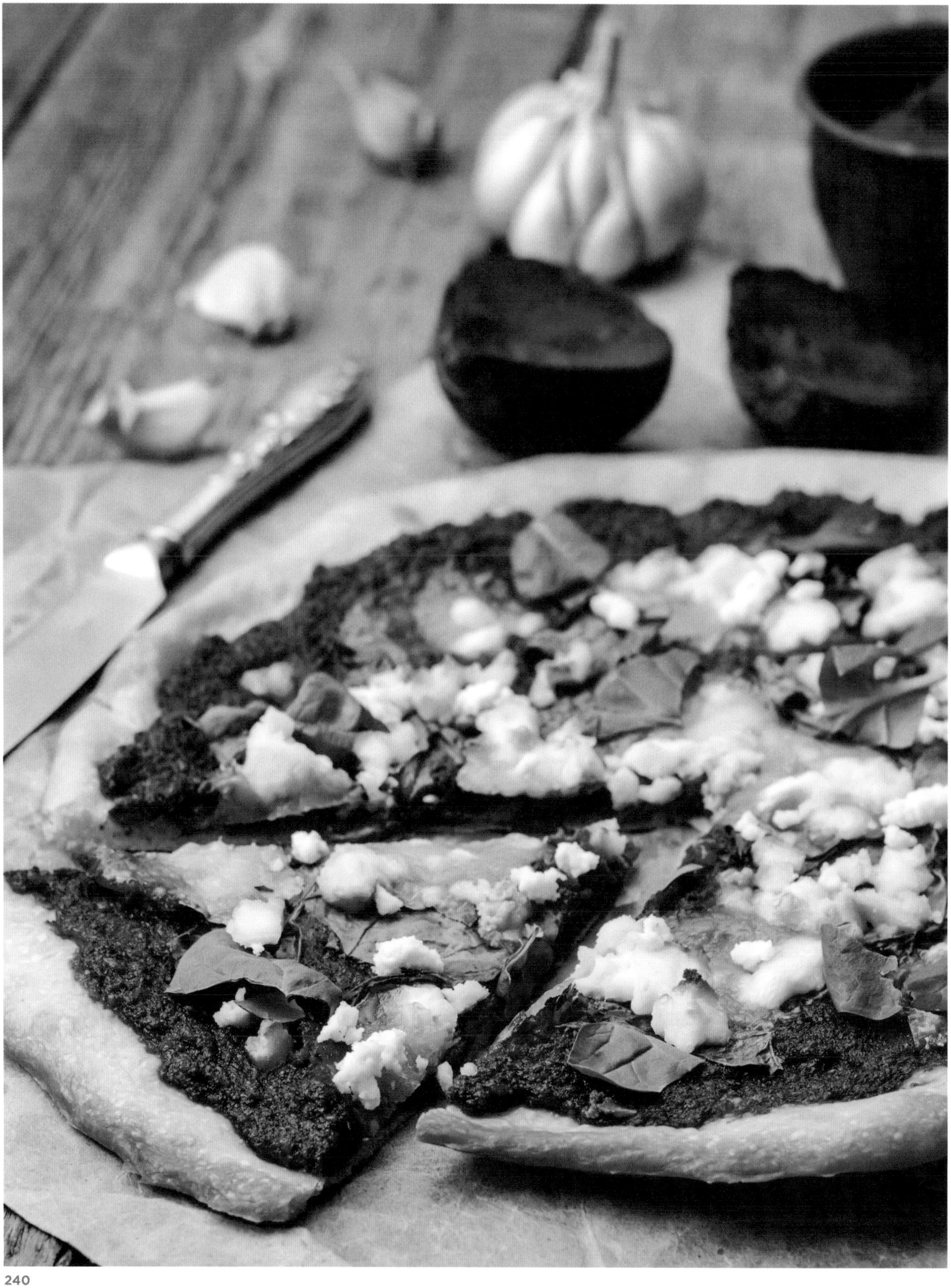

BEET AND RADICCHIO TART

SERVES 4 TO 6 ✦ ACTIVE TIME: 45 MINUTES ✦ START TO FINISH: 90 MINUTES

If you want to impress some lunch guests—or yourself, for that matter—make this beautiful tart. The flavors combine beautifully, and the deep red color is nice to look at.

1 flaky pastry crust recipe for a single crust (see page 136)

1 large beet, peeled and chopped

2 tablespoons olive oil

2 leeks, white and light green parts only, cleaned and very thinly sliced

1 head of red radicchio, thinly sliced

1 tablespoon balsamic vinegar

1 cup whole milk ricotta (don't substitute a lower-fat ricotta)

¼ cup Parmesan cheese, grated

1 egg

Salt and pepper to taste

1 tablespoon butter

1 tablespoon half-and-half

1. Preheat the oven to 400° F.

2. Put the beet pieces in a large piece of aluminum foil. Drizzle with 1 tablespoon of olive oil. Bake for 30 to 40 minutes until the beets are soft. Carefully remove from the oven, open the foil packet so that the beets cool, and reduce the temperature in the oven to 350° F.

3. In a skillet other than the cast-iron, heat 1 tablespoon olive oil over medium heat, add the leeks, and cook, while stirring, for about 5 minutes, until the leeks are soft and somewhat caramelized. Set ½ of the leeks aside, add almost all the radicchio to the pan, and reserve some for the top. Cook over low heat, while stirring occasionally, for about 8 minutes. Drizzle the balsamic vinegar over the mixture about halfway through.

4. In a bowl, combine the ricotta, Parmesan, and egg, mixing well. Stir in the beets and the leek-and-radicchio mixture, and season with salt and pepper.

5. On a lightly floured surface, roll out the crust so that it is about 1 inch larger than the bottom of the pan. Melt 1 tablespoon of butter in the skillet, remove from heat, and lay the pastry crust in the pan.

6. Place the ricotta-and-vegetable mixture in the center. Fold the edge so there is about an inch of crust along the outside. Brush the crust with half-and-half.

7. Put the skillet in the oven and bake for 25 to 30 minutes, until the crust is just golden.

8. Top with the reserved radicchio, and continue to bake for another 10 to 15 minutes.

TOMATO, CHÈVRE, AND BASIL TART

SERVES 4 TO 6 ✦ ACTIVE TIME: 30 MINUTES ✦ START TO FINISH: 90 MINUTES

If you want to throw together an elegant and easy-to-prepare tart that celebrates summer, this is it. Use a variety of tomatoes to add color and visual appeal, as the slice sizes will be different, too.

1 flaky pastry crust recipe for a single crust (see page 136)

1½ pounds tomatoes, sliced about ¼ inch thick, seeds removed

1 tablespoon kosher salt

2 tablespoons olive oil, plus more for drizzling

1 Vidalia onion, thinly sliced

Salt and freshly ground black pepper to taste

1 cup (8 oz.) fresh chèvre (goat cheese)

½ cup crumbled feta or a blend of grated Parmesan/Romano

8-10 basil leaves, cut into threads

1. Preheat the oven to 350° F.

2. Put the tomato slices on a plate lined with paper towels, and sprinkle with the salt. Let the salt sit on the tomatoes for about 15 minutes, and then turn the slices over.

3. In the cast-iron skillet, heat the olive oil over medium heat and add the onion. Cook, while stirring, until the onion is lightly browned, about 3 minutes. Season with salt and pepper. Transfer the onion to a bowl but keep the oil in the skillet.

4. On a lightly floured surface, roll out the crust so that it is just larger than the bottom of the pan and lay the pastry crust in the pan.

5. Spread the onion over bottom of the crust and dot with the goat cheese. Arrange the tomato slices so that they cover the bottom. Sprinkle with the crumbled feta or Parmesan-and-Romano blend. Drizzle lightly with olive oil.

6. Put the skillet in the oven and bake for 20 minutes. Increase the heat to 400° F and bake for an additional 10 minutes until the top of the tart is toasted.

7. While tart is still warm, sprinkle with shredded basil leaves.

FIG, PROSCIUTTO, AND CAMEMBERT TART

SERVES 4 TO 6 ✦ ACTIVE TIME: 45 MINUTES ✦ START TO FINISH: 90 MINUTES

For this tart, it's important to use a baked crust, as this doesn't need a lot of time in the oven. The figs are delicate and lose their flavor if overcooked.

1 baked crust
(see page 135)

2 tablespoons olive oil

½ onion, sliced thin

½ pound prosciutto,
cut into 1-inch slices

1 tablespoon Dijon
mustard

1 round of Camembert
at room temperature

6-8 fresh figs, stems
removed, halved

3 tablespoons aged
balsamic vinegar

1 tablespoon honey

¼ cup arugula

1. Preheat the oven to 400° F.

2. In a non-cast-iron skillet over medium heat, heat the olive oil and add the onion. Cook and stir until the onion is lightly browned, about 3 minutes. Add the prosciutto slices to the skillet and cook, while stirring, for an additional minute. Remove the skillet from heat.

3. Working with the baked crust in the cast-iron skillet, spread the Dijon mustard evenly over the bottom of the crust and top with the onion-and-prosciutto mix.

4. Cut the Camembert into ¼-inch thick wedges and place them decoratively over the onion mix. Next place the fig halves over the cheese. Make sure you don't overcrowd.

5. In a small bowl, whisk together the balsamic vinegar and honey. Drizzle the sauce over the tart.

6. Put the skillet in the oven and bake for 20 to 25 minutes until cheese is melted and figs are softened. Remove from the oven and let cool. Top with the arugula and serve.

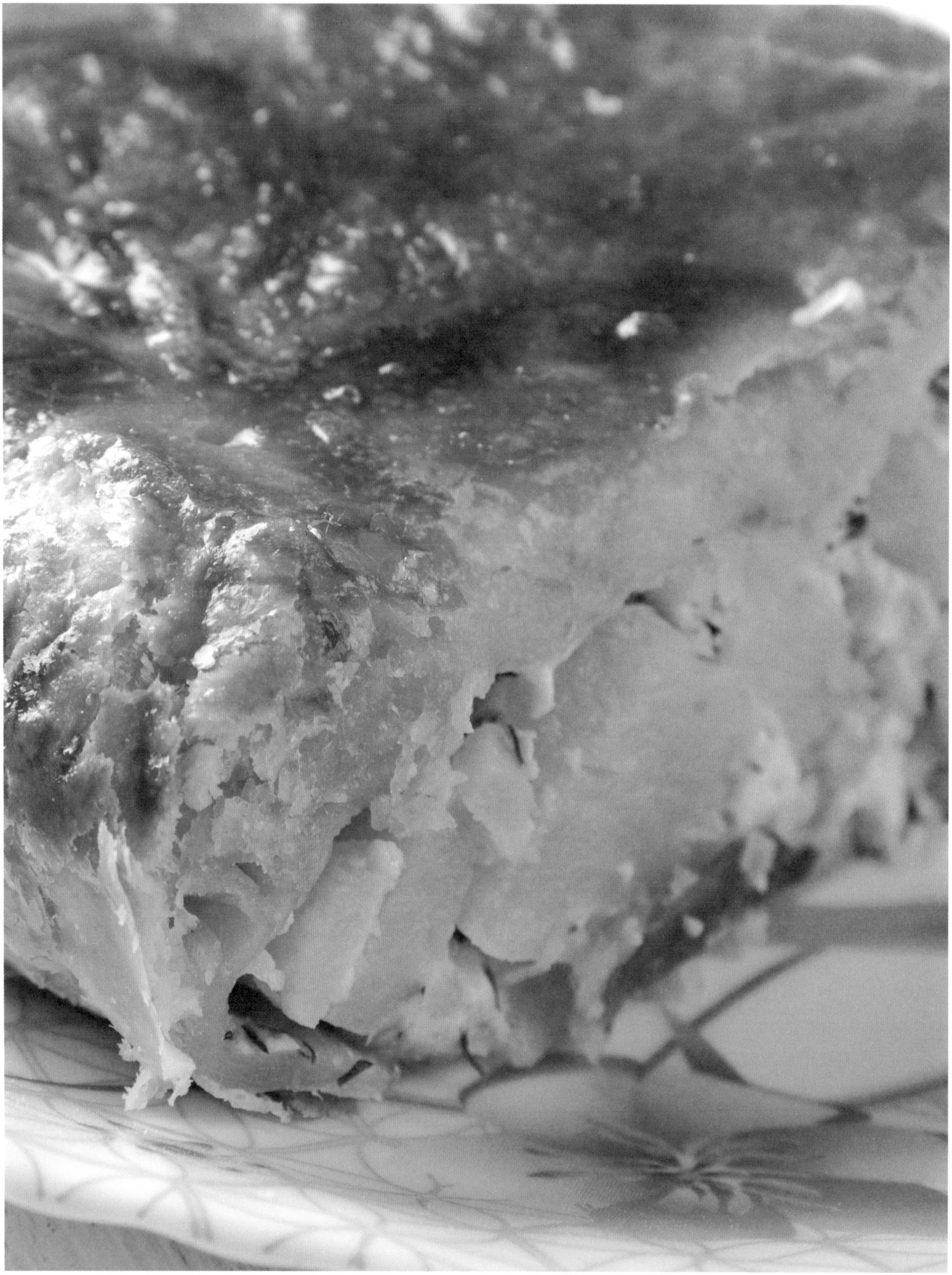

FRENCH POTATO TART

SERVES 4 TO 6 ✦ ACTIVE TIME: 45 MINUTES ✦ START TO FINISH: 2 HOURS

I refer to this as a French Potato Tart because of the crème fraîche blanketing very thin potato slices, as in a traditional au gratin. What takes it over the top is baking between two crusts. Small slices of this could also serve as a fantastic side dish for roast meat or vegetables.

1 flaky pastry crust recipe for a double crust (see page 136)

2 pounds Yukon Gold potatoes, peeled

1¼ cups crème fraîche

1 tablespoon kosher salt

½ teaspoon black pepper

Pinch of grated nutmeg

2 cloves garlic, crushed

2 teaspoons fresh thyme, chopped

1 egg yolk

1 tablespoon half-and-half

1. Preheat the oven to 400° F.

2. Using a very sharp knife, a mandoline, or a spiralizer, slice the potatoes as thin as possible.

3. In a bowl, combine the crème fraîche, salt, pepper, nutmeg, garlic, and thyme. Stir to combine.

4. Add the potato slices and fold gently to cover with the crème, making sure slices are completely covered.

5. On a lightly floured surface, roll out the crust so that it is just larger than the bottom of the pan and lay the pastry crust in the skillet.

6. Using your hands, start layering the potato slices in the crust, creating even, tight layers. When all the potatoes are in the crust, use a rubber spatula to scrape the cream mixture into the pie. Tap the edges of the skillet to distribute the mixture evenly.

7. On a lightly floured surface, roll out the top crust and crimp the edges with the bottom crust to seal. Blend the egg yolk with the half-and-half and brush the mixture over the top crust. Cut 4 to 5 slits in the middle.

8. Put the skillet in the oven and bake for 15 minutes. Reduce temperature to 350° F and continue to bake for 1 hour until potatoes are tender.

9. Serve hot or at room temperature.

SIDE DISHES

In my opinion, this is where a lot of the magic happens in cooking—especially with a cast-iron skillet—because there are so many ingredients to play with. Vegetables, starches, grains, spices, sauces—you'll see what I mean when you thumb through this chapter. Deliciousness happens over and over, and with each dish containing simple ingredients that are reasonably priced and easy to find, you'll be able to afford putting on a show for the entire family.

CLASSIC CORN BREAD

MAKES 4 TO 6 SERVINGS ✦ ACTIVE TIME: 1 HOUR ✦ START TO FINISH: 3 TO 4 HOURS

If you're going to make bread in a cast-iron skillet, you have to make corn bread. In fact, many restaurants serve corn bread in a cast-iron dish.

4 cups finely ground yellow cornmeal

¾ cup sugar

1 tablespoon salt

4 cups boiling water

1 cup flour

1 tablespoon butter, melted, plus 1 teaspoon

2 eggs, lightly beaten

2 teaspoons baking powder

1 teaspoon baking soda

1 cup milk

1. In a large bowl, combine the cornmeal, sugar, salt, and boiling water. Stir to combine and let sit for several hours in a cool, dark place or overnight in the refrigerator. Stir occasionally while the batter is resting.

2. When ready to make, preheat oven to 450° F.

3. Add flour, butter, eggs, baking powder, baking soda, and milk to the batter. Stir to thoroughly combine.

4. Heat the skillet over medium-high heat and melt the teaspoon of butter in it. Add the batter.

5. Transfer the skillet to the oven and cook for 15 minutes.

6. Reduce the heat to 250° F and cook another 40 minutes or until golden brown on top and set in the center.

Corn bread recipes are as varied and plentiful as those for chili. A fun way to discover different ones without having to go through multiple cookbooks and spend lots of time in the kitchen is to invite friends and family to a Cast-iron Corn Bread Cook-off. Make chili the way you like it (and plenty of it), then have people bring over their corn breads with the recipes.

CORNY-SPICY CORN BREAD

SERVES 6 TO 8 ✦ ACTIVE TIME: 25 MINUTES ✦ START TO FINISH: 60 MINUTES

Now that I've suggested the family or neighborhood corn bread challenge, I have to offer my own entry, since I love a corn bread that actually has kernels of corn in it. If you like spice, toss in the jalapeños, too.

2 cups finely ground yellow cornmeal

1 cup flour

¼ cup sugar

2 teaspoons baking powder

1 teaspoon baking soda

1 teaspoon salt

4 tablespoons unsalted butter

1½ cups milk

2 eggs

1 cup corn kernels (can be from fresh cooked corn on the cob, or canned, making sure to drain the liquid)

¼ to ½ cup jalapeño peppers, diced

1. Preheat the oven to 400° F.

2. In a large bowl, combine the cornmeal, flour, sugar, baking powder, baking soda, and salt. Put ½ cup of the milk in a measuring cup. Add 2 tablespoons of butter that has been cut into pieces. Put the measuring cup in the microwave and heat on high for 1 minute so that butter melts into the milk. Pour this over the dry ingredients and begin stirring. Gradually add the remaining cup of milk and stir, then add the eggs and continue stirring until thoroughly combined. When batter is mixed, fold in the corn kernels and jalapeños.

3. Heat the skillet over medium heat and melt the 2 remaining tablespoons of butter in it. Add the batter and shake the pan gently to evenly distribute.

4. Transfer the skillet to the oven and cook for 25 to 30 minutes, until the bread is a light golden brown and a toothpick inserted in the middle comes out clean.

5. Using pot holders or oven mitts, remove the skillet from the oven and let the bread cool for 10 to 15 minutes before slicing and serving.

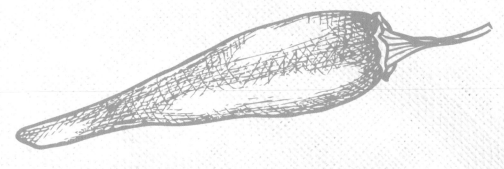

CORN CHOWDER CORN BREAD

SERVES 6 TO 8 ✦ ACTIVE TIME: 20 MINUTES ✦ START TO FINISH: 60 MINUTES

I was going through my cans of soup one day and thought, "Why not use chicken corn chowder soup instead of milk in a corn bread recipe?" So I tried it. Super easy. Nice, moist result. And this leads, of course, to thoughts of other soups as flavor additives for corn bread. I'm sure you can think of some, too.

2 cups finely ground yellow cornmeal

1 cup flour

¼ cup sugar

2 teaspoons baking powder

1 teaspoon baking soda

1 teaspoon salt

1 teaspoon cayenne pepper (optional)

¼ cup milk

4 tablespoons unsalted butter

1 (18.5 oz.) can of chicken corn chowder soup

2 eggs

1. Preheat the oven to 400° F.

2. In a large bowl, combine the cornmeal, flour, sugar, baking powder, baking soda, salt, and, if using, cayenne pepper. Put the milk in a measuring cup. Add 2 tablespoons of butter that has been cut into small pieces. Put the measuring cup in the microwave and heat on high for 1 minute so that butter is melted into the milk. Pour this over the dry ingredients and begin stirring. Add the can of soup and stir, then add the eggs and continue stirring until thoroughly combined.

3. Heat the skillet over medium heat and melt the 2 remaining tablespoons of butter in it. Add the batter and shake the pan gently to evenly distribute.

4. Transfer the skillet to the oven and cook for 25 to 30 minutes, until the bread is a light golden brown and a toothpick inserted in the middle comes out clean.

5. Using pot holders or oven mitts, remove the skillet from the oven and let the bread cool for 10 to 15 minutes before slicing and serving.

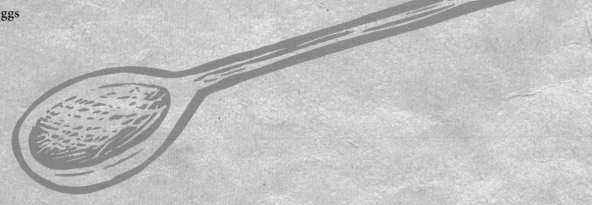

CREAMY SUCCOTASH

MAKES 8 TO 10 SERVINGS ✦ ACTIVE TIME: 30 MINUTES ✦ START TO FINISH: 60 MINUTES

Take advantage of the season when fresh corn is plentiful to create this cookout classic. This uses a lot of corn, and is a nice alternative to corn on the cob.

4 cups fresh or frozen lima beans

Kosher salt to taste

12 ears fresh corn

3 tablespoons butter

1 cup water

1 cup whole milk

Freshly ground black pepper to taste

3 tablespoons flour

½ cup warm water

1. Bring a medium pot of salted water to boil over high heat. Add the lima beans and reduce the heat. Cook until they are al dente, about 5 minutes. Drain and set aside.

2. Shuck the corn and remove all strands of silk. Rinse the ears and shake to dry.

3. Standing each ear up in the middle of a large baking dish, use a sharp knife to cut down the sides and remove all the kernels. With the kernels off, take the blade of a dull knife and press it along each side of the ears to "milk" the cob of its liquid. Discard the milked cobs.

4. Heat the skillet over medium heat. When hot, lower the heat and add the butter so it melts slowly. When melted, add the corn kernels and milk from the cobs and stir to coat the kernels with the butter. Increase the heat to medium-high and add the water and whole milk. Bring to a boil, while stirring constantly, and then reduce to low heat. Add the lima beans, salt, and pepper.

5. In a measuring cup, add the warm water to the flour and mix until thoroughly combined. Drizzle the flour mixture into the corn and lima beans, stirring and cooking over low heat until the sauce thickens. If it gets too thick, add some more water or whole milk. Serve hot.

You'll want to freeze some of this to enjoy in the dead of winter. It's easy. Allow the succotash to cool, put it in airtight containers, being sure to push all the air out, seal the container, and place in the freezer. Put the date it was cooked on the container so you remember.

SPICY SHRIMP POLENTA

SERVES 4 TO 6 ✦ ACTIVE TIME: 30 MINUTES ✦ START TO FINISH: 60 MINUTES

If you're looking for a recipe for a fun cocktail party finger food, this is it—essentially a take on fish tacos but much easier to eat while standing! Plus, it's naturally gluten-free!

3 tablespoons
canola oil

½ pound small shrimp,
thawed (if frozen),
peeled, and halved

1 cup polenta

3 cups water

1 teaspoon horseradish

1 teaspoon hot
pepper flakes

Salt and freshly ground
black pepper to taste

Fresh cilantro for
garnish

1. Preheat the oven to 400° F.

2. Heat the canola oil in a skillet over medium-high heat. When hot but not smoking, add the shrimp. Stirring constantly and with a light touch, sauté the shrimp until just pink, about 3 to 5 minutes. Remove the pan from heat and use a slotted spoon to transfer the shrimp to a plate lined with paper towels. Keep the oil in the skillet.

3. In a heavy saucepan, whisk together the polenta and water. Heat over medium heat and bring to a boil, whisking to prevent lumps from forming. When bubbling, reduce the heat to low and simmer, uncovered, for a couple of minutes or until smooth. Remove saucepan from heat and stir in the horseradish and pepper flakes. Season with salt and pepper. Taste the polenta to see if the horseradish is strong enough for you. If you think it could use more, add another ½ teaspoon and be careful not to overdo it. Stir in the shrimp.

4. Pour the polenta into the skillet, smoothing the surface with the back of a spoon. Put the skillet in the oven and bake for about 30 minutes, until the polenta is lightly golden and coming away from the edge of the pan. Allow to cool for 5 to 10 minutes, then work quickly and carefully to invert the polenta cake onto a platter. Allow to cool to room temperature.

5. Cut the polenta into wedges, and top each piece with a sprig of cilantro. Serve immediately.

POLENTA CAKE WITH GREENS

SERVES 4 TO 6 ✦ ACTIVE TIME: 30 MINUTES ✦ START TO FINISH: 60 MINUTES

Polenta is cornmeal cooked into porridge and then baked or fried. It forms a lovely, bright yellow cake that is moist yet firm. It can be topped with all kinds of things, but in this recipe, it is the base for sautéed vegetables. Delicious!

1 cup polenta

3 cups water

Salt and freshly ground black pepper to taste

1 pound bitter greens such as kale, Swiss chard, escarole, or dandelion, tough stems removed

3 tablespoons extra virgin olive oil, plus more to prepare skillet

3 cloves garlic, chopped

Red pepper flakes to taste

Romano cheese, grated, for topping

1. Preheat the oven to 400° F.

2. Liberally oil the skillet and put it in the oven for a few minutes.

3. In a heavy saucepan, whisk together the polenta and water. Heat over medium heat and bring to a boil, whisking to prevent lumps from forming. When bubbling, reduce the heat to low and simmer, uncovered, for a couple of minutes or until smooth. Season with salt and black pepper.

4. Pour the polenta into the skillet. Put the skillet in the oven and bake for about 30 minutes, until the polenta is lightly golden and coming away from the edges of the pan.

5. While it's baking, make the greens. Bring a large pot of salted water to a boil, add the greens, and boil until very tender, 15 to 20 minutes. Drain in a colander and squeeze to remove excess moisture. Cut the greens into pieces. Heat the 3 tablespoons of olive oil in a pan, add the garlic, and cook, while stirring, until fragrant, about 2 minutes. Add the red pepper flakes, stir, and then add the greens. Cook until heated through. Season with salt and pepper. Keep warm until polenta is cooked.

6. Cut the polenta into wedges, top with greens, and sprinkle with Romano.

Variation

Substitute ½ pound baby spinach leaves and ½ pound kale (tough stems removed) for the pound of mixed greens.

POLENTA CAKE WITH MUSHROOMS AND ONIONS

SERVES 4 TO 6   ACTIVE TIME: 30 MINUTES   START TO FINISH: 75 MINUTES

Think vegetarian shepherd's pie with this recipe—the mushrooms and onions are the "meat" and the polenta bakes on top the way a layer of mashed potatoes would. A cast-iron skillet seems a natural home for this kind of dish, which is hearty and rustic.

8 tablespoons (1 stick) butter

1 to 1½ cups onions, thinly sliced

2 pounds mushrooms, stems removed and cut into pieces

1 teaspoon Worcestershire sauce

1 cup polenta

3 cups water

Salt and freshly ground black pepper to taste

1. Preheat the oven to 400° F.

2. Melt 6 tablespoons of the butter in the skillet over medium heat. Add the onion slices and increase the heat to medium-high. Sauté the onions until just soft, about 3 minutes. Add the mushroom pieces and continue to cook over medium-high heat, while stirring frequently, until the mushrooms and onions are soft and reduced in volume, about 8 minutes. Stir in the Worcestershire sauce, and season with salt and pepper. Remove the skillet from the heat.

3. In a heavy saucepan, whisk together the polenta and water. Heat over medium heat and bring to a boil, whisking to prevent lumps from forming. When bubbling, reduce the heat to low and simmer, uncovered, for a couple of minutes or until smooth. Season with salt and black pepper.

4. Pour the polenta over the mushroom/onion mixture, smoothing the surface with the back of a spoon. Cut the remaining 2 tablespoons of butter into thin pieces and dot the surface of the polenta with them.

5. Put the skillet in the oven and bake for 30 minutes, until it is lightly golden and coming away from the edges of the pan (the mushroom/onion mix should be bubbling hot). Allow to cool for 10 minutes before serving.

6. Cut the polenta into wedges. Serve immediately.

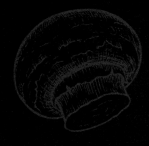

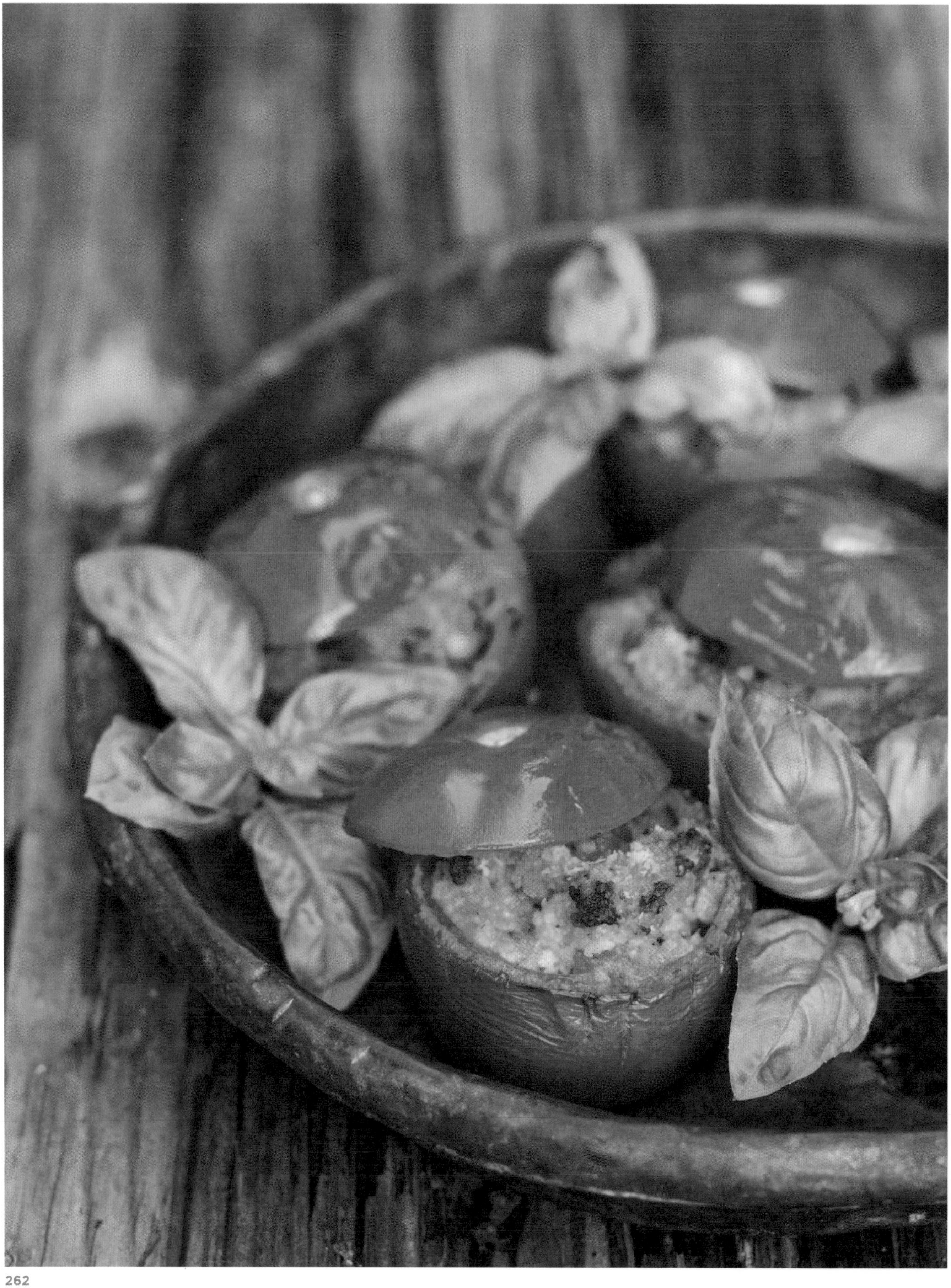

STUFFED TOMATOES

These are great filled with a stuffing with meat in it or without. The sidebar provides the recipe for a meatless version.

6 ripe large tomatoes

1 pound sausage, casings removed

1 onion, diced

4 cloves garlic, minced

2 teaspoons red pepper flakes (optional)

8 white mushrooms, stems removed, diced

½ green bell pepper, seeds removed, diced

2 cups plain bread crumbs

2 tablespoons dried sage

1 cup Parmesan cheese, grated

Salt and pepper to taste

1. Preheat the oven to 375° F.

2. Cut off the tops of the tomatoes, and use a small paring knife or a serrated grapefruit spoon to scoop out the insides. Once hollowed, sprinkle salt on the insides and turn upside down on a plate covered with a paper towel to absorb the water. Let sit for about 30 minutes.

3. Heat the skillet over medium-high heat and cook the sausage, breaking it up with a wooden spoon as it cooks. Cook until there is no pink showing in the meat. When cooked, use a slotted spoon to transfer the sausage to a large bowl. In the sausage fat, cook the onion and garlic until the onion is translucent, about 4 minutes. Add the mushrooms and pepper and cook over medium heat, while stirring, until vegetables soften, about 10 minutes. Add red pepper flakes if desired.

4. Add the mushroom mixture to the sausage and stir to combine. Then add the bread crumbs, sage, and Parmesan. Season with salt and pepper.

5. Wipe down the skillet and brush with olive oil. Position the tomatoes in the skillet bottoms down. Start filling the tomatoes gently, dividing the filling between them. Cover the tomatoes with aluminum foil and put the skillet in the oven. Bake for about 30 minutes, remove the foil, and continue baking for another 10 to 15 minutes until cooked through. Serve hot.

Meatless Stuffed Tomatoes: If you want to make this without sausage, simply omit that ingredient. Double the amount of mushrooms, and after sautéing the mushrooms and peppers, drain the excess liquid. You can also add toasted walnut pieces for additional flavor and fiber.

ONE-POT MAC AND CHEESE

MAKES 6 TO 8 SERVINGS ✦ ACTIVE TIME: 30 MINUTES ✦ START TO FINISH: 60 MINUTES

There's nothing like homemade macaroni and cheese, but it can get as messy when you have to use several pots and pans to make and serve it. Here comes your cast-iron skillet to the rescue!

1 pound elbow macaroni (I also like penne, orecchiette, or farfalle pasta.)

1 tablespoon salt

3 tablespoons butter at room temperature

3½ tablespoons flour

1½ cups milk at room temperature or slightly warmed

¼ cup sour cream

¾ pound sharp white cheddar, grated

¼ pound Gruyére cheese, grated

Salt and pepper to taste

Dash of cayenne pepper

1. Preheat the oven to 425° F.

2. Put the macaroni in the skillet and add cold water so that it reaches ¼ inch below the top. Stir in the salt, turn the heat on high, and cook the macaroni for about 10 minutes. Test a piece after about 7 minutes. The pasta should be al dente—nearly cooked through but still a bit chewy. When it is cooked, drain it in a colander over a large mixing bowl so the water is retained.

3. Put your skillet back on the stove over medium heat, and add the butter. When it's melted, stir in the flour, with a wooden spoon if possible, to prevent lumps from forming. When it is starting to bubble, start slowly adding the milk, whisking constantly as you add it. Add about a ½ cup at a time, being sure to whisk it thoroughly before continuing. When all the milk is stirred in, let the sauce simmer over low heat for about 10 minutes until thickened.

4. On low to medium heat, stir in the sour cream. When the mix is warm again, add the cheeses, stirring gently as they melt. Season with the salt, pepper, and cayenne.

5. Finally, add the macaroni gently into the cheese sauce. If it seems too thick, add some of the reserved water. The consistency should be like a thick stew. When the noodles are hot, transfer the skillet to the oven.

6. Bake in the oven for about 15 minutes, then take a peek. The dish should be bubbling and the cheese on top starting to brown. This takes somewhere between 15 and 25 minutes. Be careful not to let it burn. Let the macaroni cool slightly before serving.

Variations

Macaroni and cheese is a dish that's great fun to personalize, and there are all sorts of ways you can change it up a bit—try adding fresh herbs, jalapeños, chopped tomatoes, or even pulled pork! I also recommend sprinkling bread crumbs or bacon bits on top for some added crunch.

HOME-STYLE BAKED BEANS

MAKES 6 TO 8 SERVINGS ✦ ACTIVE TIME: 30 MINUTES ✦ START TO FINISH: 1½ TO 2 HOURS

At times, cooking in a cast-iron skillet makes me picture cowboys cooking over an open fire while their horses hang out behind them. What are they eating? In my mind, it's baked beans with bacon, which seems quintessential "skillet cooking" to me. So here's a recipe in honor of my vision.

6 strips thick-cut bacon

½ onion, diced

½ cup bell pepper, ribs and seeds removed, diced

1 teaspoon salt, plus more for seasoning

2 (15.5 oz.) cans pinto beans, rinsed and drained

1 cup barbecue sauce (not too sweet!)

1 teaspoon Dijon mustard

2 tablespoons dark brown sugar

Fresh ground pepper to taste

1. Preheat the oven to 325° F.

2. Heat the skillet over medium heat and cook half of the bacon pieces. Cook until just soft, about 8 minutes. Transfer to a plate lined with paper towels to drain.

3. Add the remaining pieces of bacon, turn up the heat, and cook, flipping often, until pieces are browned. Reduce the heat to medium. Add the onion and pepper and cook, stirring occasionally, until the vegetables soften, another 8 minutes or so.

4. Add the salt, beans, barbecue sauce, mustard, and brown sugar. Stir, season with additional salt and a generous grind of fresh pepper, and leave on the stove until the sauce just starts to simmer.

5. Lay the partially cooked pieces of bacon on top of the beans and transfer the skillet to the oven.

6. Bake for 1 hour and take a look. The bacon should be crisp and browned, and the sauce should be thick. This can go for another 15 to 30 minutes if the consistency isn't right. Just be careful not to overcook, as the beans will start to dry out. An hour and 15 to 20 minutes is about right.

7. Remove from the oven and allow to cool slightly before serving, preferably in bowls around a fire!

Baked beans are delicious and filling on their own, but they are the perfect accompaniment to grilled sausages, hot dogs, hamburgers, pork chops, or barbecued chicken. Their thickness is also complemented by coleslaw or a big green salad.

CRISP-TENDER ASPARAGUS

SERVES 4 ✦ ACTIVE TIME: 20 MINUTES ✦ START TO FINISH: 30 MINUTES

Making asparagus in the skillet is almost like making them on the grill. The outsides are crisp while the insides are tender—perfect!

1 bunch thin asparagus

3 tablespoons olive oil

1 clove garlic, minced

½ teaspoon salt

½ teaspoon freshly ground pepper

Lemon wedges

1. Cut the tough ends off the asparagus and rinse the rest of the stalks.

2. Heat the skillet over medium-high heat. When hot, add the oil and let that get hot. Add the asparagus. Using tongs, keep turning them so they are cooked evenly in the oil. Cook the asparagus until they are bright green, and hot on the outside but tender on the inside.

3. Add the garlic, salt, and pepper, and shake the pan around to distribute evenly. Cook for another 2 minutes. Transfer to a serving platter and serve with lemon wedges.

The thinner the asparagus, the faster they'll cook. If you are working with super-fresh, thin stalks, you may need to reduce the cooking times in the recipe. On the other hand, if you're using vegetables that are thicker and maybe not as fresh, the cooking times should be fine, or may even need to increase.

GLAZED SWEET POTATOES AND CARROTS

SERVES 4 ✦ ACTIVE TIME: 20 MINUTES ✦ START TO FINISH: 40 MINUTES

Sugar brings out the best in already-sweet carrots and sweet potatoes, especially when it's part of a butter sauce.

¾ **pound carrots**

¾ **pound sweet potatoes**

¾ **cup water**

4 tablespoons butter

2 tablespoons sugar

Cayenne pepper (optional)

Salt to taste

Fresh parsley, chopped, for garnish

1. Peel and trim the carrots. Cut them in half and cut the halves in half lengthwise.

2. Peel and slice the sweet potatoes into spears (about the same size as the carrots).

3. Put the carrots and sweet potatoes in the skillet with the water, butter, sugar, and cayenne pepper (if desired). Bring to a boil over medium-high heat.

4. When boiling, reduce the heat to low and simmer for another 10 minutes, stirring occasionally.

5. When the carrots and sweet potatoes are tender and there is a buttery sauce in the skillet, sprinkle with salt. Garnish with the chopped parsley and serve.

ROASTED RED POTATOES

SERVES 6 ✦ ACTIVE TIME: 20 MINUTES ✦ START TO FINISH: 60 MINUTES

The great thing about red potatoes is that the skins are very thin and don't need to be peeled off. They taste great, add extra fiber and vitamins, and look good, too.

12 to 14 small red potatoes, scrubbed clean

2 to 3 tablespoons olive oil

Freshly ground pepper to taste

Coarse sea salt to taste

Fresh parsley, chopped, for garnish

1. Preheat oven to 375˚ F.

2. In a bowl, drizzle the oil over the potatoes. Grind some fresh pepper on the potatoes. Put the potatoes in the skillet to form a single layer and sprinkle with sea salt.

3. Bake in the oven for 25 to 40 minutes, turning halfway through, until potatoes are cooked through. Serve hot with chopped parsley as a garnish.

Red potatoes are available in grocery stores most of the year. Baby potatoes harvested in late summer also taste fabulous prepared this way. Fingerling potatoes can be cut in half and roasted.

QUINOA SKILLET CASSEROLE

SERVES 6 ✦ ACTIVE TIME: 30 MINUTES ✦ START TO FINISH: 60 MINUTES

Quinoa has plenty of health benefits, but one of the drawbacks of this nutritious food is that it can become sticky, like oatmeal—a texture that isn't always appealing. With the cast-iron skillet, you can cook the quinoa so that it gets almost crackly-crunchy. Combined with the veggies and hot peppers, this is a delish dish.

1 cup quinoa

2 cups chicken broth

1½ tablespoons olive oil

1 ear of cooked corn, kernels removed

½ red bell pepper, ribs and seeds removed, diced

½ cup onion, chopped

1 jalapeño, seeded and sliced

½ teaspoon salt

1 cup cheddar cheese, grated

1. In a small saucepan with a tight-fitting lid, cook the quinoa in the broth. Bring the liquid to a boil, stir, and reduce the heat to low, simmering for about 15 minutes or until the grains are translucent. Remove from heat and let sit, still covered, for at least 5 more minutes so the quinoa fully absorbs the broth.

2. Heat the skillet over medium-high heat, add the olive oil, and then add the corn, red pepper, onion, and jalapeño slices. Stir, cooking, until the onion is soft and peppers are starting to brown, about 5 to 8 minutes.

3. Stir in the quinoa, season with salt, and combine all the ingredients. Keep the skillet on medium-high to brown the quinoa slightly.

4. Cook for another 10 minutes, while stirring occasionally. Stir in the cheese, remove from heat, and serve.

Quinoa looks and cooks like a grain, but it's actually a seed—the harvest from a grass called goosefoot that has grown in the Andes Mountains of South America for millennia. It's high in protein and fiber and loaded with magnesium, iron, and B6.

RATATOUILLE

SERVES 4 ✦ ACTIVE TIME: 40 MINUTES ✦ START TO FINISH: 2 HOURS

There are variations on this dish—some insist that zucchini is a necessary ingredient—but I like it with just eggplant, peppers, and tomatoes—and garlic, of course.

⅓ cup olive oil

6 cloves garlic, minced

1 medium eggplant, cut into bite-sized cubes

2 bell peppers, ribs and seeds removed, diced

4 tomatoes, seeded and chopped

Salt and pepper to taste

1. Heat half the olive oil in the skillet over medium-high heat. Add the garlic and eggplant and cook, while stirring, until pieces are coated with oil and just starting to sizzle, about 2 minutes. Reduce the heat slightly, add the peppers and remaining oil, and stir to combine. With the heat on medium, cover the skillet and let cook, stirring every few minutes to be sure vegetables aren't sticking to the bottom of the pan. If the mix seems too dry, add a little more olive oil. As the eggplant softens, the dish will regain moisture.

2. After about 15 minutes, when the eggplant and peppers are nearly soft, add the tomatoes and stir to combine. With the lid off, continue to cook the ratatouille, stirring occasionally, until the eggplant and peppers are soft and the tomatoes are wilted. Remove the skillet from heat, season with salt and pepper, and allow to sit for at least 1 hour. Reheat and eat.

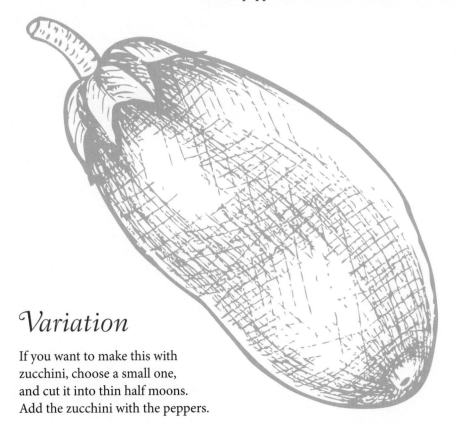

Variation

If you want to make this with zucchini, choose a small one, and cut it into thin half moons. Add the zucchini with the peppers.

CRAZY-GOOD CABBAGE

MAKES 4 TO 6 SERVINGS ✦ ACTIVE TIME: 30 MINUTES ✦ START TO FINISH: 60 MINUTES

This Southern-inspired dish is a colorful blend of pale green cabbage, bright green peppers, deep red tomatoes, and bright yellow corn—with a cayenne kick!

2 tablespoons olive oil

1 medium head cabbage, cored and shredded

1 green pepper, seeds and ribs removed, diced

1 medium onion, diced

3 cups fresh tomatoes, seeded and chopped

1 ear of corn, kernels removed, or 1 (8 oz.) can of corn, drained

1 teaspoon cayenne pepper

Salt and pepper to taste

1. Heat the skillet over medium-high heat and add the oil. Add cabbage, pepper, and onion and stir, while cooking, until onion becomes translucent, about 3 minutes. Add the tomatoes, corn, and cayenne and stir. Season with salt and pepper.

2. Cover, reduce the heat to low, and simmer until the cabbage is cooked through, about 30 minutes. Stir occasionally. Serve hot with extra salt, pepper, and cayenne.

CARAWAY SEED CABBAGE

MAKES 4 TO 6 SERVINGS ✦ ACTIVE TIME: 30 MINUTES ✦ START TO FINISH: 60 MINUTES

If you prefer a more Eastern European flavor to your cabbage, try this variation.

2 tablespoons olive oil

1 medium head cabbage, cored and shredded

½ medium onion, diced

1 teaspoon caraway seeds, toasted

Salt and pepper to taste

1. Heat the skillet over medium-high heat and add the oil. Add cabbage, onion, and toasted caraway seeds, cooking until onion becomes translucent, about 3 minutes. Season with salt and pepper.

2. Cover, reduce the heat to low, and simmer until the cabbage is cooked through, about 30 minutes. Stir occasionally. Serve hot with extra salt and pepper.

THE COMPLETE CAST-IRON COOKBOOK

SPINACH AND SHALLOTS

SERVES 6 TO 8 ✦ ACTIVE TIME: 25 MINUTES ✦ START TO FINISH: 40 MINUTES

Using mellow-flavored shallots instead of the usual garlic and onions keeps the spinach flavor bright in this quick-cooking dish. A splash of balsamic vinegar takes it over the top.

3 tablespoons olive oil

4 large shallots, thinly sliced

2 pounds fresh spinach, tough stems removed, rinsed, and thoroughly dried

1 tablespoon balsamic vinegar

Salt and pepper

1. Heat skillet over medium-high heat. Add olive oil and shallots and cook, while stirring, until shallots are translucent, about 2 minutes.

2. Add the spinach and cook, while stirring, until the leaves are covered by the oil and shallots mix, another 2 or 3 minutes. The spinach will start to wilt quickly. Reduce the heat and keep stirring so none of it burns. If desired, you can turn the heat to low and cover the skillet so the spinach steams.

3. When the spinach leaves are wilted and still bright green, splash them with the balsamic vinegar, shaking the pan to distribute. Season with salt and pepper and serve.

This dish works best with more mature spinach. Reserve baby spinach greens for salads and use the larger leaves for this dish.

Variation

If you prefer a less onion-y dish, use two shallots instead of four.

CREAMED CORN

MAKES 8 TO 10 SERVINGS ✦ ACTIVE TIME: 30 MINUTES ✦ START TO FINISH: 60 MINUTES

When you're tired of corn on the cob and in need of a little comfort, try this fresh spin on a canned classic.

12 ears of fresh corn

3 tablespoons butter

1 cup water

1 cup half-and-half

½ teaspoon salt

Freshly ground black pepper to taste

3 tablespoons flour

½ cup warm water

1. Shuck the corn and remove all strands of silk. Rinse the ears and shake to dry.

2. Standing each ear up in the middle of a large baking dish, use a sharp knife to cut down the sides and remove all the kernels. With the kernels off, take the blade of a dull knife and press it along each side of the ears to "milk" the cob of its liquid. Discard the milked cobs.

3. Heat the skillet over medium heat and, when hot, lower the heat and add the butter so it melts slowly. When melted, add the corn kernels and milk from the cobs and stir to coat. Increase the heat to medium-high and add the water and half-and-half. Bring to a boil, while stirring constantly, and then reduce to low heat. Add the salt and pepper.

4. In a measuring cup, add the warm water to the flour and mix until thoroughly combined. Drizzle the flour mixture into the corn, continuing to stir until the sauce thickens. If it gets too thick, add some more water or half-and-half. Serve hot.

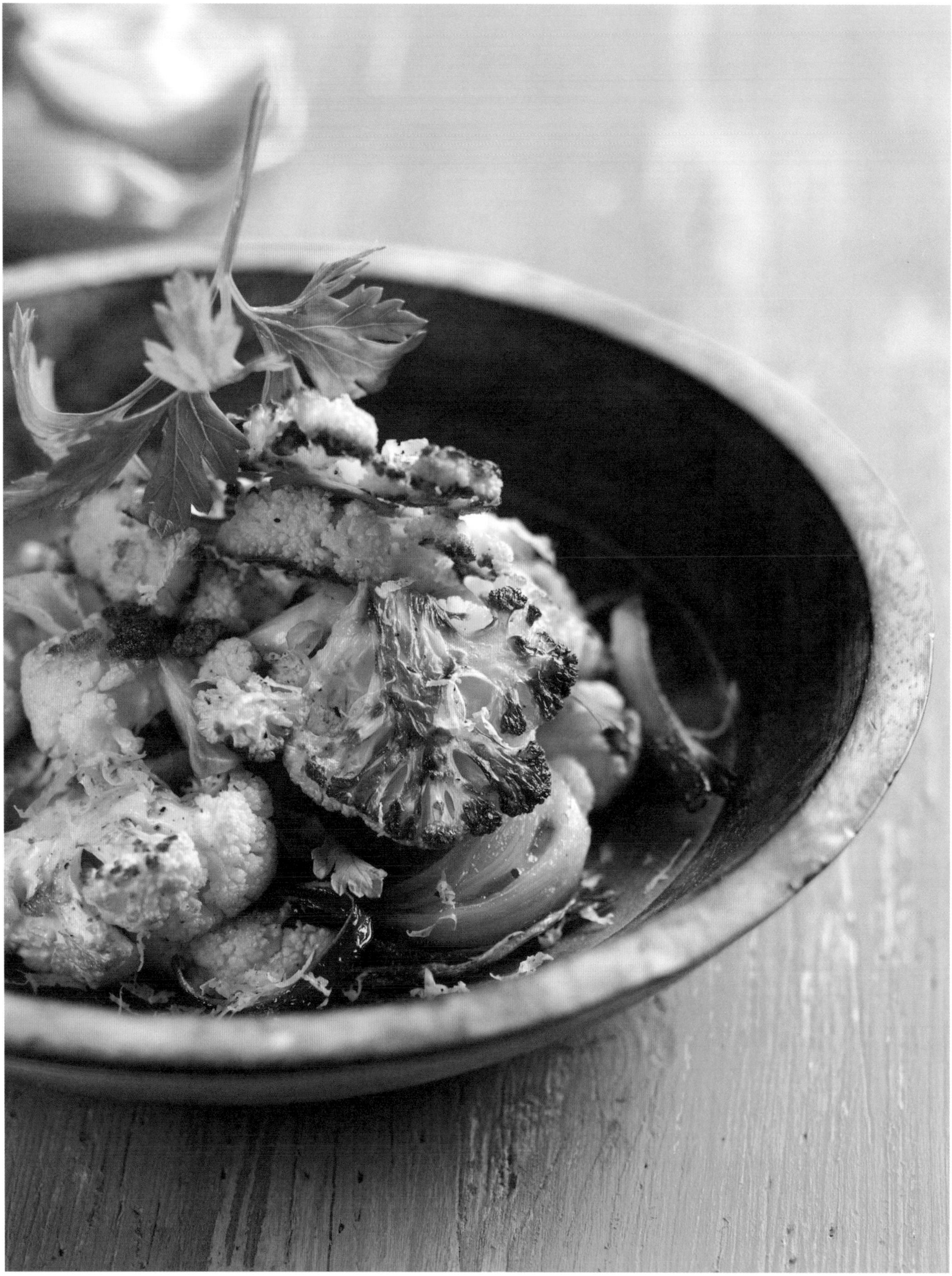

ROASTED CAULIFLOWER STEAKS

MAKES 4 TO 6 SERVINGS • **ACTIVE TIME: 30 MINUTES** • **START TO FINISH: 60 MINUTES**

There's something about roasting cauliflower that accentuates its sweet, nutty flavor. Season it with warm, earthy spices like cumin and turmeric, and you have a delicious alternative to a starchy side, full of flavor and nutrition.

1½ tablespoons olive oil

1 teaspoon salt

Freshly ground pepper to taste

½ teaspoon ground cumin

½ teaspoon ground coriander

½ teaspoon turmeric

¼ teaspoon cayenne pepper

1 medium head of cauliflower, stem and green leaves removed

1. Preheat the oven to 425° F.

2. In a bowl, combine the oil, salt, pepper, and spices and whisk to mix thoroughly.

3. Cut the cauliflower cross-wise into ½-inch slices. Put the slices in the skillet and brush the tops liberally with oil mixture. Turn the "steaks" over and brush the other side.

4. Put the skillet in the oven and roast for about 20 minutes, turning the pieces over after 10 minutes. A toothpick inserted in the flesh should go in easily to indicate that the cauliflower is cooked through.

5. Serve the slices hot, with a side of crème fraîche or sour cream if desired.

Variation

This recipe can be made with cauliflower florets, too. Instead of slicing the cauliflower into cross sections, just pick off the florets. Put them in the bowl of seasoned oil and toss to coat. Put the florets in the skillet and bake, shaking the pan halfway through to turn the pieces.

POTATO PANCAKES

MAKES 6 TO 8 SERVINGS ✦ ACTIVE TIME: 60 MINUTES ✦ START TO FINISH: 90 MINUTES

The way to make the best-tasting potato pancakes is to get as much liquid out of the grated potatoes and onions as possible. This is a bit time-consuming, but it's worth it! You can also prepare the potato-onion mixture a day or two ahead of time and keep it in an airtight container in the refrigerator.

6 large russet potatoes, washed and peeled

1 large onion

3 eggs, beaten

¼ to ½ cup matzo meal

Salt and freshly ground pepper to taste

1 cup canola or vegetable oil

1. Using a hand grater or a food processor with a shredding attachment, grate the potatoes onto a large baking dish, and then transfer to a colander in the sink.

2. Grate the onion or use a knife to dice it very finely. Put the grated onion into a bowl.

3. Squeeze as much liquid out of the potatoes as possible. Take half of the grated potatoes, mix them with the onion, and process the mixture in a food processor or blender to create a rough puree. Don't overblend or chop, as the mix will get too starchy.

4. Put the puree in a separate colander so that it can drain. Let both colanders drain for another 20 to 30 minutes. Push down on both to release more liquid and squeeze them again before continuing with the recipe.

5. Combine the puree and the remaining potatoes in a large bowl, and add the eggs and matzo meal. Stir to thoroughly combine. Season with salt and pepper.

6. Heat the skillet over medium-high heat and add the oil. Be careful making the pancakes, as the oil can splatter. Take spoonfuls of the potato mixture and place them in the oil. Cook for about 3 minutes a side. The pancakes should be golden brown on the outside and cooked through on the inside. You may need to adjust the temperature of the oil to get the right cooking temperature, especially if you have more than 3 pancakes in the skillet at one time.

7. When cooked, transfer to a plate lined with paper towels. Keep warm until ready to eat. Season with additional salt and pepper.

Variations

✻ Serve with chunky unsweetened applesauce and a small dollop of sour cream.

✻ Serve as you would French fries—with salt and vinegar, with ketchup, with gravy, or with salsa.

✻ For a nontraditional taco, top potato pancakes with chili and cheese.

SWEET POTATO PANCAKES

MAKES 6 TO 8 SERVINGS ✦ ACTIVE TIME: 60 MINUTES ✦ START TO FINISH: 90 MINUTES

Sweet potatoes aren't as moist as russet potatoes, so you won't need as much draining time with them. You will need to chop them finer to make a dough, however. Experiment until you get the right consistency.

6 large sweet potatoes, washed and peeled

1 large onion

3 eggs, beaten

½ cup matzo meal

½ teaspoon sugar

Salt and freshly ground pepper to taste

1 cup canola or vegetable oil

1. Finely chop the sweet potatoes into a colander in the sink.

2. Grate the onion or use a knife to dice very finely. Put the onion into a bowl.

3. Squeeze as much liquid out of the sweet potatoes as possible.

4. Combine the potatoes and onion and begin processing in a food processor or blender to turn the vegetables into a rough puree. Don't overblend or chop, as the mix will get too starchy.

5. Squeeze the puree through a fine-sieved colander to remove excess liquid, then let the mix sit and drain on its own for about 20 to 30 minutes.

6. Put the puree into a large bowl, and add the eggs, matzo meal, and sugar. Stir to thoroughly combine. Season with salt and pepper.

7. Heat the skillet over medium-high heat and add the oil. Be careful making the pancakes, as the oil can splatter. Take spoonfuls of the sweet potato mixture and place them in the oil. Cook for about 3 minutes a side. The pancakes should be golden brown on the outside and cooked through on the inside. You may need to adjust the temperature of the oil to get the right cooking temperature, especially if you have more than 3 pancakes in the skillet at one time.

8. When cooked, transfer the pancakes with a slotted spoon to a plate lined with paper towels. Keep warm until ready to eat. Season with additional salt and pepper.

These pancakes will probably not hold together as well as regular potato pancakes, but they are equally yummy and versatile. Serve with spinach and sour cream or refried beans. Or put some on a baking sheet, top with grated cheddar, and broil for a couple of minutes to melt the cheese.

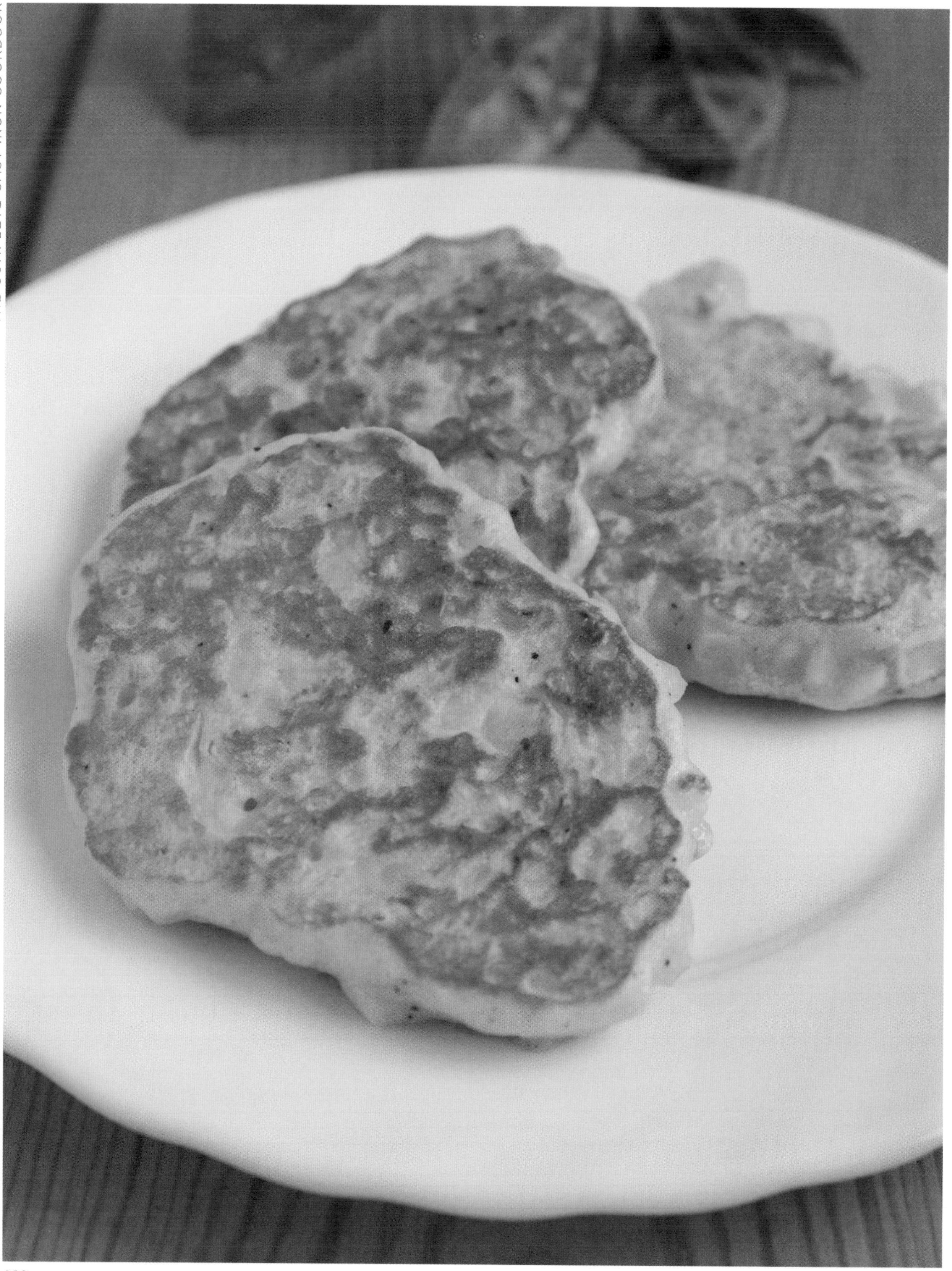

CORN FRITTERS

SERVES 4 ♦ ACTIVE TIME: 20 MINUTES ♦ START TO FINISH: 40 MINUTES

Sweet yet substantive, fancy yet simple, corn fritters are a family chef's best friend because they work no matter what the occasion.

1 egg, well beaten

1 teaspoon sugar

½ teaspoon salt

1 tablespoon butter, melted

2 teaspoons baking powder

1 cup flour

⅔ cup milk

2 cups cooked corn, cooled

1 tablespoon canola oil

1. In a large bowl, combine egg, sugar, salt, butter, baking powder, flour, and milk and stir thoroughly. Add the corn and mix.

2. Heat the skillet over medium-high heat and add the oil. Drop spoonfuls of batter into the skillet. Brown on both sides, about 3 minutes per side. Remove with a slotted spoon and put on a plate lined with paper towels to drain. Keep fritters warm while making more. Serve warm.

The best corn to use for this is leftover cooked corn on the cob that's been in the refrigerator overnight. Otherwise, you can take frozen corn and thaw the kernels, drying them before putting them in the batter. If you use canned corn, be sure all water is drained from it, and choose a high-quality brand so the kernels are firm and sweet, not mushy.

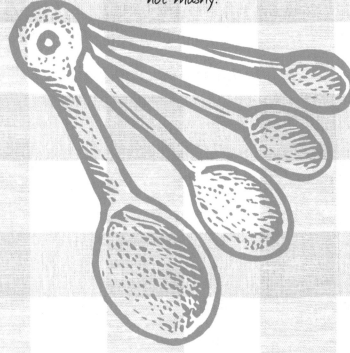

ROASTED ROOT VEGETABLES

MAKES 4 TO 6 SERVINGS ✦ ACTIVE TIME: 20 MINUTES ✦ START TO FINISH: 60 MINUTES

If you find yourself home on a fall morning with bunches of root vegetables that looked so good at the farmer's market but are now baffling you as a cook, this recipe will save you.

2 small parsnips, trimmed and scrubbed clean

1 turnip, trimmed and scrubbed clean

4 small beets, trimmed and scrubbed clean

4 medium carrots, trimmed and scrubbed clean

½ onion, sliced

1 small bulb fennel, trimmed and cut into slivers

¼ cup olive oil

Salt and pepper to taste

2 teaspoons dried rosemary, crumbled

1. Preheat the oven to 400° F.

2. Cut the cleaned vegetables in half or quarters to form bite-sized pieces.

3. In a large bowl, combine all cut vegetables and pour the olive oil over them. Season with salt and pepper and toss to coat.

4. Put the vegetables in the skillet and sprinkle the rosemary over everything.

5. Put the skillet in the oven and bake for about 40 minutes, turning the vegetables over after the first 20 minutes. Serve warm.

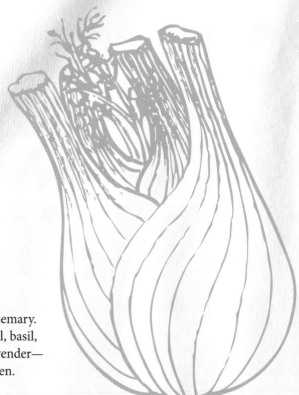

Variation

Substitute Herbes de Provence for the rosemary. This is a French blend of rosemary, fennel, basil, thyme, marjoram, basil, tarragon, and lavender— all the goodness of a Provençal herb garden.

SKILLET EGGPLANT PARM

SERVES 4 ✦ ACTIVE TIME: 20 MINUTES ✦ START TO FINISH: 60 MINUTES

Gooey goodness straight from the skillet, rich with garlic, fresh mozzarella, and Parmesan cheese—and the eggplant isn't fried, so it's not too heavy.

1 large eggplant

Salt for sprinkling on eggplant

2 tablespoons olive oil

1 cup bread crumbs (Italian seasoned)

2 tablespoons Parmesan cheese, grated

1 egg, beaten

Prepared marinara sauce (no sugar or meat added)

2 cloves garlic, pressed

8 oz. mozzarella cheese, shredded

1. Preheat the oven to 350˚ F.

2. Trim the top and bottom off the eggplant and slice the remainder into ¼-inch slices. Put the slices on paper towels in a single layer, sprinkle salt over them, and leave them for about 15 minutes. Turn the slices over, sprinkle with salt, and let sit for another 15 minutes.

3. Rinse the salt from all the pieces and dry with clean paper towels.

4. Drizzle oil over a baking sheet in preparation for the eggplant.

5. In a shallow bowl, combine the bread crumbs and Parmesan cheese. Put the beaten egg in another shallow bowl. Dip the slices of eggplant in egg, then the bread crumb mixture, coating both sides. Put them on the baking sheet.

6. Bake in the oven for about 10 minutes, turn them over, and bake another 10 minutes. Remove the sheet from the oven.

7. Put a layer of marinara sauce in the cast-iron skillet and stir in the pressed garlic. Lay the eggplant slices in the sauce, layering to fit. Top with the shredded mozzarella.

8. Put the skillet in the oven and bake for about 30 minutes, until the sauce is bubbling and the cheese is golden. Allow to cool for about 10 minutes, then serve with extra sauce if desired.

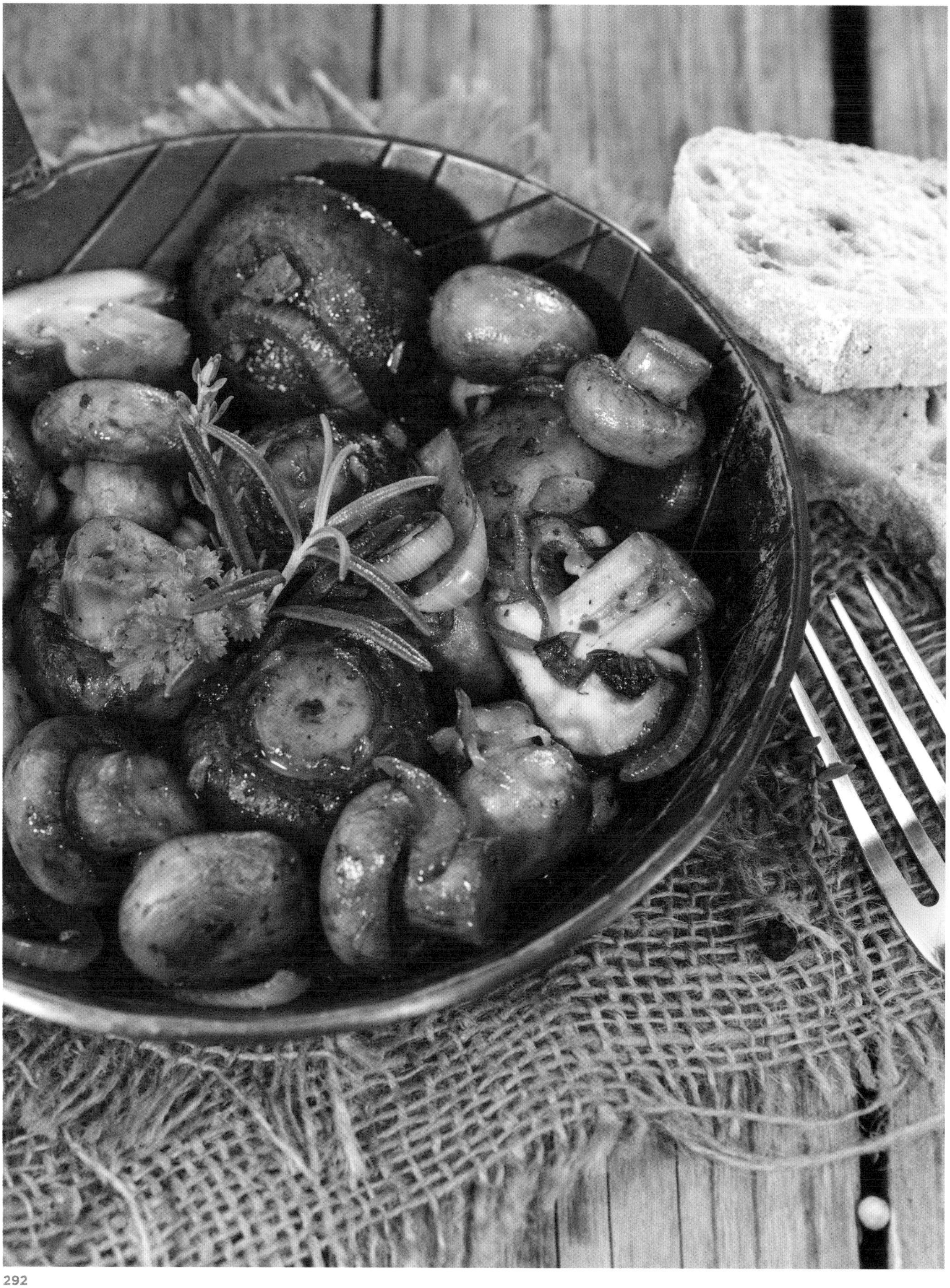

MARVELOUS MUSHROOMS

SERVES 4 ✦ ACTIVE TIME: 20 MINUTES ✦ START TO FINISH: 30 MINUTES

Sautéing mushrooms in the skillet with lots of butter yields a rich, earthy stew that is delicious with steak and potatoes. Or serve these mushrooms as a topping for burgers or baked polenta with cheese.

6 tablespoons butter, cut into pieces

1 pound mushrooms, sliced

1 teaspoon vermouth

Salt and pepper to taste

1. Heat the skillet over medium-high heat. Add the butter. When melted, add the mushrooms. Cook, while stirring, until the mushrooms begin to soften, about 5 minutes. Reduce the heat to low and let the mushrooms simmer, stirring occasionally, until they cook down, about 15 to 20 minutes.

2. Add the vermouth and stir, then season with salt and pepper. Allow to simmer until the mushrooms practically melt in your mouth. Serve hot.

There are many kinds of mushrooms available, and you can mix and match them as you desire. My favorite to use with this dish is the basic white mushroom.

YORKSHIRE PUDDING

This incredible treat is like a savory Dutch baby—a large (and delicious) popover. It's traditionally served with roast beef and is, in fact, made with the juices from the meat. Begin your preparation about an hour before the roast beef will be ready, as the batter needs to sit for a while. My mouth waters just thinking about this classic combination.

1½ cups flour

¾ teaspoon salt

¾ cup milk at room temperature

3 large eggs at room temperature

¾ cup water at room temperature

½ cup beef drippings

1. Preheat the oven to 400˚ F or increase the temperature when you take your roast beef out of the oven.

2. In a large bowl, mix the flour and salt together with a whisk. Make a well in the center of the flour, add the milk, and whisk until blended. Next beat the eggs into the batter until thoroughly combined. Add the water, stir this in thoroughly, and set the batter aside for about 1 hour.

3. When your roast beef comes out of the oven, pour off ½ cup of drippings and put them in the skillet. Put the skillet in the oven and let the drippings get very hot so that they sizzle. Stir the batter while you're waiting so it's blended. Remove the skillet from the oven, pour the batter in, and return the skillet to the oven immediately.

4. Bake for about 30 minutes or until the sides have risen and are gently browned.

5. Bring to the table where the roast beef awaits, and serve with extra juices on the side.

If you want to make this delicious side dish but you're not having roast beef, you can substitute 1/2 cup melted butter for the drippings. Butter's smoking point is lower than the drippings, so keep an eye on the skillet as it heats up in the oven. The butter will be sizzling before long.

DESSERTS

As you may have already discovered, the cast-iron skillet is remarkably versatile, doing its best "work" going from stovetop to oven, it seems, and being able to render something cooked to crunchy perfection on the outside while retaining a moist center. And desserts might be where this quality is best put to use. Did you know your cast-iron skillet is a pie plate? And a cookie sheet (OK, a small one, but still!)? And a cake pan? Best of all, it is a pan in which you can caramelize butter and sugar and sauté bananas, pears, apples, and other fruits to perfection.

KILLER VANILLA BREAD PUDDING

SERVES 4 TO 6 ✦ ACTIVE TIME: 45 MINUTES ✦ START TO FINISH: 2 HOURS

Here's a delicious and easy bread pudding that is sure to be loved by all members of the family. This is an easy dessert that will be gobbled up when it comes out of the oven—guaranteed! An important note, though: use high-quality ice cream so that it is as rich as possible.

4 tablespoons butter

4 cups croissants or a combination of baguette and croissant, cubed

2 eggs

1 teaspoon vanilla extract

1 gallon vanilla ice cream, softened

1. Place the skillet over low heat. Melt the butter, add the bread pieces to the skillet, and distribute evenly.

2. In a bowl, whisk the eggs and vanilla together. Add the softened ice cream and stir just enough to combine. Pour the mixture over the bread. Shake the skillet gently to distribute the liquid evenly.

3. Cover with tin foil, put in a cool place, and allow the mixture to rest for about 30 minutes so that the bread cubes become saturated.

4. Preheat the oven to 350° F.

5. Uncover the skillet and bake for 40 to 45 minutes until the cream mixture is set and it is slightly brown around the edges. Use pot holders or oven mitts to take the skillet out of the oven. Allow to cool for 5 to 10 minutes before inverting onto a serving dish. Serve immediately. No need for additional ice cream.

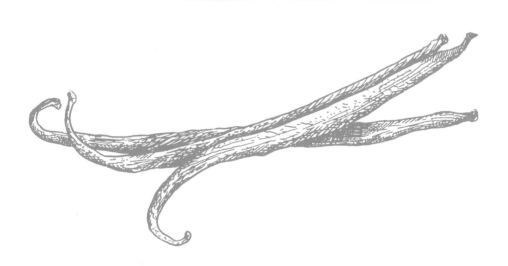

BUTTER PECAN BREAD PUDDING

SERVES 4 TO 6 ✦ ACTIVE TIME: 45 MINUTES ✦ START TO FINISH: 2 HOURS

If you want a super-simple, irresistible recipe for no-fail bread pudding, look no further. The addition of toasted pecan pieces sets this dish apart. The better the quality of the ice cream, the tastier the bread pudding will be and the better it will set up.

½ cup pecans, chopped

4 tablespoons butter

4 cups day-old bread, cubed

2 eggs

¼ cup rum

1 gallon vanilla ice cream, softened

1. Place the skillet over medium-high heat. When hot, add the chopped pecans. Using pot holders or oven mitts, shake the pecans in the skillet while they cook. You want them to toast but not brown or burn. This should take just a few minutes.

2. When toasted, transfer the pecans to a plate and allow to cool.

3. Add the butter to the skillet and, over low heat, let it melt. Add the bread pieces to the skillet and distribute evenly. Sprinkle the pecan pieces over the bread.

4. In a bowl, whisk the eggs and the rum together. Add the softened ice cream and stir just enough to combine. Pour this mixture over the bread and nuts. Shake the skillet gently to distribute the liquid evenly.

5. Cover with tin foil, put in a cool place, and allow the mixture to rest for about 30 minutes so that the bread cubes become saturated.

6. Preheat the oven to 350° F.

7. Uncover the skillet and bake for 40 to 45 minutes until the cream mixture is set and the edges are slightly browned. Use pot holders or oven mitts to take the skillet out of the oven. Allow to cool for 5 to 10 minutes before inverting onto a serving dish. Serve immediately. No need for additional ice cream.

Variation:

Make a pretty and patriotic red, white, and blue bread pudding by substituting strawberry ice cream for the vanilla and sprinkling fresh or frozen blueberries over the bread pieces before the skillet goes in the oven.

PINEAPPLE UPSIDE-DOWN CAKE

SERVES 8 TO 10 ✦ ACTIVE TIME: 60 MINUTES ✦ START TO FINISH: 2 HOURS

This is another recipe that is cooked to perfection in cast-iron. You'll see!

For the Fruit

4 tablespoons butter

1 (18 oz.) can pineapple rings, plus juice

½ cup dark brown sugar

Maraschino cherries (optional)

For the Cake

4 tablespoons butter, chilled

1 cup light brown sugar

2 eggs

1 cup buttermilk

1 teaspoon vanilla extract

1½ cups flour

1½ teaspoons baking powder

½ teaspoon salt

1. Preheat the oven to 350° F.

2. Heat the skillet over medium-high heat. Add the butter, the juice from the can of pineapples, and the brown sugar. Stir continuously while the sugar melts, and continue stirring until the liquid boils and starts to thicken. Cook until the sauce darkens and gains the consistency of caramel.

3. Remove from heat and place the pineapple rings in the liquid, working from the outside in. Place a cherry in the center of each ring, if adding cherries. Put the skillet in the oven while preparing the batter.

4. To make the cake, beat the cold butter and light brown sugar with an electric mixer until light and creamy. Beat in the eggs one at a time, making sure the first is thoroughly incorporated before adding the next. Add the buttermilk and vanilla extract.

5. In a small bowl, whisk together the flour, baking powder, and salt. Combine the dry and liquid mixtures and stir until combined but not overly smooth.

6. Remove the skillet from the oven and pour the batter over the pineapple rings. Return to the oven and bake for 45 minutes until the cake is golden and a knife inserted in the middle comes out clean.

7. Take the skillet out of the oven and let it rest for about 10 minutes.

8. Find a plate that is an inch or two larger than the top of the skillet and place it over the top. You will be inverting the cake onto the plate. Be sure to use oven mitts or secure pot holders, as the skillet will be hot. Holding the plate tightly against the top of the skillet, turn the skillet over so the plate is on the bottom. If some of the pineapple is stuck to the bottom of the skillet, gently remove it and place it on the cake.

9. Allow to cool a few more minutes, or set aside until ready to serve (it's better if it's served warm).

In 1925, Dole sponsored a pineapple recipe contest, promising to publish winning recipes in a book. The company received over 50,000 recipes, and over 2,000 of them were for pineapple upside-down cake. It's been a classic of American cooking ever since.

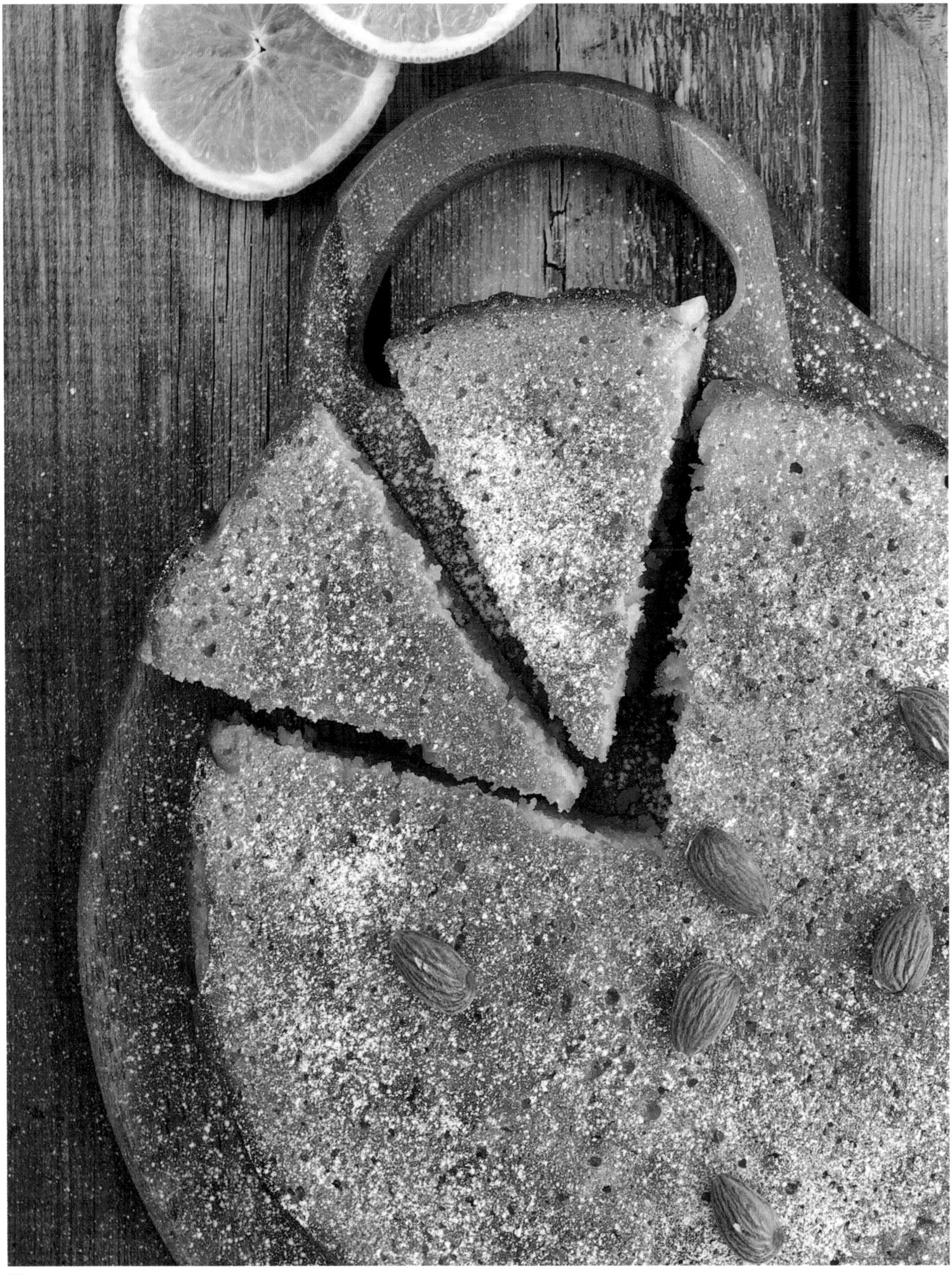

ORANGE CAKE

SERVES 6 TO 8 ✦ ACTIVE TIME: 40 MINUTES ✦ START TO FINISH: 90 MINUTES

When all your friends have flown south for the winter and you're listening to a forecast for snow, stop everything and make this cake. As it's cooling, take a fragrant bubble bath, wrap yourself in a fluffy robe, put on warm slippers, and have a piece of this cake with a glass of champagne.

¾ cup sugar

Zest of 2 oranges (about 2 tablespoons)

8 tablespoons (1 stick) butter, cut in pieces

3 eggs

1½ cups flour

1 teaspoon baking powder

½ cup orange juice (preferably fresh squeezed)

1. Preheat the oven to 350° F. Put the skillet in the oven.

2. In a large bowl, combine the sugar and orange zest, working them together so the zest penetrates the sugar. Add the butter and beat until the mixture is light and fluffy. Add the eggs one at a time, stirring to combine thoroughly after each addition.

3. In the measuring cup you use for the flour, add the baking powder and mix together. Alternately add the flour mixture and the orange juice to the butter-sugar mixture and stir until thoroughly combined.

4. Remove the skillet from the oven using pot holders or oven mitts. Pour the batter into it.

5. Put the skillet in the oven and bake for about 30 to 35 minutes, until the top is golden, the cake springs to the touch, and a toothpick inserted in the middle comes out clean. Remove skillet, let cool, and cut into wedges.

6. Serve with fresh whipped cream laced with Grand Marnier liqueur and a glass of champagne.

LEMON RASPBERRY CAKE

SERVES 6 TO 8   ACTIVE TIME: 40 MINUTES   START TO FINISH: 90 MINUTES

Bright, beautiful, and as delicious to eat as it is to look at, this is a cake you'll find yourself making repeatedly in the summer. Serve it with fresh raspberries, blueberries, or blackberries and a dollop of whipped cream laced with framboise *liqueur.*

½ cup fresh raspberries (substitute frozen if you don't have fresh, but drain them)

1 cup sugar, plus 1 tablespoon

Zest of 2 lemons (about 1 tablespoon)

6 tablespoons butter, cut in pieces

2 eggs

1 cup flour

1 teaspoon baking powder

½ cup sour cream

1. Preheat the oven to 350° F. Put the skillet in the oven.

2. In a small bowl, gently mash the raspberries and sprinkle with 1 tablespoon of sugar. Set aside.

3. In a large bowl, combine the remaining sugar and the lemon zest, working them together so the zest penetrates the sugar. Add the butter and beat until the mixture is light and fluffy. Add the eggs one at a time, stirring to combine thoroughly after each addition.

4. In the measuring cup you use for the flour, add the baking powder and mix the ingredients together. Alternately add the flour mix and the sour cream to the butter-sugar mix until thoroughly combined. Gently stir in the mashed raspberries. Be careful not to overmix.

5. Remove the skillet from the oven with pot holders or oven mitts, and fill with the batter.

6. Put the skillet in the oven and bake for about 30 to 35 minutes, until the top is golden, the cake springs to the touch, and a toothpick inserted in the middle comes out clean. Remove the skillet, let cool, and cut into wedges.

DOUBLE CHOCOLATE DECADENCE CAKE

SERVES 8 ✦ ACTIVE TIME: 20 MINUTES ✦ START TO FINISH: 60 MINUTES

When you are in the mood for a fudgy, easy chocolate cake, look no further than this recipe. It's so easy to make and so good. Beware!

6 tablespoons butter

1 cup semi-sweet chocolate morsels

1 (15.25 oz.) box of chocolate cake mix

1 cup water

½ cup vegetable oil

6 oz. unsweetened applesauce

4 eggs

1. Preheat the oven to 350˚ F.

2. In the skillet, melt the butter over medium heat. When it's melted, add the chocolate morsels. Reduce heat and cook until the chocolate is melted.

3. In a large bowl, combine the cake mix, water, oil, applesauce, and eggs. Stir to combine.

4. When the chocolate/butter mixture is melted and hot, but not bubbling, turn off the heat and pour the batter over the chocolate.

5. Place the skillet in the oven and bake for 35 to 40 minutes until the cake browned on the top and sides and a toothpick inserted in the middle comes out clean.

6. Remove the skillet from the oven and allow the cake to cool for about 10 minutes. The skillet will still be hot. Put a large serving plate on the counter and, working quickly and purposefully, flip the skillet so the cake is inverted onto the plate.

7. Allow to cool slightly before serving.

CHOCOLATE CAKE

SERVES 4 ✦ ACTIVE TIME: 20 MINUTES ✦ START TO FINISH: 60 MINUTES

This is a classic that you'll want to serve again and again, either plain or with a topping of your choice.

6 tablespoons butter, cut in pieces, plus more for greasing the skillet

1 cup sugar

2 eggs

½ teaspoon vanilla extract

1 cup flour

1 teaspoon baking powder

2 tablespoons unsweetened cocoa powder

½ cup milk

1. Preheat the oven to 350° F.

2. In a large bowl, beat the butter and sugar together until the mixture is light and fluffy. Add the eggs one at a time, stirring to combine thoroughly after each addition. Stir in the vanilla extract.

3. In a small bowl, combine the flour, baking powder, and cocoa powder, and mix together. Alternately add the flour mix and the milk to the butter-sugar mixture and stir until thoroughly combined.

4. Grease the skillet with butter and add the cake batter.

5. Put the skillet in the oven and bake for about 30 to 35 minutes, until the cake springs to the touch and a toothpick inserted in the middle comes out clean. Remove the skillet from the oven, let the cake cool, and cut into wedges.

Variation

There are so many ways to top this simple chocolate cake, including whipped cream, frosting, fresh berries, chocolate syrup, ice cream (almost any flavor), or marshmallow fluff.

BASIC CARROT CAKE

SERVES 8 ✦ ACTIVE TIME: 20 MINUTES ✦ START TO FINISH: 60 MINUTES

This recipe makes a delicious and moist carrot cake. It's especially tasty when frosted with an easy-to-make cream cheese frosting (see recipe below).

8 tablespoons (1 stick) butter

1 cup julienned carrots, finely chopped

1½ cups golden raisins

1 (15.25 oz.) box of carrot cake mix

¾ cup water

⅔ cup vegetable oil

6 oz. unsweetened applesauce

4 eggs

1. Preheat the oven to 350° F.

2. In the skillet, melt the butter over medium heat. When it's melted, add the carrots and raisins. Simmer over low to medium heat.

3. In a large bowl, combine the cake mix, water, oil, applesauce, and eggs. Stir to combine.

4. When the butter in the skillet is bubbling, turn off the heat and pour the cake batter over the carrot/raisin mixture.

5. Place the skillet in the oven and bake for 35 to 40 minutes, until the cake is browned on top and a toothpick inserted in the middle comes out clean.

6. Remove the skillet from the oven and allow the cake to cool for about 10 minutes. The skillet will still be hot. Put a large serving plate on the counter and, working quickly and purposefully, flip the skillet so the cake is inverted onto the plate. Allow to cool completely before frosting.

EASY CREAM CHEESE FROSTING

This makes enough to frost a single-layer skillet cake.

6 oz. cream cheese, at room temperature

4 tablespoons unsalted butter at room temperature

1¼ cups confectioners' sugar

½ teaspoon vanilla extract

1. In a large bowl, combine all ingredients. With an electric mixer, beat on medium until well combined and smooth.

2. Spread over cooled cake.

CARAMEL RAISIN SPICE CAKE

SERVES 8 ◆ ACTIVE TIME: 20 MINUTES ◆ START TO FINISH: 60 MINUTES

It's so much fun to shop for add-ins to cake mixes! When I discovered caramel raisins, I couldn't resist adding them to a spice cake mix—along with some chopped nuts. Here's the recipe. See if your family enjoys it as much as mine did (with a scoop of butter pecan ice cream).

8 tablespoons (1 stick) butter

1 (15.25 oz.) box of spice cake mix

1 (8 oz.) package caramel raisins

½ cup walnuts (or almonds or pecans), chopped

1 cup water

½ cup vegetable oil

6 oz. unsweetened applesauce

4 eggs

1. Preheat the oven to 350° F.

2. In the skillet, melt the butter over low to medium heat.

3. In a large bowl, combine the cake mix, caramel raisins, nuts, water, oil, applesauce, and eggs. Stir to combine.

4. When the butter in the skillet is hot, pour the batter over it.

5. Place the skillet in the oven and bake for 30 minutes, until the top of the cake is browned and a toothpick inserted in the middle comes out clean.

6. Remove the skillet from the oven and allow the cake to cool for about 10 minutes. The skillet will still be hot. Put a large serving plate on the counter and, working quickly and purposefully, flip the skillet so the cake is inverted onto the plate. Allow to the cake cool an additional 15 to 20 minutes before serving.

COCONUT BROWN SUGAR CAKE

SERVES 8 ✦ ACTIVE TIME: 20 MINUTES ✦ START TO FINISH: 60 MINUTES

It's so great to be able to make cakes that don't need frosting! The butter/sugar mixture that the cake cooks in adds all the deliciousness that a frosting would. Not only is it fewer calories, it's infinitely easier.

8 tablespoons (1 stick) butter

2 tablespoons dark brown sugar

1 (15.25 oz.) box of white cake mix

1 cup unsweetened coconut flakes

½ cup unsweetened shredded coconut

1¼ cups water

⅓ cup vegetable oil

6 oz. unsweetened applesauce

4 eggs

1. Preheat the oven to 350° F.

2. In the skillet, melt the butter over medium heat. When it's melted, sprinkle the brown sugar over it. Reduce the heat and let the sugar melt, taking care to not let the butter get too hot.

3. In a large bowl, combine the cake mix, coconut flakes, shredded coconut, water, oil, applesauce, and eggs. Stir to combine.

4. Pour the batter into the skillet. The butter/sugar mixture will come up over the sides of the batter, which is all part of the magic.

5. Place the skillet in the oven and bake for 25 to 30 minutes, until the cake is browned on top and a toothpick inserted in the middle comes out clean.

6. Remove the skillet from the oven and allow the cake to cool for about 10 minutes. The skillet will still be hot. Put a large serving plate on the counter and, working quickly and purposefully, flip the skillet so the cake is inverted onto the plate. Allow the cake to cool an additional 15 to 20 minutes before slicing and serving.

7. If you want to dress up this cake, serve with a scoop of vanilla ice cream and a drizzle of raspberry or chocolate sauce.

GERMAN CHOCOLATE CAKE

SERVES 8 ✦ ACTIVE TIME: 20 MINUTES ✦ START TO FINISH: 60 MINUTES

By adding some chocolate malt to a devil's food cake mix—and lots of yummy coconut— this cake takes on a distinctive flavor that's rich without being overly sweet. Which means you can put a layer of gooey coconut-pecan frosting (see recipe below) on it and really indulge.

8 tablespoons (1 stick) butter

1 (15.25 oz.) box of devil's food cake mix

⅓ cup chocolate Ovaltine

1 cup unsweetened coconut flakes

1 cup water

½ cup vegetable oil

6 oz. unsweetened applesauce

4 eggs

1. Preheat the oven to 350° F.

2. In the skillet, melt the butter over low to medium heat.

3. In a large bowl, combine the cake mix, Ovaltine, coconut flakes, water, oil, applesauce, and eggs. Stir to combine.

4. Pour the batter over the butter. Place the skillet in the oven and bake for 25 to 30 minutes, until the cake is browned on the top and a toothpick inserted in the middle comes out clean.

5. Remove the skillet from the oven and allow the cake to cool for about 10 minutes. The skillet will still be hot. Put a large serving plate on the counter and, working quickly and purposefully, flip the skillet so the cake is inverted onto the plate. Allow the cake to cool an additional 15 to 20 minutes before slicing and serving.

COCONUT-PECAN FROSTING

Makes enough to top one layer.

½ cup evaporated milk

½ cup sugar

1 egg yolk

4 tablespoons butter, cut into slices

½ teaspoon vanilla extract

½ cup sweetened flaked coconut

½ cup pecans, chopped

1. In a large saucepan, combine the evaporated milk, sugar, egg yolk, butter, and vanilla. Cook over medium heat, stirring frequently, until thickened, about 10 to 12 minutes. Add the coconut and pecans, stirring to combine. Remove the saucepan from heat and let cool, while stirring occasionally. Spread over the top of the cooled cake.

STRAWBERRY CAKE

SERVES 8 ✦ ACTIVE TIME: 20 MINUTES ✦ START TO FINISH: 60 MINUTES

Pink cake makes you feel happy, that's just a fact. This one won't disappoint. Make it as an everyday cake, or dress it up with a whipped cream frosting and pink sugar for Valentine's Day, Mother's Day, or a loved one's birthday.

1 (14 oz.) bag frozen sliced strawberries, thawed and juice reserved

1 cup strawberry juice and water

8 tablespoons (1 stick) butter

1 (15.25 oz.) box of strawberry or white cake mix

½ cup vegetable oil

6 oz. unsweetened applesauce

4 eggs

1. Preheat the oven to 350° F.

2. Set the bag of frozen strawberry pieces in a colander or strainer over a large measuring cup while they thaw so the juice is collected. Transfer thawed berries to a bowl, and add enough water to put 1 cup of liquid in the measuring cup.

3. In the skillet, melt the butter over low to medium heat.

4. In a large bowl, combine the strawberries, cake mix, strawberry water, oil, applesauce, and eggs. Stir to combine.

5. Pour the batter over the butter. Place the skillet in the oven and bake for 35 to 40 minutes, until the cake is golden brown on the top and a toothpick inserted in the middle comes out clean.

6. Remove the skillet from the oven and allow the cake to cool for about 10 minutes. The skillet will still be hot. Put a large serving plate on the counter and, working quickly and purposefully, flip the skillet so the cake is inverted onto the plate. Cool cake to room temperature before serving.

VANILLA-BUTTERSCOTCH PUDDING PIE

SERVES 6 TO 8 ✦ ACTIVE TIME: 40 MINUTES ✦ START TO FINISH: 2 HOURS

The layers in this pie are fashioned from the two flavors of pudding. The result is a pie that's as pleasing to the eye as it is to the tummy. Sprinkle with mini chocolate morsels for an extra treat.

1 graham cracker crust (see page 142)

1 (3.5 oz.) box instant vanilla pudding

1 (3.5 oz.) box instant butterscotch pudding

3 cups whole milk

½ cup semi-sweet mini chocolate morsels, or finely chopped white chocolate pieces (optional)

1. In a medium bowl, combine the vanilla pudding mix and 1½ cups of milk. Whisk until all the lumps are broken up, the pudding is smooth, and it has started to thicken, about 5 minutes.

2. Put the pudding in the graham cracker crust and refrigerate.

3. In another bowl, combine the butterscotch pudding mix and the remaining milk. Whisk until all the lumps are broken up, the pudding is smooth, and it has started to thicken, about 5 minutes.

4. Gently spread the butterscotch pudding over the vanilla pudding to form a second layer. Cover with plastic wrap and refrigerate for an hour or longer.

5. Before serving, sprinkle with the chocolate morsels or white chocolate pieces.

BANANA CREAM PIE

SERVES 6 TO 8 ✦ ACTIVE TIME: 30 MINUTES ✦ START TO FINISH: 6+ HOURS

This is simply a more decadent version of a classic banana pudding pie, as it is made from scratch and layered. Be prepared for the whole thing to be eaten in one sitting!

1 flaky pastry crust recipe for a single crust, baked (see page 136)

1 cup sugar

¼ cup cornstarch

½ teaspoon salt

3 cups milk

2 eggs

3 tablespoons butter, cut into pieces

1½ teaspoons vanilla

2 large bananas, not overly ripe

1 cup Cool Whip or fresh whipped cream

1. In a large saucepan, combine the sugar, cornstarch, salt, and milk and whisk together until smooth. Cook over medium heat, while stirring continuously, until thickened and just starting to boil, about 7 minutes. Reduce heat and cook, while continuing to stir, 2 minutes longer. Remove the saucepan from heat.

2. In a small bowl, whisk the eggs together. Add a scoop of the hot custard, stirring briskly so the eggs don't congeal or cook. When the hot custard is completely combined with the eggs, stir the egg mixture into the saucepan of custard.

3. Place the saucepan over medium heat and cook, while stirring constantly, until the mixture comes to a gentle boil. Continue to stir and cook for about 2 minutes. Remove from heat and stir in butter and vanilla. Cover with plastic wrap, pressing it onto the surface of the custard. Refrigerate for at least 30 minutes.

4. Spread half of the custard into the baked crust. Slice bananas and arrange over filling. Pour remaining custard over bananas. Spread Cool Whip or whipped cream on top.

5. Refrigerate at least 6 hours before serving.

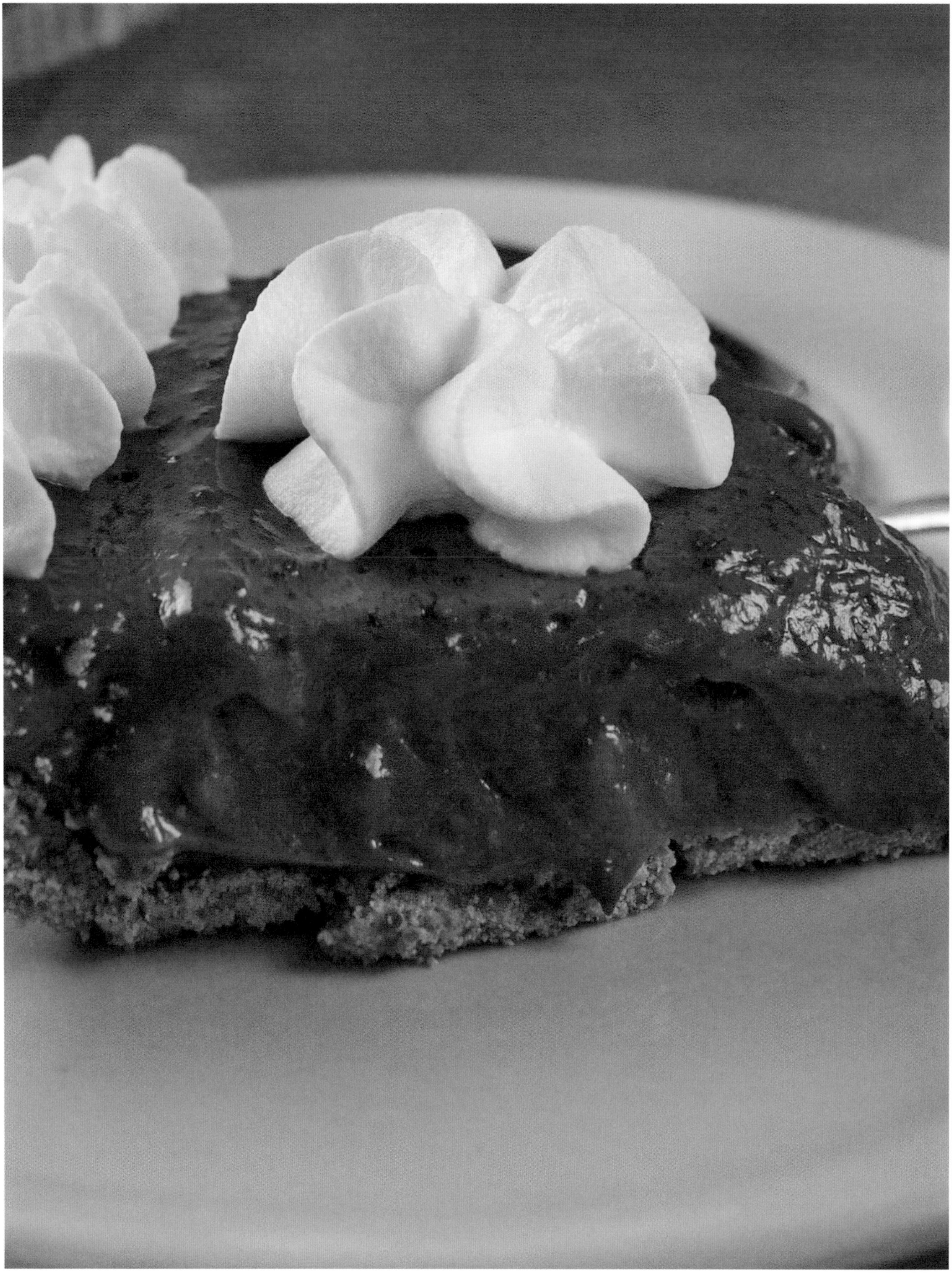

CHOCOLATE PUDDING PIE

SERVES 6 TO 8 ✦ ACTIVE TIME: 20 MINUTES ✦ START TO FINISH: 90 MINUTES

Whatever you do, don't skip adding the whipped topping on this pie. It truly is the "secret ingredient" that brings it all together. Garnishing with fresh raspberries or strawberry pieces adds flavor and color.

1 graham cracker crust (see page 142)

2 (3.5 oz.) boxes instant chocolate pudding (dark chocolate is preferable)

3 cups whole milk

2 cups Cool Whip or fresh whipped cream

Whole fresh raspberries or sliced strawberries for garnish (optional)

1. In a large bowl, combine the pudding mix and milk. Whisk until all the lumps are broken up, the pudding is smooth, and it has started to thicken, about 5 minutes.

2. Working with the crust in the skillet, transfer the pudding into the crust and cover with plastic wrap. Refrigerate for an hour or longer.

3. Before serving, top with your preferred whipped topping and garnish with the fruit, if desired.

CHOCOLATE SALTED PISTACHIO PUDDING PIE

SERVES 6 TO 8 ◆ ACTIVE TIME: 60 MINUTES ◆ START TO FINISH: 2 HOURS

So easy to make and so good! And so colorful, too. Kids love this one. And guess what? So do adults. It'll become a go-to recipe.

7 tablespoons butter, melted

8 oz. vanilla wafer cookies, crushed

2 oz. semi-sweet baking chocolate

¼ cup sweetened condensed milk

1 cup salted, shelled pistachio pieces

2 (3.4 oz.) boxes instant pistachio pudding mix

2 cups milk

1 cup Cool Whip or fresh whipped cream (optional)

1. Warm a cast-iron skillet over low heat and then place 1 tablespoon of the butter into it.

2. In a large bowl, mix the cookie crumbs with the remaining butter until combined. Carefully remove the cast-iron skillet from the heat and press the cookie mixture into the bottom of the pan to form a crust. Allow to cool and set.

3. In a small, microwave-safe bowl, microwave the chocolate in 15-second increments, removing to stir after each, until just melted. Stir in the sweetened condensed milk.

4. Pour the chocolate mixture over the pie crust. Sprinkle with half of the salted pistachio pieces. Refrigerate for about 30 minutes.

5. In a large bowl, whisk together the pudding mix and milk for about 3 minutes, until the mixture is smooth and thick. Put the pudding into the crust and spread evenly. Sprinkle with remaining pistachios. Add a layer of whipped topping, if desired.

6. Cover with plastic wrap and refrigerate for at least 1 hour and up to 1 day. When ready to serve, remove plastic wrap and sprinkle with additional salted pistachio pieces.

LEMON RICE PUDDING PIE

SERVES 6 TO 8 ✦ ACTIVE TIME: 30 MINUTES ✦ START TO FINISH: 3 OR MORE HOURS

I had leftover rice one night and I thought it would be a nice texture and flavor addition to a pudding pie. I chose lemon pudding for the filling and enhanced the flavor with some fresh squeezed lemon juice and vanilla extract. This is now a family favorite.

1 graham cracker crust (see page 142)

1 (3.4 oz.) box instant lemon pudding mix

2 cups whole milk

1 tablespoon fresh squeezed lemon juice

1 teaspoon vanilla extract

1½ to 2 cups cooked rice (brown rice is best)

1 cup Cool Whip or fresh whipped cream

Cinnamon (optional)

1. In a large bowl, combine the lemon pudding mix and milk. Whisk until all the lumps are broken up, the pudding is smooth, and it has started to thicken, about 3 minutes. Stir in the lemon juice and vanilla, then stir in the rice.

2. Working with the crust in the skillet, transfer the filling into the piecrust. Put a piece of plastic wrap over it, covering the filling, and refrigerate for 2 or more hours before serving.

3. Top with your preferred whipped topping and sprinkle with cinnamon, if desired.

PINEAPPLE CREAM PIE

**SERVES 6 TO 8 ✦ ACTIVE TIME: 40 MINUTES ✦
START TO FINISH: 3 TO 24 HOURS**

*This creamy pie has the great zing of pineapple, plus it's really fun to decorate with
the pineapple rings and maraschino cherries. The result is a modern take on pineapple
upside–down cake.*

**1 baked crust
(see page 135)**

½ cup sugar

**3 tablespoons
cornstarch**

¼ teaspoon salt

1¾ cups milk

**¾ cup pineapple juice
from a can of sliced
pineapple rings**

3 egg yolks

1 tablespoon butter

**1 (20 oz.) can pineapple
rings**

Maraschino cherries

1. In a medium saucepan, combine the sugar, cornstarch, and salt. Whisk to
combine. Stir in the milk until smooth. Cook over medium-low heat, stirring
constantly, until mixture begins to thicken and just begins to boil. Reduce heat
so that the mixture does not come to a rolling boil. Add the pineapple juice
and continue to stir until thoroughly combined. Remove from heat.

2. In a small bowl, whisk the egg yolks. Add a large spoonful of the pineapple
cream and stir rapidly to prevent curdling or cooking. Repeat, being sure
to stir rapidly. Next, stir the egg mixture into the saucepan containing
the pineapple cream, and stir briskly to combine. Return saucepan to low
heat, and stir in the butter. Continue to stir while cooking, until the mixture
thickens considerably, about 5 minutes.

3. Working with the crust in the skillet, transfer the mixture into the piecrust
and spread evenly. Cover with plastic wrap and refrigerate several hours or
up to 1 day.

4. When ready to serve, remove plastic wrap and decorate with pineapple rings
and maraschino cherries, putting the cherries in the centers of the rings or
as desired.

327

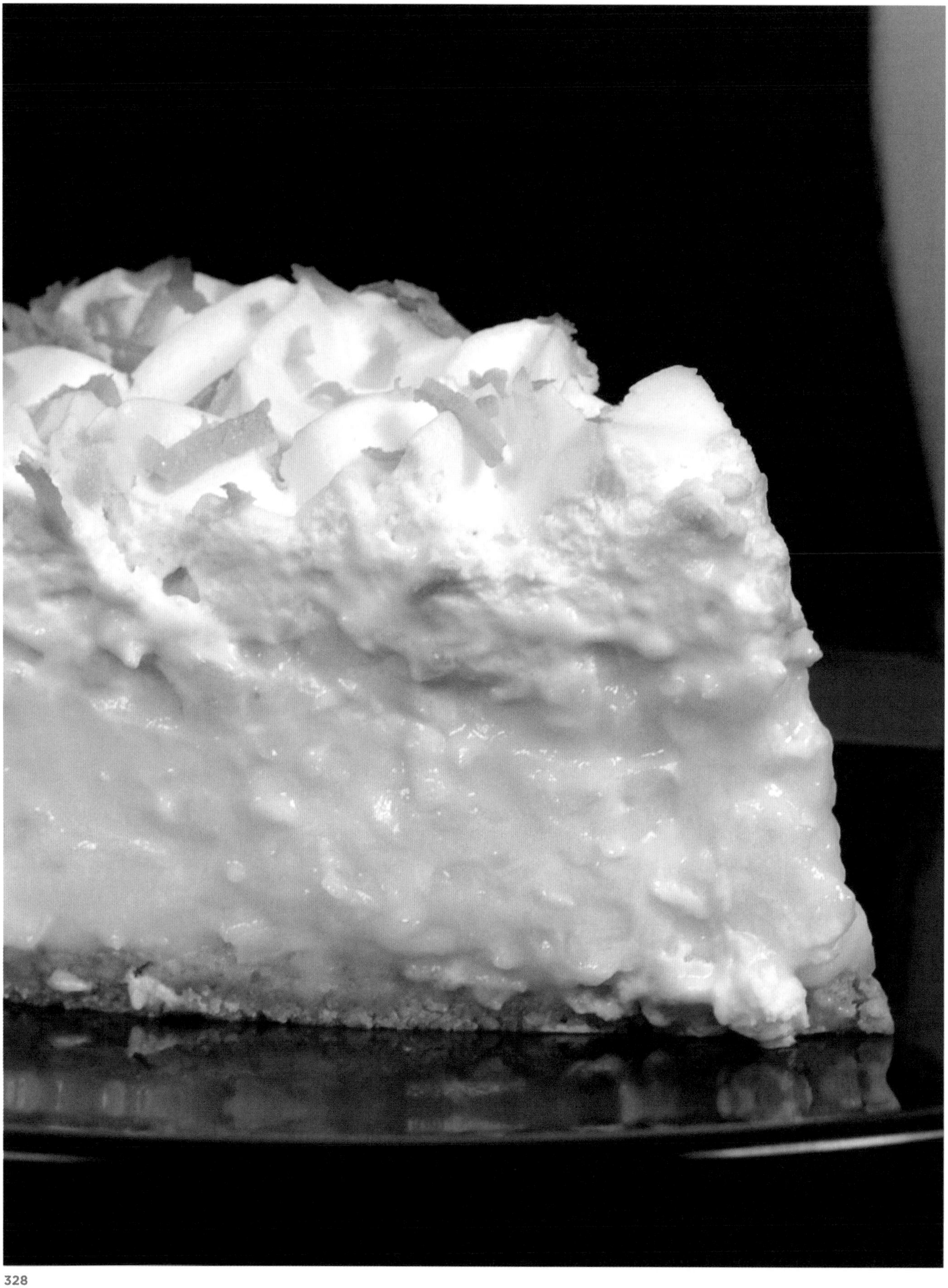

COCONUT CREAM PIE

SERVES 6 TO 8 ✦ ACTIVE TIME: 60 MINUTES ✦ START TO FINISH: 2 OR MORE HOURS

Make this pie on a cold day if you want to feel like you're taking a vacation in the tropics. Make it on a warm day if you love the taste of coconut and all the beachy associations it brings with it. Make it any time, because it's really good.

1 baked crust
(see page 135)

1 cup sugar

¼ cup cornstarch

½ teaspoon salt

3 cups milk

2 eggs

3 tablespoons butter,
cut into pieces

1 teaspoons vanilla
extract

½ teaspoon coconut
extract or coconut rum

1½ cups unsweetened
coconut flakes

1. In a large saucepan, combine the sugar, cornstarch, salt, and milk and whisk together until smooth. Cook over medium heat, stirring continuously, until thickened and just starting to boil, about 7 minutes. Reduce heat and continue stirring for 2 minutes. Remove saucepan from heat.

2. In a small bowl, stir the eggs together until combined. Add a scoop of the hot custard, stirring briskly so the eggs don't congeal or cook. When the hot custard is completely combined with the eggs, stir the egg mixture into the saucepan.

3. Bring the saucepan to a gentle boil over medium heat, while stirring constantly. Continue to cook, while stirring, for about 2 minutes. Remove from heat and stir in butter, vanilla, and coconut extract or rum. Gently fold in the unsweetened coconut, stirring just to combine. Cover with plastic wrap, pressing it onto surface the custard. Refrigerate for at least 30 minutes.

4. Working with the crust in the skillet, transfer the pudding into it, cover with plastic wrap again, and refrigerate for at least 1 hour before serving.

CHOCOLATE-ESPRESSO CREAM PIE

SERVES 6 TO 8 ✦ ACTIVE TIME: 45 MINUTES ✦
START TO FINISH: 2 TO 24 HOURS

For those of us who love the combination of chocolate and coffee, this pie is a winner. The espresso adds an earthiness and additional layer of flavor that is rich and satisfying. I like to use a chocolate graham cracker crust for this pie, but if that seems like too much, use a baked crust instead.

1 chocolate graham cracker crust (see page 142)

3½ cups heavy cream

1 (11.5 oz.) bag of semi-sweet chocolate morsels

1 teaspoon vanilla extract

1 tablespoon instant espresso powder or coffee

Pinch of salt

½ cup almond pieces, toasted (optional)

1. In a heavy-bottomed saucepan, heat 2 cups of heavy cream over medium heat until heated through. Stir in the chocolate morsels and stir until melted. Add the vanilla, espresso powder or coffee, and the salt, and continue to stir until thoroughly combined. Remove from heat and set aside.

2. In a large bowl, beat the remaining cream with an electric mixer until it forms stiff peaks. Fold the whipped cream into the chocolate-espresso mixture. Working with the crust in the skillet, transfer the filling to the piecrust, spreading evenly to fill. Cover with plastic wrap and refrigerate for at least 1 hour and up to 1 day.

3. Top with toasted almond pieces if desired.

CHOCOLATE MOUSSE PIE

SERVES 6 TO 8 ✦ ACTIVE TIME: 45 MINUTES ✦
START TO FINISH: SEVERAL HOURS OR OVERNIGHT

Doesn't this sound amazingly good? The secret is the darkness and richness of the chocolate filling, which is why it's made with heavy cream and dark chocolate morsels. You can change this one up, too, by making different kinds of cookie crusts or by using a nut crust (hazelnut would be wonderful).

1 chocolate graham cracker crust (see page 142)

4 cups heavy cream

1 (10 oz.) bag of dark chocolate morsels

2 cups mini marshmallows

1 teaspoon vanilla extract

Pinch of salt

¼ cup confectioners' sugar

2 tablespoons unsweetened cocoa powder

1. In a heavy-bottomed saucepan, heat 2 cups of the heavy cream over medium heat until heated through. Stir in the chocolate morsels and stir until melted. Add the marshmallows, vanilla, and salt, and continue to stir until marshmallows are melted and combined. Remove from heat and set aside.

2. In a large bowl, beat 1 cup of the cream with an electric mixer until it forms stiff peaks. Fold the whipped cream into the chocolate mixture. Working with the crust in the skillet, transfer chocolate filling to the piecrust, spreading evenly to fill. Cover with plastic wrap and refrigerate for at least 1 hour and up to 1 day.

3. Before serving, beat the remaining 1 cup of heavy cream in a bowl with an electric mixer. As the cream stiffens, add the confectioners' sugar and cocoa powder. Continue to beat until stiff peaks form.

4. Remove the pie from refrigerator and top with the whipped cream before serving.

LEMON MERINGUE PIE

SERVES 6 TO 8 ✦ ACTIVE TIME: 60 MINUTES ✦ START TO FINISH: 90 MINUTES

This is one of my very favorite pies, and while there are several ways you can make it, this one is the best. Be sure to use fresh squeezed lemon juice, not the juice that's already pressed. It makes a huge difference.

1 baked crust (see page 135)

⅓ cup cornstarch

1½ cups sugar

1½ cups water

Zest of 1 lemon

½ cup fresh squeezed lemon juice

4 eggs, separated

1 tablespoon butter

¼ teaspoon salt, plus a pinch

1. Preheat the oven to 400° F.

2. In a saucepan, combine the cornstarch, 1 cup of the sugar, and pinch of salt. Whisk to combine. Stir in the water, lemon zest, and lemon juice. Cook over medium heat, stirring constantly until mixture comes to a boil. Remove the saucepan from heat.

3. In the bowl with the egg yolks, add a spoonful of the hot lemon mixture. Stir rapidly to combine so the eggs don't cook or curdle. Add another spoonful of the lemon mixture and repeat. Transfer the egg yolk mixture to the saucepan and stir constantly to combine well.

4. Cook over medium heat while continuing to stir. Add the butter. Stir until butter is completely melted and blended and the mixture has thickened, about 3 minutes.

5. Working with the crust in the skillet, transfer the filling into the piecrust.

6. In a large bowl, beat the egg whites and the remaining salt with an electric mixer on high until soft peaks form. Continue to beat, adding 2 tablespoons of the remaining sugar at a time until all the sugar has been beaten in and the egg whites have formed stiff peaks.

7. Spoon onto the lemon filling and spread to cover evenly.

8. Put the skillet in the oven for about 10 minutes until the meringue is just golden.

9. Remove skillet and allow to cool completely before serving.

GLUTEN-FREE GRAPEFRUIT CUSTARD PIE

SERVES 6 TO 8 ✦ ACTIVE TIME: 60 MINUTES ✦
START TO FINISH: 3 TO 24 HOURS

This came to a dinner party I attended by way of a native Texan. She claimed that the grapefruits that grew in her yard produced something far tastier than what she made for us in New York, and if so, I'm not sure how she ever moved. The pie became an instant favorite of mine. I like it with vanilla ice cream.

1 gluten-free crust
(see page 138)

2½ cups sugar

½ cup all-purpose
gluten-free flour

4 egg yolks

4 red grapefruits,
peeled, pith removed,
and sections halved

2 cups water

1 (16 oz.) can sweetened
condensed milk

1 teaspoon vanilla
extract

Vanilla ice cream

Grapefruit or kiwi slices
for garnish

1. In a small bowl, stir 2 cups of sugar and the flour together until combined. In another bowl, whisk the egg yolks until well combined. Set aside.

2. Place the grapefruit pieces in a saucepan and add the water. Cook over medium heat, while stirring constantly, until the water comes to a boil. Add remaining ½ cup sugar and continue to stir while the mixture boils, another 10 or so minutes. The grapefruit sections will fall apart and yield a thick, pulpy mixture.

3. Remove the saucepan from heat and stir in the sugar/flour mixture. Add the sweetened condensed milk and stir gently to combine.

4. Put a large spoonful of the hot grapefruit mixture into the egg yolks and whisk or stir briskly to combine. Repeat, and then transfer the egg yolk mixture to the saucepan and stir to combine. Return the saucepan to the heat and bring to a boil, while stirring constantly, and cook for about 10 minutes more. Remove from heat and stir in the vanilla.

5. Working with the crust in the skillet, transfer the filling into the piecrust and distribute evenly. Cover with plastic wrap and refrigerate for several hours or up to 1 day. When ready to serve, remove the plastic wrap and garnish with fruit slices, if desired. Top with vanilla ice cream.

YOGURT CUSTARD PIE WITH BLACKBERRY PRESERVES

**SERVES 6 TO 8   ACTIVE TIME: 60 MINUTES
START TO FINISH: 3 TO 24 HOURS**

If you want a pie that's a bit healthier than the rich desserts featured in this chapter, this one's for you. Greek yogurt is thick and creamy and just a little tart, and makes a delicious, custard-y filling. Put it in a nut crust (you could use any of the ones described on page 144, but I prefer the almond crust), and top with warmed preserves and you have an easy, instant hit.

**1 almond crust
(see page 144)**

**1 cup low-fat plain
Greek yogurt**

2 eggs, lightly beaten

¼ cup sugar

**3 tablespoons fresh
squeezed lemon juice**

**1 teaspoon pure vanilla
extract**

**½ cup blackberry
preserves, warmed**

Fresh berries for garnish

1. Preheat the oven to 350° F.

2. In a large bowl, whisk together the yogurt, eggs, sugar, lemon juice, and vanilla.

3. Working with the crust in the skillet, transfer the filling into the piecrust and distribute evenly.

4. Put the skillet in the oven and bake for 25 minutes, until the filling is just set. A toothpick inserted in the side of the pie will come out clean, but the center can still look slightly undercooked.

5. Remove the skillet from the oven and allow the pie to cool for 5 to 10 minutes. Heat the preserves in a small saucepan or a microwave-safe bowl. Spread over the yogurt filling, add fruit for garnish, cover with plastic wrap, and refrigerate for several hours to 1 day.

DESSERTS

339

BANANAS FOSTER

MAKES 3 TO 6 SERVINGS ✦ ACTIVE TIME: 10 MINUTES ✦ START TO FINISH: 20 MINUTES

As elegant as it is delicious, Bananas Foster is a New Orleans classic. It's great fun (and a fabulous spectacle) to light this dessert on fire, but there's a gastronomic reason to do it, too—the intense heat caramelizes the butter and rum on the bananas!

3 ripe bananas

6 tablespoons butter

½ cup brown sugar, packed

½ teaspoon cinnamon

¼ cup dark rum

3 tablespoons banana liqueur

Long matches or a lighter

Vanilla ice cream

Pecans, chopped (optional)

Mint leaves for garnish (optional)

1. Peel the bananas and cut them in half lengthwise.

2. Heat the skillet over medium-high heat and add the butter, cooking until it melts. Add the brown sugar and cinnamon and stir until incorporated.

3. Lay the banana pieces on the bubbling butter mixture and let cook for about 2 minutes per side. When the bananas are soft and coated with the butter, pour the rum over them. Have someone else turn off the lights in the kitchen while you get ready to strike the match or lighter. Swirl the rum around in the pan and light it on fire. The flame will burn for just a minute or so as the alcohol burns off. When the flame dies down, the dessert is ready.

4. Put the bananas on plates with a scoop of vanilla ice cream—or put the ice cream over them in the skillet and eat out of it. Top with chopped pecans and mint leaves, if desired.

Proceed with caution on this one. The long-stemmed lighters that are made for lighting grills and fireplaces are great for this. You want to make sure there's nothing flammable near the stove when you light the bananas. Move the bottle of rum, be sure your hair is tied back, and hold the pan with an oven mitt, not a dish towel.

PRALINE RED VELVET CAKE

SERVES 8 ✦ ACTIVE TIME: 20 MINUTES ✦ START TO FINISH: 60 MINUTES

This cake verges on the elegant—there's something about red velvet that looks exotic and special—and it can be served with no regrets at a dinner party. The butter-brown sugar-pecan topping is crunchy and delicious.

8 tablespoons (1 stick) butter

½ cup dark brown sugar

1 cup pecans, chopped

1 (15.25 oz.) box of red velvet cake mix

1 cup water

½ cup vegetable oil

6 oz. unsweetened applesauce

4 eggs

1. Preheat the oven to 350˚ F.

2. In the skillet, melt the butter over medium heat. When thoroughly melted and just starting to bubble, sprinkle the brown sugar over it, then distribute the chopped pecans evenly over the mixture. Lower the heat but continue to cook until the butter is just bubbling.

3. In a large bowl, combine the cake mix, water, oil, applesauce, and eggs. Stir to combine.

4. When the butter in the skillet is melted, turn off the heat and pour in the batter.

5. Place the skillet in the oven and bake 35 to 40 minutes until the cake is golden brown on the top and a toothpick inserted in the middle comes out clean.

6. Remove the skillet and allow the cake to cool for about 15 minutes. Run a spatula around the edges and toward the bottom to loosen any sugar or nuts. Put a large serving plate on the counter and, working quickly and purposefully, flip the skillet so the cake is inverted onto the plate. Cool to room temperature before serving.

LEMON BRÛLÉE PIE

SERVES 6 TO 8 ✦ ACTIVE TIME: 30 MINUTES ✦ START TO FINISH: 2 HOURS

Another zinger of a lemon pie, loaded with fresh lemon juice and heavy cream, two nearly perfect ingredients. As this pie bakes in the oven for nearly an hour, it fills your home with its lemony goodness. Delicious in every way.

1 baked crust
(see page 135)

6 eggs

1¼ cups sugar

Zest from 2 lemons

¾ cup fresh squeezed
lemon juice (don't use
bottled lemon juice)

2 teaspoons lemon
liqueur (optional but
worth it)

⅔ cup heavy cream

1. Preheat the oven to 300° F.

2. In a large bowl, beat the eggs until just combined. Add the sugar, zest, lemon juice and lemon liqueur, and whisk or stir until well combined and sugar is dissolved.

3. Stir in heavy cream.

4. Fill crust with lemon/cream mixture, tapping to distribute filling evenly.

5. Bake for 50 to 60 minutes, testing after 50 minutes to see if center is set. If it is, remove from oven. If it's still runny, continue baking, testing after another 5 minutes, etc., until set in center.

6. Allow to cool before serving.

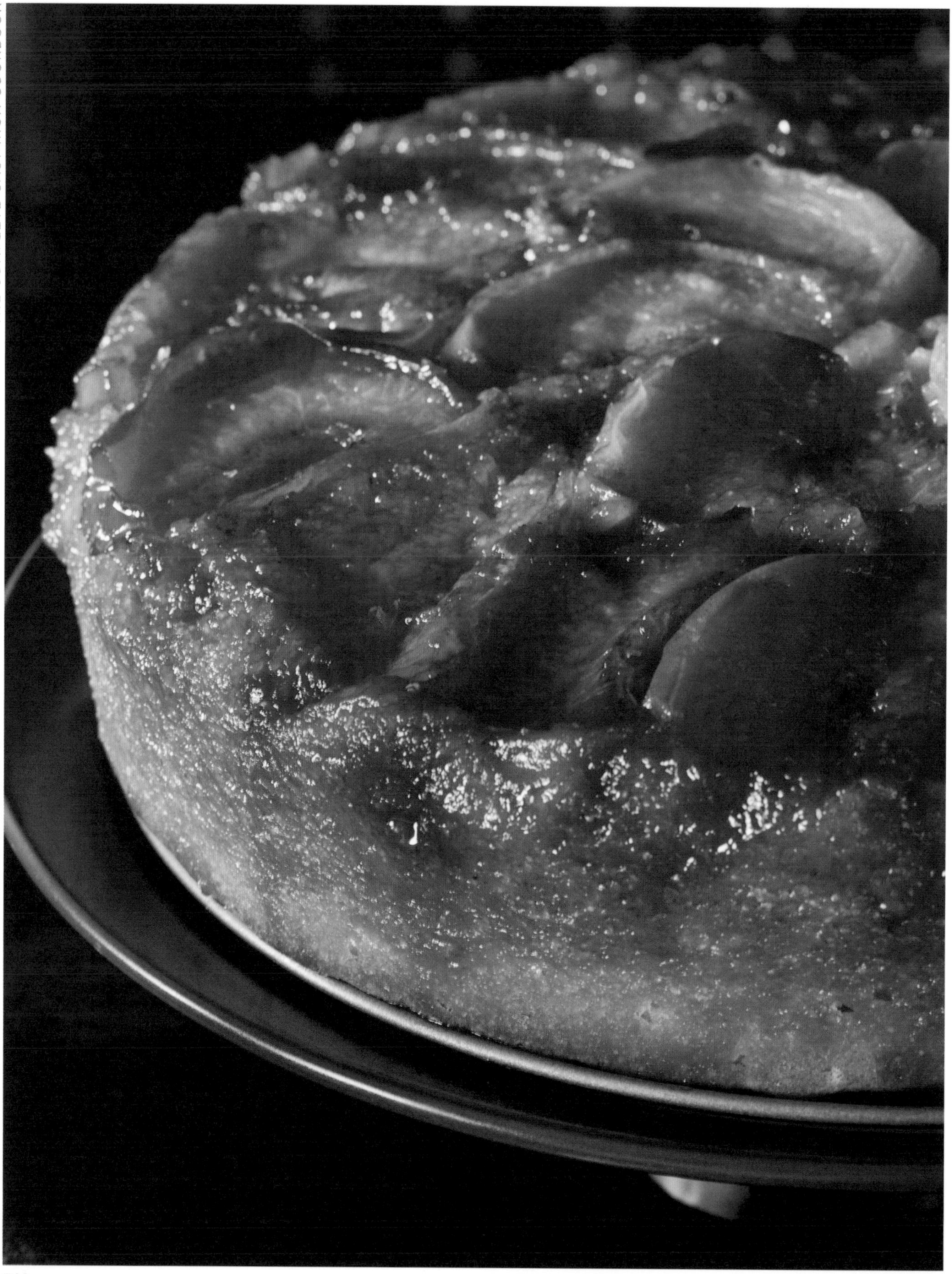

PEACHY KEEN CAKE

SERVES 8 ✦ ACTIVE TIME: 20 MINUTES ✦ START TO FINISH: 60 MINUTES

If you find yourself yearning for the taste of juicy peaches and they're not in season, whip up this cake. It'll get you through until the real thing is available. And when you can use ripe peaches instead of canned peaches, just make the switch. The cake will taste equally wonderful. I like to add a touch of almond extract as I think it enhances the peach flavor.

8 tablespoons (1 stick) butter

½ pound fresh peaches, sliced, or 1 can sliced or chopped peaches with no sugar added, drained

1 (15.25 oz.) box of yellow cake mix

1 cup water

½ cup vegetable oil

6 oz. unsweetened applesauce

4 eggs

¼ teaspoon almond extract

1. Preheat the oven to 350° F.

2. In the skillet, melt the butter over medium heat. When it's melted, add the fruit. Allow the fruit to simmer in the butter over low to medium heat until the butter is bubbling but not browning.

3. In a large bowl, combine the cake mix, water, oil, applesauce, eggs, and almond extract. Stir to combine.

4. When the butter in the skillet is bubbling, turn off the heat and pour the batter over the fruit.

5. Place the skillet in the oven and bake 35 to 40 minutes until the cake is browned on the top and a toothpick inserted in the middle comes out clean.

6. Remove the skillet from the oven and allow to cool for about 10 minutes. The skillet will still be hot. Put a large serving plate on the counter and, working quickly and purposefully, flip the skillet so the cake is inverted onto the plate. Serve with butter pecan ice cream for a flavor sensation.

THE BEST SKILLET BROWNIES

SERVES 6 TO 8 ✦ ACTIVE TIME: 40 MINUTES ✦ START TO FINISH: 90 MINUTES

If you're serious about chocolate brownies, you'll love this recipe. When shopping for the ingredients, remember that the better the chocolate, the better the taste and texture of the brownie. What gets baked up in the cast-iron skillet is a gooey yet crunchy confection that is heaven in every bite. Don't even wait to slice and serve them—serve them right out of the skillet (when cool enough). Be sure to have friends and family around when you do, as you may be tempted to eat the whole pan by yourself, and that wouldn't be good.

10 tablespoons unsalted butter

8 oz. semi-sweet chocolate, coarsely chopped

1 cup sugar

3 eggs at room temperature

1 teaspoon vanilla extract

½ cup all-purpose flour, plus 2 tablespoons

2 tablespoons unsweetened cocoa powder

¼ teaspoon salt

1 cup semi-sweet chocolate chips

1. Preheat the oven to 350° F.

2. In a microwave-safe bowl, microwave 9 tablespoons of the butter and chopped chocolate pieces together, cooking in 15-second increments and stirring after each. The butter and chocolate should be just melted together and smooth.

3. In a large bowl, whisk the sugar in with the eggs. Add the vanilla and stir to combine. Working in batches, start mixing the melted chocolate into the mixture, stirring vigorously to combine after each addition. In a small bowl, mix the flour, cocoa powder, and salt. Gently fold the dry ingredients into the chocolate mixture. Next, fold in the chocolate chips.

4. Over medium heat, melt 1 tablespoon butter in the skillet. When melted, pour in the batter. Place the skillet in the oven and bake for about 30 minutes or until a toothpick inserted in the center comes out with a few moist crumbs. It may need a couple more minutes, but be careful not to over-bake this or you'll lose the great gooeyness. When it's ready, remove the skillet from the oven and allow to cool for about 10 minutes.

5. Dig right in, or scoop into bowls and serve with your favorite ice cream.

Variation

Enhance the flavor further and add a ½ teaspoon of peppermint extract and 1½ cups of chopped York Peppermint Patties to the batter.

STRAWBERRY RHUBARB BISCUIT COBBLER

MAKES 4 SERVINGS ✦ ACTIVE TIME: 30 MINUTES ✦ START TO FINISH: 60 MINUTES

Nothing says early summer like fresh, juicy strawberries. Rhubarb adds texture and tartness to cooked strawberries. Together, they're magic.

1 biscuits recipe (see page 78) or 1 (26.4 oz.) package frozen biscuits

1½ cups rhubarb, cut into ½ inch pieces

1½ cups strawberries, sliced

2 tablespoons sugar

2 teaspoons flour

1 teaspoon cinnamon

1. Preheat oven to 400° F.

2. In a bowl, combine the rhubarb pieces, strawberry slices, sugar, and flour, and toss to coat the fruit. Transfer to the skillet and bake for 10 minutes.

3. Remove the skillet from the oven and drop spoonfuls of biscuit dough across the strawberry rhubarb mixture, making sure the spoonfuls are evenly distributed. Sprinkle cinnamon on top.

4. Return the skillet to the oven and bake for about 15 minutes or until the biscuits are golden and the fruit mixture is bubbling. Serve warm with whipped cream or ice cream.

In the early 1900s, American rhubarb farmers successfully lobbied for their vegetable to be officially designated as a fruit so that they could get lower tax rates and less stringent interstate shipping laws.

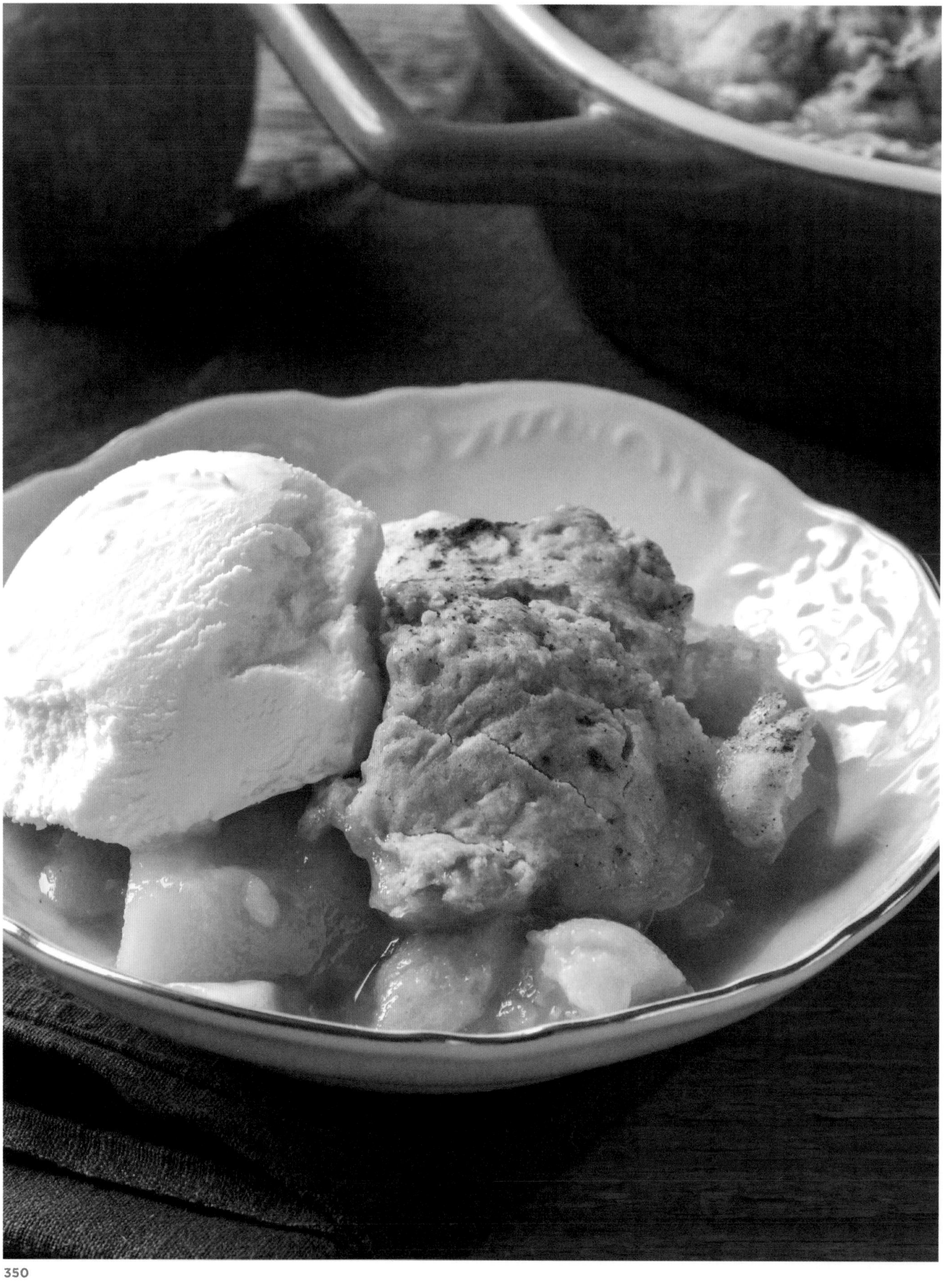

PEACH BISCUIT COBBLER

MAKES 4 TO 6 SERVINGS ✦ ACTIVE TIME: 30 MINUTES ✦ START TO FINISH: 60 MINUTES

Just like a strawberry rhubarb cobbler says early summer, a fresh peach cobbler says late summer. Use ripe fruit and plenty of it and you may end up making this every night while peaches are in season.

1 biscuits recipe (see page 78) or 1 (26.5 oz.) package frozen biscuits

5 or 6 peaches, pitted and sliced (skin on or off)

¼ cup sugar

1 to 2 tablespoons flour

1 teaspoon cinnamon

1. Preheat oven to 400° F.

2. In a bowl, combine the peach slices with sugar and flour. The amount of flour you use will depend on how juicy the peaches are; more juice means more flour. Put the mixture in the skillet and bake for 10 minutes.

3. Take the skillet out of the oven and drop spoonfuls of biscuit dough on top, making sure the spoonfuls are evenly distributed. Sprinkle cinnamon on top and return the skillet to the oven.

4. Bake for about 15 minutes or until the biscuits are golden and the peaches are bubbling. Be careful not to burn the topping.

5. Serve warm with fresh whipped cream or ice cream.

KETTLE CORN COOKIE TREATS

SERVES 6 TO 8 ✦ ACTIVE TIME: 20 MINUTES ✦ START TO FINISH: 45 MINUTES

I was excited to learn about this variation on the classic Rice Krispie treat, so I had to try it. Well, it's a winner! These sweet-salty-chewy-crunchy cookies are great for potlucks and tailgating.

2½ cups flour

1 teaspoon baking soda

½ teaspoon salt

1 cup (2 sticks) butter, softened

½ cup white sugar

1 cup brown sugar

2 eggs

½ teaspoon vanilla extract

1½ cups kettle corn

1. Preheat the oven to 375° F. Heat the skillet in the oven while making the batter.

2. In a bowl, whisk together the flour, baking soda, and salt.

3. In a large bowl, beat the butter and sugars until light and creamy. Add the eggs one at a time, being sure to combine thoroughly before proceeding. Stir in the vanilla.

4. Add the flour mixture to the butter mixture, stirring to combine thoroughly. Fold in the kettle corn.

5. Remove the skillet from the oven and put the batter in it, distributing evenly with a spatula.

6. Place the skillet in the oven and bake for about 15 to 20 minutes until the top is golden. Remove the skillet from the oven and allow to cool about 10 minutes before serving.

GLUTEN-FREE MACAROON BITES

SERVES 8 ✦ ACTIVE TIME: 15 MINUTES ✦ START TO FINISH: 45 MINUTES

What I love about this recipe—besides the gooey, sweet, sticky, absolutely delicious result— is the fact that it's a much easier way to make this treat than scooping the macaroons onto a baking sheet. That is messy and time-consuming. With this version, just pour the confection into the skillet, bake, cool, serve, eat.

1½ cups sugar

4 cups unsweetened coconut flakes

4 egg whites

2 teaspoons vanilla extract

¼ teaspoon salt

1. Preheat the oven to 350° F. While the oven is preheating, put the skillet in it to warm up.

2. In a large bowl, combine the sugar, coconut, egg whites, vanilla, and salt. Stir to combine well.

3. When the oven is preheated, remove the skillet. Put the batter into the pan and put it back in the oven.

4. Bake for 20 to 30 minutes until browned on top.

5. Remove the skillet and allow to cool for about 30 minutes before serving. Slice into wedges and use a pie server to remove from the skillet.

GIANT CHOCOLATE CHIP COOKIE

MAKES 1 LARGE COOKIE   **ACTIVE TIME: 20 MINUTES**   **START TO FINISH: 45 MINUTES**

Yes, your cast-iron skillet is also a great baking sheet—just smaller, and with sides. So why not cook a giant cookie in it? Here's how.

1 cup butter (2 sticks), softened

½ cup sugar

1 cup brown sugar

2 eggs

2 teaspoons vanilla extract

1 teaspoon baking soda

2 teaspoons hot water

½ teaspoon salt

2½ cups flour

2 cups semi-sweet chocolate chips

1. Preheat oven to 375° F. Heat the skillet in the oven while making the batter.

2. In a large bowl, beat the butter and sugars together until light and fluffy. Add the eggs one at a time, being sure to combine thoroughly before proceeding. Stir in the vanilla.

3. Dissolve the baking soda in the hot water and add to the batter with the salt. Stir in the flour and chocolate chips.

4. Remove the skillet from the oven and put the batter in it, smoothing the top with a spatula.

5. Put the skillet in the oven and cook until golden, about 15 minutes. Serve with ice cream.

Variation

If you like nuts in your chocolate chip cookies, mix in ½ cup walnut or almond pieces when adding the flour and chocolate chips.

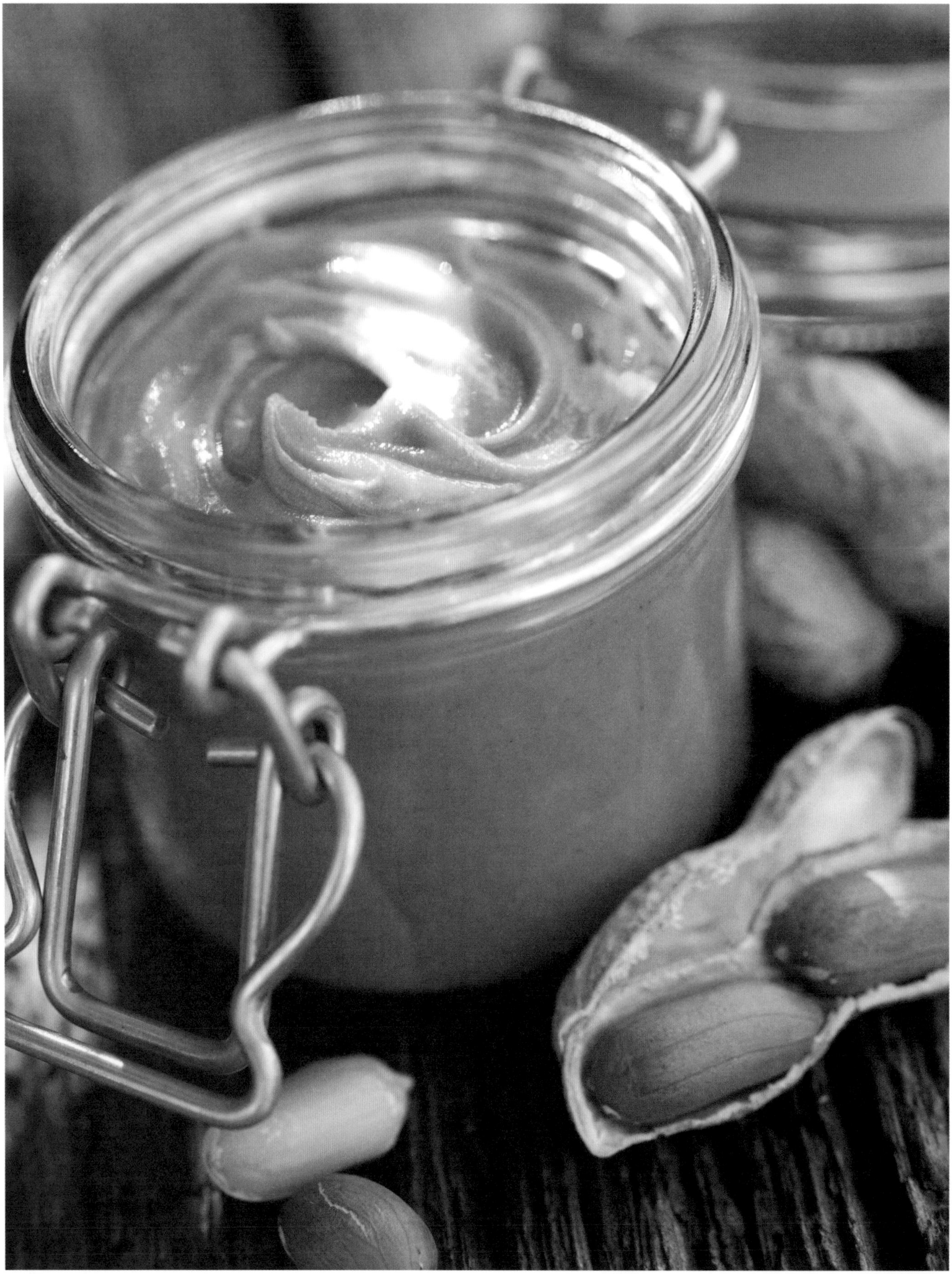

PEANUT BUTTER COOKIE WEDGES

SERVES 6 TO 8 ✦ ACTIVE TIME: 20 MINUTES ✦ START TO FINISH: 45 MINUTES

This is a recipe that melts in your mouth. Making thin wedges before baking makes it easier to break away pieces of the cookie when it's cooked. There are all kinds of peanut butters available these days. You can choose creamy or chunky, traditional, or all-natural. I prefer creamy, all-natural peanut butter. The oil has a tendency to separate with this kind of peanut butter, so stir it in the jar before measuring it out.

1½ cups flour

1 teaspoon baking soda

Dash of salt

8 tablespoons (1 stick) butter, softened

½ cup dark brown sugar

½ cup granulated sugar

1 egg

½ teaspoon vanilla extract

½ cup peanut butter

1. Preheat the oven to 350° F. Heat the skillet in the oven while making the batter.

2. In a bowl, whisk together the flour, baking soda, and salt.

3. In a large bowl, beat the butter and sugars until light and creamy. Add the egg and vanilla and mix until combined. Stir in the flour mixture, and when it's incorporated, stir in the peanut butter.

4. Remove the skillet from the oven and spread the cookie batter with a spatula to distribute evenly in the skillet. Use a butter knife to cut the dough into 8 to 10 wedges.

5. Place the skillet in the oven and bake for about 15 to 20 minutes until the cookie is golden brown and cooked through. Remove the skillet from the oven and allow to cool for 10 minutes before serving.

Variations

Substitute ½ cup almond butter or cashew butter for the peanut butter, or experiment with a nut butter "blend." Experiment with different consistencies of nut butters, too—try using a chunky peanut butter rather than smooth.

OATMEAL BUTTERSCOTCH COOKIE BARS

SERVES 6 TO 8 ✦ ACTIVE TIME: 20 MINUTES ✦ START TO FINISH: 45 MINUTES

Sure you've heard of oatmeal raisin cookies, but as you can see, I like to experiment with different flavor combinations. And in this case, the slightly savory taste of the butterscotch morsels works really well with the oatmeal base!

1¼ cups flour

2 cups quick-cooking oatmeal

1 teaspoon baking soda

½ teaspoon salt

¾ cup (1½ sticks) butter, softened

½ cup dark brown sugar

½ cup granulated sugar

1 egg

½ teaspoon vanilla extract

1½ cups butterscotch morsels

1. Preheat the oven to 350° F. Heat the skillet in the oven while making the batter.

2. In a bowl, mix together the flour, oatmeal, baking soda, and salt.

3. In a large bowl, beat the butter and sugars until light and creamy. Add the egg and vanilla and mix to combine. Stir in the flour mixture, and when it's incorporated, stir in the butterscotch morsels.

4. Remove the skillet from the oven and put the batter in it, distributing evenly with a spatula. Use a butter knife to cut the dough into 8 to 10 wedges.

5. Place the skillet in the oven and bake for about 20 to 25 minutes until the cookie is golden brown and cooked through. Remove the skillet and allow to cool for 10 minutes before serving.

Variation

Substitute toffee chips for the butterscotch chips.

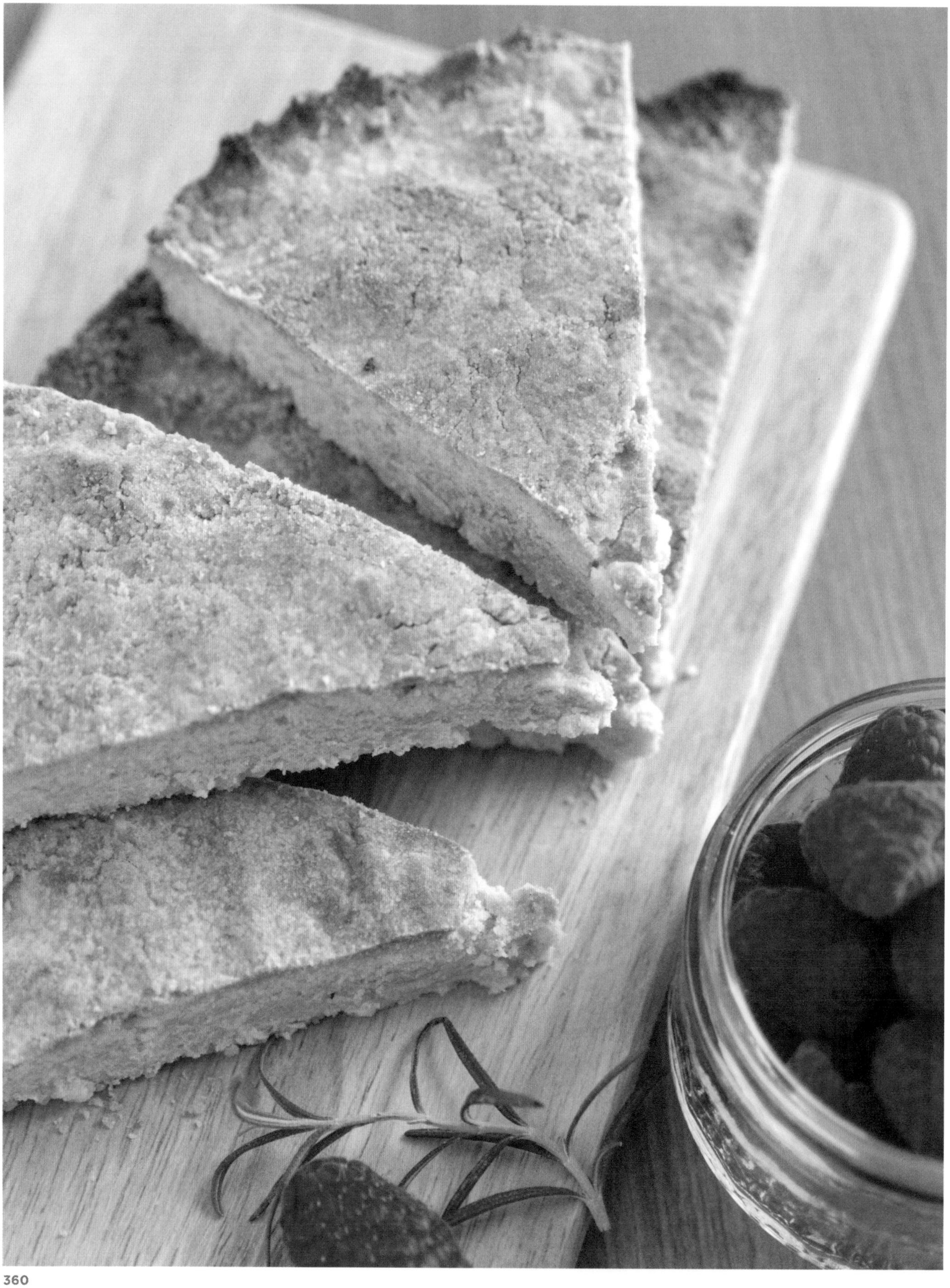

CLASSIC SHORTBREAD COOKIE BARS

SERVES 6 TO 8 ✦ ACTIVE TIME: 25 MINUTES ✦ START TO FINISH: 60 MINUTES

Shortbread cookies are wonderfully simple to prepare and so, so yummy. The butter shines through in each flaky bite. They are the perfect late afternoon pick-me-up when served with coffee, tea, or hot chocolate.

1 cup flour

¼ teaspoon salt

¼ cup sugar

8 tablespoons (1 stick) unsalted butter, chilled

½ teaspoon vanilla extract

1. Preheat the oven to 300° F. Heat the skillet in the oven while making the dough.

2. In a large bowl, combine the flour, salt, and sugar, whisking to combine.

3. Cut the butter into slices and add to the flour mixture. The best way to work it into the flour is with your hands. As it starts to come together, add the vanilla extract. Work with the mixture until it resembles coarse meal.

4. Gather the dough into a ball. On a lightly floured surface, roll it out into a circle that's just smaller than the surface of the skillet—about 8 inches in diameter. Slice the round into 8 wedges.

5. Remove the skillet from the oven and place the wedges in it to recreate the circle of dough. Bake for about 45 minutes or until the shortbread is a pale golden color. Remove the skillet from the oven and allow to cool for about 10 minutes before transferring the cookies to a plate.

APPLE-PEAR CRISP

SERVES 6 TO 8 ✦ ACTIVE TIME: 40 MINUTES ✦ START TO FINISH: 60 MINUTES

The flavors of fall shine in this dish, which is a winner each and every time.

For the Topping

½ cup walnut pieces, preferably toasted

3 tablespoons light brown sugar

2 tablespoons butter, softened

½ teaspoon cinnamon

¼ teaspoon freshly grated nutmeg

¼ teaspoon salt

For the Apples & Pears

1 tablespoon butter

1 apple, peeled, cored, and sliced

1 pear, cored and sliced

1 teaspoon fresh lemon juice

1 teaspoon maple syrup

Butter pecan ice cream

1. Preheat the oven to 350° F.

2. In a small bowl, combine the walnuts, sugar, butter, cinnamon, nutmeg, and salt. Using your fingers, crumble the mixture up until it's somewhat combined. No need to get too particular about it.

3. Heat the butter in a skillet over medium-high heat. Add the apple slices and cook, while stirring gently, for a minute or so, then add the pear slices and continue to cook until the fruits soften. Sprinkle the lemon juice and maple syrup over the fruits and remove from heat.

4. Using your fingers, spread the nut/sugar mixture over the top of the fruits. Put the skillet in the oven and cook for about 10 minutes, until the fruits are bubbling and the topping is lightly toasted. Serve with butter pecan ice cream.

Variations

✸ Instead of walnuts, use pecan pieces or crushed almonds.

✸ Cut the amount of nuts by half and make up the difference with oatmeal.

✸ Instead of an apple-pear combo, make it with just one of the fruits, doubling up on the one you select. Add a handful of dried cranberries while the fruits are sautéing.

STRAWBERRY RHUBARB CRISP

SERVES 4 ✦ ACTIVE TIME: 30 MINUTES ✦ START TO FINISH: 60 MINUTES

This magnificent combo traditionally appears in a pie, but this crisp allows you to enjoy it without all of that fuss.

1½ cups rhubarb, cut into ½-inch pieces

1½ cups strawberries, sliced

2 tablespoons sugar

⅓ cup flour, plus 2 teaspoons

¾ cup quick-cooking oats

4 tablespoons butter, chilled, cut into pieces

¼ cup dark brown sugar

flour

1. Preheat the oven to 450° F.

2. In a bowl, combine the rhubarb pieces, strawberry slices, sugar, and 2 teaspoons flour, and toss to coat the fruit. Transfer to the skillet.

3. In another bowl, work the butter in with the sugar using a fork. Add the oats and remaining flour and continue to use the fork to create a crumbly mixture. Sprinkle it over the fruit in the skillet.

4. Put the skillet in the oven and bake for about 30 minutes until the topping is golden and the fruit is bubbly. Serve warm with whipped cream or ice cream.

PEACH CRISP

SERVES 4 TO 6 ✦ ACTIVE TIME: 30 MINUTES ✦ START TO FINISH: 60 MINUTES

When you've got ripe peaches to work with, you want to find as many recipes as possible to use them in. This one is so quick and easy, it just may rise to the top of that list.

5 or 6 peaches, pitted and sliced (skin on or off)

¾ cup sugar

¾ cup flour, plus 1 to 2 tablespoons

¼ teaspoon salt

¼ cup dark brown sugar

½ cup quick-cooking oats (quick-cooking but not instant)

8 tablespoons (1 stick) chilled butter, cut into pieces

1. Preheat the oven to 350° F.

2. In a bowl, combine the peach slices with ¼ cup of the sugar and 1 or 2 tablespoons of the flour. The amount of flour you use will depend on how juicy the peaches are—more juice means more flour. Let the peaches sit in the bowl while you make the topping. If there's juice left in the bowl after sitting, add another tablespoon of flour.

3. In another bowl, make the topping. Blend the remaining flour, the remaining sugar, salt, and the brown sugar together, and add the butter, using a fork to combine. When somewhat mixed and crumbly, add the oats and stir. The topping should be crumbly.

4. Put the peaches in the skillet and add the topping.

5. Put the skillet in the oven and bake for about 1 hour until the topping is golden and the peaches are bubbling. If it doesn't look crispy enough, turn the oven up to 375° F and continue to bake, checking every 5 minutes until it looks just right. Be careful not to burn the topping.

6. Serve warm with fresh whipped cream and a sprinkling of toasted nuts.

Variation

Many fruit crisp recipes feature nuts in the topping. These can be whatever you like: walnuts, pecans, or almonds. Break the raw nuts into pieces and use about ½ cup in the topping.

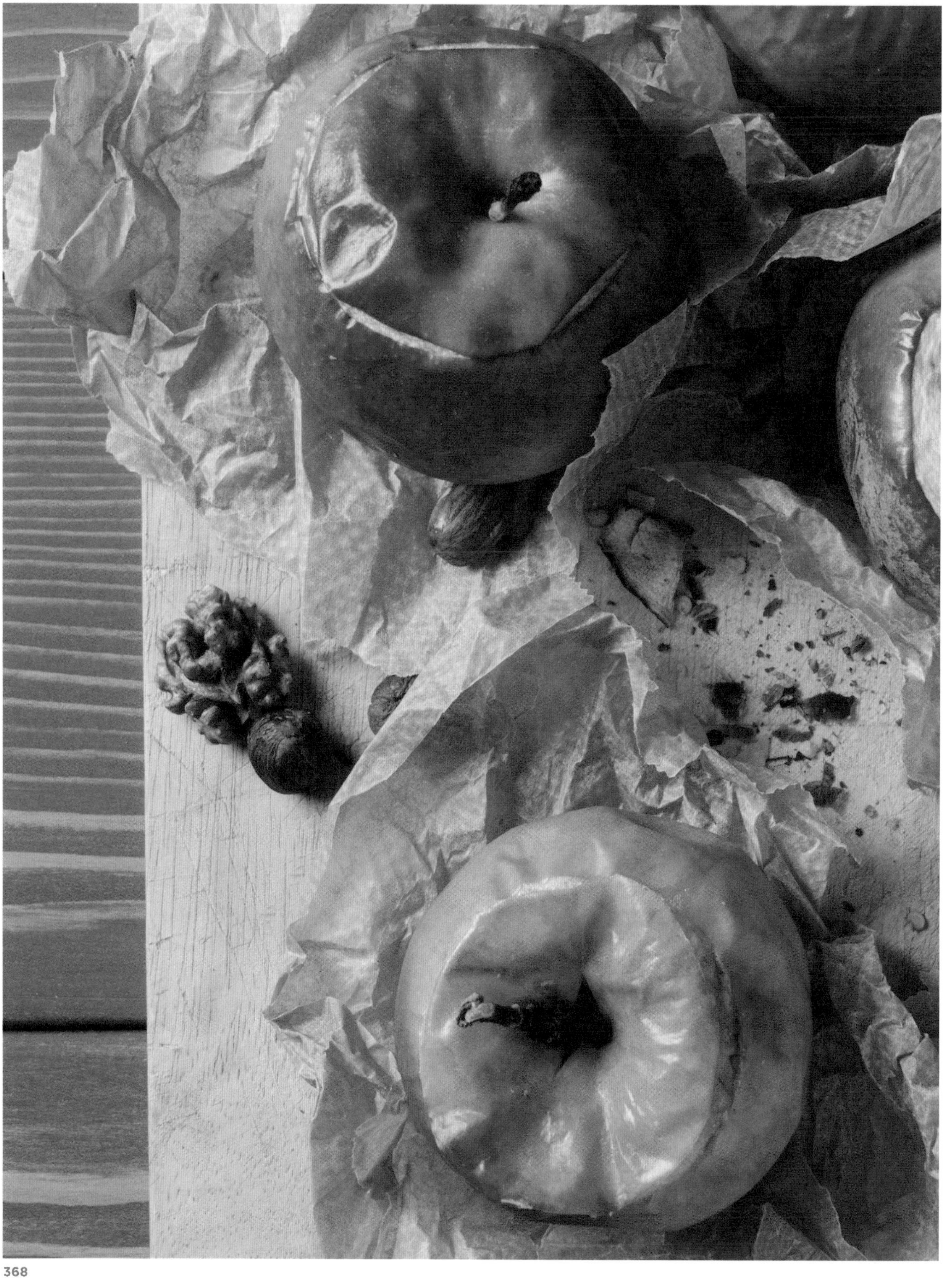

BAKED APPLES

SERVES 4 ✦ ACTIVE TIME: 30 MINUTES ✦ START TO FINISH: 50 MINUTES

These are easy to make and are delicious served warm or at room temperature the next day. Of course, they're best with a side of vanilla ice cream or even maple Greek yogurt.

4 firm apples

2 tablespoons butter

½ cup water

Maple syrup

1. Preheat the oven to 350° F.

2. Peel the apples, leaving a ring of peel on the bottom where the apple will stand in the skillet. Remove as much of the core as you can without cutting the apple in half.

3. Heat the skillet over medium-high heat. Add the butter and let it melt. Place the apples bottom-down in the skillet. Add the water from the center so that it distributes evenly around the apples. Drizzle the tops of the apples with maple syrup.

4. Put the skillet in the oven and cook for about 20 minutes, or until apples are soft. Drizzle with additional maple syrup if desired.

Variations

- Use apple cider instead of water to make a nice apple–butter sauce, which you can reduce after the apples are cooked to make a concentrated sauce.

- Paleo-friendy: This recipe is Paleo-appropriate with the substitution of 2 tablespoons coconut oil or ghee (clarified butter) for the butter.

DUTCH APPLE BABY

SERVES 4 ♦ ACTIVE TIME: 45 MINUTES ♦ START TO FINISH: 75 MINUTES

This is a classic cast-iron skillet recipe for a pastry that puffs in the oven. It is reminiscent of the recipe for David Eyre's Pancake in the Breakfast Treats & Pastries chapter.

2 firm, semi-tart apples, like Mutsu or Golden Delicious

4 tablespoons butter

¼ cup sugar, plus 3 tablespoons

1 tablespoon cinnamon

¾ cup flour

¼ teaspoon salt

¾ cup milk

4 eggs

1 teaspoon vanilla or almond extract

Confectioners' sugar for dusting

1. Preheat the oven to 425° F and position a rack in the middle.

2. Peel and core the apples, and cut into slices. Heat a skillet over medium-high heat. Add the butter and apples and cook, stirring, for 3 to 4 minutes until the apples soften. Add the ¼ cup of sugar and cinnamon and continue cooking for another 3 or 4 minutes. Distribute the apples evenly over the bottom of the skillet and remove from heat.

3. In a large bowl, mix the remaining sugar, flour, and salt together. In a smaller bowl, whisk together the milk, eggs, and vanilla or almond extract. Add the wet ingredients to the dry ingredients and stir to combine. Pour the batter over the apples.

4. Put the skillet in the oven and bake for 15 to 20 minutes until the "baby" is puffy and browned on the top.

5. Remove the skillet from the oven and allow to cool for a few minutes. Run a knife along the edge of the skillet to loosen the dessert. Put a plate over the skillet and, using oven mitts or pot holders, flip the skillet over so the dessert is transferred to the plate. Serve warm with a dusting of confectioners' sugar.

The Dutch Apple Baby is attributed to early Pennsylvania Dutch settlers.

CHERRY CLAFOUTI

SERVES 4 TO 6 ✦ ACTIVE TIME: 20 MINUTES ✦ START TO FINISH: 45 MINUTES

This is a French specialty that originated in the Limousin region and used the sour cherries that grew there. This dessert is so delicious that it is now known around the world. It's essentially full-flavored cherries baked in a custard. How can you go wrong?

10 tablespoons (1 stick) butter

1 cup sugar, plus 2 teaspoons

⅔ cup flour

½ teaspoon salt

1 teaspoon vanilla extract

3 eggs, beaten

1 cup milk

3 cups ripe cherries (pits in)

Confectioners' sugar for dusting (optional)

1. Place 8 tablespoons of the butter in a microwave-safe bowl and microwave until melted. Preheat the oven to 400° F.

2. In a large bowl, mix together 6 tablespoons of the melted butter, ½ cup of the sugar, flour, salt, vanilla, eggs, and milk until all ingredients are blended and smooth. Set aside.

3. Put 2 tablespoons of the melted butter in the skillet and put the skillet in the oven to heat up.

4. Transfer the skillet to the stovetop and add the remaining butter. When it is melted, put ½ cup of the sugar in the skillet and shake it so it distributes evenly. Add the cherries. Pour the batter over the cherries, sprinkle with the last teaspoons of sugar, and put the skillet back in the oven. Bake for about 30 minutes, or until the topping is golden brown and set in the center.

5. Dust with confectioners' sugar, if desired, and serve warm—and be sure to let diners know that the cherries contain their pits.

The Limousin region of France is located in the center of the country, with Bordeaux to the west and Lyon to the east. Limoges is the largest city in the region. It is known for its agricultural heritage, including the griottes (sour morello cherries) grown there. There is some debate about whether the pits should be removed from the cherries before baking, but Julia Child left them in, going off the belief that the pits add flavor.

PEAR CLAFOUTI

SERVES 4 TO 6 ✦ ACTIVE TIME: 20 MINUTES ✦ START TO FINISH: 45 MINUTES

When you get the hang of making clafouti, you'll want to experiment with different fruits. This one is made with pears and uses almond extract to accentuate their mild nuttiness.

12 tablespoons (1 stick) butter

1 cup sugar, plus 2 teaspoons

⅔ cup flour

½ teaspoon salt

1 teaspoon almond extract

3 eggs

1 cup milk

4 pears, sliced

1. Place 8 tablespoons of the butter in a microwave-safe bowl and microwave until melted. Preheat the oven to 400° F.

2. In a large bowl, mix together 6 tablespoons of the melted butter, ½ cup of the sugar, flour, salt, almond extract, eggs, and milk until all ingredients are blended and smooth. Set aside.

3. Put 2 tablespoons of the melted butter in the skillet and put it in the oven to heat up.

4. In another skillet on the stove, working over medium-high heat, add the remaining butter and cook until melted. Add the pears and ½ cup of the sugar to the butter and cook, while stirring, until the pears are just soft and glazed, about 3 minutes.

5. Remove the skillet from the oven and pour in half of the batter. Spoon the cooked pears over the batter, and then add the remaining batter. Sprinkle with the remaining sugar.

6. Place the skillet in the oven and bake in the oven for 25 to 30 minutes until the clafouti is golden brown and set in the center. Serve warm with whipped cream or confectioners' sugar, or just by itself.

Although clafouti is most delicious served warm, it is plenty tasty served at room temperature or even chilled.

CHOCOLATE CHEESECAKE BROWNIES

SERVES 6 TO 8 ✦ ACTIVE TIME: 40 MINUTES ✦ START TO FINISH: 90 MINUTES

For this brownie, a swirl of cheesecake batter adds an extra creamy goodness.

For the Brownie Batter

8 tablespoons (1 stick) butter

¼ cup unsweetened cocoa powder

1 cup sugar

½ cup flour

½ teaspoon salt

2 large eggs, lightly beaten

1 teaspoon vanilla extract

1 cup semi-sweet chocolate chips

For the Cream Cheese Batter

4 oz. cream cheese, softened

¼ cup sugar

1 egg

1 teaspoon vanilla extract

1. Preheat the oven to 325° F.

2. Prepare the cream cheese batter by combining the cream cheese, sugar, egg, and vanilla in a bowl. Set aside.

3. Melt the butter in the skillet over medium-low heat.

4. Put the cocoa powder in a medium-sized bowl. When the butter is melted, pour it over the cocoa powder, leaving a film of butter on the skillet. Whisk the butter into the powder, then add the sugar, stirring to combine. Combine the flour and salt, and stir this mixture into the batter. Add the eggs, vanilla, and chocolate chips and stir to combine.

5. Put the batter into the skillet. Drop the cream cheese batter in spoonfuls onto the brownie, distributing evenly. Use a small knife to gently swirl the cream cheese into the chocolate.

6. Put the skillet in the oven and bake for 30 to 35 minutes until the edges of the brownie start to brown and a toothpick inserted in the middle comes out clean. Use pot holders or oven mitts to remove the hot skillet. Let it cool for about 10 minutes before serving.

Serve with fresh strawberries or raspberries.

BANANAS FLAMBÉ

MAKES 2 TO 4 SERVINGS ✦ **ACTIVE TIME: 10 MINUTES** ✦ **START TO FINISH: 20 MINUTES**

Sure, it's fun lighting things on fire, but the taste those flames provide are essential to this dish.

2 ripe bananas

6 tablespoons butter

¼ cup dark rum

Long matches or
a lighter

1. Peel the bananas and cut them in half lengthwise.

2. Heat the skillet over medium-high heat and add the butter, cooking until it melts. Lay the banana pieces on the bubbling butter and cook for about 2 minutes per side. When the bananas have softened and are coated with the butter, pour the rum over them. Have someone else turn off the lights in the kitchen while you get ready to strike the match or lighter. Swirl the rum around in the pan and light it on fire. The flame will burn for just a minute or so as the alcohol burns off. When the flame dies down, the dessert is ready.

3. Put the bananas on plates with a scoop of vanilla ice cream—or put the ice cream over them in the skillet and eat out of it.

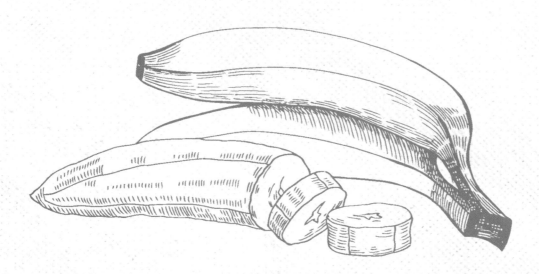

PECAN PIE

SERVES 8 TO 10   **ACTIVE TIME: 30 MINUTES**   **START TO FINISH: 90 MINUTES**

This simple dessert of nuts, eggs, sugar, and vanilla is associated with the goodness of the South, especially Louisiana. However, credit for its creation is partly due to the French, who used the newly discovered nut in a dessert during their early days in the territory. It's also been attributed to a founder of Karo corn syrup. I say merci and thank you to both!

1 flaky pastry crust recipe for a single crust (see page 136)

3 eggs

1 cup dark corn syrup

½ cup sugar

¼ cup butter, melted

1 teaspoon vanilla extract

1 cup pecan halves or broken pieces

1. Preheat the oven to 350° F.

2. In a large bowl, whisk the eggs until thoroughly combined. Add the corn syrup, sugar, melted butter, and vanilla. Whisk until combined, and then stir in the pecan pieces.

3. Working with the crust in the skillet, transfer the filling into the piecrust, shaking the skillet gently to distribute evenly.

4. Put the skillet in the oven and bake for about 60 minutes or until a knife inserted toward the middle comes out clean. If the edge of the crust becomes overly brown, remove the skillet from the oven and put tin foil over the exposed crust until the filling is set.

5. Remove the skillet and allow to cool to cool to room temperature before serving.

If you intend to remove the pie before serving, make sure you grease the skillet with butter or cooking spray before cooking. When the pie is cooked and completely cooled, it will be possible to slide the pie out with the help of a thin plastic spatula. However, greasing the pan in this manner will lend the bottom crust a slightly rough texture.

CHOCOLATE-BOURBON PECAN PIE

SERVES 8 TO 10 ✦ ACTIVE TIME: 45 MINUTES ✦ START TO FINISH: 2 HOURS

Here's another notch up in the pecan pie department—the additions of chocolate and bourbon! If you're looking to make a pie that will have your guests raving about your cooking, this is the one!

1 flaky pastry crust recipe for a single crust, baked (see page 136)

1½ cups pecans, toasted and chopped

6 oz. semi-sweet chocolate morsels

1 cup dark corn syrup

⅓ cup sugar

½ cup light brown sugar, firmly packed

¼ cup bourbon

4 large eggs

¼ cup butter, melted

2 teaspoons vanilla extract

½ teaspoon table salt

1. To toast the pecan pieces, preheat the oven to 350° F. Spread the pecan pieces on a baking sheet in a single layer. Bake for 6 to 10 minutes, checking often to make sure they don't burn. When fragrant, remove from oven and let cool. Chop pecans into small pieces and set aside.

2. Reduce the heat in the oven to 325° F.

3. Working with the crust in the skillet, sprinkle the toasted pecan pieces and chocolate morsels evenly onto the crust.

4. In a saucepan over medium heat, combine the corn syrup, sugar, light brown sugar, and bourbon. Stir to combine and cook, while stirring constantly, until mixture just comes to a boil. Remove from heat.

5. In a large bowl, whisk the eggs until thoroughly combined. Add the melted butter, vanilla, and salt, and whisk to combine. Add about ¼ of the sugar-and-bourbon mixture to the egg mixture, whisking briskly to combine so the eggs don't curdle or cook. When thoroughly combined, continue to add the hot liquid to the egg mixture in small amounts, whisking to combine thoroughly after each addition until all of it is incorporated. Pour the this mixture over the nuts and chocolate pieces and shake the skillet gently to distribute evenly.

6. Put the skillet in the oven and bake for about 60 minutes or until a knife inserted toward the middle comes out clean. If the edge of the crust becomes overly brown, remove the skillet from the oven and put tin foil over the exposed crust until the filling is set. Remove the skillet from the oven and allow to cool completely before serving.

CHOCOLATE MOUSSE PECAN PIE

SERVES 6 TO 8 ✦ ACTIVE TIME: 40 MINUTES
START TO FINISH: SEVERAL HOURS OR OVERNIGHT

Doesn't this pie sound decadent? A combination of chocolate mousse and the buttery richness of pecans? Well, it is decadent, but it is also super-simple to make—it doesn't even need to be baked. Time to indulge!

**1 baked crust
(see page 135)**

**½ cup pecans, toasted
and coarsely chopped**

**12 oz. semi-sweet
chocolate morsels**

2½ cups heavy cream

1 tablespoon bourbon

**1 teaspoon vanilla
extract**

1. Preheat the oven to 350° F.

2. Spread the pecan pieces on a cookie sheet. Bake for about 8 minutes, checking on the nuts after 5 minutes to be sure they don't burn. Remove when just starting to brown. Allow to cool and then coarsely chop.

3. Put the chocolate morsels in a microwave-safe bowl. Add ½ cup of the cream and stir. Microwave on high in 30-second increments, stirring after each. When just melted, stir in the bourbon and vanilla. Let stand for about 5 minutes.

4. In a large bowl, use an electric mixer to beat the remaining 2 cups of cream at medium-high speed for about 3 minutes or until medium peaks form. Fold the chocolate mixture into the whipped cream. Pour this mixture into the crust, spreading with the back of a spoon to distribute evenly. Sprinkle the toasted pecans over the top.

5. Refrigerate for several hours, or overnight, before serving.

Try using a cast-iron muffin tin to make delicious individual pies, topping them with individual pecans. Perfect for a party!

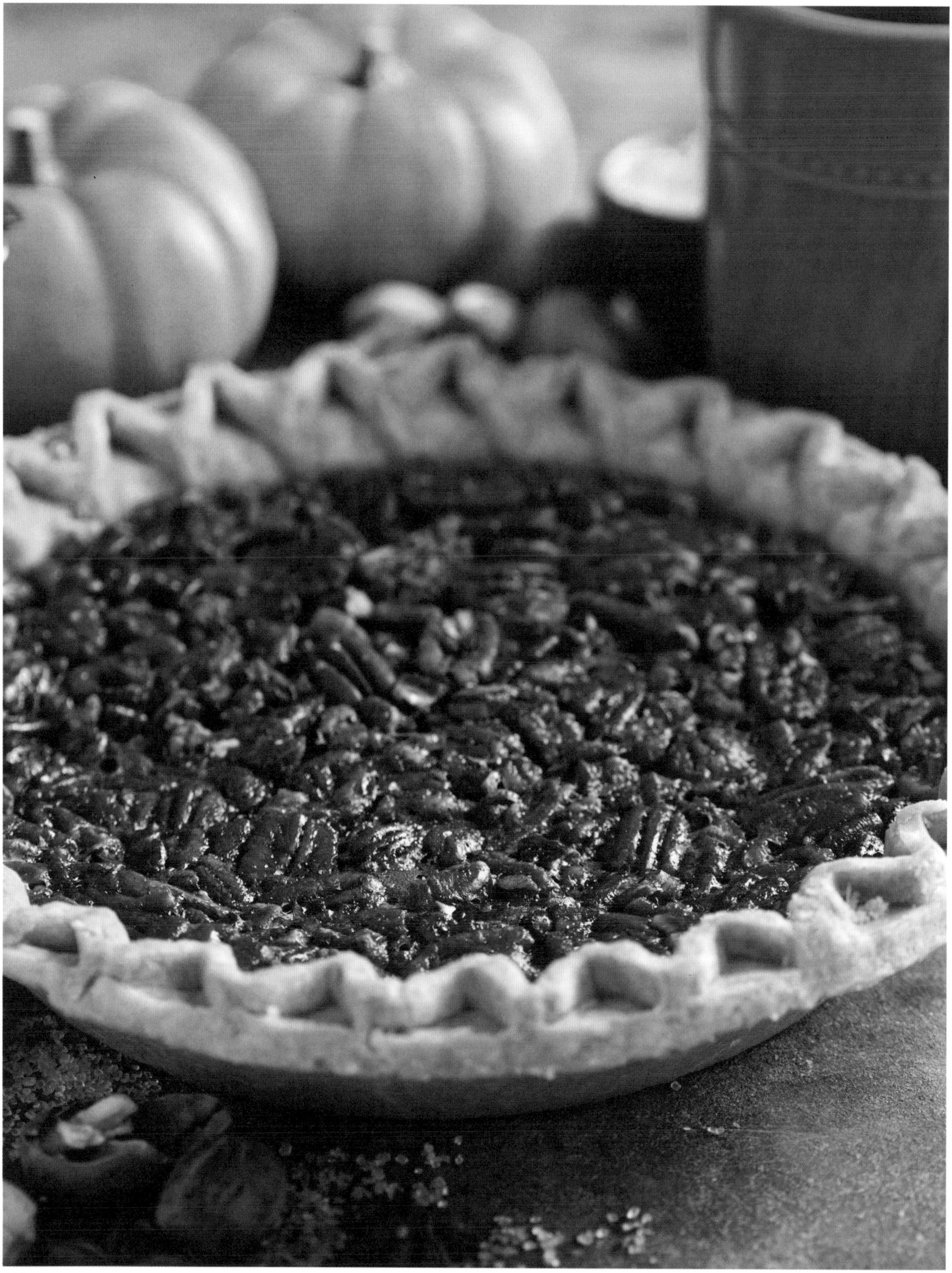

PUMPKIN-PECAN PIE

SERVES 6 TO 8 ✦ ACTIVE TIME: 30 MINUTES ✦ START TO FINISH: 75 MINUTES

If you want to dress up a basic pumpkin pie and add a delicious nutty-buttery taste, try this recipe. The topping is so tasty!

1 flaky pastry crust recipe for a single crust (see page 136)

1 (15 oz.) can pumpkin puree (not pumpkin pie filling)

1 (14 oz.) can sweetened condensed milk (not evaporated)

2 eggs

2 tablespoons 100% natural maple syrup

½ teaspoon ground cinnamon

¼ teaspoon ground ginger

¼ teaspoon ground nutmeg

¼ cup brown sugar, packed

¼ cup pecans, finely chopped

2 tablespoons flour

2 tablespoons butter, chilled and cut into pieces

1. Preheat the oven to 425° F.

2. In a large bowl, combine the pumpkin puree, sweetened condensed milk, eggs, maple syrup, and spices. Whisk or stir until thoroughly combined. Pour into unbaked crust. Put the skillet in the oven and bake for 10 minutes.

3. While pie is baking, in a small bowl, combine the brown sugar, pecans, and flour. Work in the butter with your fingers until the mixture is crumbly.

4. Reduce the oven temperature to 350° F. Carefully take the pie out of the oven and top with the brown sugar-and-pecan mixture, distributing evenly. Use foil to cover the edges of the crust to prevent them from burning.

5. Return the skillet to the oven and bake for 30 to 35 minutes or until a knife inserted about an inch from the edge comes out clean. Remove from the oven, allow to cool completely, and then refrigerate until ready to serve.

6. Serve with fresh whipped cream or French vanilla ice cream.

Variation

For an extra nutty version of this delicious pie, try making it with a pecan nut crust (see page 144).

PEANUT BUTTER PIE

SERVES 8 TO 10 ✦ ACTIVE TIME: 30 MINUTES ✦ START TO FINISH: 90 MINUTES

Yes, this pie tastes as amazing as it sounds. If you're looking for a peanut butter cup kind of experience, you can also bathe the top in chocolate when cool. Try it, you'll love it.

1 chocolate graham cracker crust (see page 142)

3 eggs

1 cup dark corn syrup

½ cup sugar

½ cup creamy all-natural peanut butter (with no added sugar)

½ teaspoon vanilla extract

1 cup salted peanuts (the higher the quality, the better)

6 oz. semi-sweet chocolate morsels (optional)

Pecans, peanuts, or walnuts as garnish (optional)

1. Preheat the oven to 350˚ F.

2. In a large bowl, whisk the eggs until thoroughly combined. Add the corn syrup and sugar, and whisk until sugar is completely dissolved. Add the peanut butter and vanilla and whisk until smooth and combined. Don't over-whisk the mixture.

3. Working with the crust in the skillet, transfer the filling into the crust and sprinkle with the salted whole peanuts.

4. Put the skillet in the oven and bake for about 60 minutes or until a knife inserted toward the middle comes out clean. If the edge of the crust becomes overly brown, remove the skillet from the oven and put tin foil over the exposed crust until the filling is set. Remove the skillet from the oven and allow to cool completely.

5. If you'd like to top with chocolate, put the morsels in a microwave-safe bowl and heat in 15-second increments, stirring after each, until pieces are just melted. Drizzle over cooled pie and refrigerate until hard. Garnish with pecans, peanuts, or walnuts, if desired.

PUMPKIN-WALNUT PIE

The crunch provided by walnuts is a great complement for the creamy pumpkin.

1 flaky pastry crust recipe for a single crust (see page 136)

1 (15 oz.) can pumpkin puree (not pumpkin pie filling)

1 (14 oz.) can sweetened condensed milk (not evaporated)

2 eggs

2 tablespoons 100% natural maple syrup (preferably Grade B dark)

½ teaspoon ground cinnamon

¼ teaspoon ground ginger

¼ teaspoon ground nutmeg

¼ cup brown sugar, packed

¼ cup walnuts, finely chopped

2 tablespoons flour

2 tablespoons butter, chilled and cut into pieces

1. Preheat the oven to 425° F.

2. In a large bowl, combine the pumpkin puree, sweetened condensed milk, eggs, maple syrup, and spices. Whisk or stir until thoroughly combined. Pour into unbaked crust. Put the skillet in the oven and bake for 10 minutes.

3. While pie is baking, combine the brown sugar, walnuts, and flour in a small bowl. Work in the butter with your fingers until the mixture is crumbly.

4. Reduce the oven temperature to 350° F. Carefully take the pie out of the oven and top with the brown sugar-and-walnut mixture, distributing evenly. Use foil to cover the edges of the crust to prevent them from burning.

5. Return skillet to the oven and bake 30 to 35 minutes or until a knife inserted about an inch from the edge comes out clean. Remove the skillet from the oven, allow to cool completely, and then refrigerate until ready to serve.

6. Serve with fresh whipped cream or French vanilla ice cream.

PEACH PIE

SERVES 6 TO 8 ✦ ACTIVE TIME: 60 MINUTES ✦ START TO FINISH: 2 HOURS

There's something otherworldly about a pie made with fresh peaches. It is just so good! With the way the cast-iron skillet yields a sugary, somewhat crunchy bottom crust, this just may become your favorite recipe when peaches are in season.

1 flaky crust recipe for a double crust (see page 136)

2–3 pounds peaches to yield 4 cups peeled and sliced

1 tablespoon lemon juice

¾ cup sugar

4 tablespoons flour

8 tablespoons (1 stick) butter

1 cup light brown sugar

1 egg white

2 tablespoons sugar

1. Preheat the oven to 350° F.

2. Bring a large pot of water to boil. Fill another large pot with cold water. When the water is boiling, submerge the peaches for a minute or 2, then remove them with a slotted spoon and put them immediately into the cold water. This loosens the skin and makes them much easier to peel. Use enough peaches to yield 4 cups of peeled slices. Put the slices in a bowl and add the lemon juice, sugar, and flour. Stir to combine.

3. Put the skillet over medium heat and melt the butter in it. Add the brown sugar and cook, while stirring constantly, for a minute or 2, until the sugar is dissolved. Remove pan from heat.

4. Roll out 1 of the piecrusts and gently place it over the butter-and-brown sugar mixture. Fill with the peaches and place the other crust over the peaches, crimping the edges together.

5. Brush the top crust with the egg white and then sprinkle the sugar over it. Cut 4 or 5 slits in the middle.

6. Put the skillet in the oven and bake for 60 to 70 minutes until the pie is golden brown and bubbly. Cover the outermost edge with aluminum foil in the last 10 minutes of baking to prevent it from burning.

7. Remove the skillet from the oven and allow to cool before serving. Serve with bourbon whipped cream.

For this pie you have to try serving it with bourbon whipped cream. You'll understand why this is so popular in the South, from whence the best peaches (and bourbon) hail. Simply beat heavy or whipping cream until soft peaks form. Add about ¼ cup sugar and continue beating until stiff peaks form. Gently beat in ¼ cup bourbon.

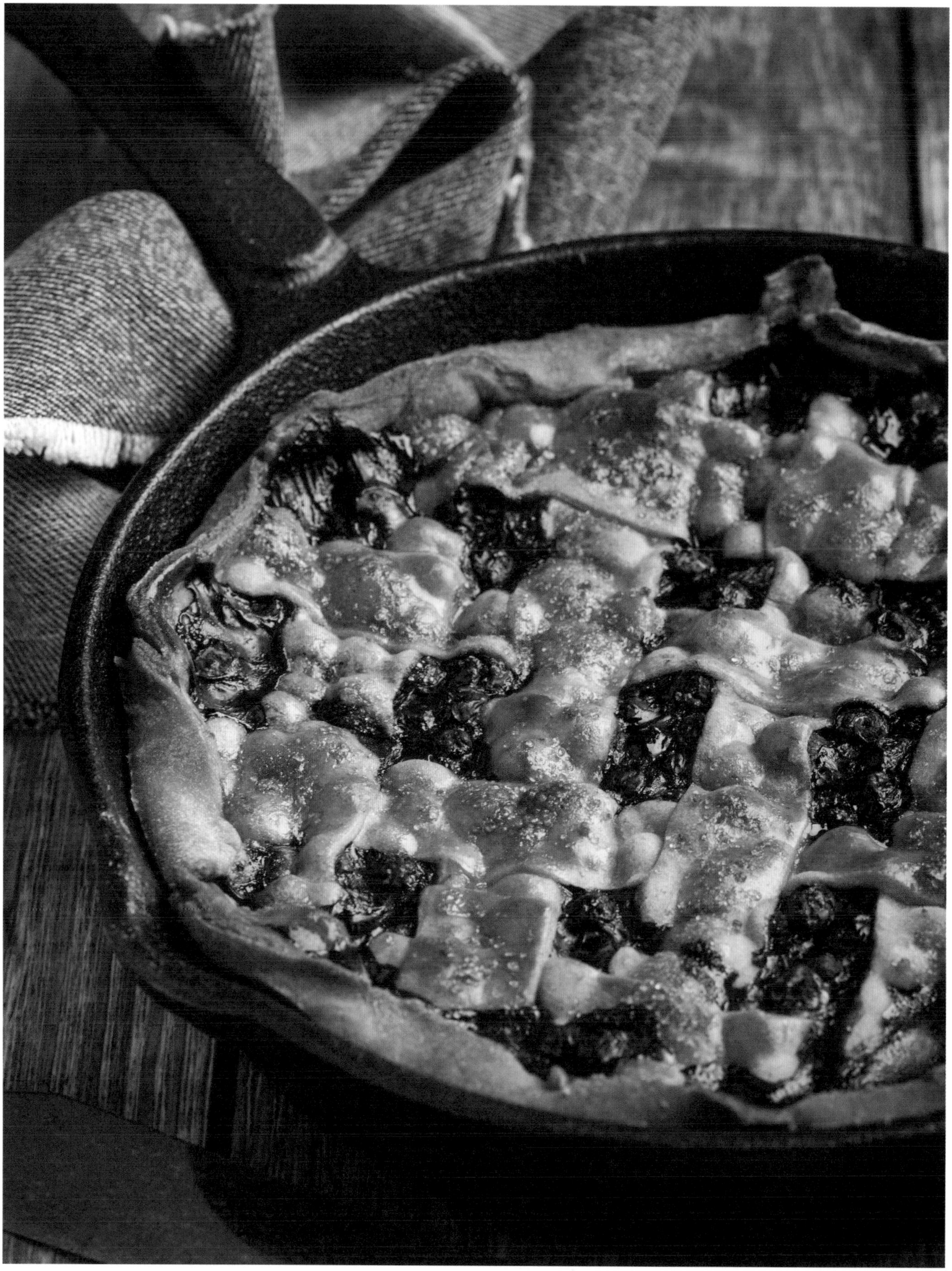

BLUEBERRY PIE

SERVES 6 TO 8 ✦ ACTIVE TIME: 60 MINUTES ✦ START TO FINISH: 2 HOURS

Blueberry pie is so easy to make and tastes so good with rich, creamy vanilla ice cream. It's summer in a slice!

1 flaky pastry crust recipe for a double crust (see page 136)

4 cups fresh or frozen blueberries

1 tablespoon lemon juice

1 cup sugar

3 tablespoons flour

8 tablespoons (1 stick) butter

1 cup light brown sugar

1 egg white

2 tablespoons sugar

1. Preheat the oven to 350° F.

2. If using frozen blueberries, it's not necessary to thaw them completely. Put the blueberries in a large bowl, add the lemon juice, sugar, and flour. Stir to combine.

3. Put the skillet over medium heat and melt the butter in it. Add the brown sugar and cook, while stirring constantly, until sugar is dissolved, 1 or 2 minutes. Remove pan from heat.

4. Gently place one crust over the sugar mixture. Fill with the blueberries and place the other crust over the blueberries, crimping the edges together.

5. Brush the top crust with the egg white and then sprinkle the sugar over it. Cut 4 or 5 slits in the middle.

6. Put the skillet in the oven and bake for 50 to 60 minutes until the pie is golden brown and bubbly. Cover the outermost edge with aluminum foil in the last 10 minutes of baking to prevent it from burning.

7. Remove the skillet from the oven and allow to cool before serving.

Tip: If you feel like adding a decorative touch to your pie, cut your second crust into strips and lay them across the top in a crisscross pattern!

VERY CHERRY PIE

SERVES 6 TO 8 ✦ ACTIVE TIME: 60 MINUTES ✦ START TO FINISH: 2 HOURS

What I love about making this pie is working with the cherries. It takes time to slice and pit them, and I use this time to whet my appetite for the final result by eating as I work. A few for the pie, a few for me … it's the simple things! I also prefer to use fresh cherries for this pie, as there is no substitute for the flavor. Use one variety or a combination.

1 flaky pastry crust recipe for a double crust (see page 136)

4 cups fresh cherries, pitted

1 tablespoon lemon juice

1 cup sugar

1½ tablespoons flour

8 tablespoons (1 stick) butter

1 cup light brown sugar

1 egg white

2 tablespoons sugar

1. Preheat the oven to 350° F.

2. Pitting the cherries takes time, but it's worth it. Work with clean cherries and put a piece of waxed paper over the area where you'll be working, as the juice will drip and stain. Have your measuring cup nearby to put the cherries in when they're pitted.

3. Use toothpicks or tweezers with a pointed end or something small and sharp on the end. Remove the stem from the cherry, insert the toothpick or tool next to the pit, and circle the pit until it can be scooped out.

4. When you have 4 cups of pitted cherries, put them in a large bowl and add the lemon juice, sugar, and flour. Stir to combine.

5. Put the skillet over medium heat and melt the butter in it. Add the brown sugar and cook, while stirring constantly, until sugar is dissolved, 1 or 2 minutes. Remove pan from heat.

6. Gently place one of the crusts over the sugar mixture. Fill with the cherries and place the other crust over the cherries, crimping the edges together.

7. Brush the top crust with the egg white and then sprinkle the sugar over it. Cut 4 or 5 slits in the middle.

8. Put the skillet in the oven and bake for 50 to 60 minutes until the pie is golden brown and bubbly. Cover the outermost edge with aluminum foil in the last 10 minutes of baking to prevent it from burning.

9. Remove the skillet from the oven and allow to cool before serving.

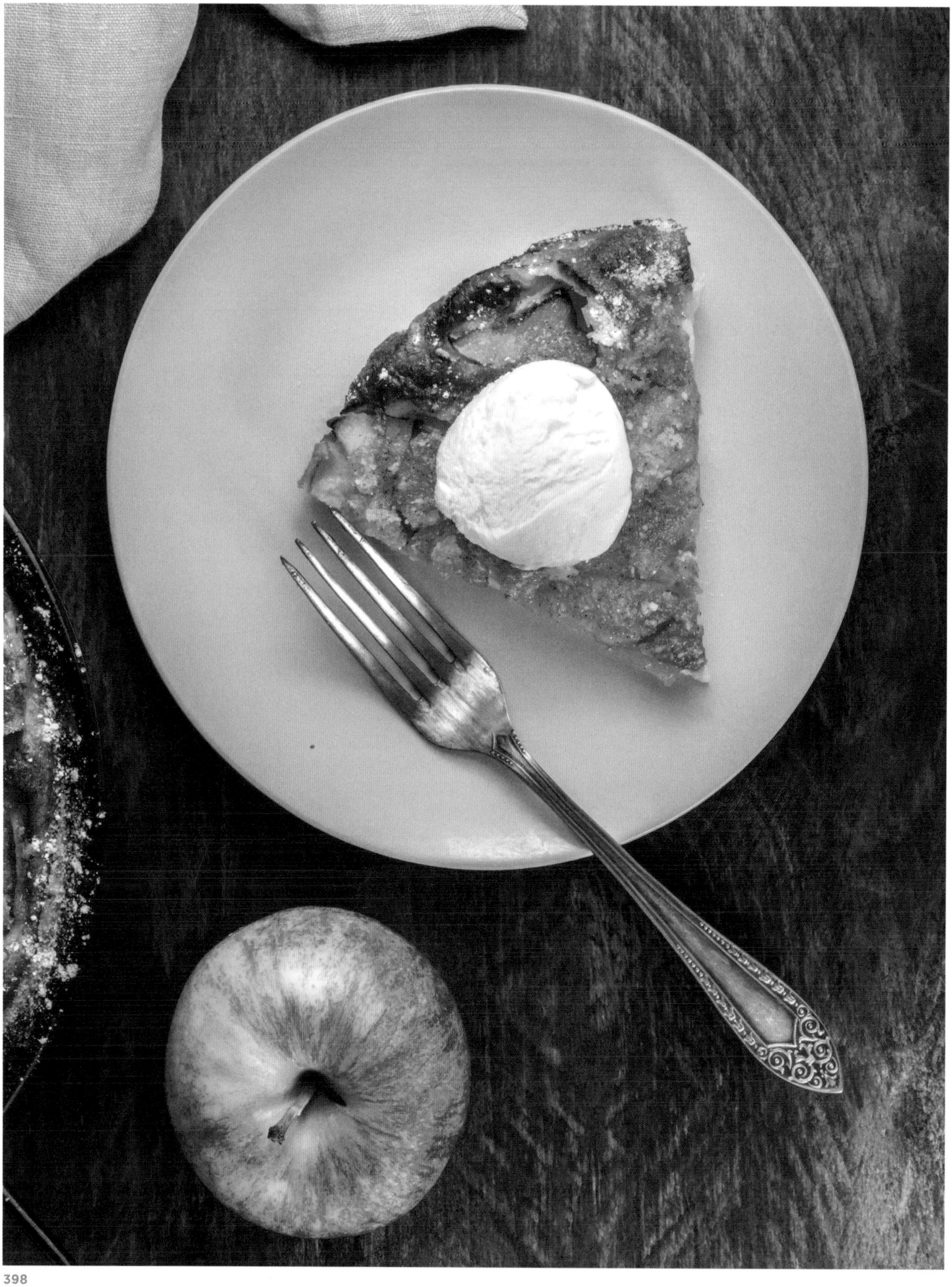

APPLE PIE

SERVES 6 TO 8 ✦ ACTIVE TIME: 60 MINUTES ✦ START TO FINISH: 2 HOURS

Impress your friends. Impress your family. Impress yourself—you won't believe how easy this is and how delicious the result.

1 flaky crust recipe for a double crust (see page 136)

6 Granny Smith apples, peeled, cored, and sliced

1 teaspoon ground cinnamon

¾ cup sugar

1 teaspoon fresh squeezed lemon juice

1 tablespoon butter

1 tablespoon light brown sugar

1 egg white

1. Preheat the oven to 350° F.

2. In a large bowl, toss apples with cinnamon, sugar, and lemon juice.

3. Put the skillet over medium heat and melt the butter in it. Add the brown sugar and cook, while stirring constantly, for a minute or 2, until the sugar is dissolved. Carefully remove pan from heat.

4. Place one of the crusts over the sugar mixture. Fill with the apple mix and place the other crust over the apples, crimping the edges together.

5. Brush the top crust with the egg white. Cut 4 or 5 slits in the middle.

6. Put the skillet in the oven and bake for about 60 minutes until the pie is golden brown and bubbly. Cover the outermost edge with aluminum foil in the last 10 minutes of baking to prevent it from burning.

7. Allow to cool before serving. Serve with whipped cream or ice cream.

You can flavor whipped cream with liqueur for an especially yummy topping. Beat heavy or whipping cream until soft peaks form. Add about ¼ cup sugar and continue beating until stiff peaks form. Gently beat in ¼ cup liqueur, such as apple brandy or Cointreau. Serve immediately or cover with plastic wrap and refrigerate until ready to serve.

BLACKBERRY-PEACH PIE

SERVES 6 TO 8 ✦ ACTIVE TIME: 60 MINUTES ✦ START TO FINISH: 2 HOURS

Colorful, flavorful, and smacking of summer, this is the perfect pie for nights when the sun doesn't set until after 9. Ah, summertime!

1 flaky pastry crust recipe for a double crust (see page 136)

4 cups fresh peaches, peeled, pitted, and cut into small pieces

¾ cup sugar

3 tablespoons flour

½ teaspoon lemon zest

1 tablespoon fresh squeezed lemon juice

¼ teaspoon ground ginger

2 cups fresh blackberries

1 tablespoon butter

1 egg white

2 tablespoons sugar

1. Preheat the oven to 375° F.

2. In a large bowl, toss the peaches with the sugar, flour, lemon zest, lemon juice, and ginger. Gently stir in the blackberries.

3. Put the skillet over medium heat and melt the butter in it. Carefully remove pan from heat.

4. Place one of the piecrusts in the skillet. Fill with fruit mixture. Roll out the top crust on a lightly floured surface, and cut 8 strips from the dough. Arrange them in a lattice pattern, crimping the edges to connect them to the bottom crust, or use whole and cut 4–5 slits in the top.

5. Brush the top crust with the egg white and sprinkle the sugar over it.

6. Put the skillet in the oven and bake for about 55 to 60 minutes, until the pie is golden brown and bubbly.

7. Remove the skillet from the oven, allow to cool before serving, and top with fresh whipped cream.

BANANA PUDDING PIE

SERVES 6 TO 8 ✦ ACTIVE TIME: 45 MINUTES ✦ START TO FINISH: SEVERAL HOURS

You can go several ways with this pie and end up with something really tasty in all instances. One is to use instant vanilla pudding and top the pie with banana slices. Another is to use banana-flavored instant pudding, into which you could stir in some whipped topping for a lighter texture, and top with sliced bananas. The third is the recipe given here. It's made from scratch, flavored with real bananas—and topped with banana slices.

1 graham cracker crust (see page 142)

1 cup whole milk

1 cup heavy cream

2 large bananas, very ripe, thinly sliced

1 medium banana, slightly ripe, sliced into ¼-inch thick rounds

3 tablespoons cornstarch

3 egg yolks

⅓ cup 100% natural maple syrup or ½ cup sugar

1 teaspoon vanilla extract

Dash of salt

1. In a small saucepan over medium-high heat, stir together the milk and heavy cream. Cook, while stirring constantly, until heated through. Gently add the thin slices of very ripe banana, reduce the heat to low, and use a fork to mash the milk, cream, and fruit together, leaving some slices whole. Continue to cook over low heat, while stirring occasionally, until the mixture is hot but not boiling. Slowly stir in the cornstarch, 1 tablespoon at a time.

2. Keep the milk mixture cooking over very low heat. In another bowl, beat the egg yolks until they're combined. Stir in the maple syrup or sugar. Add a large spoonful of the hot milk mixture to the egg mixture and whisk briskly to combine. Do this 2 more times until you've put about ½ cup of the milk mixture into the egg mixture.

3. Next, gently whisk the egg mixture into the saucepan. Slowly bring the mixture to a gentle boil and, while stirring constantly, boil for a couple of minutes. Remove from heat and stir in the vanilla and salt.

4. Allow the mixture to cool for about 15 minutes, then pour it into the crust. Top with slices of the slightly ripe banana, cover with plastic wrap, and refrigerate for several hours before serving.

KEY LIME CHIFFON PIE

SERVES 6 TO 8 ✦ ACTIVE TIME: 30 MINUTES ✦ START TO FINISH: 2 HOURS

This is a fluffier version of a classic key lime pie. What I love about this one is the cloud-like consistency of the filling, which is the perfect complement to the tangy taste of lime. Don't omit the lime zest from the recipe.

1 graham cracker crust (see page 142)

2 cups heavy cream

¼ cup sugar

⅓ cup fresh squeezed key lime juice

Zest from 2 key limes

1 envelope (about 1 tablespoon) unflavored gelatin

½ cup sweetened condensed milk

Whipped cream and key lime zest or key lime wheels for garnish

1. In a large mixing bowl, beat the cream on high until peaks start to form. Add the sugar and continue to beat on high until stiff peaks form.

2. In a small saucepan, combine the lime juice, zest, and gelatin, and stir until gelatin is dissolved. Turn the heat on to medium and cook the mixture until it begins to thicken, while stirring constantly, about 3 to 5 minutes. Do not let it boil or burn. Remove from heat and allow to cool slightly. Stir in the sweetened condensed milk.

3. Fold this mixture into the whipped cream and stir until combined and smooth. Don't overwork it.

4. Working with the crust in the skillet, transfer the filling into the crust. Cover with plastic wrap and refrigerate until set, about 45 minutes (or keep in the refrigerator for up to a day). Garnish with whipped cream and either key lime zest or key lime wheels

SWEET POTATO PIE

SERVES 6 TO 8 ✦ ACTIVE TIME: 30 MINUTES ✦ START TO FINISH: 90 MINUTES

With the butter/sugar combo underneath the pie shell, the result is a crisp, sweet crust topped with an earthy, smooth sweet potato filling. It really works.

1 flaky pastry crust recipe for a single crust (see page 136)

2 cups sweet potatoes, mashed

1 (12 oz.) can evaporated milk

2 eggs, lightly beaten

½ cup sugar

½ teaspoon salt

1 teaspoon cinnamon

¼ teaspoon ground ginger

¼ teaspoon ground nutmeg

8 tablespoons (1 stick) butter

1 cup light brown sugar

1. Preheat the oven to 400° F.

2. In a large bowl, combine the sweet potato, evaporated milk, eggs, sugar, salt, cinnamon, ginger, and nutmeg. Stir to combine thoroughly.

3. Put the skillet over medium heat and melt the butter in it. Add the brown sugar and cook, while stirring constantly, for a minute or 2, until the sugar is dissolved. Remove pan from heat.

4. Roll out the piecrust and gently place it over the sugar mixture. Fill with the sweet potato mixture.

5. Put the skillet in the oven and bake for 15 minutes, then reduce the heat to 325° F and bake an additional 30 to 45 minutes until the filling is firm and a toothpick inserted in the middle comes out clean. Don't overcook.

6. Remove the skillet from the oven and allow to cool before serving. Serve with fresh whipped cream or ice cream.

APPLE-PEAR PIE

MAKES 6 TO 8 SERVINGS ✦ ACTIVE TIME: 30 MINUTES ✦ START TO FINISH: 90 MINUTES

Using a combination of apples and pears results in a pie that's not quite as sweet as an apples-only pie. Dark brown sugar instead of light brown sugar also contributes to the earthy flavor.

1 flaky pastry crust recipe for a double crust (see page 136)

3 Granny Smith apples, peeled, cored, and sliced

3 firm pears (Anjou or Bartlett), peeled, cored, and sliced

½ teaspoon ground cinnamon

½ teaspoon ground nutmeg

½ cup sugar

1 teaspoon fresh squeezed lemon juice

1 tablespoon flour

1 tablespoon butter

1 tablespoon dark brown sugar

1 egg white

1. Preheat the oven to 350˚ F.

2. In a large bowl, toss the fruit with the cinnamon, nutmeg, sugar, lemon juice, and flour, being sure to coat the pieces.

3. Put the skillet over medium heat and melt the butter in it. Add the brown sugar and cook, while stirring constantly, for a minute or 2 until the sugar is dissolved. Carefully remove pan from heat.

4. Place 1 of the piecrusts over the sugar mixture. Fill with the apple-pear mixture, and place the other crust over the fruit, crimping the edges together.

5. Brush the top crust with the egg white. Cut 4 or 5 slits in the middle.

6. Put the skillet in the oven and bake for 60 to 70 minutes until the pie is golden brown and bubbly. Cover the outermost edge with aluminum foil in the last 10 minutes of baking to prevent it from burning.

7. Remove the skillet and allow to cool before serving. Serve with whipped cream or ice cream.

APPLE-RASPBERRY PIE

MAKES 6 TO 8 SERVINGS ✦ ACTIVE TIME: 35 MINUTES ✦ START TO FINISH: 90 MINUTES

The sweet summery taste of fresh raspberries makes for a lovely pairing with apples. If you're inspired, make a lattice crust on this one so the dark liquid of the cooked raspberries bubbles up through the gaps. This makes for a divine presentation.

1 flaky pastry crust recipe for a double crust (see page 136)

6 to 8 crisp and tart apples (such as Macoun, Granny Smith, or Jonagold) peeled, cored, and sliced

2 tablespoons flour

¼ cup light brown sugar

¼ teaspoon salt

¼ cup unsweetened raspberry preserves

1 cup fresh raspberries

1 tablespoon butter

1 egg white

2 tablespoons sugar

1. Preheat the oven to 350° F.

2. In a large bowl, toss the apples with the flour, brown sugar, and salt, being sure to coat the pieces. Add the raspberry preserves and stir. Add the fresh raspberries last, gently stirring so as not to overly macerate the fresh fruit.

3. Put the skillet over medium heat and melt the butter in it. Carefully remove pan from heat.

4. Place 1 of the crusts in the skillet. Fill with the fruit mixture.

5. Roll out the top crust on a lightly floured surface, and cut 8 strips from the dough. Arrange them in a lattice pattern, crimping the edges to connect them to the bottom crust.

6. Brush the top crust with the egg white and sprinkle the sugar over it.

7. Cover the pie with foil and bake for about 35 minutes. Remove the foil and finish baking, another 25 to 30 minutes, until the pie is golden and bubbling.

8. Remove the skillet from the oven and allow to cool before serving.

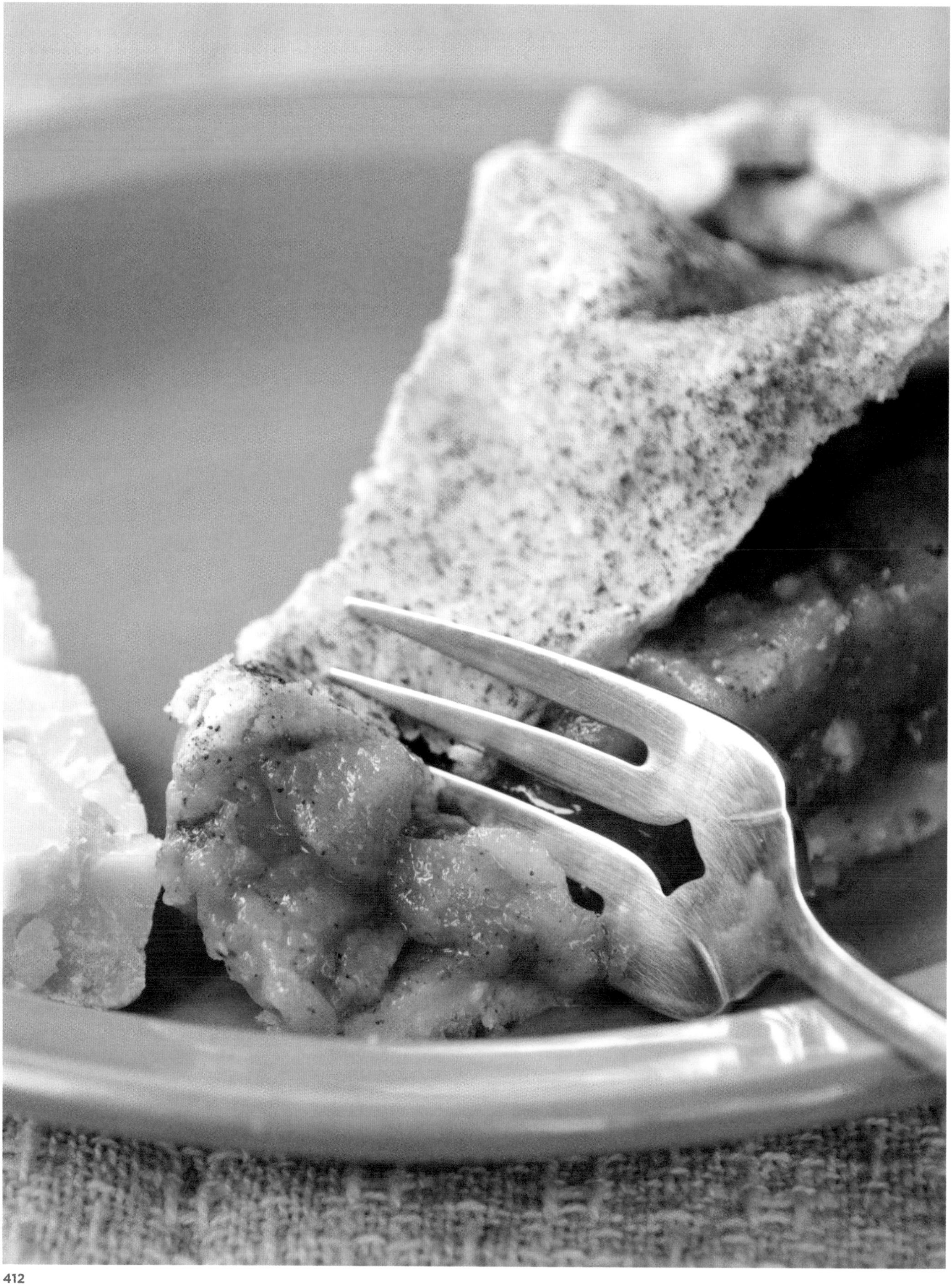

CHEDDAR APPLE PIE

MAKES 6 TO 8 SERVINGS ✦ ACTIVE TIME: 45 MINUTES ✦ START TO FINISH: 2 HOURS

Cheddar cheese adds a savory "something" to apple pie. You can add the cheese to the crust when you make it, or you can add it directly to the apples. I prefer the latter.

1 flaky pastry crust recipe for a double crust (see page 136)

6 crisp and tart apples (such as Macoun, Granny Smith, or Jonagold) peeled, cored, and sliced

¾ cup light brown sugar

2 tablespoons flour

¼ teaspoon salt

1 cup sharp cheddar cheese, shredded or cut into small pieces

1 tablespoon butter

1 egg white

2 tablespoons sugar

1. Preheat the oven to 350° F.

2. In a large bowl, toss the apples with the brown sugar, flour, and salt, being sure to coat the pieces. Add the cheese and stir.

3. Put the skillet over medium heat and melt the butter in it. Carefully remove pan from heat.

4. Place 1 of the crusts in the skillet. Fill with the apple mixture and place the other crust over the apples, crimping the edges together.

5. Brush the top crust with the egg white and sprinkle the sugar over it. Cut 4 or 5 slits in the middle.

6. Put the skillet in the oven and bake for about 60 minutes until the pie is golden brown and bubbly. Cover the outermost edge with aluminum foil in the last 10 minutes of baking to prevent it from burning.

7. Remove the skillet from the oven and allow to cool before serving. Serve with whipped cream or ice cream.

GRAPE PIE

SERVES 6 TO 8 ✦ ACTIVE TIME: 60 MINUTES ✦ START TO FINISH: 90 MINUTES

A refreshing twist on tarte Tatin: fruit embedded in pastry cream. Sliced grapes make for beautiful presentation, and the taste is just as nice. Serve this with a white dessert wine.

1 flaky pastry crust recipe for a single crust (see page 136)

1 (10 oz.) jar lemon curd

1 tablespoon fresh squeezed lemon juice

1 teaspoon lemon zest

1 tablespoon butter

1 tablespoon light brown sugar

2-3 cups seedless grapes (white, red, or a combination), halved

2 tablespoons sugar

1. Preheat the oven to 350˚ F.

2. In a small bowl, combine the lemon curd, lemon juice, and lemon zest. Set aside.

3. Put the skillet over medium heat and melt the butter in it. Add the brown sugar and cook, while stirring constantly, for a minute or 2, until the sugar is dissolved. Carefully remove pan from heat.

4. Place the piecrust over the sugar mixture. Spread the lemon curd mixture over the piecrust. Place the grape halves in a decorative pattern on top of the lemon curd, skin side up. Sprinkle with the sugar.

5. Put the skillet in the oven and bake for 45 to 50 minutes until set.

6. Remove the skillet from the oven and allow to cool before serving.

STRAWBERRY RHUBARB PIE

SERVES 6 TO 8 ✦ ACTIVE TIME: 45 MINUTES ✦ START TO FINISH: 2 HOURS

In the spring, rhubarb is one of the first things to reappear in the gardens of those of us who live in the Northeast, and so it is celebrated. Rhubarb is naturally tart, which is why it works so well with strawberries.

1 flaky pastry crust recipe for a double crust (see page 136)

4-5 stalks rhubarb, cleaned and cut into 1-inch pieces (use about 1½ pounds frozen rhubarb, thawed, if fresh isn't available)

1 quart fresh strawberries, washed and tops trimmed, and halved or quartered (use ½ pound frozen strawberries, thawed, if fresh aren't available)

¾ cup sugar

⅓ cup flour

1 tablespoon butter

1 egg white

1. Preheat the oven to 375° F.

2. In a large bowl, toss the rhubarb and strawberries with the sugar and flour.

3. Put the skillet over medium heat and melt the butter in it. Carefully remove pan from heat.

4. Place 1 of the piecrusts in the skillet. Fill with the rhubarb/strawberry mixture, and place the other crust over the fruit, crimping the edges together.

5. Brush the top crust with the egg white. Cut 4 or 5 slits in the middle.

6. Put the skillet in the oven and bake for about 45 to 55 minutes until the pie is golden brown and bubbly. Cover the outermost edge with aluminum foil in the last 10 minutes of baking to prevent it from burning.

7. Remove the skillet from the oven and allow to cool before serving. Serve with whipped cream.

MIXED BERRY PIE

I especially like this pie in a cornmeal crust. It gives it texture since the berries soften as they cook. Of course, it's best to use all fresh fruit, but if one of them isn't available, you can substitute frozen fruit (thaw it first).

1 cornmeal crust
(see page 141)

1½ cups fresh
blueberries

1 cup fresh blackberries

1 cup fresh raspberries

1½ cups fresh
strawberries, washed
and tops trimmed, and
halved

1 tablespoon fresh
lemon juice

½ cup light brown sugar

2 tablespoons
cornstarch

½ cup unsweetened
raspberry preserves

1. Preheat oven to 375° F.

2. In a large bowl, toss the berries with the lemon juice, brown sugar, and cornstarch. Transfer the mixture to a large saucepan and cook over medium heat for about 3 minutes, until the fruit starts to warm and break down.

3. Working with the crust in the skillet, scrape the fruit and resulting juices onto crust.

4. In a small bowl, stir the preserves until slightly liquefied. Drizzle over pie.

5. Put the skillet in the oven and bake for about 30 to 40 minutes until the filling is bubbling.

6. Remove the skillet from the oven and allow to cool before serving. Serve with fresh whipped cream.

NECTARINE–PLUM PIE

SERVES 6 TO 8 ✦ ACTIVE TIME: 45 MINUTES ✦ START TO FINISH: 90 MINUTES

There's something sublime about this pie. I think it's the addition of Amaretto, which imparts a sweet nuttiness that's a perfect complement to the fruits.

1 flaky pastry crust recipe for a double crust (see page 136)

6 to 8 medium nectarines, peeled, pitted, and cut into ¼-inch thick slices

6 to 8 fresh plums, pitted and quartered

¾ cup light brown sugar

¼ cup flour

3 tablespoons Amaretto liqueur

1 tablespoon butter, plus 3 tablespoons cold, unsalted butter for dotting top of pie filling

1 tablespoon half-and-half

1. Preheat the oven to 400° F.

2. In a large bowl, combine the nectarine and plum pieces. Toss with the brown sugar, flour, and Amaretto.

3. Put the skillet over medium heat and melt the 1 tablespoon of butter in it. Carefully remove pan from heat.

4. Place 1 of the piecrusts in the skillet. Fill with the fruit mixture. Cut the unsalted butter into slivers and dot the top of the fruit mixture with it. Place the other crust over the fruit, crimping the edges together.

5. Brush the top crust with the half-and-half.

6. Put the skillet in the oven and bake for about 40 minutes, until golden brown and bubbly.

7. Remove the skillet from the oven and allow to cool before serving.

GLUTEN-FREE PLUM PIE

SERVES 6 TO 8 ✦ ACTIVE TIME: 45 MINUTES ✦ START TO FINISH: 3 HOURS

There's something so simple and fresh about this pie, and putting it into a gluten-free crust makes it feel that much healthier. Of course, if you don't need or want to, you can use a regular crust. Whichever you choose, you'll discover that this is really good!

1 gluten-free crust recipe (see page 138)

10 to 12 fresh plums, pitted and quartered

½ cup granulated sugar, plus 2 tablespoons

2 tablespoons gluten-free flour

¼ teaspoon ground nutmeg

1 tablespoon fresh squeezed lemon juice

2 tablespoons cold unsalted butter, cut into slivers

2 tablespoons half-and-half

Confectioners' sugar for dusting (optional)

1. When the bottom crust is prepared in the skillet, put it in the refrigerator for 30 minutes.

2. In a large bowl, toss the plums with the ½ cup of sugar, gluten-free flour, nutmeg, and lemon juice. Put the mixture in the cold bottom crust and dot with the butter slivers.

3. Brush with the half-and-half and sprinkle with the remaining sugar. Refrigerate for another 30 minutes or more.

4. While it's refrigerating, preheat the oven to 375° F.

5. Put the skillet in the oven and bake for about 40 minutes, until the plums are tender.

6. Remove the skillet from the oven and allow to cool before serving. Dust with confectioners' sugar if desired.

SOUR CREAM PEAR-WALNUT PIE

SERVES 6 TO 8 ✦ ACTIVE TIME: 60 MINUTES ✦ START TO FINISH: 2 HOURS

Creamy, fruity, nutty….this pie is a potpourri of deliciousness. Be sure the pears you use are ripe, otherwise you'll want to substitute canned pears.

1 flaky pastry crust recipe for a single crust (see page 136)

1¼ cups sour cream

¾ cup granulated sugar

¾ cup flour

¼ teaspoon salt, plus ⅛ teaspoon

2 teaspoons vanilla extract

1 egg

4 to 5 cups ripe pears, peeled, cored, and sliced; or 2 (15 oz.) cans pear slices in natural or unsweetened syrup, drained

½ cup walnuts, chopped

3 tablespoons 100% natural maple syrup (preferably Grade B dark)

¼ cup light brown sugar, packed

½ teaspoon ground cardamom

3 tablespoons cold butter, cut into slivers

1. Preheat the oven to 400° F.

2. In a large bowl, whisk together the sour cream, sugar, ¼ cup of the flour, ¼ teaspoon salt, vanilla, and egg until combined. Stir in the pear slices. Transfer the fruit mixture to the crust in the skillet.

3. In a separate bowl, mix the remaining flour, the remaining salt, the walnuts, maple syrup, brown sugar, and cardamom together. Add butter slivers and work with a fork or pastry blender to form coarse crumbs. Chill in refrigerator until ready to use.

4. Put the skillet in the oven and bake for 15 minutes, then reduce the oven temperature to 350° F and bake for another 30 minutes.

5. Remove pie from oven, take topping out of the refrigerator, and sprinkle it over the pie. Bake for another 20 to 25 minutes until topping is golden brown.

6. Remove the skillet from the oven and allow to cool before serving.

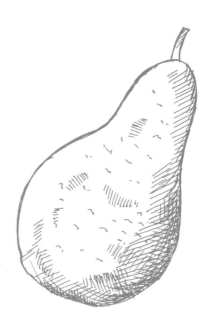

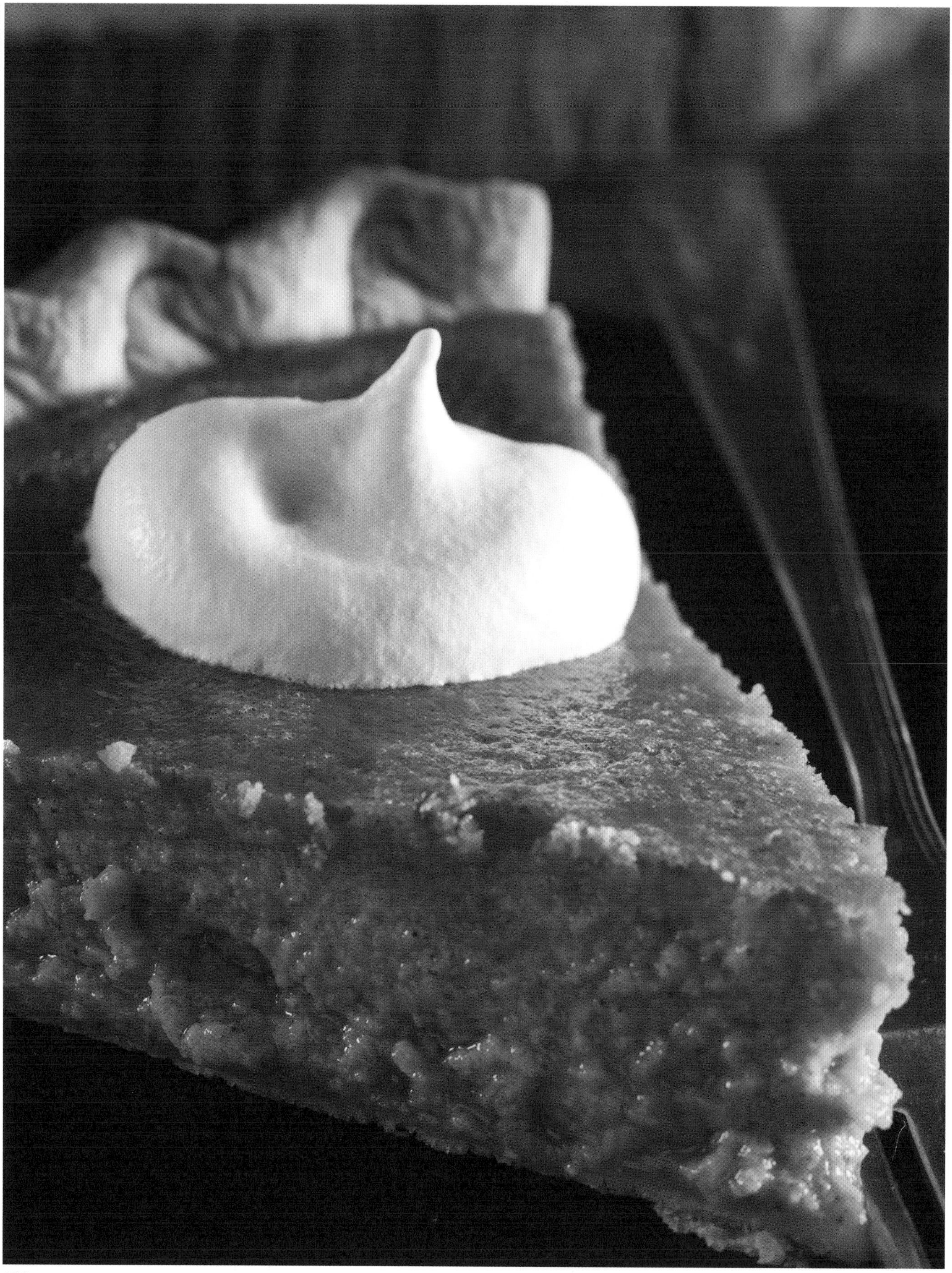

PUMPKIN PIE

SERVES 6 TO 8 ✦ ACTIVE TIME: 30 MINUTES ✦ START TO FINISH: 90 MINUTES

With the butter/sugar combo underneath the pie shell, the result is a crisp, sweet crust topped with an earthy, smooth pumpkin filling. It really works.

1 flaky pastry crust
recipe for a single crust
(see page 136)

1 (15 oz.) can pumpkin
puree (not pumpkin pie
filling)

1 (12 oz.) can
evaporated milk

2 eggs, lightly beaten

½ cup sugar

½ teaspoon salt

1 teaspoon cinnamon

¼ teaspoon ground
ginger

¼ teaspoon ground
nutmeg

1 tablespoon butter

1 tablespoon light
brown sugar

1. Preheat the oven to 400° F.

2. In a large bowl, combine the pumpkin puree, evaporated milk, eggs, sugar, salt, cinnamon, ginger, and nutmeg. Stir to combine thoroughly.

3. Put the skillet over medium heat and melt the butter in it. Add the brown sugar and cook, while stirring constantly, for a minute or 2, until the sugar is dissolved. Carefully remove pan from heat.

4. Place the piecrust over the sugar mixture. Fill with the pumpkin mixture.

5. Put the skillet in the oven and bake for 15 minutes, then reduce the heat to 325° F and bake for an additional 30 to 45 minutes until the filling is firm and a toothpick inserted in the middle comes out clean. Don't overcook.

6. Remove the skillet from the oven and allow to cool before serving. Serve with fresh whipped cream.

NUTTY APPLE– CRANBERRY PIE

SERVES 6 TO 8 ✦ ACTIVE TIME: 60 MINUTES ✦ START TO FINISH: 2 HOURS

If you and your family like something a bit sweet-tart, you'll love this pie. The sweetness of the apples pairs wonderfully with the tartness of fresh cranberries, and the toasted walnuts add a buttery earthiness.

1 cup walnuts, chopped

4 pounds Granny Smith apples

1 cup fresh cranberries

1 teaspoon ground cinnamon

¼ teaspoon ground ginger

1 cup sugar, plus 2 tablespoons

1 teaspoon lemon juice

8 tablespoons (1 stick) butter

1 cup light brown sugar

1 pre-made refrigerator pie dough (14.1 oz) or 1 flaky crust recipe for a double crust (see page 136)

1 egg white

1. Preheat the oven to 450° F.

2. Spread the walnut pieces out on a cookie sheet and bake until toasted, about 5 to 8 minutes, removing the cookie sheet after 4 minutes to shake and turn the nuts. Keep an eye on them so they don't burn. Remove the cookie sheet from the oven and allow the nuts to cool. Reduce the oven temperature to 350° F.

3. Peel and core the apples, and cut into ½-inch thick wedges. In a large bowl, combine the apples with the cranberries, cinnamon, ginger, 1 cup of sugar, and lemon juice. Stir in the walnut pieces.

4. Put the skillet over medium heat and melt the butter in it. Add the brown sugar and cook, while stirring constantly, for a minute or 2, until the sugar is dissolved. Remove pan from heat.

5. Roll out 1 of the piecrusts and gently place it over the sugar mixture. Fill with the apple mixture, and place the other crust over the apples, crimping the edges together.

6. Brush the top crust with the egg white and sprinkle the remaining sugar over it. Cut 4 or 5 slits in the middle.

7. Put the skillet in the oven and bake for 60 to 70 minutes until the pie is golden brown and bubbly. Cover the outermost edge with aluminum foil in the last 10 minutes of baking to prevent it from burning.

8. Remove the skillet from the oven and allow to cool before serving.

CARAMELIZED PINEAPPLE

MAKES 6 TO 8 SERVINGS ✦ ACTIVE TIME: 30 MINUTES ✦ START TO FINISH: 30 MINUTES

Experience the wonder that is the browned, crispy outside and the juicy inside of a seared pineapple. It's like a fresh fruit steak off the grill.

4 tablespoons butter

½ cup dark brown sugar

¼ cup dark rum

1 fresh pineapple, peeled, cored, and cut into ½-inch slices

1. Preheat the oven to 200° F. Heat the skillet over medium-high heat. When it's hot, add the butter, brown sugar, and rum. Stir until the butter is melted and bubbling.

2. Add the pineapple slices to the skillet one at a time and cook until warmed through, about 2 minutes a side.

3. Keep the cooked pineapple warm in the oven while cooking the remaining slices.

Variations

These are delicious by themselves, but there are lots of ways to dress them up and make them part of a fancier dessert.

✺ Put a scoop of vanilla ice cream in the hole in the center and top with a sprig of mint.

✺ Cut the slices into cubes and toss with chunks of mango or cantaloupe.

✺ Sprinkle shredded coconut over the pineapple.

✺ Use the pineapple as a topping for pound cake.

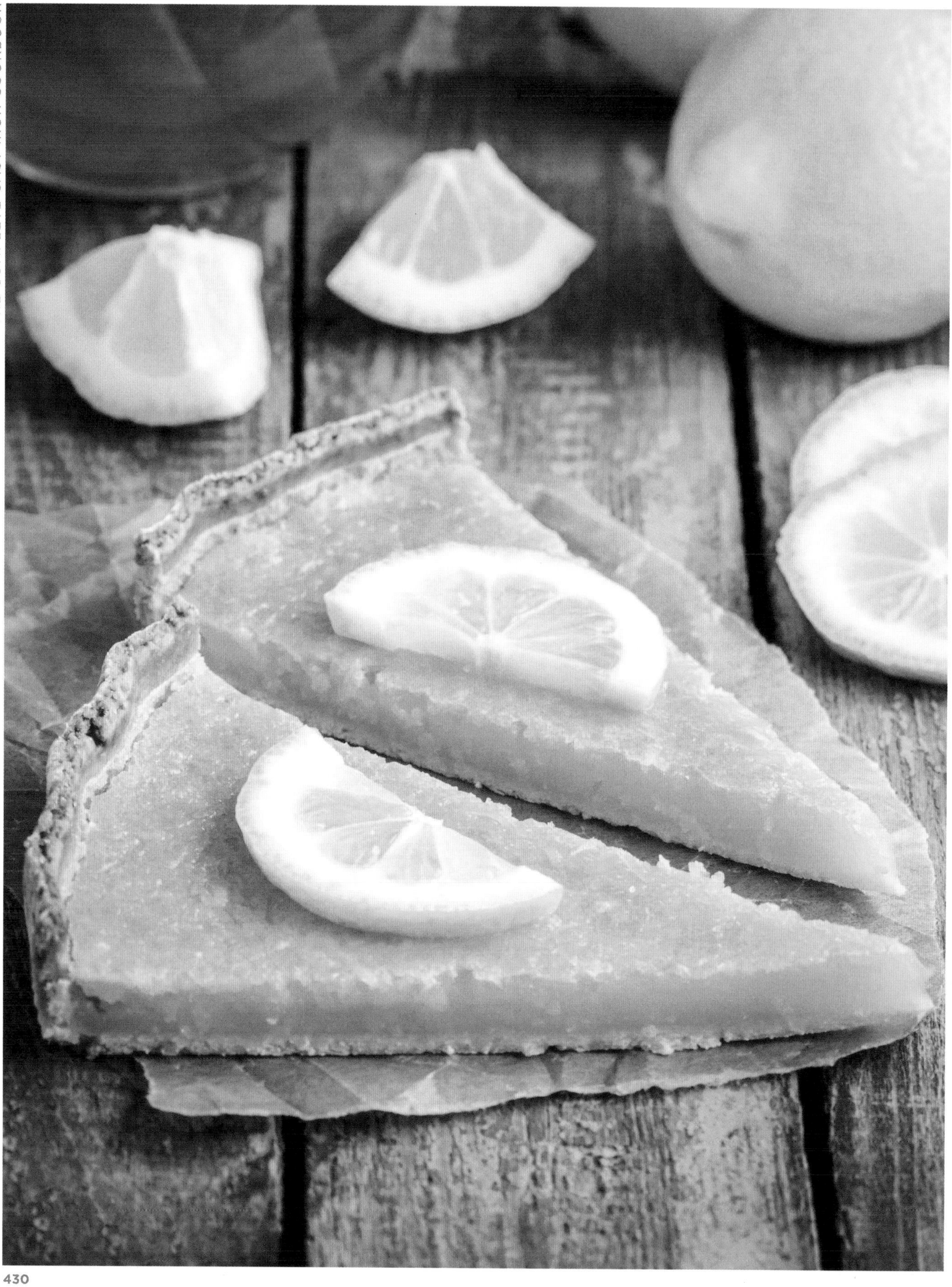

DOUBLE LEMON TART

SERVES 6 TO 8 ✦ ACTIVE TIME: 30 MINUTES ✦ START TO FINISH: 60 MINUTES

Lemons are like sunshine—they brighten everything! Very thinly sliced lemons sit atop a lemon-drenched custard to make a dessert whose flavor shines from the first bite to the last.

1 graham cracker crust (see page 142)

1 (14 oz.) can sweetened condensed milk

½ cup fresh squeezed lemon juice

4 large egg yolks

1 tablespoon vanilla extract

1 lemon, very thinly sliced, seeds removed

1. Preheat the oven to 325° F.

2. In a medium bowl, combine the condensed milk, lemon juice, egg yolks, and vanilla. Working with the crust in the skillet, pour the filling into the crust. Top with the very thin slices of lemon, arranged in a decorative pattern.

3. Put the skillet in the oven and bake for about 15 to 20 minutes, until the liquid has set into a soft custard.

4. Remove the skillet from the oven and allow to cool completely before serving.

FRENCH APPLE TART

SERVES 6 TO 8 ✦ ACTIVE TIME: 60 MINUTES ✦
START TO FINISH: SEVERAL HOURS OR OVERNIGHT

Cast-iron skillets caramelize fruits to perfection. This recipe is the quintessential example. It's what the French call "tarte Tatin," and for them it's a national treasure.

1 cup flour

½ teaspoon salt

1½ cups sugar, plus
1 tablespoon

2¾ cups unsalted butter,
cut into small pieces

3 tablespoons ice water

8 to 10 apples, peeled,
cored, and halved

1. To make the pastry, whisk together the flour, salt, and 1 tablespoon of sugar in a large bowl. Using your fingers, work 6 tablespoons of the butter into the flour mixture until you have coarse clumps. Sprinkle the ice water over the mixture and continue to work it with your hands until the dough just holds together. Shape it into a ball, wrap it in plastic wrap, and refrigerate it for at least 1 hour, or overnight.

2. Preparation for the tart starts in the skillet. Place the remaining pieces of butter evenly over the bottom of the skillet, then sprinkle the remaining sugar evenly over everything. Next, start placing the apple halves in a circular pattern, starting on the inner edge of the pan and working in. The halves should overlap and face the same direction. Place either 1 or 2 halves in the center when finished working around the outside. As the tart bakes, the slices will slide down a bit.

3. Place the skillet on the stove and turn the heat to medium-high. Cook the apples in the pan, uncovered, until the sugar and butter start to caramelize, about 35 minutes. While they're cooking, spoon some of the juices over the apples (but don't overdo it).

4. Preheat the oven to 400° F, and position a rack in the center.

5. Take the chilled dough out of the refrigerator and, working on a lightly floured surface, roll it out into a circle just big enough to cover the skillet (about 12 to 14 inches). Gently drape the pastry over the apples, tucking it in around the sides.

6. Put the skillet in the oven and bake for about 25 minutes, until the pastry is golden brown.

7. Remove the skillet from the oven and allow to cool for about 5 minutes. Find a plate that is an inch or 2 larger than the top of the skillet and place it over the top. You will be inverting the tart onto the plate. Be sure to use oven mitts or secure pot holders, as the skillet will be hot.

8. Holding the plate tightly against the top of the skillet, turn the skillet over so the plate is now on the bottom. If some of the apples are stuck to the bottom, gently remove them and place them on the tart. Allow to cool a few more minutes, or set aside until ready to serve (it's better if it's served warm).

GLUTEN-FREE RASPBERRY ALMOND TART

SERVES 6 TO 8 ✦ ACTIVE TIME: 30 MINUTES ✦ START TO FINISH: 90 MINUTES

What's amazing about this dessert is the sweetness of the raspberries and the nutty hints of almond. They are a great pair. And of course the custard is creamy, the colors are gorgeous, and the overall effect is irresistible.

1 gluten-free crust (see page 138)

5 tablespoons unsalted butter, softened

½ cup sugar, plus 1 tablespoon

Dash of salt

1 egg, plus 1 egg white

¾ cup almond flour

½ teaspoon almond extract

1½ cups fresh raspberries

1. Preheat the oven to 375° F.

2. In a large bowl, beat the butter and ½ cup of sugar until the mixture is light and fluffy. Add salt.

3. Stir in the egg and egg white until thoroughly combined, then add the almond flour and almond extract. Stir to combine. In a separate bowl, combine the raspberries and the remaining tablespoon of sugar.

4. Working with the crust in the skillet, sprinkle with about ⅓ of the berries. Top with the almond flour-and-egg mixture, and put the remaining raspberries on top.

5. Put the skillet in the oven and bake for about 40 to 45 minutes, until a knife inserted near the center comes out clean.

6. Remove the skillet from the oven and allow to cool completely before serving.

GINGER KEY LIME TART

SERVES 6 TO 8 ✦ ACTIVE TIME: 40 MINUTES ✦ START TO FINISH: 60 MINUTES

To complement the zestiness of the key lime, the tart is baked in a gingersnap crust spiked with fresh ginger, which itself has a bright, zingy flavor. The result is an explosion in your mouth.

8-10 gingersnap cookies

1 teaspoon fresh ginger, grated

½ cup (8 tablespoons) unsalted butter

1 (14 oz.) can sweetened condensed milk

½ cup key lime juice

4 large egg yolks

1 tablespoon vanilla extract

1. Place 6 tablespoons of the butter in a microwave-safe bowl and microwave until melted. Preheat the oven to 350° F.

2. In a food processor, grind the cookies until they are crumbs. If you don't have a food processor, you can also put the cookies in a resealable plastic bag and use a rolling pin to grind them into crumbs.

3. Put the crumbs in a bowl and add the ginger. Stir in the 6 tablespoons of melted butter. Heat the remaining 2 tablespoons of butter in the cast-iron skillet to coat the bottom. Press the cookie crumb mixture into the skillet, extending the crust about halfway up the side of the skillet.

4. Place the skillet in the oven and bake until the crust is firm, about 10 minutes. Remove the skillet from the oven and allow to cool. Reduce oven temperature to 325° F.

5. In a medium bowl, combine the condensed milk, key lime juice, egg yolks, and vanilla. Pour the filling into the crust.

6. Put the skillet in the oven and bake for about 20 to 30 minutes, until the liquid has set into a soft custard.

7. Remove the skillet from the oven and allow to cool completely before serving.

STRAWBERRY-KIWI TART

SERVES 6 TO 8 ✦ ACTIVE TIME: 90 MINUTES ✦ START TO FINISH: SEVERAL HOURS

This is one of those desserts you marvel at in the display case of a high-end grocery store. It always looks perfect. When you make one yourself, you'll find that it's quite simple, and looks just as impressive.

1 baked crust
(see page 135)

½ cup cream cheese
at room temperature

½ cup sugar

1 teaspoon vanilla
extract

1 cup heavy cream

1½ cups fresh
strawberries, stems
removed, halved

3 medium kiwis, peeled
and sliced

3 tablespoons seedless
strawberry jam

1 tablespoon water

1. In a large bowl, beat the softened cream cheese and the sugar, stirring until very smooth. Add the vanilla.

2. In a separate bowl, whip the cream with an electric mixer on high until it forms stiff peaks. Fold the cream into the cream cheese mixture until fully incorporated. Working with the crust in the skillet, scrape the mixture into the crust and spread evenly.

3. Arrange the fruit in the skillet, alternating the kiwis and the strawberries and working from the outside toward the center. Refrigerate until set, about 1 hour.

4. Place the jam and the water in a small saucepan and cook over low heat until the jam is melted. Remove pan from heat, let cool slightly, then brush it over the entire surface of the tart.

5. Chill for several hours before serving.

6. Serve with fresh whipped cream, crème fraîche, or vanilla ice cream.

PUMPKIN PECAN TART

SERVES 6 TO 8 ✦ ACTIVE TIME: 30 MINUTES ✦ START TO FINISH: 90 MINUTES

In a twist on a traditional pumpkin pie, this tart has the pecans as the crust. The result? Delicious!

1 pecan crust
(see page 144)

1 (15 oz.) can pumpkin
puree (not pumpkin
pie filling)

1 (12 oz.) can
evaporated milk

2 eggs, lightly beaten

¾ cup granulated sugar

1 teaspoon ground
cinnamon

¼ teaspoon ground
ginger

¼ teaspoon ground
allspice

½ teaspoon salt

1 cup heavy cream

2 tablespoons
confectioners' sugar

1. Preheat the oven to 350° F.

2. In a large bowl, stir together the pumpkin puree and evaporated milk. Add the eggs and stir to combine. Add the sugar, cinnamon, ginger, allspice, and salt and stir to combine thoroughly.

3. Working with the crust in the skillet, transfer the pumpkin mixture into the crust.

4. Put the skillet in the oven and bake for about 50 minutes, until a knife inserted near the center comes out clean. Remove the skillet from the oven and allow to cool completely.

5. Before serving, beat the heavy cream with an electric mixer until soft peaks form. Add the confectioners' sugar 1 tablespoon at a time until it has dissolved and stiff peaks form.

6. Serve the tart with the whipped cream.

CHOCOLATE CHEESECAKE TART

SERVES 6 TO 8 ✦ ACTIVE TIME: 40 MINUTES ✦ START TO FINISH: 90 MINUTES

There's something so decadent about cheesecake! It's fantastic in a cookie crust, and this one is enhanced with cocoa powder and a dash of Kahlúa liqueur.

8-10 Oreo cookies, filling scraped off

1 tablespoon unsweetened cocoa powder

2 tablespoons Kahlúa or coffee liqueur

½ cup (8 tablespoons) unsalted butter, melted

2 (8 oz.) packages cream cheese, softened

1 cup sugar

1 tablespoon cocoa powder

½ teaspoon vanilla extract

2 eggs

1. Preheat the oven to 350° F.

2. In a food processor, grind the cookies until they are crumbs. If you don't have a food processor, you can also put the cookies in a resealable plastic bag and use a rolling pin to grind them into crumbs.

3. Put the crumbs in a bowl and add the unsweetened cocoa powder and the Kahlúa. Stir in 6 tablespoons of the butter. Place the other 2 tablespoons of the butter in the cast-iron skillet to coat the bottom. Press the cookie crumb mixture into the skillet, extending the crust about halfway up the side of the skillet.

4. Bake until the crust is firm, about 10 minutes. Remove the skillet from the oven and allow to cool. Reduce oven temperature to 325° F.

5. In a large bowl, add the cream cheese with the sugar, cocoa powder, vanilla, and eggs, and stir until thoroughly combined. Scrape the cream cheese mixture into the cooled crust.

6. Put the skillet in the oven and bake for 40 to 60 minutes, until set.

7. Remove the skillet from the oven, allow to cool, and refrigerate for 1 hour or overnight before serving.

CHOCOLATE FUDGE TART

SERVES 6 TO 8 ✦ ACTIVE TIME: 45 MINUTES ✦ START TO FINISH: 90 MINUTES

When you know that nothing else will do for dessert except chocolate, you'll want to make this tart. The crust is crunchy chocolate, the filling is fudgy chocolate, and you can even drizzle white chocolate over it for the hat trick.

For the Crust

8-10 Oreo cookies, filling scraped off

½ cup (8 tablespoons) unsalted butter, melted

For the Filling

10 oz. semi-sweet chocolate (morsels or a bar broken into pieces)

½ cup (8 tablespoons) unsalted butter, cut into pieces

2 eggs

1 cup heavy cream

½ cup sugar

1 teaspoon vanilla extract

1 pinch of salt

4 oz. white chocolate morsels or pieces

1. Preheat the oven to 350° F.

2. In a food processor, grind the cookies until they are crumbs. If you don't have a food processor, you can also put the cookies in a resealable plastic bag and use a rolling pin to grind them into crumbs.

3. Put the crumbs in a bowl and add 6 tablespoons of the melted butter. Heat the remaining 2 tablespoons in the cast-iron skillet to coat the bottom. Press the cookie crumb mixture into the skillet, extending the crust about halfway up the side of the skillet.

4. Place the skillet in the oven and bake until the crust is firm, about 10 minutes. Remove the skillet from the oven and allow to cool.

5. Prepare the filling. In a small saucepan, combine the chocolate and butter. Heat over low heat and cook, while stirring frequently, until both are melted and combined. Set aside.

6. In a bowl, whisk together the eggs, heavy cream, sugar, vanilla, and salt. Pouring gently and steadily, add the chocolate mixture to the egg mixture, whisking as the chocolate is added. Whisk or stir to combine thoroughly.

7. Pour the mixture into the crust and shake the skillet gently to evenly distribute the liquid.

8. Put the skillet in the oven and bake for 15 to 20 minutes until the filling is set around the edges but still soft in the center. It will continue to cook when it's removed from the oven.

9. Remove the skillet from the oven, transfer to a wire rack, and allow to cool completely.

10. Before serving, put the white chocolate in a microwave-safe bowl and microwave on high for 15-second intervals, stirring after each, until the chocolate is just melted. Drizzle over the tart.

GLUTEN-FREE PEAR-CRANBERRY CRUMBLE

SERVES 4 TO 6 ✦ ACTIVE TIME: 30 MINUTES ✦ START TO FINISH: 60 MINUTES

A dessert that will impress and delight in the fall, when cranberries are at their freshest. Not only that, the almond flour complements the pears beautifully.

4 pears

1 teaspoon ground ginger

1 cup almond flour

½ cup dark brown sugar

9 tablespoons unsalted butter, chilled

½ cup unsweetened coconut flakes

¾ cup fresh cranberries or ½ cup dried cranberries

1. Preheat the oven to 350° F.

2. Melt 1 tablespoon of the butter in the skillet over medium heat.

3. Trim the tops and bottoms from the pears, cut them into quarters, remove the cores, and cut each quarter in half. Lay the slices in the melted butter. Sprinkle the pear slices with ginger and then remove the skillet from the heat.

4. In a bowl, combine the almond flour and brown sugar. Cut the remaining butter into slices. Using your fingers, work the butter into the mixture until coarse crumbles form. Add the coconut, stirring to combine thoroughly, and then fold in the cranberries.

5. Spread the coconut-and-cranberry mixture over the pears. Put the skillet in the oven and bake for 15 to 20 minutes, until the contents of the skillet are bubbly. Remove the skillet from the oven and let cool for a few minutes before serving. Top with whipped cream or Greek yogurt.

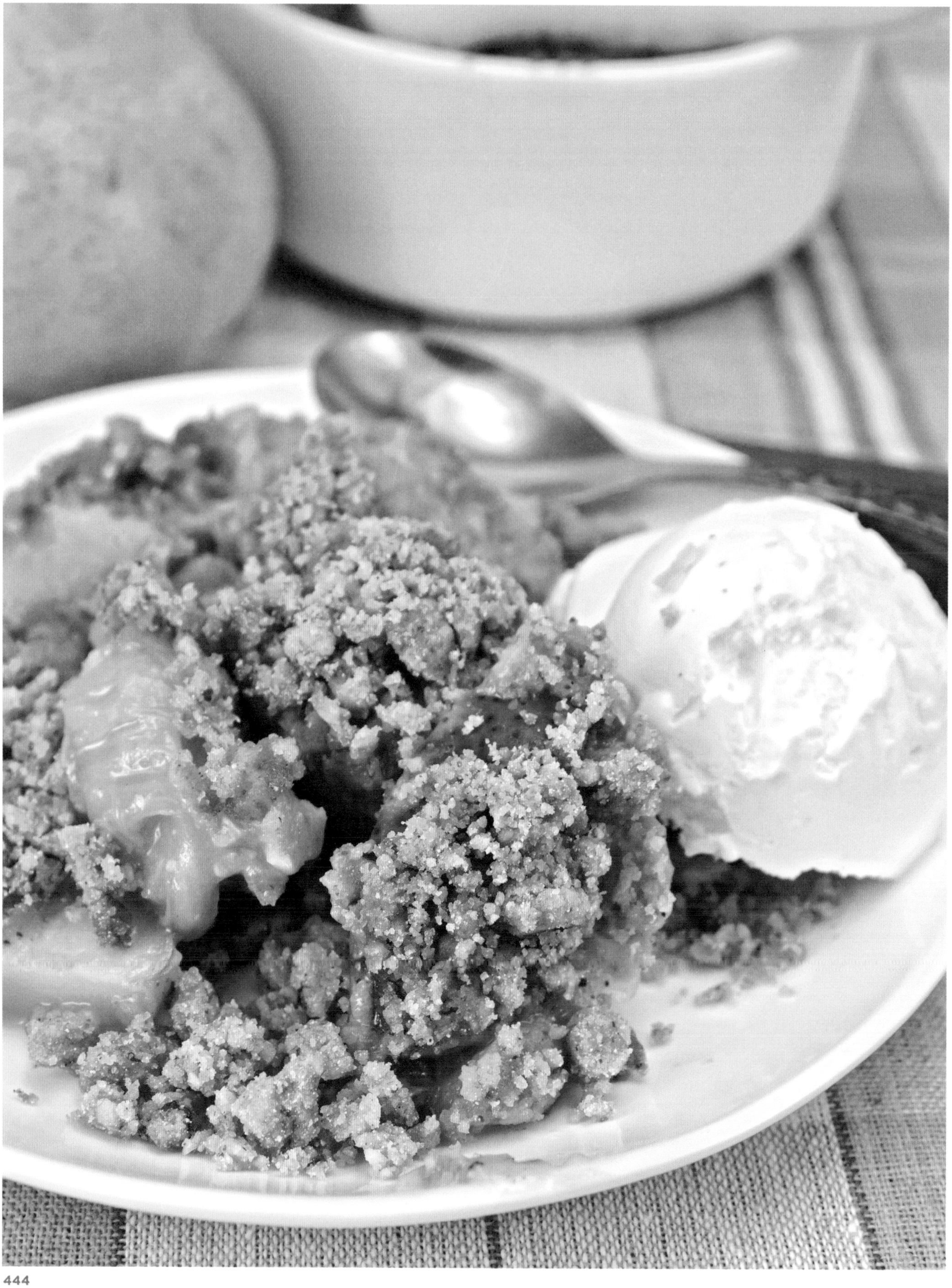

PEAR-GINGER CRUMBLE

SERVES 4 TO 6 ✦ ACTIVE TIME: 30 MINUTES ✦ START TO FINISH: 90 MINUTES

The ginger adds a deep warmth to this dish, which can come up huge on a cool autumn night. Serving it warm is most delicious, but if you can't, no worries—it still tastes great!

4 pears

1 teaspoon ground ginger

1 cup flour

½ cup dark brown sugar

9 tablespoons unsalted butter, chilled

½ cup rolled oats

Vanilla ice cream or whipped cream

1. Preheat the oven to 350° F.

2. Melt 1 tablespoon of the butter in the skillet over medium heat.

3. Trim the tops and bottoms from the pears, cut into quarters, remove the cores, and cut each quarter in half. Lay the slices in the melted butter. Sprinkle the pear slices with the ginger and remove the skillet from the heat.

4. In a bowl, combine the flour and brown sugar. Cut the remaining butter into slices. Using your fingers, work the butter into the mixture until coarse crumbles form. Add the rolled oats, combine, and then spread the mixture over the pears. Put the skillet in the oven and bake for 15 minutes, until the contents of the saucepan are melted and bubbly. Remove the skillet from the oven and let cool for a few minutes before serving. Top with ice cream or whipped cream.

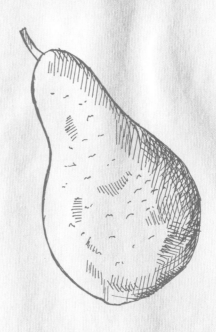

PEACH GALETTE

SERVES 6 TO 8 ✦ ACTIVE TIME: 45 MINUTES ✦ START TO FINISH: 90 MINUTES

When peaches are ripe in the mid-to-late summer, this is a super-simple way to turn them into a great dessert. Smearing some peach jam on the crust before adding the fruit will intensify the flavor, and if you want something a little more "adult," consider adding some Amaretto liqueur or bourbon to the jam instead of water.

1 flaky pastry crust recipe for a single crust (see page 136)

3 cups fresh peaches, peeled, pitted, and sliced

½ cup sugar, plus 1 tablespoon

Juice of ½ lemon

3 tablespoons cornstarch

Pinch of salt

2 tablespoons peach jam

1 teaspoon Amaretto liqueur (optional)

1 egg, beaten

1. Preheat the oven to 400° F.

2. The crust in the skillet should be slightly larger than the bottom of the pan so that it can be folded over.

3. In a large bowl, mix the peaches with the ½ cup of sugar, lemon juice, cornstarch, and salt. Stir well to be sure to coat all the fruit.

4. If using the liqueur, mix it with the jam in a small bowl before smearing the jam on the center of the crust.

5. Place the fruit in a mound in the center of the crust. Fold the edge of the crust over to cover about 1 inch of filling. Brush the crust with the beaten egg and sprinkle it with the remaining sugar.

6. Put the skillet in the oven and bake until the filling is bubbly, which is necessary for it to thicken sufficiently, about 35 to 40 minutes.

7. Remove the skillet from the oven and allow to cool before serving.

TRIPLE BERRY GALETTE

SERVES 4 TO 6 ✦ ACTIVE TIME: 30 MINUTES ✦ START TO FINISH: 60 MINUTES

You'll soon discover why this triple berry galette is a real home run. The fruits marry perfectly, with the raspberries sweetening everything just enough. If you want to kick it up some more, consider spreading some raspberry jam on the crust before adding the fruit and baking it.

1 flaky pastry crust recipe for a single crust (see page 136)

1 cup fresh blueberries

1 cup fresh blackberries

1 cup fresh raspberries

½ cup sugar, plus 1 tablespoon

Juice of ½ lemon

3 tablespoons cornstarch

Pinch of salt

1 egg, beaten

1. Preheat the oven to 400° F.

2. The crust in the skillet should be slightly larger than the bottom of the pan so that it can be folded over the berry filling.

3. In a large bowl, mix the fruit with ½ cup of the sugar, lemon juice, cornstarch, and salt. Stir well to coat all the fruit.

4. Place the fruit in a mound in the center of the crust. Fold the edge of the crust over to cover about 1 inch of the filling. Brush the crust with the beaten egg and sprinkle it with the remaining sugar.

5. Put the skillet in the oven and bake until the filling is bubbly, which is necessary for it to thicken sufficiently, about 35 to 40 minutes.

6. Remove the skillet from the oven and allow to cool before serving.

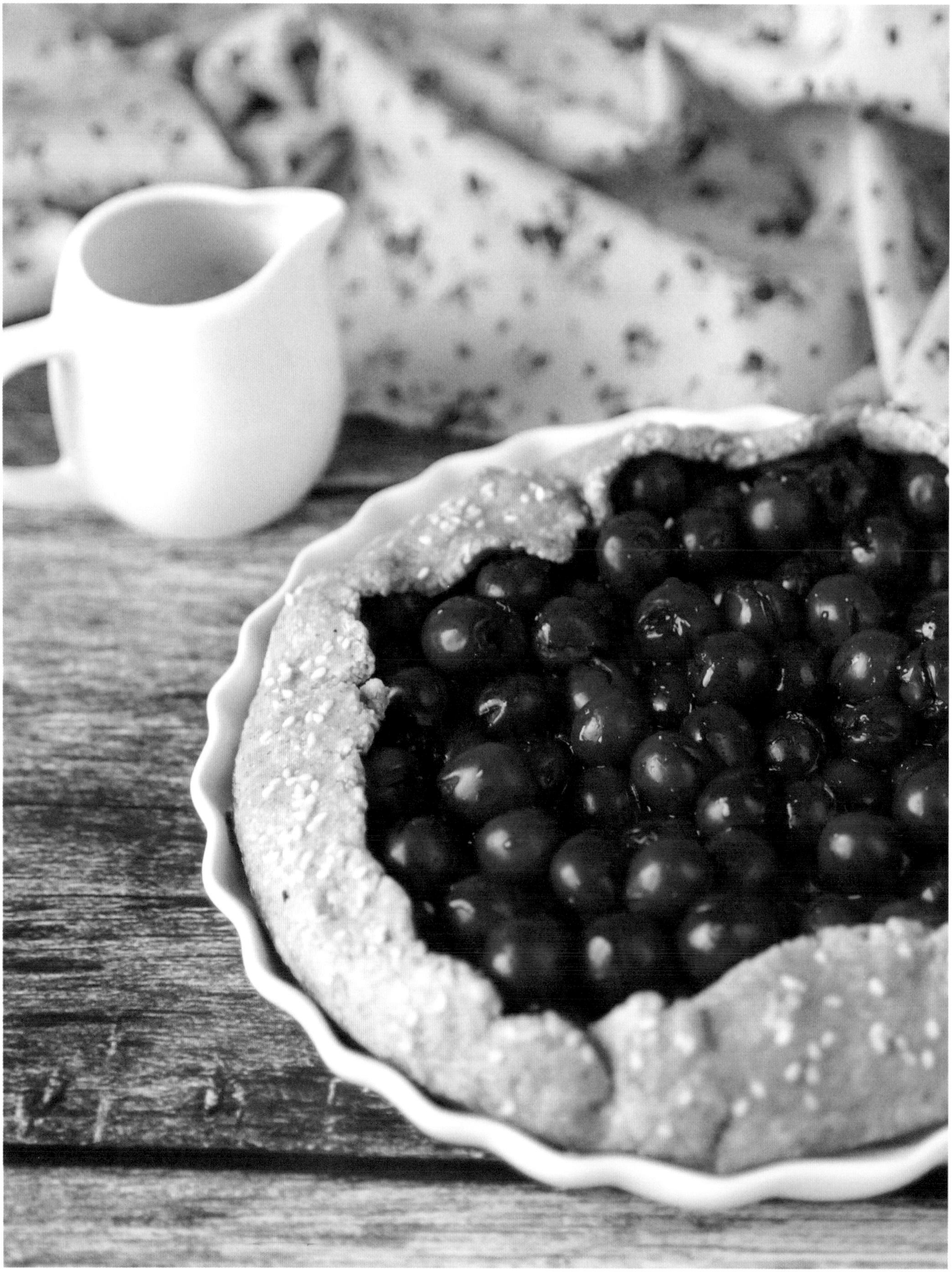

SUMMER CHERRY GALETTE

SERVES 4 TO 6 ✦ ACTIVE TIME: 30 MINUTES ✦ START TO FINISH: 60 MINUTES

You can use all of the same type of cherry for this galette, or you can mix varietals. It takes some work to remove the pits from the cherries, but it's so worth it!

1 flaky pastry crust recipe for a single crust (see page 136)

3 cups cherries, pitted and halved

½ cup light brown sugar

Juice of ½ lemon

3 tablespoons cornstarch

Pinch of salt

1 egg, beaten

1 tablespoon granulated sugar

1. Preheat the oven to 400° F.

2. The crust in the skillet should be slightly larger than the bottom of the pan so that it can be folded over the filling.

3. In a large bowl, mix the cherries with the brown sugar, lemon juice, cornstarch, and salt. Stir well to be sure to coat all the fruit.

4. Place the fruit in a mound in the center of the crust. Fold the edge of the crust over to cover about 1 inch of the filling. Brush the crust with the beaten egg and sprinkle it with the remaining sugar.

5. Put the skillet in the oven and bake until the filling is bubbly, which is necessary for it to thicken sufficiently, about 35 to 40 minutes.

6. Remove the skillet from the oven and allow to cool before serving.

PLUM GALETTE

SERVES 4 TO 6 ✦ ACTIVE TIME: 40 MINUTES ✦ START TO FINISH: 90 MINUTES

Here's another summer fruit-laden treat that is so easy to put together and tastes great! The flavor of the plums is definitely enhanced by the jam, and the whole thing is sublime when topped with ice cream and—try this—roasted and salted pumpkin seeds (just a sprinkle).

1 flaky pastry crust recipe for a single crust (see page 136)

3 cups fresh plums, pitted and sliced

½ cup sugar, plus 1 tablespoon

Juice of ½ lemon

3 tablespoons cornstarch

Pinch of salt

2 tablespoons blackberry jam

1 egg, beaten

1. Preheat the oven to 400° F.

2. The crust in the skillet should be slightly larger than the bottom of the pan so that it can be folded over along the edges.

3. In a large bowl, mix the plums with ½ cup of the sugar, lemon juice, cornstarch, and salt. Stir well to coat all the fruit.

4. Brush or smear the jam in the center of the crust. Place the fruit in a mound in the center. Fold the edges of the crust over to cover about 1 inch of the filling. Brush the filling with the beaten egg and sprinkle it with the remaining sugar.

5. Put the skillet in the oven and bake until the filling is bubbly, which is necessary for it to thicken sufficiently, about 35 to 40 minutes.

6. Remove the skillet from the oven and allow to cool before serving.

NECTARINE-RASPBERRY GALETTE

SERVES 4 TO 6 ✦ ACTIVE TIME: 40 MINUTES ✦ START TO FINISH: 90 MINUTES

I love this flavor combination, and I love the colors, too. The best part is that it tastes even better than it looks.

1 flaky pastry crust recipe for a single crust (see page 136)

1½ cups fresh nectarines, pitted and sliced

1½ cups fresh raspberries

½ cup sugar, plus 1 tablespoon

Juice of ½ lemon

1 teaspoon lemon zest

3 tablespoons cornstarch

Pinch of salt

1 egg, beaten

1. Preheat the oven to 400° F.

2. The crust in the skillet should be slightly larger than the bottom of the pan so that it can be folded over along the edges.

3. In a large bowl, mix the fruit with ½ cup of the sugar, lemon juice, lemon zest, cornstarch, and salt. Stir well to coat all the fruit.

4. Place the fruit in a mound in the center of the crust. Fold the edges of the crust over to cover about 1 inch of the filling. Brush the crust with the beaten egg and sprinkle it with the remaining sugar.

5. Put the skillet in the oven and bake until the filling is bubbly, which is necessary for it to thicken sufficiently, about 35 to 40 minutes.

6. Remove the skillet from the oven and allow to cool before serving.

METRIC CONVERSION CHART

US measurement	Approximate metric liquid measurement	Approximate metric dry measurement
1 teaspoon	5 mL	
1 tablespoon or 1/2 ounce	15 mL	14 g
1 ounce or 1/8 cup	30 mL	28 g
1/4 cup or 2 ounces	60 mL	57 g
1/3 cup	80 mL	
1/2 cup or 4 ounces	120 mL	113 g
2/3 cup	160 mL	
3/4 cup or 6 ounces	180 mL	
1 cup or 8 ounces or 1/2 pint	240 mL	227 g
1 1/2 cups or 12 ounces	350 mL	
2 cups or 1 pint or 16 ounces	475 mL	453 g
3 cups or 1 1/2 pints	700 mL	
4 cups or 2 pints or 1 quart	950 mL	

The names of the recipes included in the book are in italics.

ABOUT CIDER MILL PRESS
BOOK PUBLISHERS

Good ideas ripen with time. From seed to harvest, Cider Mill Press brings fine reading, information, and entertainment together between the covers of its creatively crafted books. Our Cider Mill bears fruit twice a year, publishing a new crop of titles each spring and fall.

CIDER MILL PRESS

BOOK PUBLISHERS

KENNEBUNKPORT, MAINE

"Where Good Books Are Ready for Press"

Visit us online at
www.cidermillpress.com
or write to us at
PO Box 454
12 Spring Street
Kennebunkport, Maine 04046